STAN LEE PRESENTS

# SPIDER-GIRL



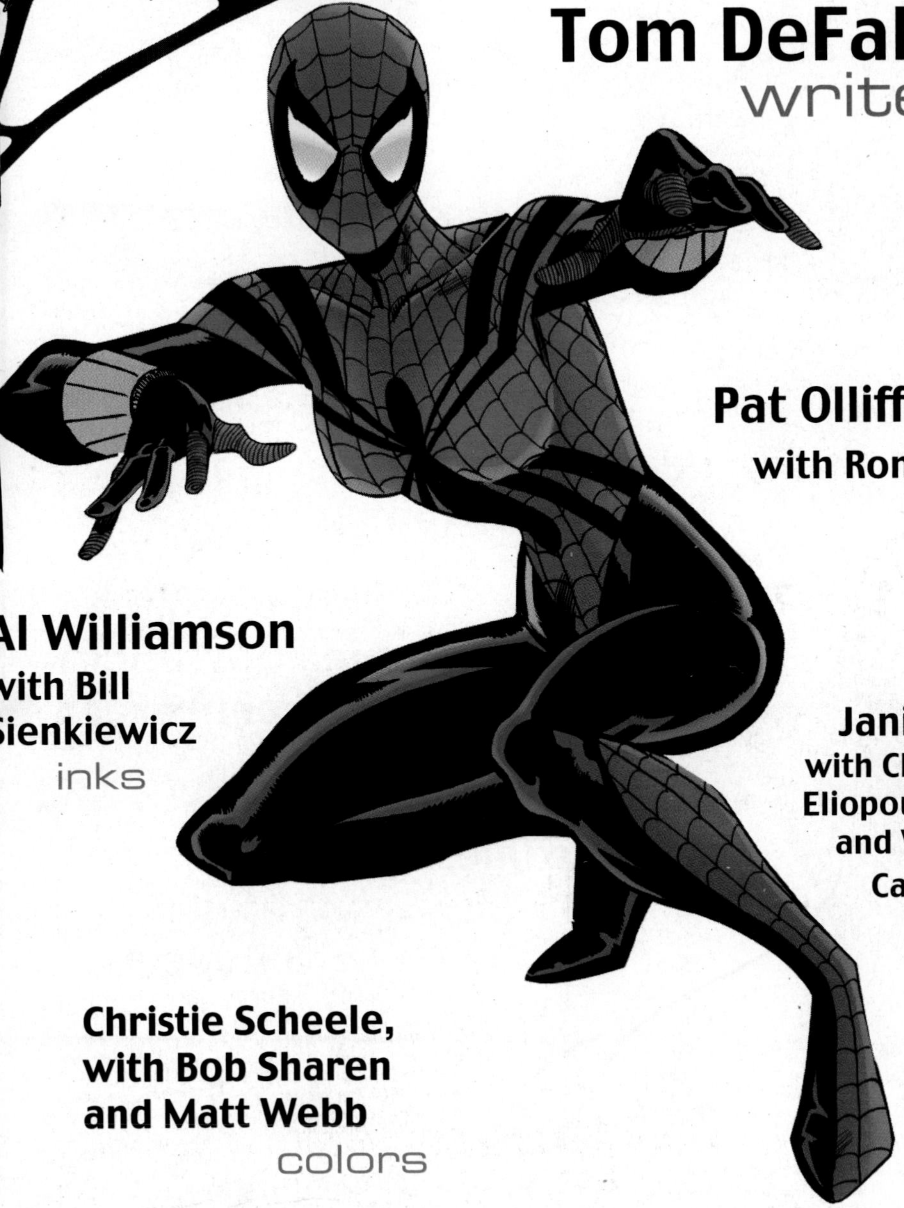

**Tom DeFalco**
writer

**Pat Olliffe**
**with Ron Frenz**
pencils

**Al Williamson**
**with Bill Sienkiewicz**
inks

**Janice Chiang**
**with Chris Eliopoulos and Virtual Calligraphy**
letters

**Christie Scheele, with Bob Sharen and Matt Webb**
colors

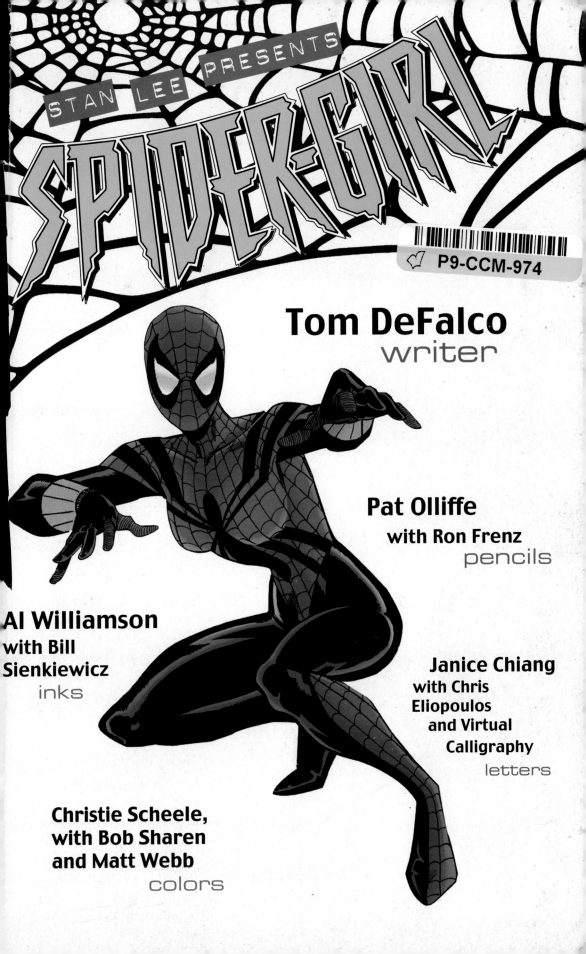

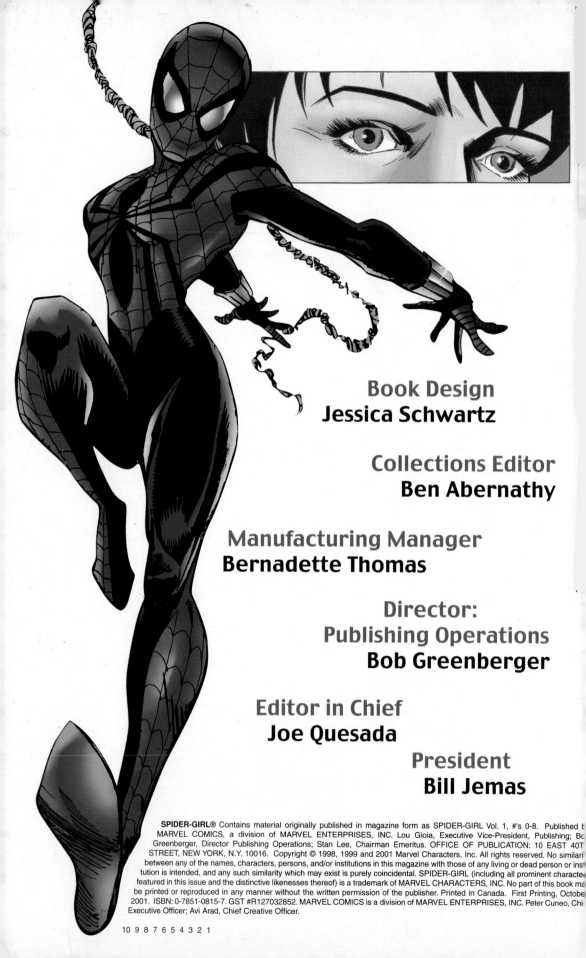

**Book Design**
**Jessica Schwartz**

**Collections Editor**
**Ben Abernathy**

**Manufacturing Manager**
**Bernadette Thomas**

**Director:**
**Publishing Operations**
**Bob Greenberger**

**Editor in Chief**
**Joe Quesada**

**President**
**Bill Jemas**

SPIDER-GIRL® Contains material originally published in magazine form as SPIDER-GIRL Vol. 1, #'s 0-8. Published by MARVEL COMICS, a division of MARVEL ENTERPRISES, INC. Lou Gioia, Executive Vice-President, Publishing; Bob Greenberger, Director Publishing Operations; Stan Lee, Chairman Emeritus. OFFICE OF PUBLICATION: 10 EAST 40T STREET, NEW YORK, N.Y. 10016. Copyright © 1998, 1999 and 2001 Marvel Characters, Inc. All rights reserved. No similari between any of the names, characters, persons, and/or institutions in this magazine with those of any living or dead person or ins tution is intended, and any such similarity which may exist is purely coincidental. SPIDER-GIRL (including all prominent character featured in this issue and the distinctive likenesses thereof) is a trademark of MARVEL CHARACTERS, INC. No part of this book ma be printed or reproduced in any manner without the written permission of the publisher. Printed in Canada. First Printing, Octobe 2001. ISBN: 0-7851-0815-7. GST #R127032852. MARVEL COMICS is a division of MARVEL ENTERPRISES, INC. Peter Cuneo, Chi Executive Officer; Avi Arad, Chief Creative Officer.

10 9 8 7 6 5 4 3 2 1

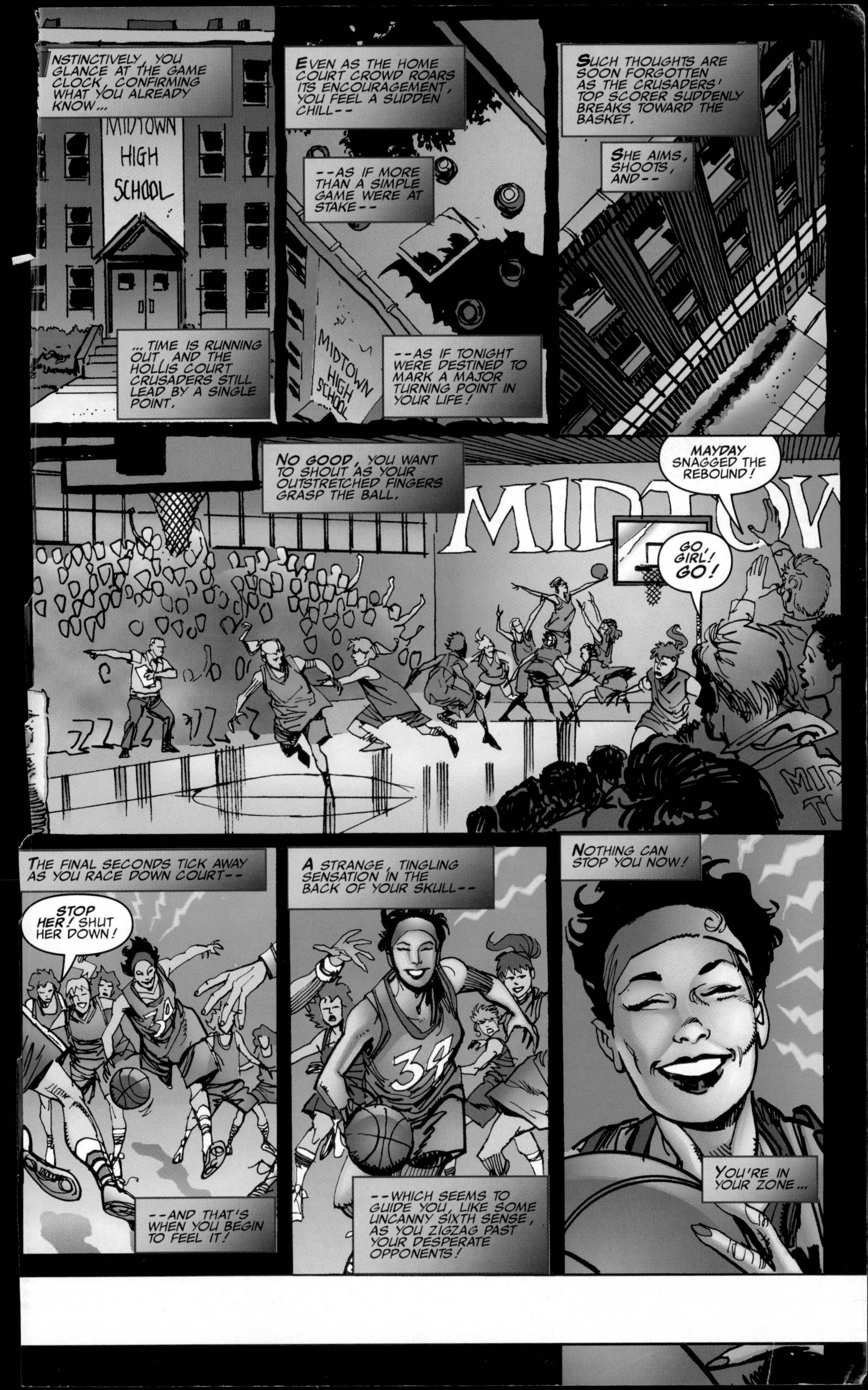
INSTINCTIVELY, YOU GLANCE AT THE GAME CLOCK, CONFIRMING WHAT YOU ALREADY KNOW...
MIDTOWN HIGH SCHOOL
...TIME IS RUNNING OUT, AND THE HOLLIS COURT CRUSADERS STILL LEAD BY A SINGLE POINT.
EVEN AS THE HOME COURT CROWD ROARS ITS ENCOURAGEMENT, YOU FEEL A SUDDEN CHILL--
--AS IF MORE THAN A SIMPLE GAME WERE AT STAKE--
MIDTOWN HIGH SCHOOL
--AS IF TONIGHT WERE DESTINED TO MARK A MAJOR TURNING POINT IN YOUR LIFE!
SUCH THOUGHTS ARE SOON FORGOTTEN AS THE CRUSADERS' TOP SCORER SUDDENLY BREAKS TOWARD THE BASKET.
SHE AIMS, SHOOTS, AND--
NO GOOD, YOU WANT TO SHOUT AS YOUR OUTSTRETCHED FINGERS GRASP THE BALL.
MAYDAY SNAGGED THE REBOUND!
GO, GIRL! GO!
THE FINAL SECONDS TICK AWAY AS YOU RACE DOWN COURT--
STOP HER! SHUT HER DOWN!
--AND THAT'S WHEN YOU BEGIN TO FEEL IT!
A STRANGE, TINGLING SENSATION IN THE BACK OF YOUR SKULL--
--WHICH SEEMS TO GUIDE YOU, LIKE SOME UNCANNY SIXTH SENSE, AS YOU ZIGZAG PAST YOUR DESPERATE OPPONENTS!
NOTHING CAN STOP YOU NOW!
YOU'RE IN YOUR ZONE...

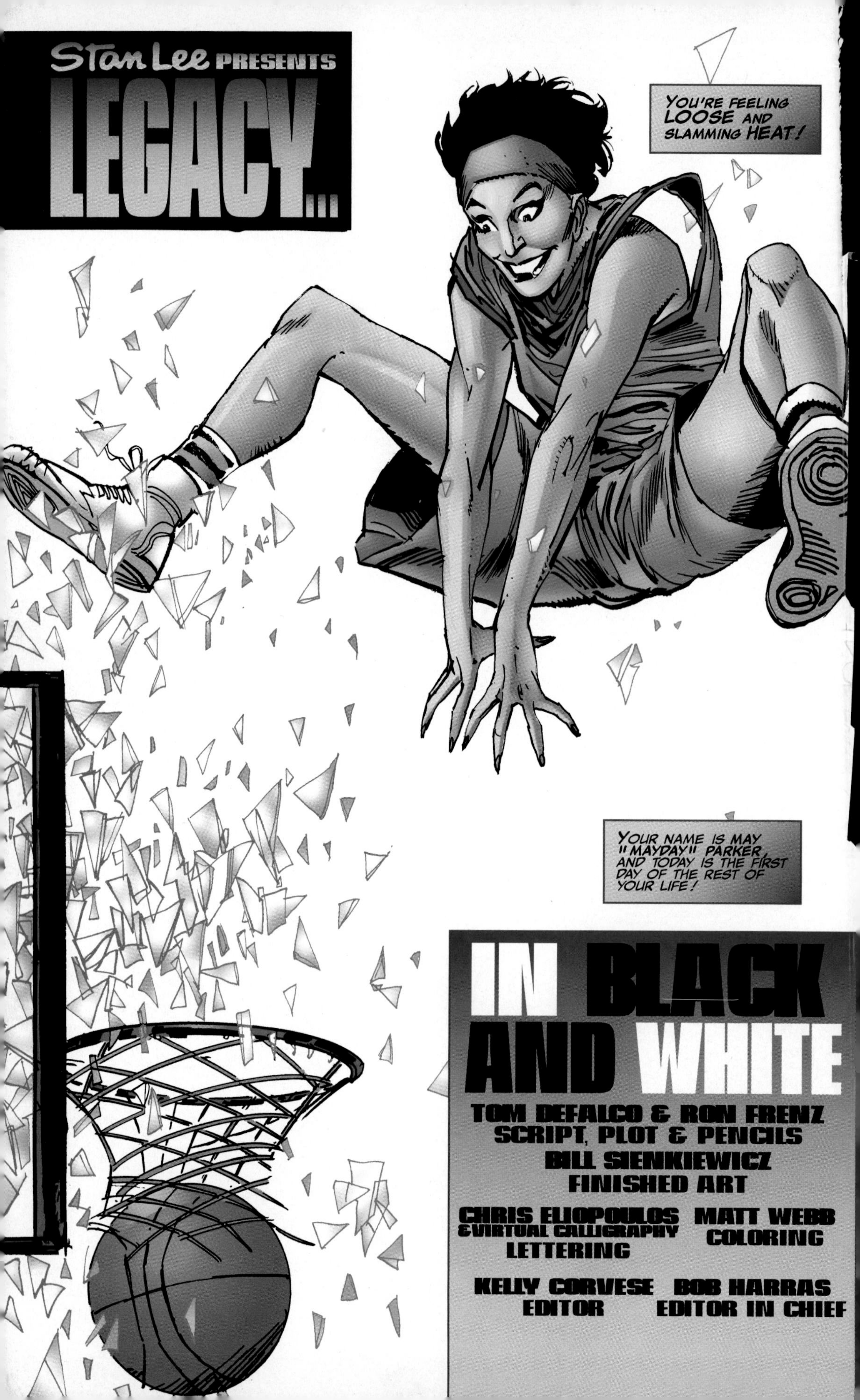
Stan Lee PRESENTS
LEGACY...
YOU'RE FEELING LOOSE AND SLAMMING HEAT!
YOUR NAME IS MAY "MAYDAY" PARKER, AND TODAY IS THE FIRST DAY OF THE REST OF YOUR LIFE!
IN BLACK AND WHITE
TOM DEFALCO & RON FRENZ SCRIPT, PLOT & PENCILS
BILL SIENKIEWICZ FINISHED ART
CHRIS ELIOPOULOS & VIRTUAL CALLIGRAPHY LETTERING
MATT WEBB COLORING
KELLY CORVESE EDITOR
BOB HARRAS EDITOR IN CHIEF

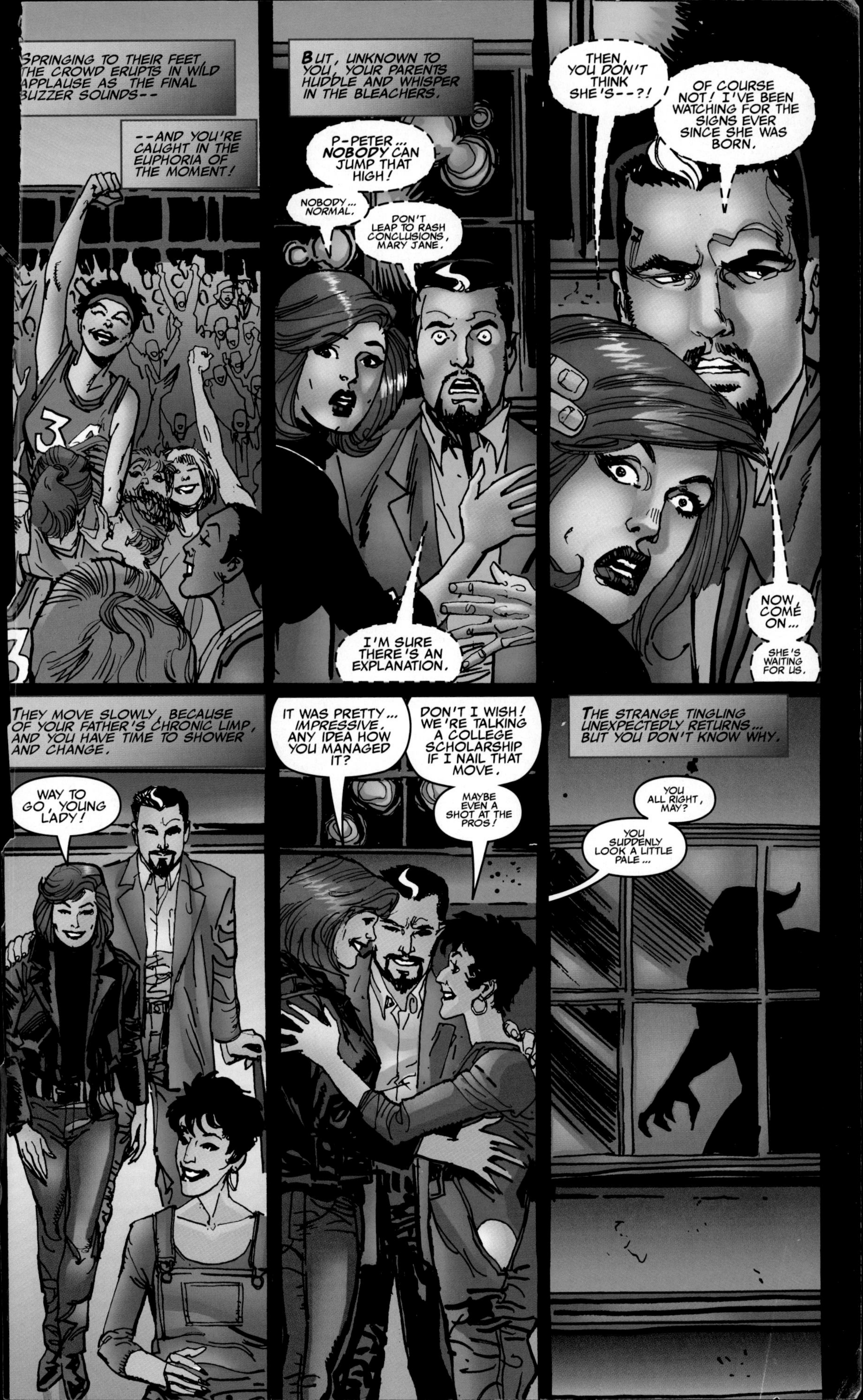
SPRINGING TO THEIR FEET, THE CROWD ERUPTS IN WILD APPLAUSE AS THE FINAL BUZZER SOUNDS--
--AND YOU'RE CAUGHT IN THE EUPHORIA OF THE MOMENT!
BUT, UNKNOWN TO YOU, YOUR PARENTS HUDDLE AND WHISPER IN THE BLEACHERS.
P-PETER... NOBODY CAN JUMP THAT HIGH!
NOBODY... NORMAL.
DON'T LEAP TO RASH CONCLUSIONS, MARY JANE.
I'M SURE THERE'S AN EXPLANATION.
THEN, YOU DON'T THINK SHE'S--?!
OF COURSE NOT! I'VE BEEN WATCHING FOR THE SIGNS EVER SINCE SHE WAS BORN.
NOW, COME ON...
SHE'S WAITING FOR US.
THEY MOVE SLOWLY, BECAUSE OF YOUR FATHER'S CHRONIC LIMP, AND YOU HAVE TIME TO SHOWER AND CHANGE.
WAY TO GO, YOUNG LADY!
IT WAS PRETTY... IMPRESSIVE. ANY IDEA HOW YOU MANAGED IT?
DON'T I WISH! WE'RE TALKING A COLLEGE SCHOLARSHIP IF I NAIL THAT MOVE.
MAYBE EVEN A SHOT AT THE PROS!
THE STRANGE TINGLING UNEXPECTEDLY RETURNS... BUT YOU DON'T KNOW WHY.
YOU ALL RIGHT, MAY?
YOU SUDDENLY LOOK A LITTLE PALE...

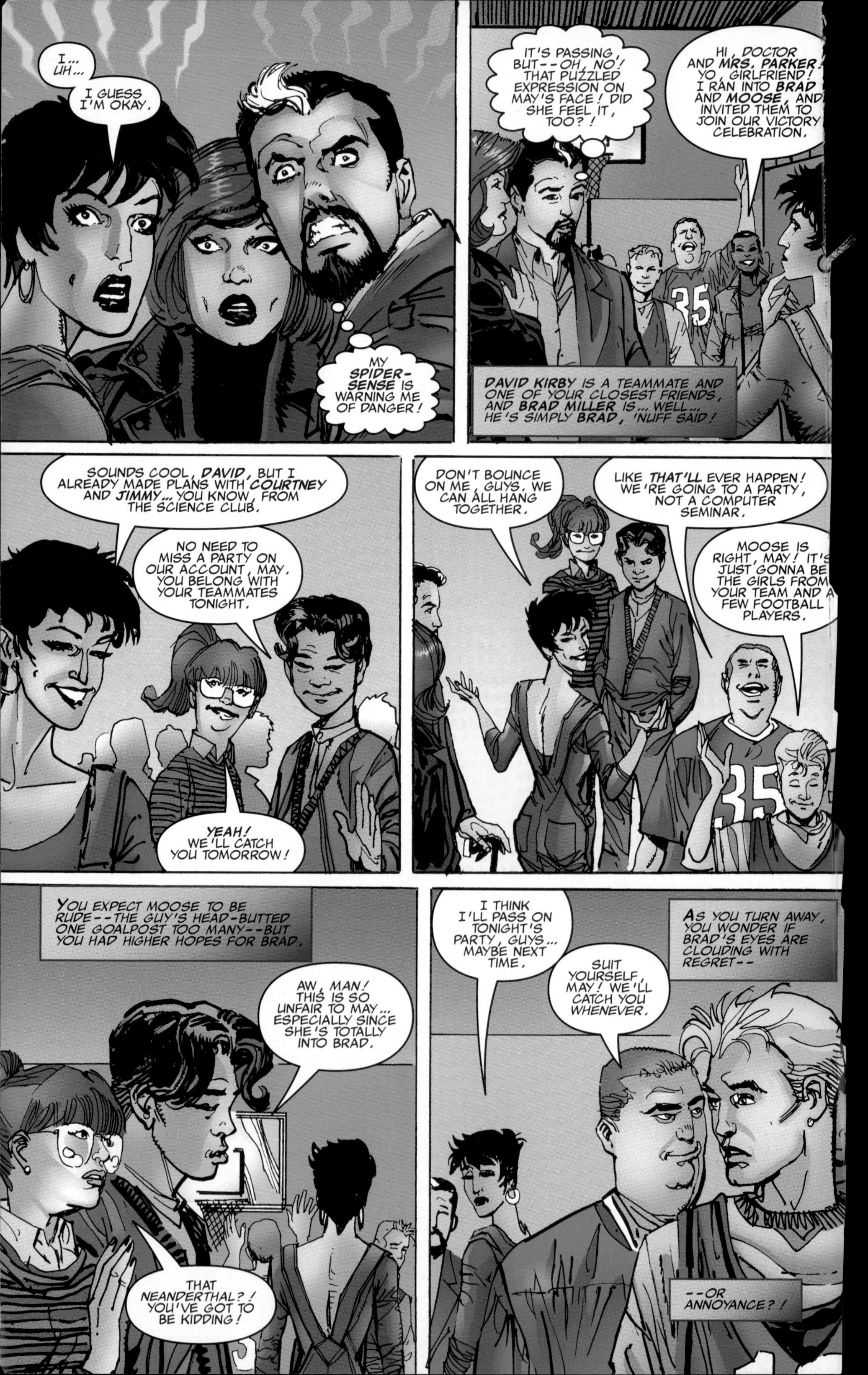
I... UH...
I GUESS I'M OKAY.
MY SPIDER-SENSE IS WARNING ME OF DANGER!
IT'S PASSING, BUT--OH, NO! THAT PUZZLED EXPRESSION ON MAY'S FACE! DID SHE FEEL IT, TOO?!
HI, DOCTOR AND MRS. PARKER! YO, GIRLFRIEND! I RAN INTO BRAD AND MOOSE, AND INVITED THEM TO JOIN OUR VICTORY CELEBRATION.
DAVID KIRBY IS A TEAMMATE AND ONE OF YOUR CLOSEST FRIENDS, AND BRAD MILLER IS... WELL... HE'S SIMPLY BRAD, 'NUFF SAID!
SOUNDS COOL, DAVID, BUT I ALREADY MADE PLANS WITH COURTNEY AND JIMMY... YOU KNOW, FROM THE SCIENCE CLUB.
NO NEED TO MISS A PARTY ON OUR ACCOUNT, MAY. YOU BELONG WITH YOUR TEAMMATES TONIGHT.
YEAH! WE'LL CATCH YOU TOMORROW!
DON'T BOUNCE ON ME, GUYS. WE CAN ALL HANG TOGETHER.
LIKE THAT'LL EVER HAPPEN! WE'RE GOING TO A PARTY, NOT A COMPUTER SEMINAR.
MOOSE IS RIGHT, MAY! IT'S JUST GONNA BE THE GIRLS FROM YOUR TEAM AND A FEW FOOTBALL PLAYERS.
YOU EXPECT MOOSE TO BE RUDE--THE GUY'S HEAD-BUTTED ONE GOALPOST TOO MANY--BUT YOU HAD HIGHER HOPES FOR BRAD.
AW, MAN! THIS IS SO UNFAIR TO MAY... ESPECIALLY SINCE SHE'S TOTALLY INTO BRAD.
THAT NEANDERTHAL?! YOU'VE GOT TO BE KIDDING!
I THINK I'LL PASS ON TONIGHT'S PARTY, GUYS... MAYBE NEXT TIME.
SUIT YOURSELF, MAY! WE'LL CATCH YOU WHENEVER.
AS YOU TURN AWAY, YOU WONDER IF BRAD'S EYES ARE CLOUDING WITH REGRET--
--OR ANNOYANCE?!

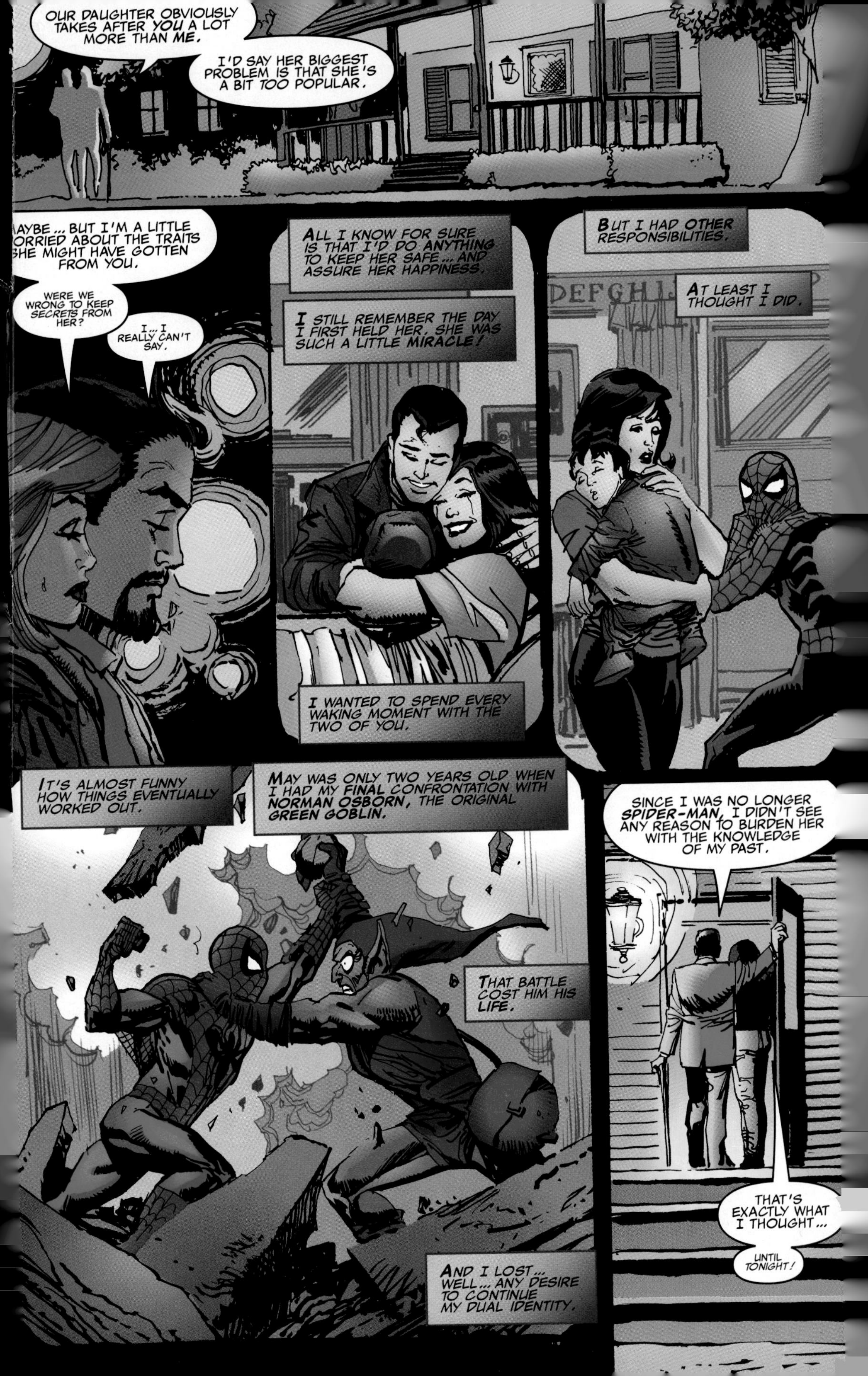
OUR DAUGHTER OBVIOUSLY TAKES AFTER YOU A LOT MORE THAN ME.
I'D SAY HER BIGGEST PROBLEM IS THAT SHE'S A BIT TOO POPULAR.
AYBE... BUT I'M A LITTLE ORRIED ABOUT THE TRAITS HE MIGHT HAVE GOTTEN FROM YOU.
WERE WE WRONG TO KEEP SECRETS FROM HER?
I... I REALLY CAN'T SAY.
ALL I KNOW FOR SURE IS THAT I'D DO ANYTHING TO KEEP HER SAFE... AND ASSURE HER HAPPINESS.
I STILL REMEMBER THE DAY I FIRST HELD HER. SHE WAS SUCH A LITTLE MIRACLE!
I WANTED TO SPEND EVERY WAKING MOMENT WITH THE TWO OF YOU.
BUT I HAD OTHER RESPONSIBILITIES.
AT LEAST I THOUGHT I DID.
DEFGHI
IT'S ALMOST FUNNY HOW THINGS EVENTUALLY WORKED OUT.
MAY WAS ONLY TWO YEARS OLD WHEN I HAD MY FINAL CONFRONTATION WITH NORMAN OSBORN, THE ORIGINAL GREEN GOBLIN.
THAT BATTLE COST HIM HIS LIFE.
AND I LOST... WELL... ANY DESIRE TO CONTINUE MY DUAL IDENTITY.
SINCE I WAS NO LONGER SPIDER-MAN, I DIDN'T SEE ANY REASON TO BURDEN HER WITH THE KNOWLEDGE OF MY PAST.
THAT'S EXACTLY WHAT I THOUGHT...
UNTIL TONIGHT!

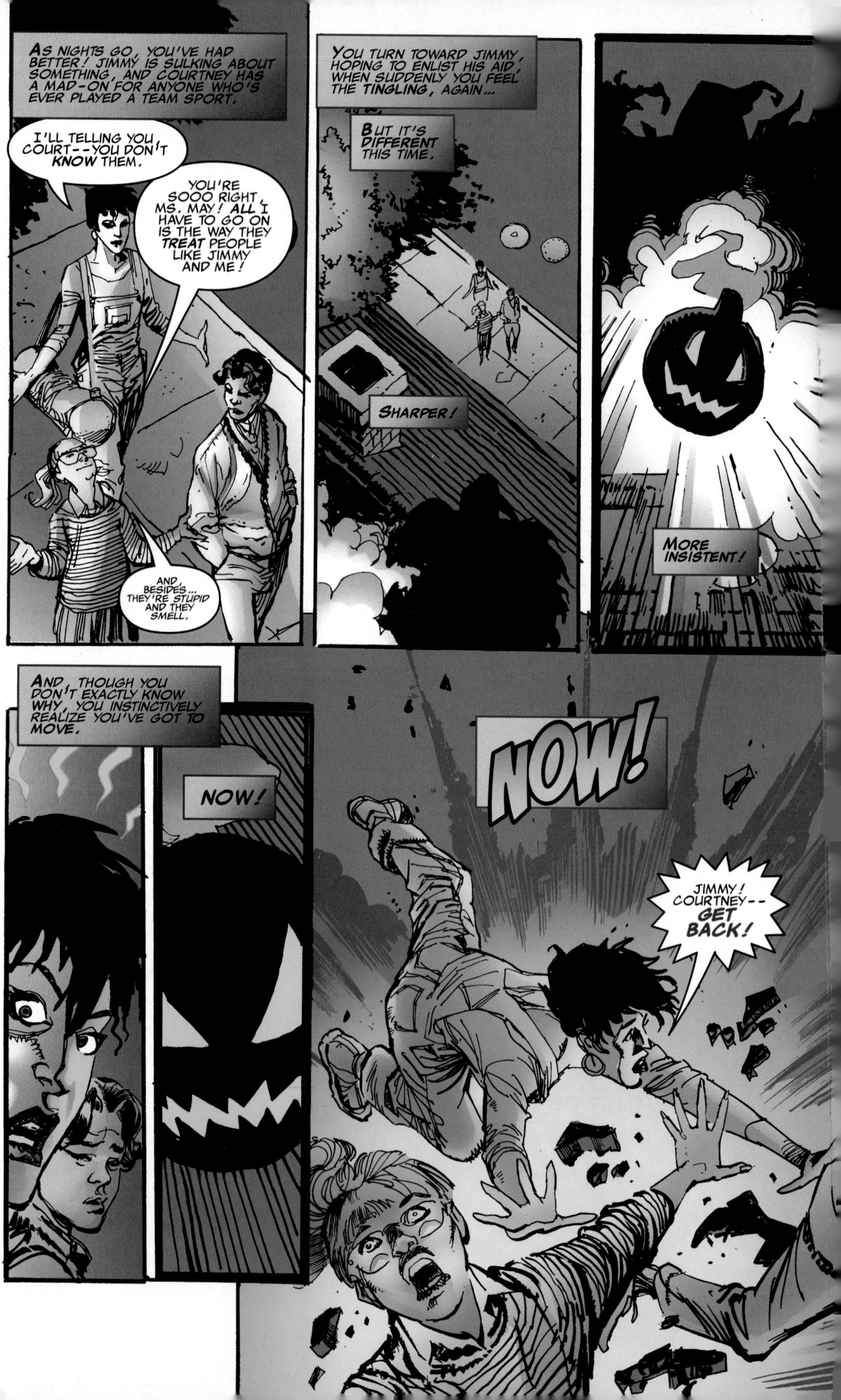
AS NIGHTS GO, YOU'VE HAD BETTER! JIMMY IS SULKING ABOUT SOMETHING, AND COURTNEY HAS A MAD-ON FOR ANYONE WHO'S EVER PLAYED A TEAM SPORT.
I'LL TELLING YOU, COURT--YOU DON'T KNOW THEM.
YOU'RE SOOO RIGHT, MS. MAY! ALL I HAVE TO GO ON IS THE WAY THEY TREAT PEOPLE LIKE JIMMY AND ME!
AND, BESIDES... THEY'RE STUPID AND THEY SMELL.
YOU TURN TOWARD JIMMY, HOPING TO ENLIST HIS AID, WHEN SUDDENLY YOU FEEL THE TINGLING, AGAIN...
BUT IT'S DIFFERENT THIS TIME.
SHARPER!
MORE INSISTENT!
AND, THOUGH YOU DON'T EXACTLY KNOW WHY, YOU INSTINCTIVELY REALIZE YOU'VE GOT TO MOVE.
NOW!
NOW!
JIMMY! COURTNEY--GET BACK!

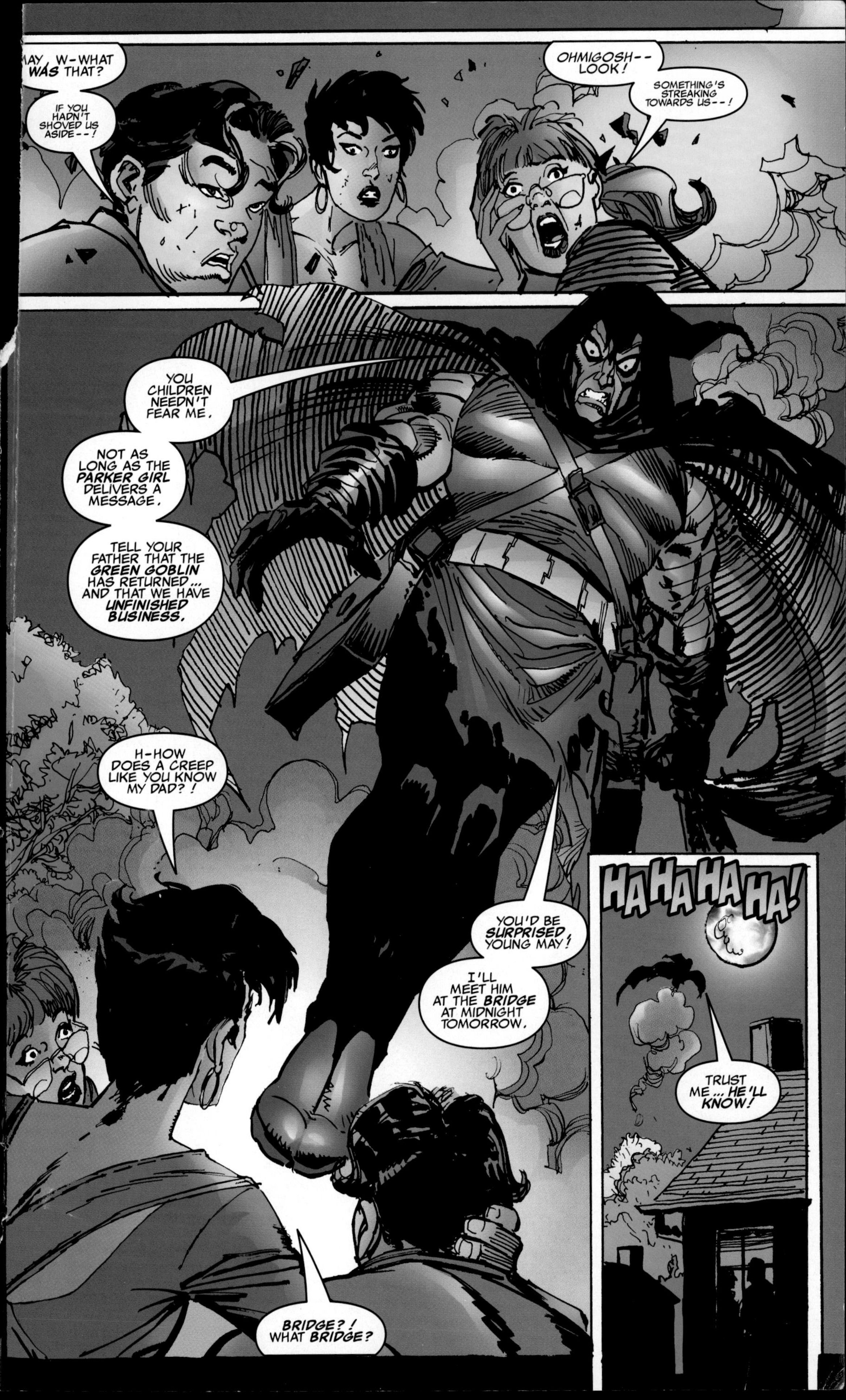
MAY, W-WHAT WAS THAT?
IF YOU HADN'T SHOVED US ASIDE--!
OHMIGOSH--LOOK!
SOMETHING'S STREAKING TOWARDS US--!
YOU CHILDREN NEEDN'T FEAR ME.
NOT AS LONG AS THE PARKER GIRL DELIVERS A MESSAGE.
TELL YOUR FATHER THAT THE GREEN GOBLIN HAS RETURNED... AND THAT WE HAVE UNFINISHED BUSINESS.
H-HOW DOES A CREEP LIKE YOU KNOW MY DAD?!
YOU'D BE SURPRISED, YOUNG MAY!
I'LL MEET HIM AT THE BRIDGE AT MIDNIGHT TOMORROW.
BRIDGE?! WHAT BRIDGE?
HAHAHAHAHA!
TRUST ME... HE'LL KNOW!

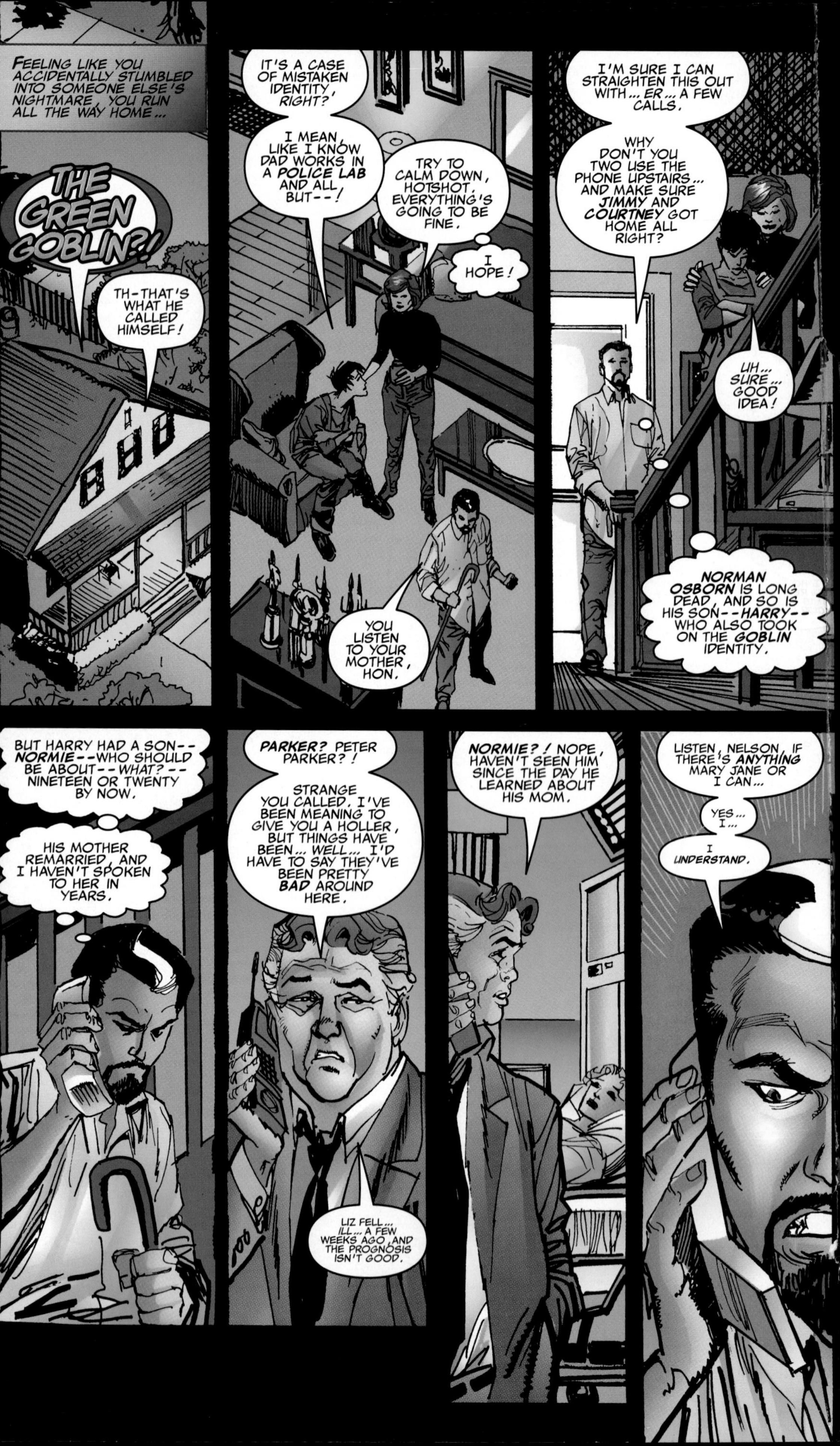
FEELING LIKE YOU ACCIDENTALLY STUMBLED INTO SOMEONE ELSE'S NIGHTMARE, YOU RUN ALL THE WAY HOME...
THE GREEN GOBLIN?!
TH-THAT'S WHAT HE CALLED HIMSELF!
IT'S A CASE OF MISTAKEN IDENTITY, RIGHT?
I MEAN, LIKE I KNOW DAD WORKS IN A POLICE LAB AND ALL, BUT--!
TRY TO CALM DOWN, HOTSHOT. EVERYTHING'S GOING TO BE FINE.
I HOPE!
YOU LISTEN TO YOUR MOTHER, HON.
I'M SURE I CAN STRAIGHTEN THIS OUT WITH... ER... A FEW CALLS.
WHY DON'T YOU TWO USE THE PHONE UPSTAIRS... AND MAKE SURE JIMMY AND COURTNEY GOT HOME ALL RIGHT?
UH... SURE... GOOD IDEA!
NORMAN OSBORN IS LONG DEAD, AND SO IS HIS SON--HARRY--WHO ALSO TOOK ON THE GOBLIN IDENTITY.
BUT HARRY HAD A SON--NORMIE--WHO SHOULD BE ABOUT--WHAT?--NINETEEN OR TWENTY BY NOW.
HIS MOTHER REMARRIED, AND I HAVEN'T SPOKEN TO HER IN YEARS.
PARKER? PETER PARKER?!
STRANGE YOU CALLED. I'VE BEEN MEANING TO GIVE YOU A HOLLER, BUT THINGS HAVE BEEN... WELL... I'D HAVE TO SAY THEY'VE BEEN PRETTY BAD AROUND HERE.
LIZ FELL... ILL... A FEW WEEKS AGO, AND THE PROGNOSIS ISN'T GOOD.
NORMIE?! NOPE, HAVEN'T SEEN HIM SINCE THE DAY HE LEARNED ABOUT HIS MOM.
LISTEN, NELSON, IF THERE'S ANYTHING MARY JANE OR I CAN...
YES... I...
I UNDERSTAND.

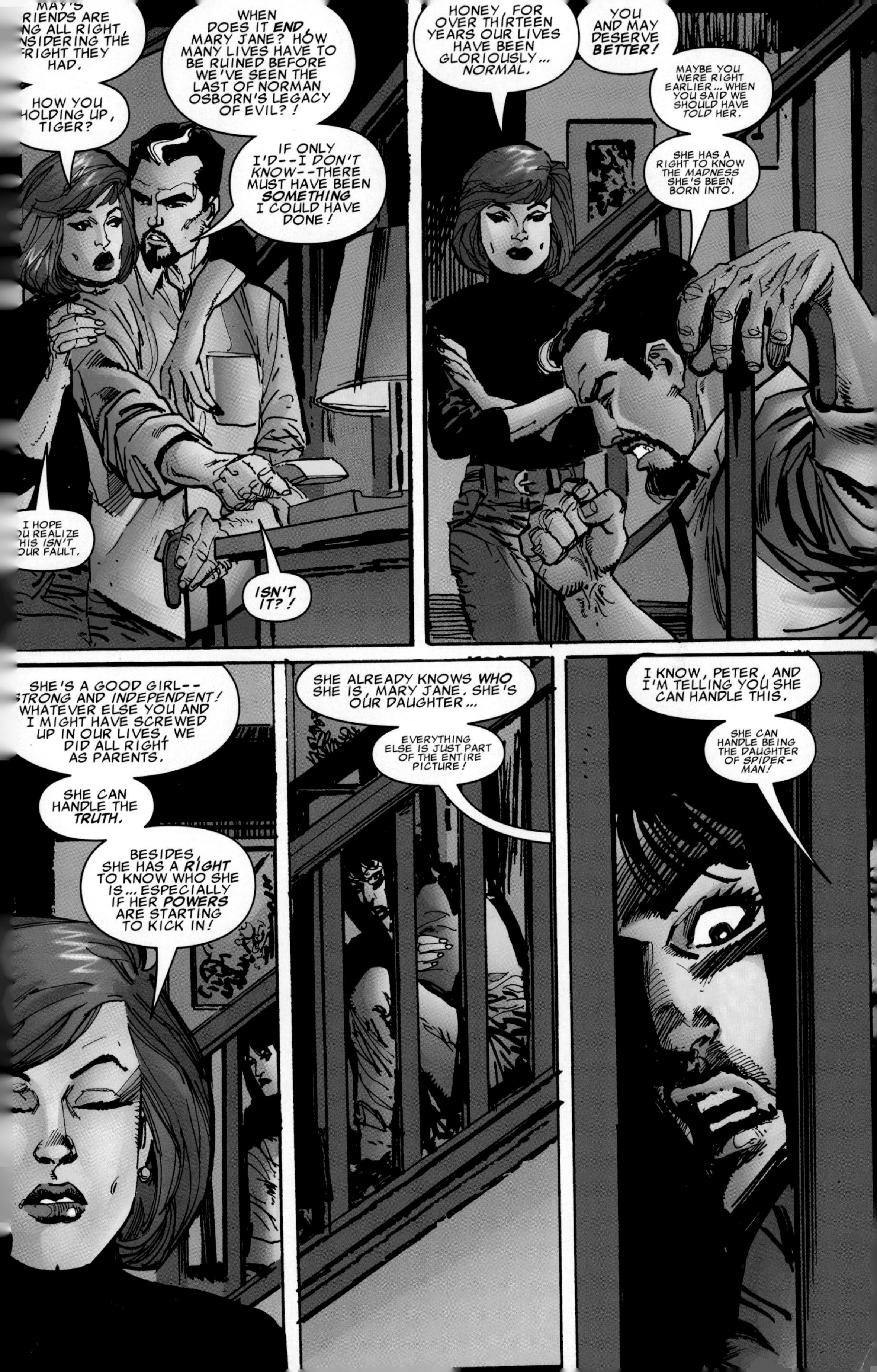
MAY'S RIENDS ARE NG ALL RIGHT, NSIDERING THE FRIGHT THEY HAD.
HOW YOU HOLDING UP, TIGER?
WHEN DOES IT END, MARY JANE? HOW MANY LIVES HAVE TO BE RUINED BEFORE WE'VE SEEN THE LAST OF NORMAN OSBORN'S LEGACY OF EVIL?!
IF ONLY I'D--I DON'T KNOW--THERE MUST HAVE BEEN SOMETHING I COULD HAVE DONE!
I HOPE OU REALIZE THIS ISN'T OUR FAULT.
ISN'T IT?!
HONEY, FOR OVER THIRTEEN YEARS OUR LIVES HAVE BEEN GLORIOUSLY... NORMAL.
YOU AND MAY DESERVE BETTER!
MAYBE YOU WERE RIGHT EARLIER... WHEN YOU SAID WE SHOULD HAVE TOLD HER.
SHE HAS A RIGHT TO KNOW THE MADNESS SHE'S BEEN BORN INTO.
SHE'S A GOOD GIRL-- STRONG AND INDEPENDENT! WHATEVER ELSE YOU AND I MIGHT HAVE SCREWED UP IN OUR LIVES, WE DID ALL RIGHT AS PARENTS.
SHE CAN HANDLE THE TRUTH.
BESIDES, SHE HAS A RIGHT TO KNOW WHO SHE IS... ESPECIALLY IF HER POWERS ARE STARTING TO KICK IN!
SHE ALREADY KNOWS WHO SHE IS, MARY JANE. SHE'S OUR DAUGHTER...
EVERYTHING ELSE IS JUST PART OF THE ENTIRE PICTURE!
I KNOW, PETER, AND I'M TELLING YOU SHE CAN HANDLE THIS.
SHE CAN HANDLE BEING THE DAUGHTER OF SPIDER-MAN!

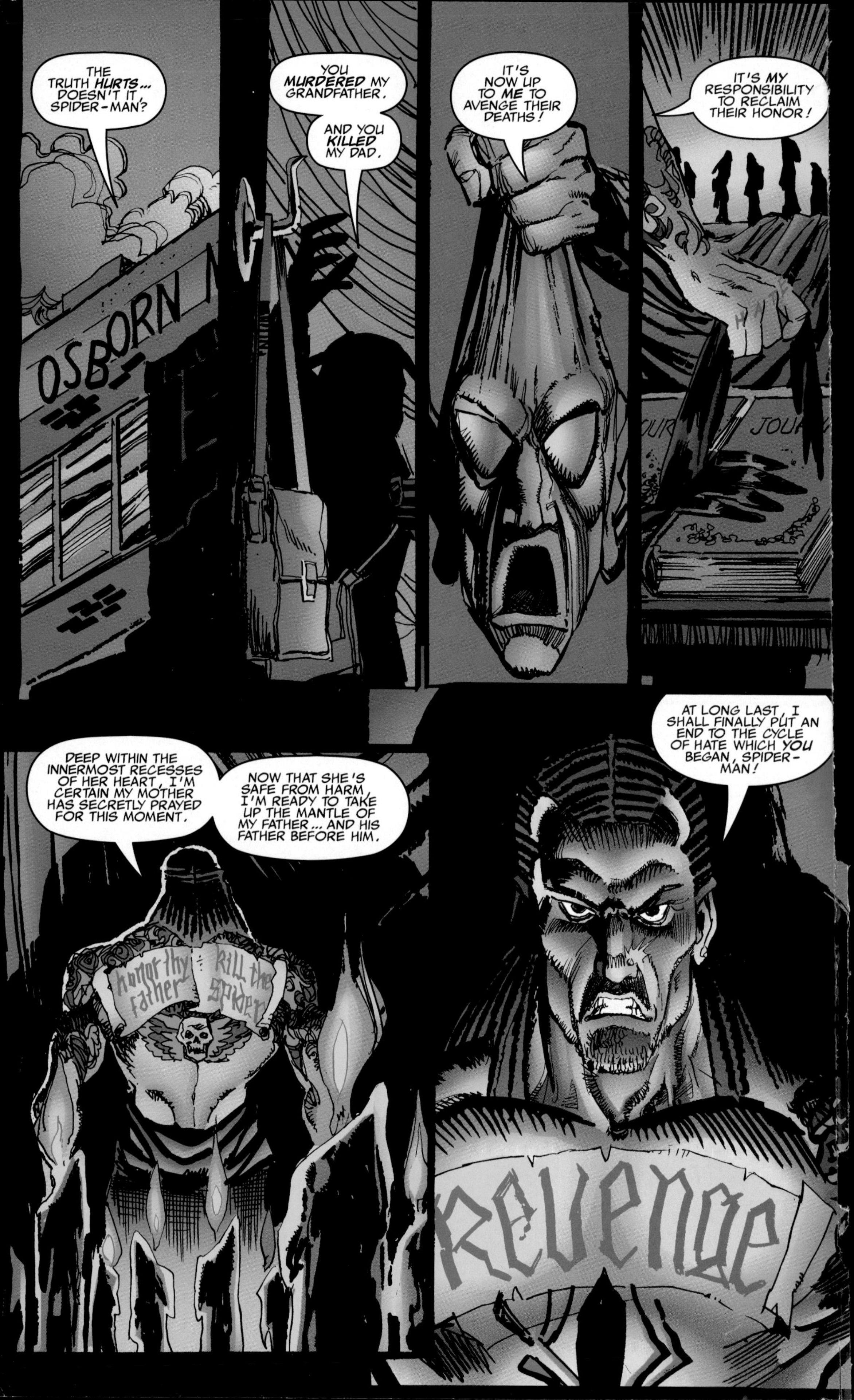
THE TRUTH HURTS... DOESN'T IT, SPIDER-MAN?
YOU MURDERED MY GRANDFATHER.
AND YOU KILLED MY DAD.
IT'S NOW UP TO ME TO AVENGE THEIR DEATHS!
IT'S MY RESPONSIBILITY TO RECLAIM THEIR HONOR!
OSBORN
OSB
DEEP WITHIN THE INNERMOST RECESSES OF HER HEART, I'M CERTAIN MY MOTHER HAS SECRETLY PRAYED FOR THIS MOMENT.
NOW THAT SHE'S SAFE FROM HARM, I'M READY TO TAKE UP THE MANTLE OF MY FATHER... AND HIS FATHER BEFORE HIM.
honor thy father
kill the spider
AT LONG LAST, I SHALL FINALLY PUT AN END TO THE CYCLE OF HATE WHICH YOU BEGAN, SPIDER-MAN!
REVENGE

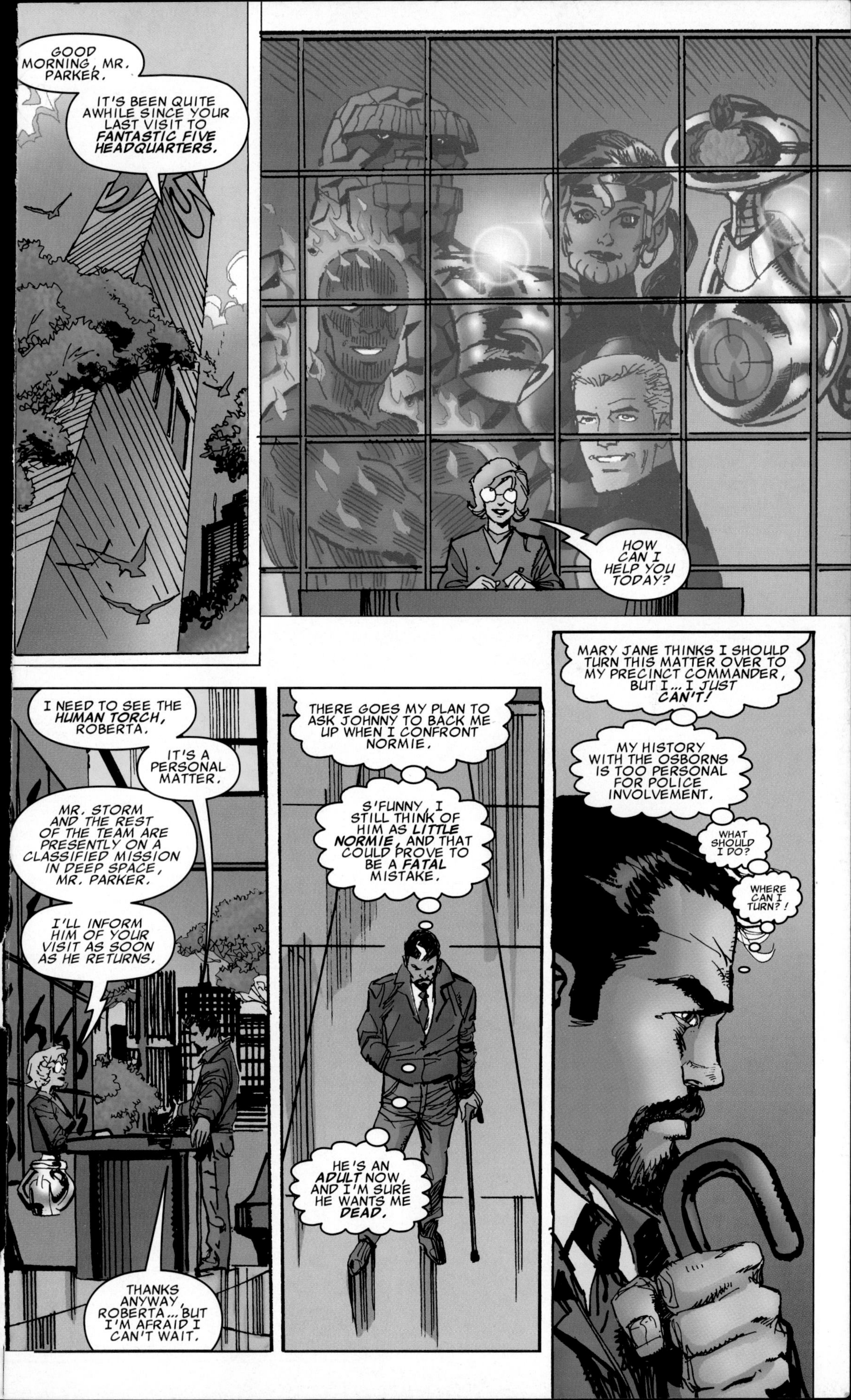
GOOD MORNING, MR. PARKER.
IT'S BEEN QUITE AWHILE SINCE YOUR LAST VISIT TO FANTASTIC FIVE HEADQUARTERS.
HOW CAN I HELP YOU TODAY?
I NEED TO SEE THE HUMAN TORCH, ROBERTA.
IT'S A PERSONAL MATTER.
MR. STORM AND THE REST OF THE TEAM ARE PRESENTLY ON A CLASSIFIED MISSION IN DEEP SPACE, MR. PARKER.
I'LL INFORM HIM OF YOUR VISIT AS SOON AS HE RETURNS.
THANKS ANYWAY, ROBERTA... BUT I'M AFRAID I CAN'T WAIT.
THERE GOES MY PLAN TO ASK JOHNNY TO BACK ME UP WHEN I CONFRONT NORMIE.
S'FUNNY, I STILL THINK OF HIM AS LITTLE NORMIE, AND THAT COULD PROVE TO BE A FATAL MISTAKE.
HE'S AN ADULT NOW, AND I'M SURE HE WANTS ME DEAD.
MARY JANE THINKS I SHOULD TURN THIS MATTER OVER TO MY PRECINCT COMMANDER, BUT I... I JUST CAN'T!
MY HISTORY WITH THE OSBORNS IS TOO PERSONAL FOR POLICE INVOLVEMENT.
WHAT SHOULD I DO?
WHERE CAN I TURN?!

**THWIPPP!**

TWENTY STRAIGHT SWISHES!

I USED TO THINK MY ATHLETIC SKILLS WERE THE RESULT OF TRAINING, PRACTICE, AND HARD WORK...

BUT I'M JUST SOME KIND OF FREAK!

SAAAAAY...

EXACTLY HOW FREAKY AM I?!

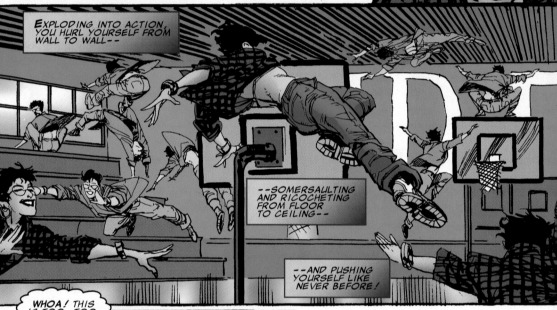

EXPLODING INTO ACTION, YOU HURL YOURSELF FROM WALL TO WALL--

--SOMERSAULTING AND RICOCHETING FROM FLOOR TO CEILING--

--AND PUSHING YOURSELF LIKE NEVER BEFORE!

WHOA! THIS IS TOO, TOO COOOOOL!

BEING A FREAK MAY ACTUALLY BE ALL IT'S CRACKED UP TO BE-- AND MORE!

UH-OH! THAT TINGLING'S BACK, AND--HEY! IT'S DAVIDA, BUT SOMETHING TELLS ME I'D BETTER KEEP THE LID ON MY POWERS!

WHAT'S THE WORD, GIRLY GIRL?

WE STILL TIGHT AFTER LAST NIGHT?

LIKE FOREVER, GIRLFRIEND! YOU'RE STILL MY BEST BUD... EVEN THOUGH I GOTTA BOUNCE NOW.

CALL ME LATER?

BELIEVE IT!

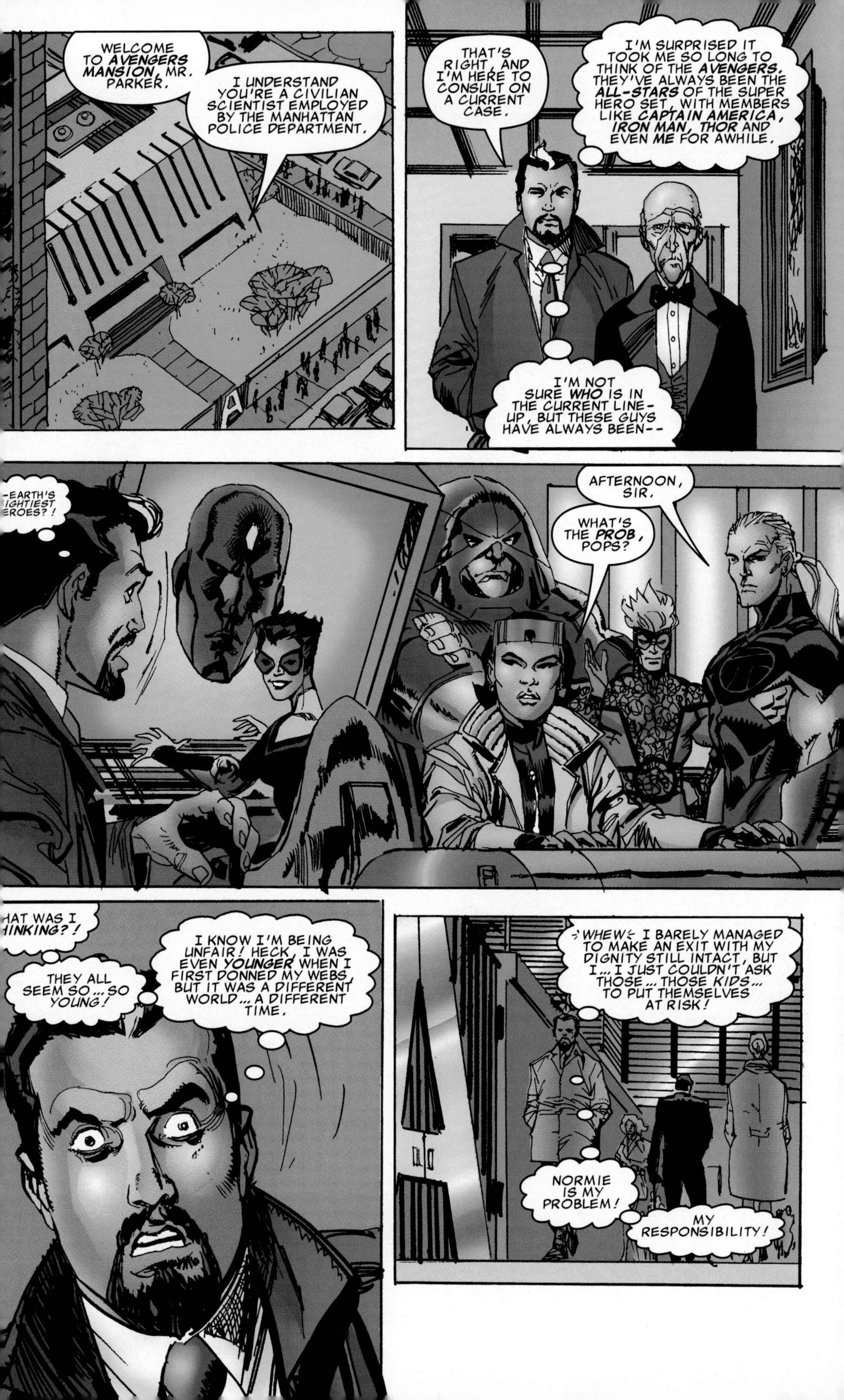
WELCOME TO AVENGERS MANSION, MR. PARKER.
I UNDERSTAND YOU'RE A CIVILIAN SCIENTIST EMPLOYED BY THE MANHATTAN POLICE DEPARTMENT.
THAT'S RIGHT, AND I'M HERE TO CONSULT ON A CURRENT CASE.
I'M SURPRISED IT TOOK ME SO LONG TO THINK OF THE AVENGERS. THEY'VE ALWAYS BEEN THE ALL-STARS OF THE SUPER HERO SET, WITH MEMBERS LIKE CAPTAIN AMERICA, IRON MAN, THOR AND EVEN ME FOR AWHILE.
I'M NOT SURE WHO IS IN THE CURRENT LINE-UP, BUT THESE GUYS HAVE ALWAYS BEEN--
AFTERNOON, SIR.
WHAT'S THE PROB, POPS?
I KNOW I'M BEING UNFAIR! HECK, I WAS EVEN YOUNGER WHEN I FIRST DONNED MY WEBS, BUT IT WAS A DIFFERENT WORLD... A DIFFERENT TIME.
THEY ALL SEEM SO... SO YOUNG!
WHEW! I BARELY MANAGED TO MAKE AN EXIT WITH MY DIGNITY STILL INTACT, BUT I... I JUST COULDN'T ASK THOSE... THOSE KIDS... TO PUT THEMSELVES AT RISK!
NORMIE IS MY PROBLEM!
MY RESPONSIBILITY!

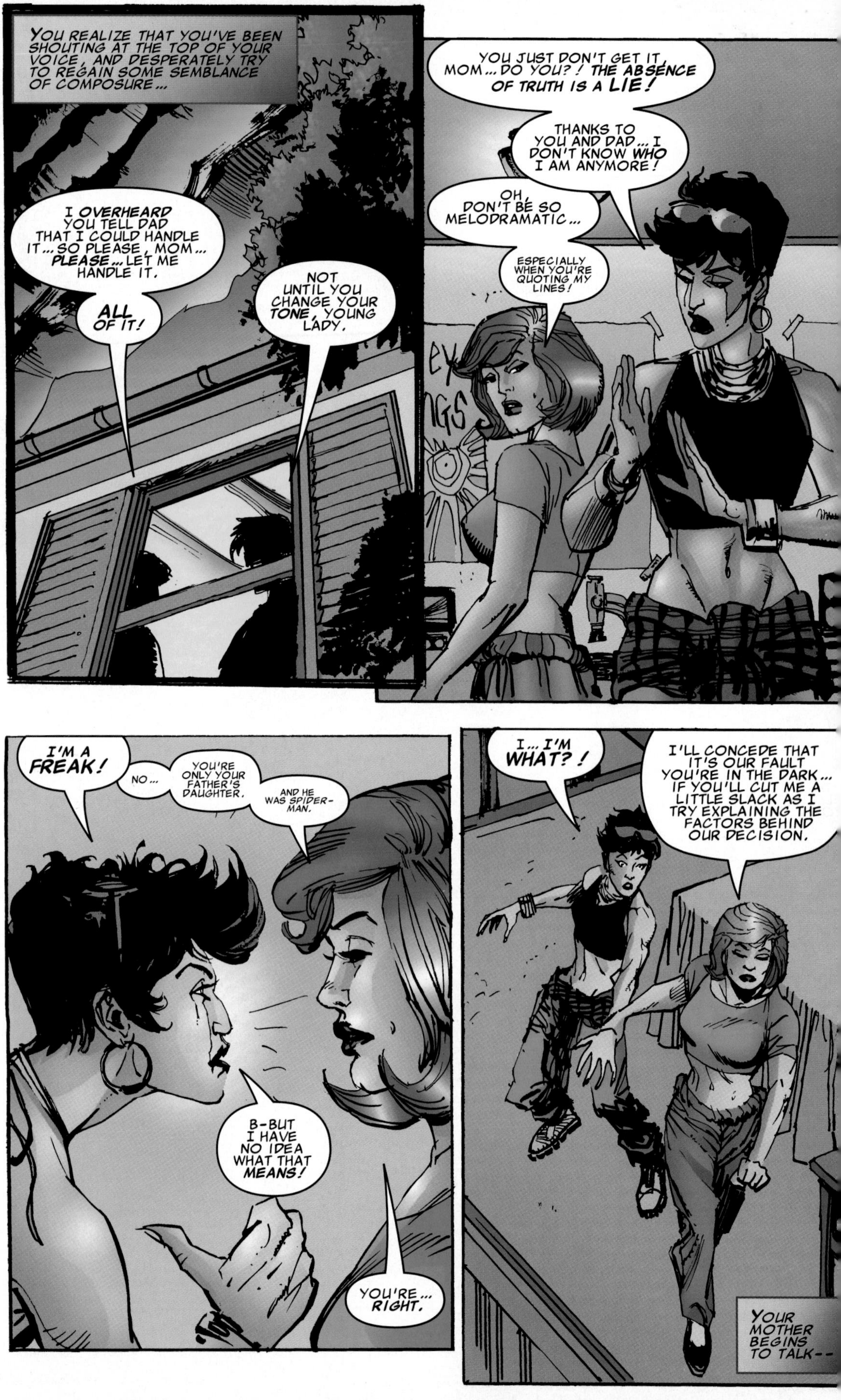
YOU REALIZE THAT YOU'VE BEEN SHOUTING AT THE TOP OF YOUR VOICE, AND DESPERATELY TRY TO REGAIN SOME SEMBLANCE OF COMPOSURE...
I OVERHEARD YOU TELL DAD THAT I COULD HANDLE IT...SO PLEASE, MOM... PLEASE...LET ME HANDLE IT.
ALL OF IT!
NOT UNTIL YOU CHANGE YOUR TONE, YOUNG LADY.
YOU JUST DON'T GET IT, MOM...DO YOU?! THE ABSENCE OF TRUTH IS A LIE!
THANKS TO YOU AND DAD...I DON'T KNOW WHO I AM ANYMORE!
OH, DON'T BE SO MELODRAMATIC...
ESPECIALLY WHEN YOU'RE QUOTING MY LINES!
I'M A FREAK!
NO...
YOU'RE ONLY YOUR FATHER'S DAUGHTER.
AND HE WAS SPIDER-MAN.
B-BUT I HAVE NO IDEA WHAT THAT MEANS!
YOU'RE... RIGHT.
I... I'M WHAT?!
I'LL CONCEDE THAT IT'S OUR FAULT YOU'RE IN THE DARK... IF YOU'LL CUT ME A LITTLE SLACK AS I TRY EXPLAINING THE FACTORS BEHIND OUR DECISION.
YOUR MOTHER BEGINS TO TALK--

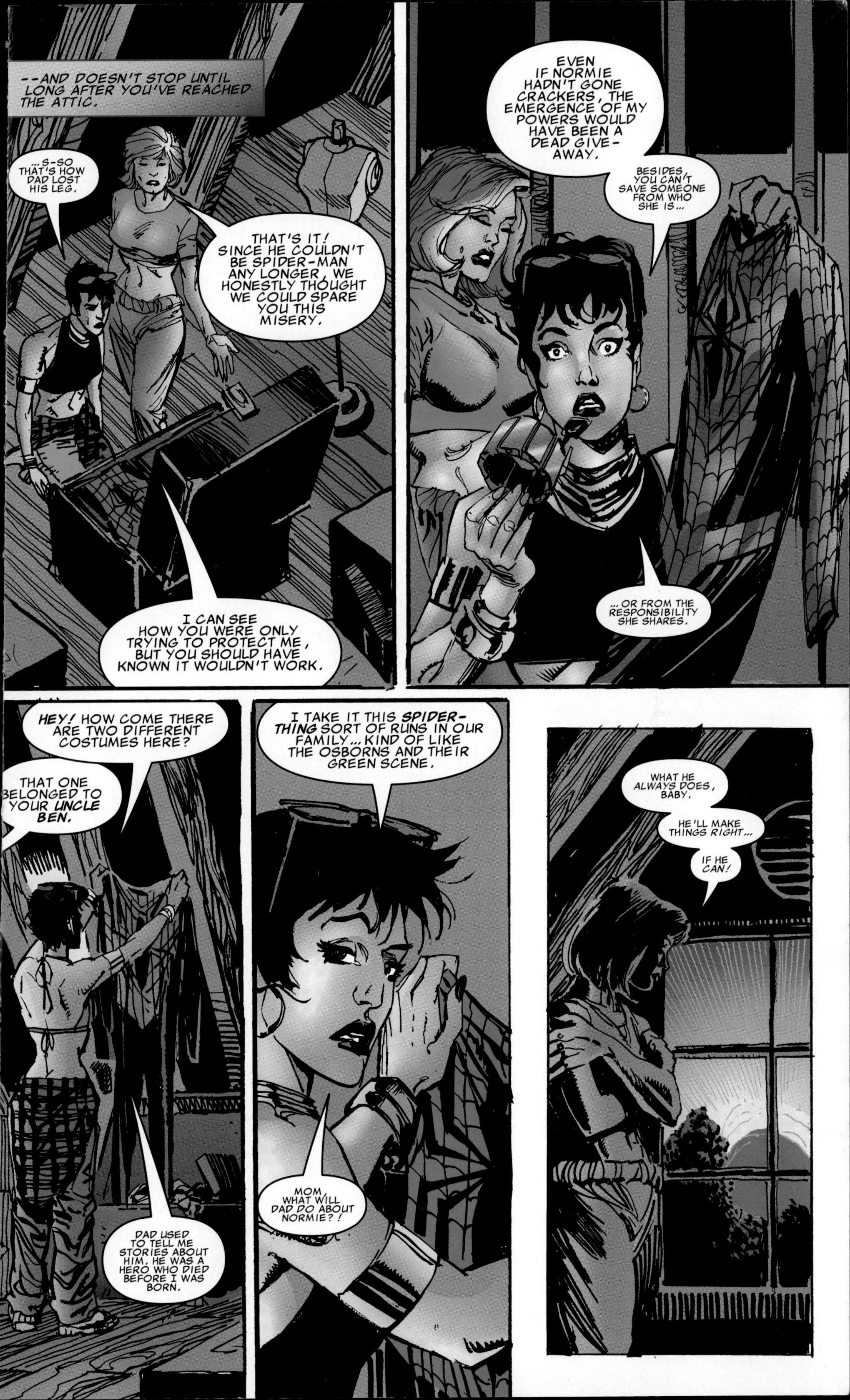
--AND DOESN'T STOP UNTIL LONG AFTER YOU'VE REACHED THE ATTIC.
...S-SO THAT'S HOW DAD LOST HIS LEG.
THAT'S IT! SINCE HE COULDN'T BE SPIDER-MAN ANY LONGER, WE HONESTLY THOUGHT WE COULD SPARE YOU THIS MISERY.
I CAN SEE HOW YOU WERE ONLY TRYING TO PROTECT ME, BUT YOU SHOULD HAVE KNOWN IT WOULDN'T WORK.
EVEN IF NORMIE HADN'T GONE CRACKERS, THE EMERGENCE OF MY POWERS WOULD HAVE BEEN A DEAD GIVE-AWAY.
BESIDES, YOU CAN'T SAVE SOMEONE FROM WHO SHE IS...
...OR FROM THE RESPONSIBILITY SHE SHARES.
HEY! HOW COME THERE ARE TWO DIFFERENT COSTUMES HERE?
THAT ONE BELONGED TO YOUR UNCLE BEN.
DAD USED TO TELL ME STORIES ABOUT HIM. HE WAS A HERO WHO DIED BEFORE I WAS BORN.
I TAKE IT THIS SPIDER-THING SORT OF RUNS IN OUR FAMILY... KIND OF LIKE THE OSBORNS AND THEIR GREEN SCENE.
MOM, WHAT WILL DAD DO ABOUT NORMIE?!
WHAT HE ALWAYS DOES, BABY.
HE'LL MAKE THINGS RIGHT...
IF HE CAN!

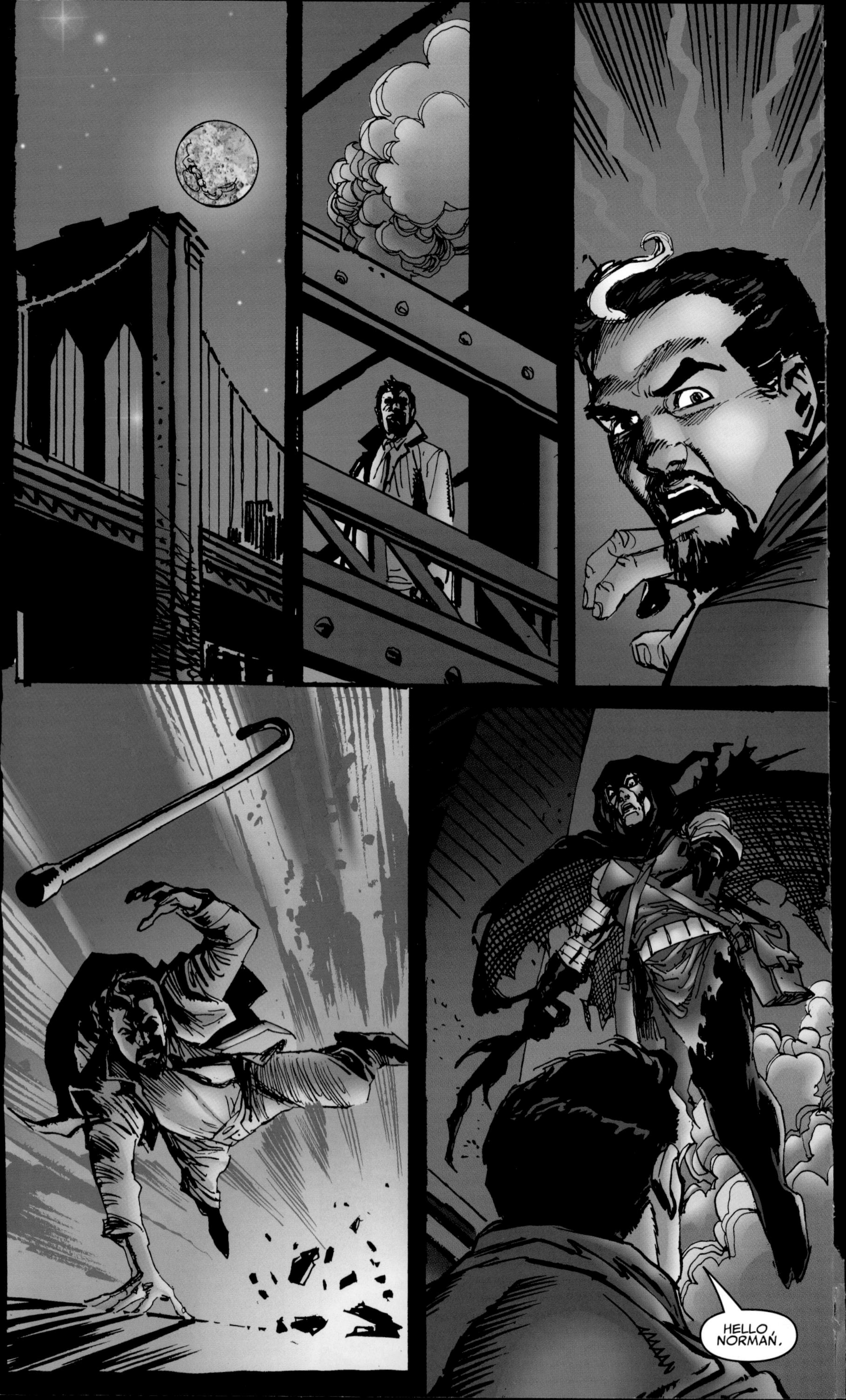
HELLO, NORMAN.

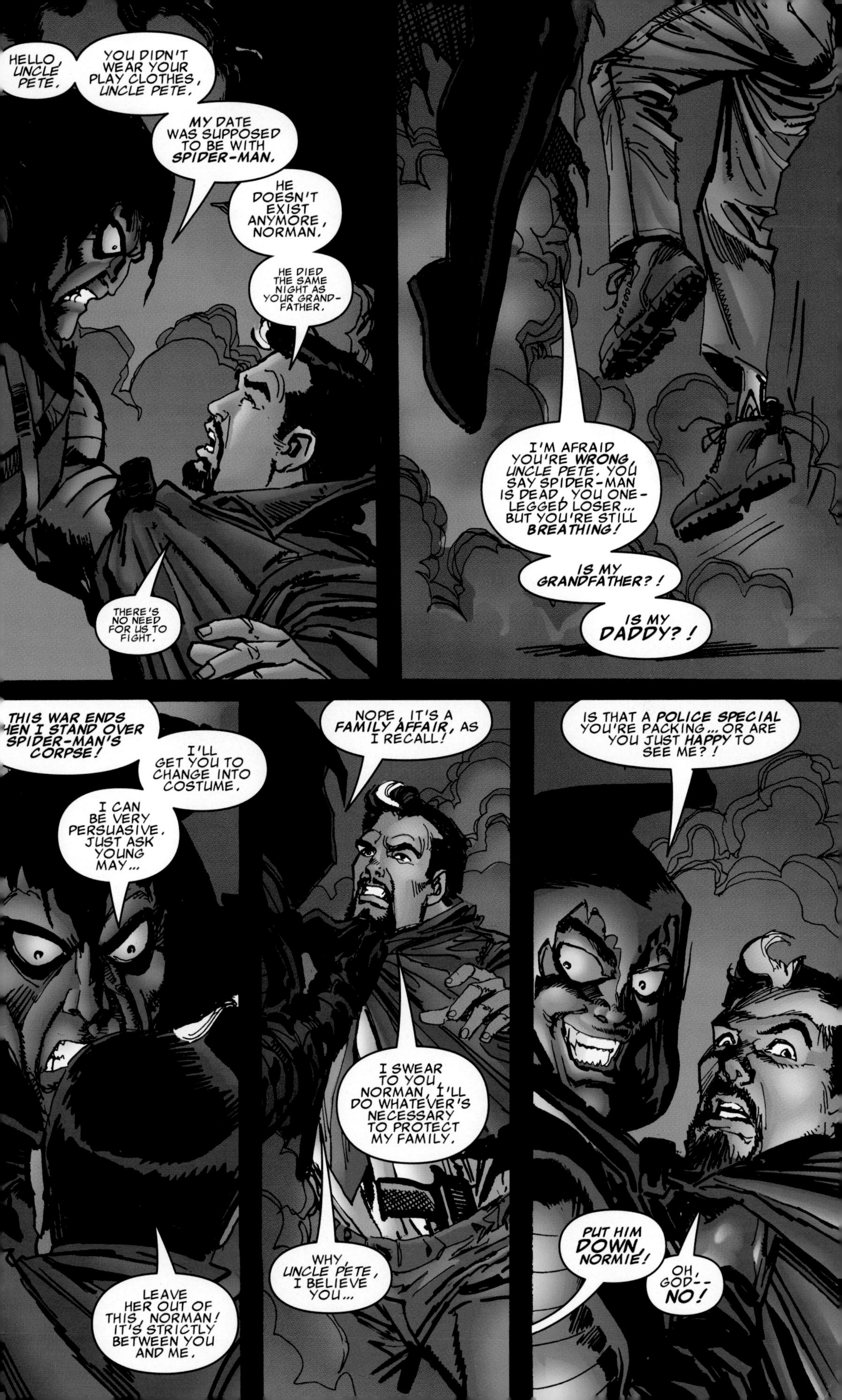

HELLO, UNCLE PETE.
YOU DIDN'T WEAR YOUR PLAY CLOTHES, UNCLE PETE.
MY DATE WAS SUPPOSED TO BE WITH SPIDER-MAN.
HE DOESN'T EXIST ANYMORE, NORMAN.
HE DIED THE SAME NIGHT AS YOUR GRAND-FATHER.
THERE'S NO NEED FOR US TO FIGHT.
I'M AFRAID YOU'RE WRONG, UNCLE PETE. YOU SAY SPIDER-MAN IS DEAD, YOU ONE-LEGGED LOSER... BUT YOU'RE STILL BREATHING!
IS MY GRANDFATHER?!
IS MY DADDY?!
THIS WAR ENDS HEN I STAND OVER SPIDER-MAN'S CORPSE!
I'LL GET YOU TO CHANGE INTO COSTUME.
I CAN BE VERY PERSUASIVE. JUST ASK YOUNG MAY...
LEAVE HER OUT OF THIS, NORMAN! IT'S STRICTLY BETWEEN YOU AND ME.
NOPE, IT'S A FAMILY AFFAIR, AS I RECALL!
I SWEAR TO YOU, NORMAN, I'LL DO WHATEVER'S NECESSARY TO PROTECT MY FAMILY.
WHY, UNCLE PETE, I BELIEVE YOU...
IS THAT A POLICE SPECIAL YOU'RE PACKING... OR ARE YOU JUST HAPPY TO SEE ME?!
PUT HIM DOWN, NORMIE!
OH, GOD-- NO!

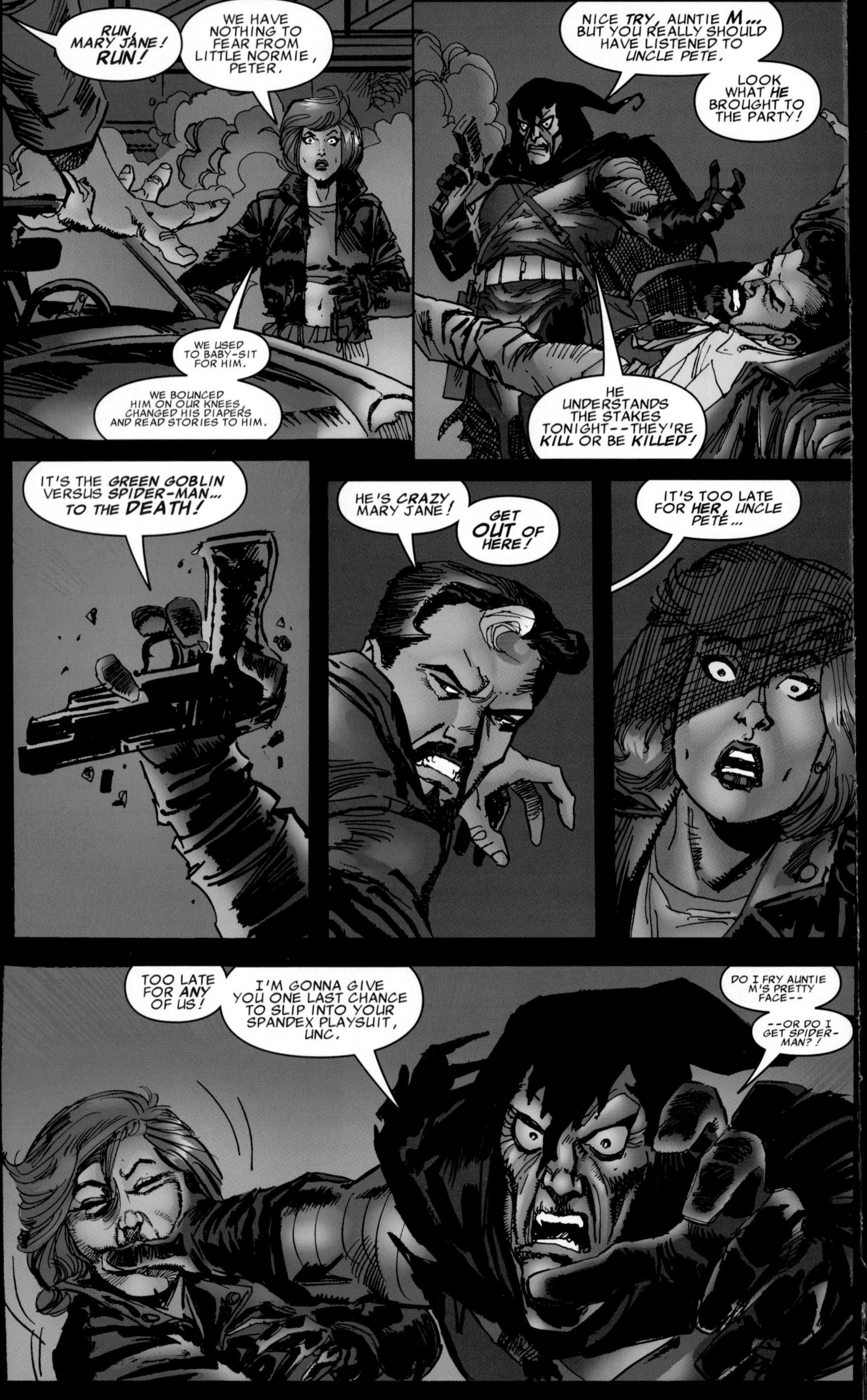
RUN, MARY JANE! RUN!
WE HAVE NOTHING TO FEAR FROM LITTLE NORMIE, PETER.
WE USED TO BABY-SIT FOR HIM.
WE BOUNCED HIM ON OUR KNEES, CHANGED HIS DIAPERS AND READ STORIES TO HIM.
NICE TRY, AUNTIE M... BUT YOU REALLY SHOULD HAVE LISTENED TO UNCLE PETE.
LOOK WHAT HE BROUGHT TO THE PARTY!
HE UNDERSTANDS THE STAKES TONIGHT--THEY'RE KILL OR BE KILLED!
IT'S THE GREEN GOBLIN VERSUS SPIDER-MAN... TO THE DEATH!
HE'S CRAZY, MARY JANE!
GET OUT OF HERE!
IT'S TOO LATE FOR HER, UNCLE PETE...
TOO LATE FOR ANY OF US!
I'M GONNA GIVE YOU ONE LAST CHANCE TO SLIP INTO YOUR SPANDEX PLAYSUIT, UNC.
DO I FRY AUNTIE M'S PRETTY FACE--
--OR DO I GET SPIDER-MAN?!

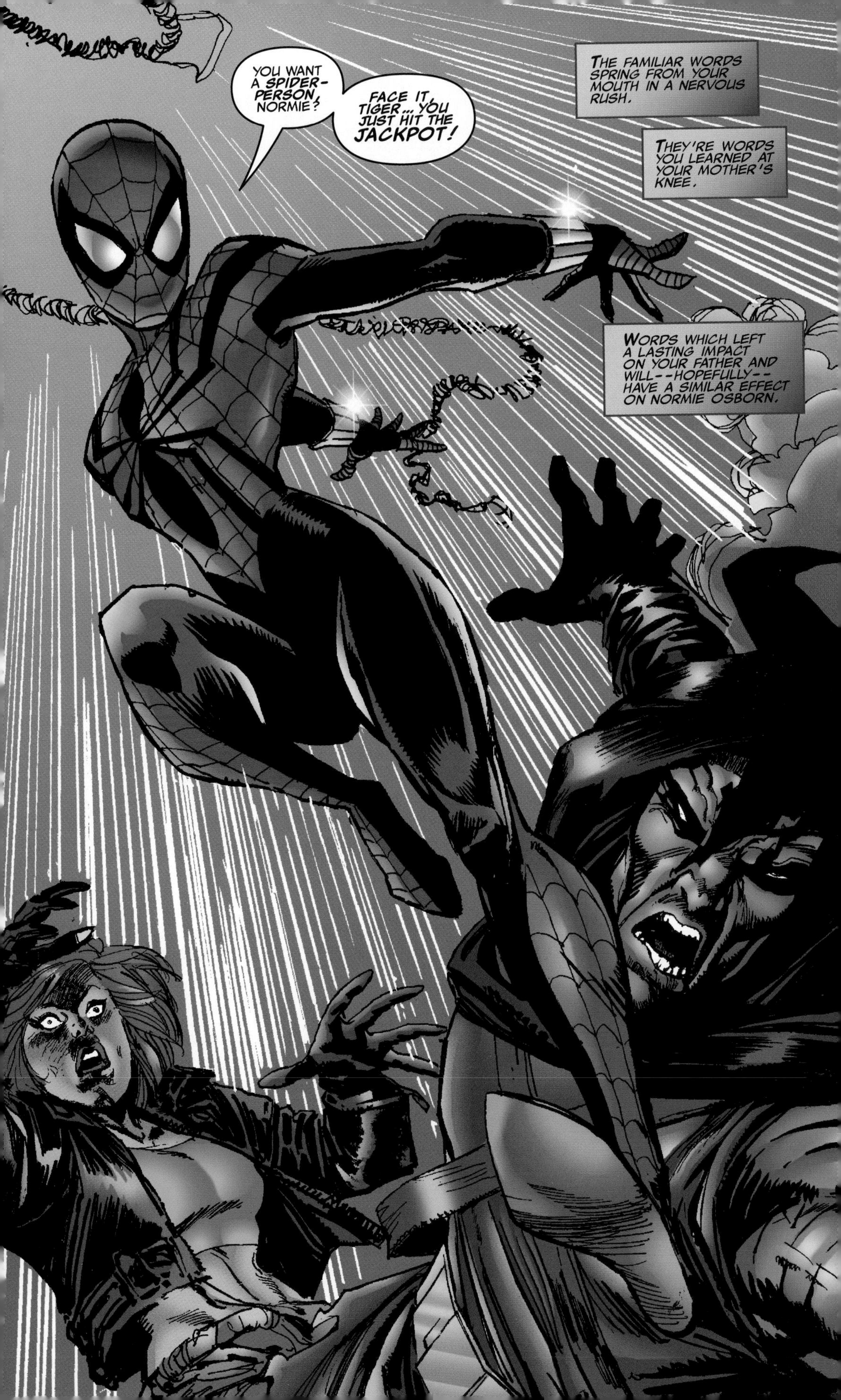
YOU WANT A SPIDER-PERSON, NORMIE?
FACE IT, TIGER... YOU JUST HIT THE JACKPOT!
THE FAMILIAR WORDS SPRING FROM YOUR MOUTH IN A NERVOUS RUSH.
THEY'RE WORDS YOU LEARNED AT YOUR MOTHER'S KNEE.
WORDS WHICH LEFT A LASTING IMPACT ON YOUR FATHER AND WILL--HOPEFULLY--HAVE A SIMILAR EFFECT ON NORMIE OSBORN.

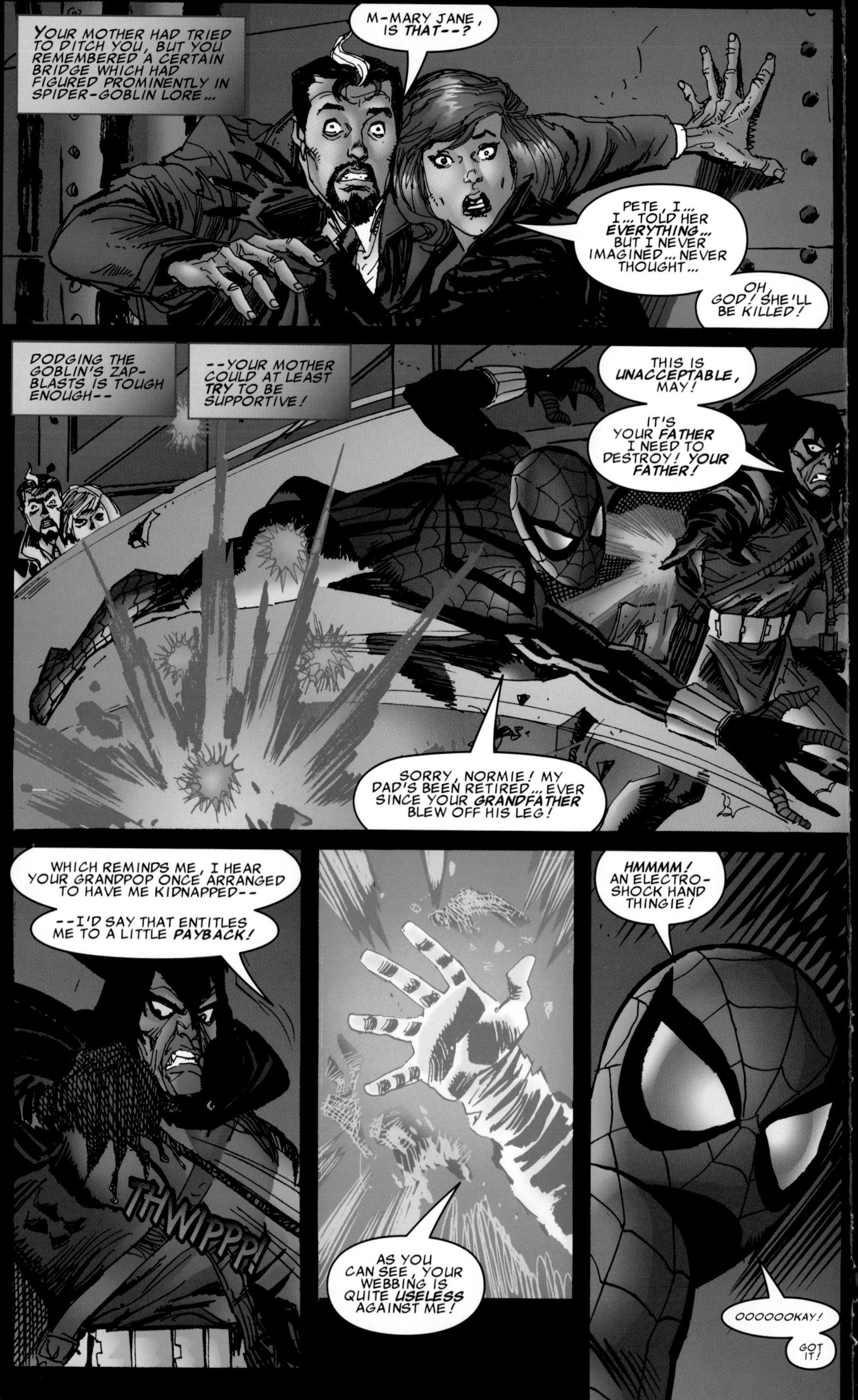
YOUR MOTHER HAD TRIED TO DITCH YOU, BUT YOU REMEMBERED A CERTAIN BRIDGE WHICH HAD FIGURED PROMINENTLY IN SPIDER-GOBLIN LORE...
M-MARY JANE, IS THAT--?
PETE, I... I... TOLD HER EVERYTHING... BUT I NEVER IMAGINED... NEVER THOUGHT...
OH, GOD! SHE'LL BE KILLED!
DODGING THE GOBLIN'S ZAP-BLASTS IS TOUGH ENOUGH--
--YOUR MOTHER COULD AT LEAST TRY TO BE SUPPORTIVE!
THIS IS UNACCEPTABLE, MAY!
IT'S YOUR FATHER I NEED TO DESTROY! YOUR FATHER!
SORRY, NORMIE! MY DAD'S BEEN RETIRED... EVER SINCE YOUR GRANDFATHER BLEW OFF HIS LEG!
WHICH REMINDS ME, I HEAR YOUR GRANDPOP ONCE ARRANGED TO HAVE ME KIDNAPPED--
--I'D SAY THAT ENTITLES ME TO A LITTLE PAYBACK!
THWIPPP!
AS YOU CAN SEE, YOUR WEBBING IS QUITE USELESS AGAINST ME!
HMMMM! AN ELECTRO-SHOCK HAND THINGIE!
OOOOOOKAY!
GOT IT!

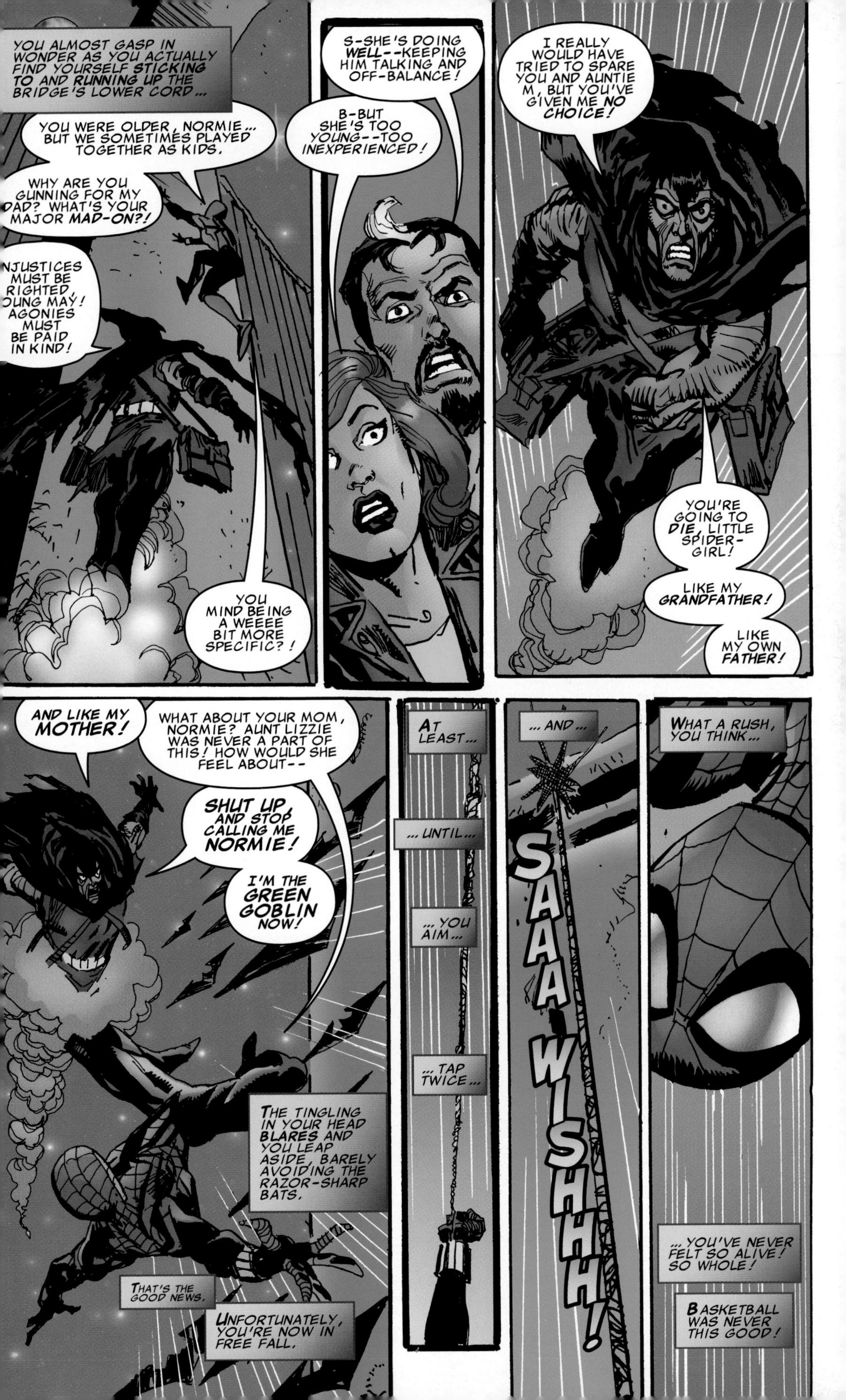
YOU ALMOST GASP IN WONDER AS YOU ACTUALLY FIND YOURSELF STICKING TO AND RUNNING UP THE BRIDGE'S LOWER CORD...
YOU WERE OLDER, NORMIE... BUT WE SOMETIMES PLAYED TOGETHER AS KIDS.
WHY ARE YOU GUNNING FOR MY DAD? WHAT'S YOUR MAJOR MAD-ON?!
INJUSTICES MUST BE RIGHTED, YOUNG MAY! AGONIES MUST BE PAID IN KIND!
YOU MIND BEING A WEEEE BIT MORE SPECIFIC?!
S-SHE'S DOING WELL--KEEPING HIM TALKING AND OFF-BALANCE!
B-BUT SHE'S TOO YOUNG--TOO INEXPERIENCED!
I REALLY WOULD HAVE TRIED TO SPARE YOU AND AUNTIE M, BUT YOU'VE GIVEN ME NO CHOICE!
YOU'RE GOING TO DIE, LITTLE SPIDER-GIRL!
LIKE MY GRANDFATHER!
LIKE MY OWN FATHER!
AND LIKE MY MOTHER!
WHAT ABOUT YOUR MOM, NORMIE? AUNT LIZZIE WAS NEVER A PART OF THIS! HOW WOULD SHE FEEL ABOUT--
SHUT UP, AND STOP CALLING ME NORMIE!
I'M THE GREEN GOBLIN NOW!
THE TINGLING IN YOUR HEAD BLARES AND YOU LEAP ASIDE, BARELY AVOIDING THE RAZOR-SHARP BATS.
THAT'S THE GOOD NEWS.
UNFORTUNATELY, YOU'RE NOW IN FREE FALL.
AT LEAST...
...UNTIL...
...YOU AIM...
...TAP TWICE...
...AND...
SAAAWISHHH!
WHAT A RUSH, YOU THINK...
...YOU'VE NEVER FELT SO ALIVE! SO WHOLE!
BASKETBALL WAS NEVER THIS GOOD!

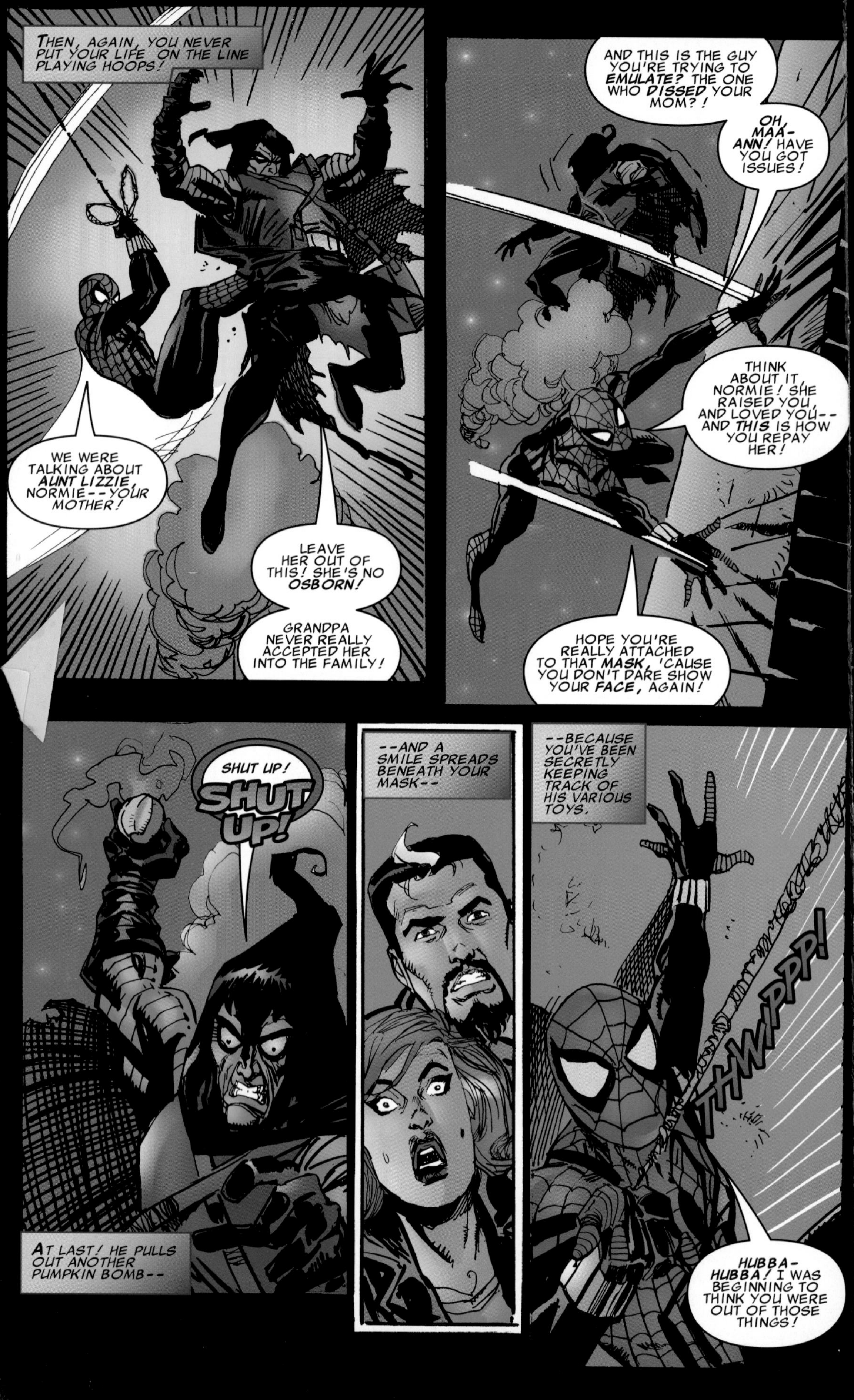
THEN, AGAIN, YOU NEVER PUT YOUR LIFE ON THE LINE PLAYING HOOPS!
WE WERE TALKING ABOUT AUNT LIZZIE, NORMIE--YOUR MOTHER!
LEAVE HER OUT OF THIS! SHE'S NO OSBORN!
GRANDPA NEVER REALLY ACCEPTED HER INTO THE FAMILY!
AND THIS IS THE GUY YOU'RE TRYING TO EMULATE? THE ONE WHO DISSED YOUR MOM?!
OH, MAA-ANN! HAVE YOU GOT ISSUES!
THINK ABOUT IT, NORMIE! SHE RAISED YOU, AND LOVED YOU--AND THIS IS HOW YOU REPAY HER!
HOPE YOU'RE REALLY ATTACHED TO THAT MASK, 'CAUSE YOU DON'T DARE SHOW YOUR FACE, AGAIN!
SHUT UP!
SHUT UP!
AT LAST! HE PULLS OUT ANOTHER PUMPKIN BOMB--
--AND A SMILE SPREADS BENEATH YOUR MASK--
--BECAUSE YOU'VE BEEN SECRETLY KEEPING TRACK OF HIS VARIOUS TOYS.
THWIPPP!
HUBBA-HUBBA! I WAS BEGINNING TO THINK YOU WERE OUT OF THOSE THINGS!

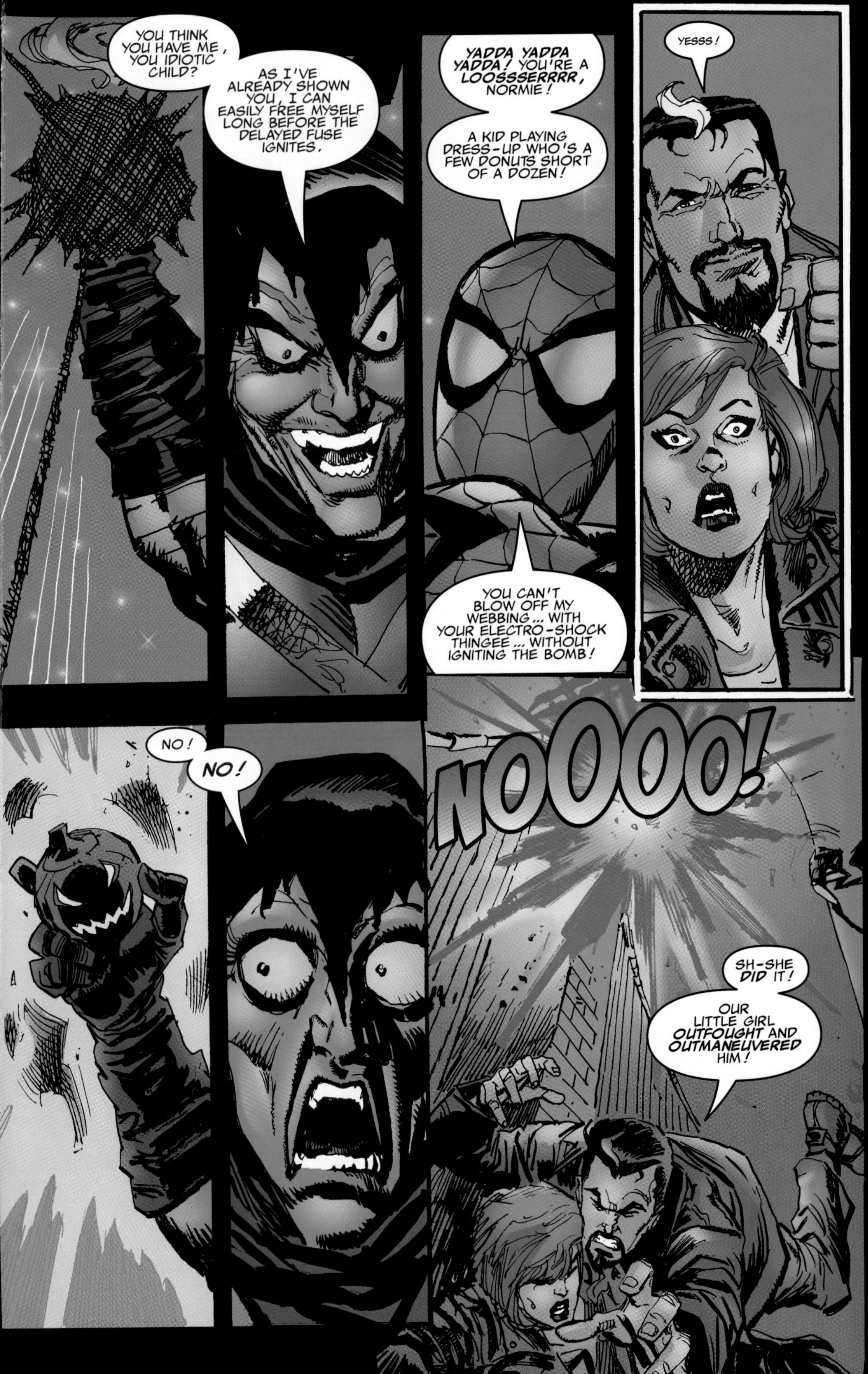
YOU THINK YOU HAVE ME, YOU IDIOTIC CHILD?
AS I'VE ALREADY SHOWN YOU, I CAN EASILY FREE MYSELF LONG BEFORE THE DELAYED FUSE IGNITES.
YADDA YADDA YADDA! YOU'RE A LOOSSSERRRR, NORMIE!
A KID PLAYING DRESS-UP WHO'S A FEW DONUTS SHORT OF A DOZEN!
YOU CAN'T BLOW OFF MY WEBBING... WITH YOUR ELECTRO-SHOCK THINGEE... WITHOUT IGNITING THE BOMB!
YESSS!
NO!
NO!
NOOOO!
SH-SHE DID IT!
OUR LITTLE GIRL OUTFOUGHT AND OUTMANEUVERED HIM!

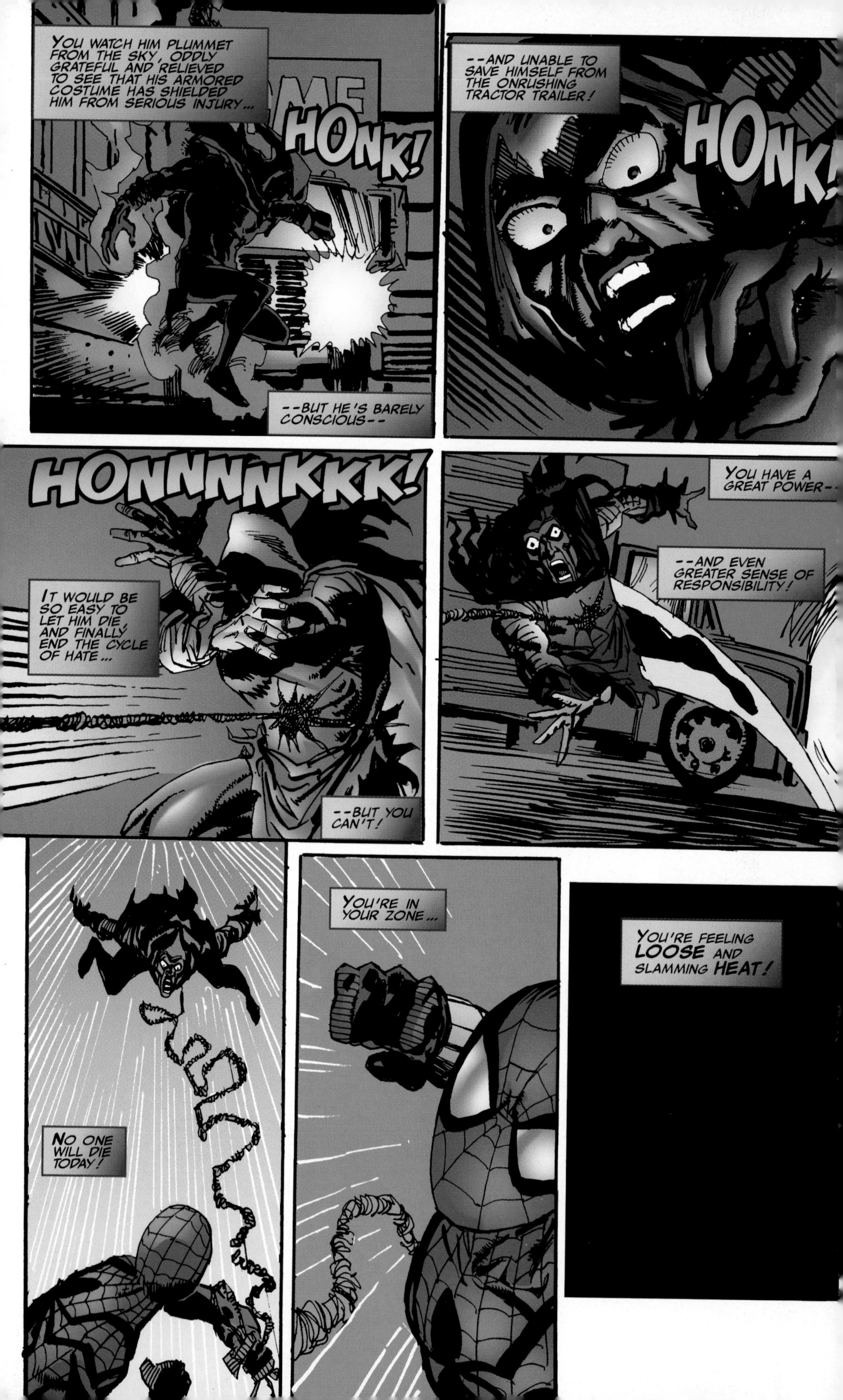

YOU WATCH HIM PLUMMET FROM THE SKY, ODDLY GRATEFUL AND RELIEVED TO SEE THAT HIS ARMORED COSTUME HAS SHIELDED HIM FROM SERIOUS INJURY...
HONK!
--BUT HE'S BARELY CONSCIOUS--
--AND UNABLE TO SAVE HIMSELF FROM THE ONRUSHING TRACTOR TRAILER!
HONK!
HONNNNKKK!
IT WOULD BE SO EASY TO LET HIM DIE, AND FINALLY END THE CYCLE OF HATE...
--BUT YOU CAN'T!
YOU HAVE A GREAT POWER--
--AND EVEN GREATER SENSE OF RESPONSIBILITY!
NO ONE WILL DIE TODAY!
YOU'RE IN YOUR ZONE...
YOU'RE FEELING LOOSE AND SLAMMING HEAT!

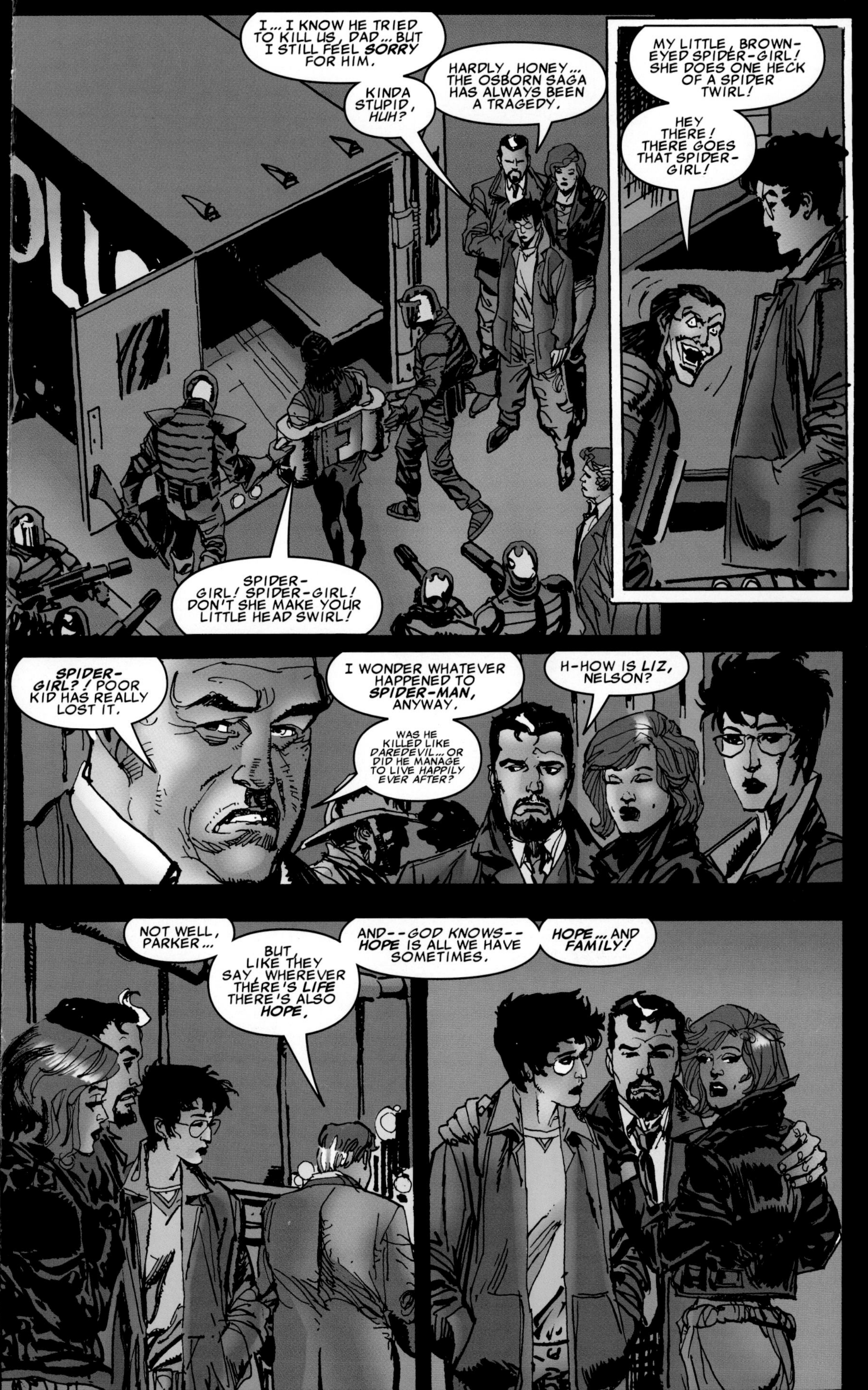
I... I KNOW HE TRIED TO KILL US, DAD... BUT I STILL FEEL SORRY FOR HIM.
KINDA STUPID, HUH?
HARDLY, HONEY... THE OSBORN SAGA HAS ALWAYS BEEN A TRAGEDY.
MY LITTLE, BROWN-EYED SPIDER-GIRL! SHE DOES ONE HECK OF A SPIDER TWIRL!
HEY THERE! THERE GOES THAT SPIDER-GIRL!
SPIDER-GIRL! SPIDER-GIRL! DON'T SHE MAKE YOUR LITTLE HEAD SWIRL!
SPIDER-GIRL?! POOR KID HAS REALLY LOST IT.
I WONDER WHATEVER HAPPENED TO SPIDER-MAN, ANYWAY.
WAS HE KILLED LIKE DAREDEVIL... OR DID HE MANAGE TO LIVE HAPPILY EVER AFTER?
H-HOW IS LIZ, NELSON?
NOT WELL, PARKER...
BUT, LIKE THEY SAY, WHEREVER THERE'S LIFE THERE'S ALSO HOPE.
AND--GOD KNOWS--HOPE IS ALL WE HAVE SOMETIMES.
HOPE... AND FAMILY!

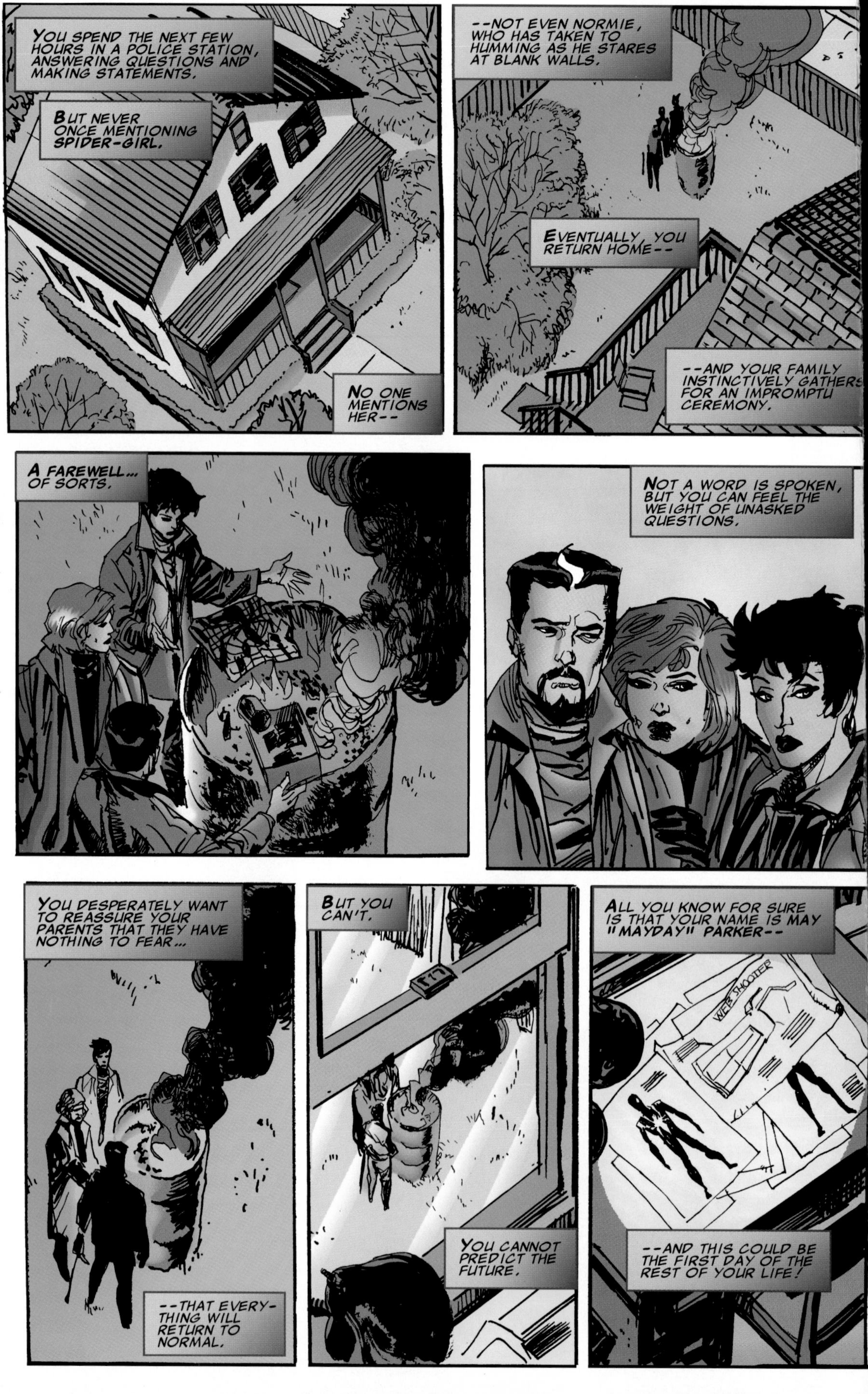
YOU SPEND THE NEXT FEW HOURS IN A POLICE STATION, ANSWERING QUESTIONS AND MAKING STATEMENTS.
BUT NEVER ONCE MENTIONING SPIDER-GIRL.
NO ONE MENTIONS HER--
--NOT EVEN NORMIE, WHO HAS TAKEN TO HUMMING AS HE STARES AT BLANK WALLS.
EVENTUALLY, YOU RETURN HOME--
--AND YOUR FAMILY INSTINCTIVELY GATHERS FOR AN IMPROMPTU CEREMONY.
A FAREWELL... OF SORTS.
NOT A WORD IS SPOKEN, BUT YOU CAN FEEL THE WEIGHT OF UNASKED QUESTIONS.
YOU DESPERATELY WANT TO REASSURE YOUR PARENTS THAT THEY HAVE NOTHING TO FEAR...
--THAT EVERY-THING WILL RETURN TO NORMAL.
BUT YOU CAN'T.
YOU CANNOT PREDICT THE FUTURE.
ALL YOU KNOW FOR SURE IS THAT YOUR NAME IS MAY "MAYDAY" PARKER--
WEB SHOOTER
--AND THIS COULD BE THE FIRST DAY OF THE REST OF YOUR LIFE!

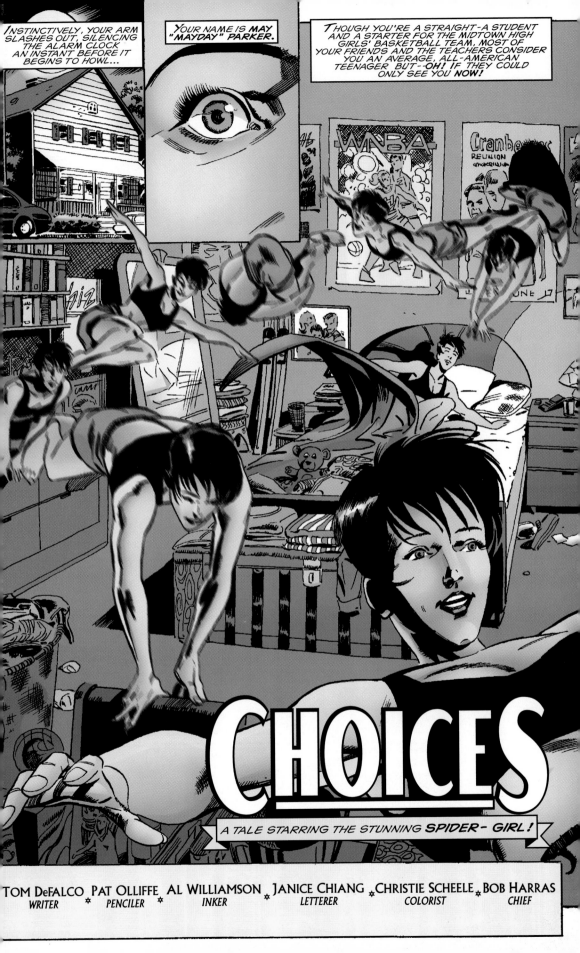

INSTINCTIVELY, YOUR ARM SLASHES OUT, SILENCING THE ALARM CLOCK AN INSTANT BEFORE IT BEGINS TO HOWL...

YOUR NAME IS MAY "MAYDAY" PARKER.

THOUGH YOU'RE A STRAIGHT-A STUDENT AND A STARTER FOR THE MIDTOWN HIGH GIRLS' BASKETBALL TEAM, MOST OF YOUR FRIENDS AND THE TEACHERS CONSIDER YOU AN AVERAGE, ALL-AMERICAN TEENAGER BUT--OH! IF THEY COULD ONLY SEE YOU NOW!

# CHOICES

A TALE STARRING THE STUNNING SPIDER-GIRL!

TOM DeFALCO ✱ PAT OLLIFFE ✱ AL WILLIAMSON ✱ JANICE CHIANG ✱ CHRISTIE SCHEELE ✱ BOB HARRAS
WRITER ✱ PENCILER ✱ INKER ✱ LETTERER ✱ COLORIST ✱ CHIEF

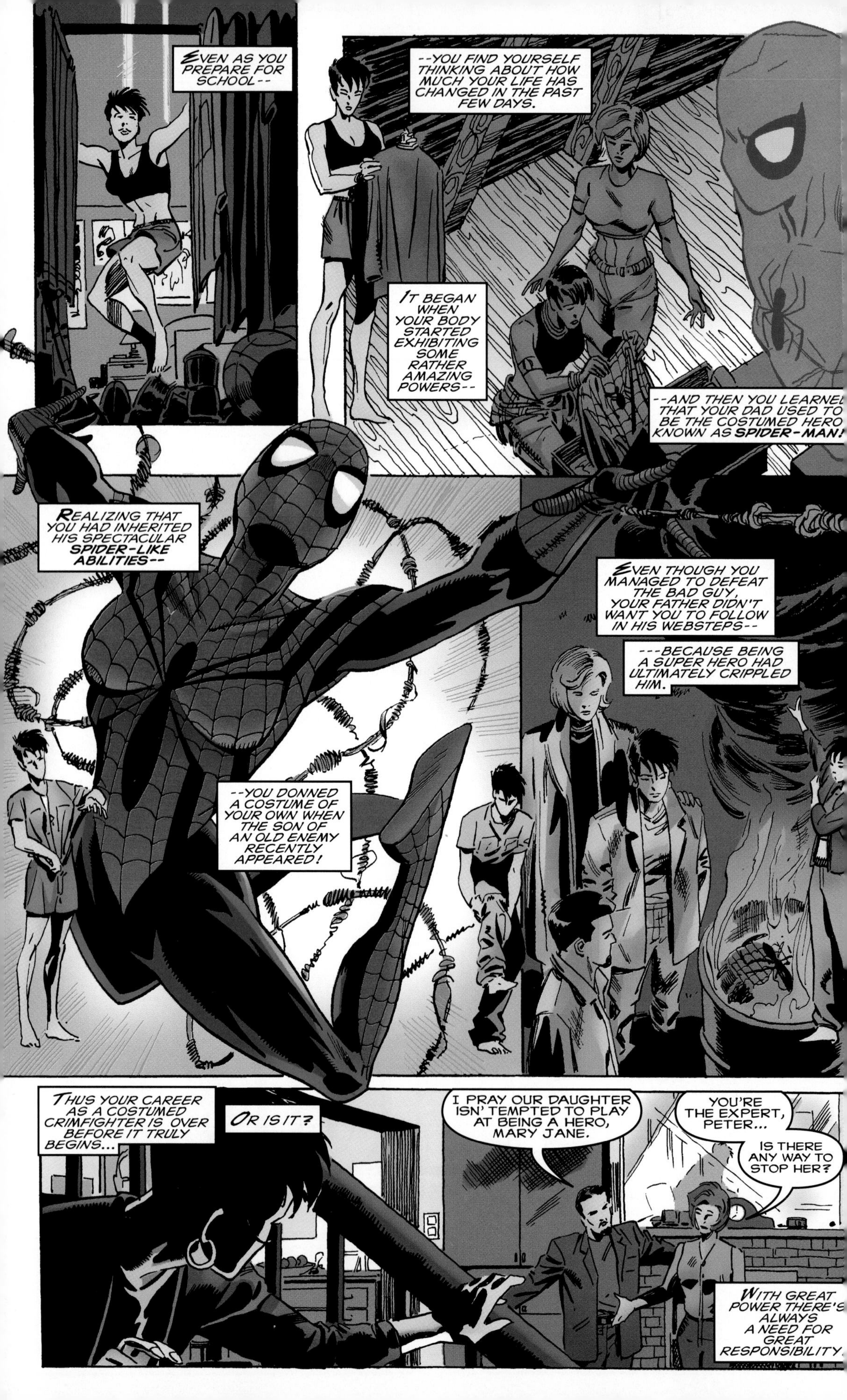
EVEN AS YOU PREPARE FOR SCHOOL--
--YOU FIND YOURSELF THINKING ABOUT HOW MUCH YOUR LIFE HAS CHANGED IN THE PAST FEW DAYS.
IT BEGAN WHEN YOUR BODY STARTED EXHIBITING SOME RATHER AMAZING POWERS--
--AND THEN YOU LEARNED THAT YOUR DAD USED TO BE THE COSTUMED HERO KNOWN AS SPIDER-MAN!
REALIZING THAT YOU HAD INHERITED HIS SPECTACULAR SPIDER-LIKE ABILITIES--
--YOU DONNED A COSTUME OF YOUR OWN WHEN THE SON OF AN OLD ENEMY RECENTLY APPEARED!
EVEN THOUGH YOU MANAGED TO DEFEAT THE BAD GUY, YOUR FATHER DIDN'T WANT YOU TO FOLLOW IN HIS WEBSTEPS--
---BECAUSE BEING A SUPER HERO HAD ULTIMATELY CRIPPLED HIM.
THUS YOUR CAREER AS A COSTUMED CRIMFIGHTER IS OVER BEFORE IT TRULY BEGINS...
OR IS IT?
I PRAY OUR DAUGHTER ISN' TEMPTED TO PLAY AT BEING A HERO, MARY JANE.
YOU'RE THE EXPERT, PETER...
IS THERE ANY WAY TO STOP HER?
WITH GREAT POWER THERE'S ALWAYS A NEED FOR GREAT RESPONSIBILITY.

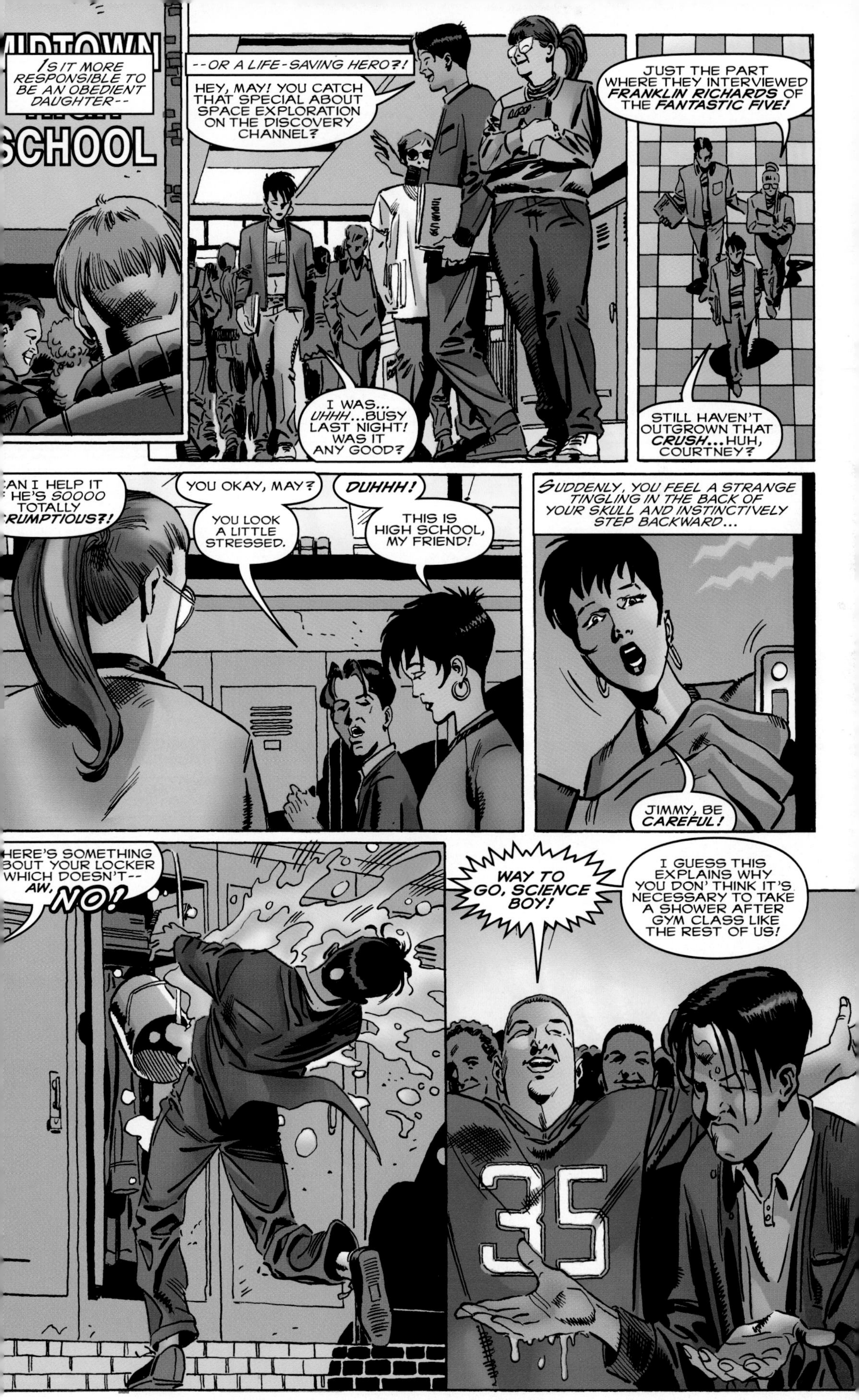

MIDTOWN HIGH SCHOOL
IS IT MORE RESPONSIBLE TO BE AN OBEDIENT DAUGHTER--
--OR A LIFE-SAVING HERO?!
HEY, MAY! YOU CATCH THAT SPECIAL ABOUT SPACE EXPLORATION ON THE DISCOVERY CHANNEL?
I WAS... UHHH...BUSY LAST NIGHT! WAS IT ANY GOOD?
JUST THE PART WHERE THEY INTERVIEWED FRANKLIN RICHARDS OF THE FANTASTIC FIVE!
STILL HAVEN'T OUTGROWN THAT CRUSH...HUH, COURTNEY?
CAN I HELP IT IF HE'S SOOOO TOTALLY SCRUMPTIOUS?!
YOU OKAY, MAY?
YOU LOOK A LITTLE STRESSED.
DUHHH!
THIS IS HIGH SCHOOL, MY FRIEND!
SUDDENLY, YOU FEEL A STRANGE TINGLING IN THE BACK OF YOUR SKULL AND INSTINCTIVELY STEP BACKWARD...
JIMMY, BE CAREFUL!
THERE'S SOMETHING ABOUT YOUR LOCKER WHICH DOESN'T-- AW, NO!
WAY TO GO, SCIENCE BOY!
I GUESS THIS EXPLAINS WHY YOU DON' THINK IT'S NECESSARY TO TAKE A SHOWER AFTER GYM CLASS LIKE THE REST OF US!
35

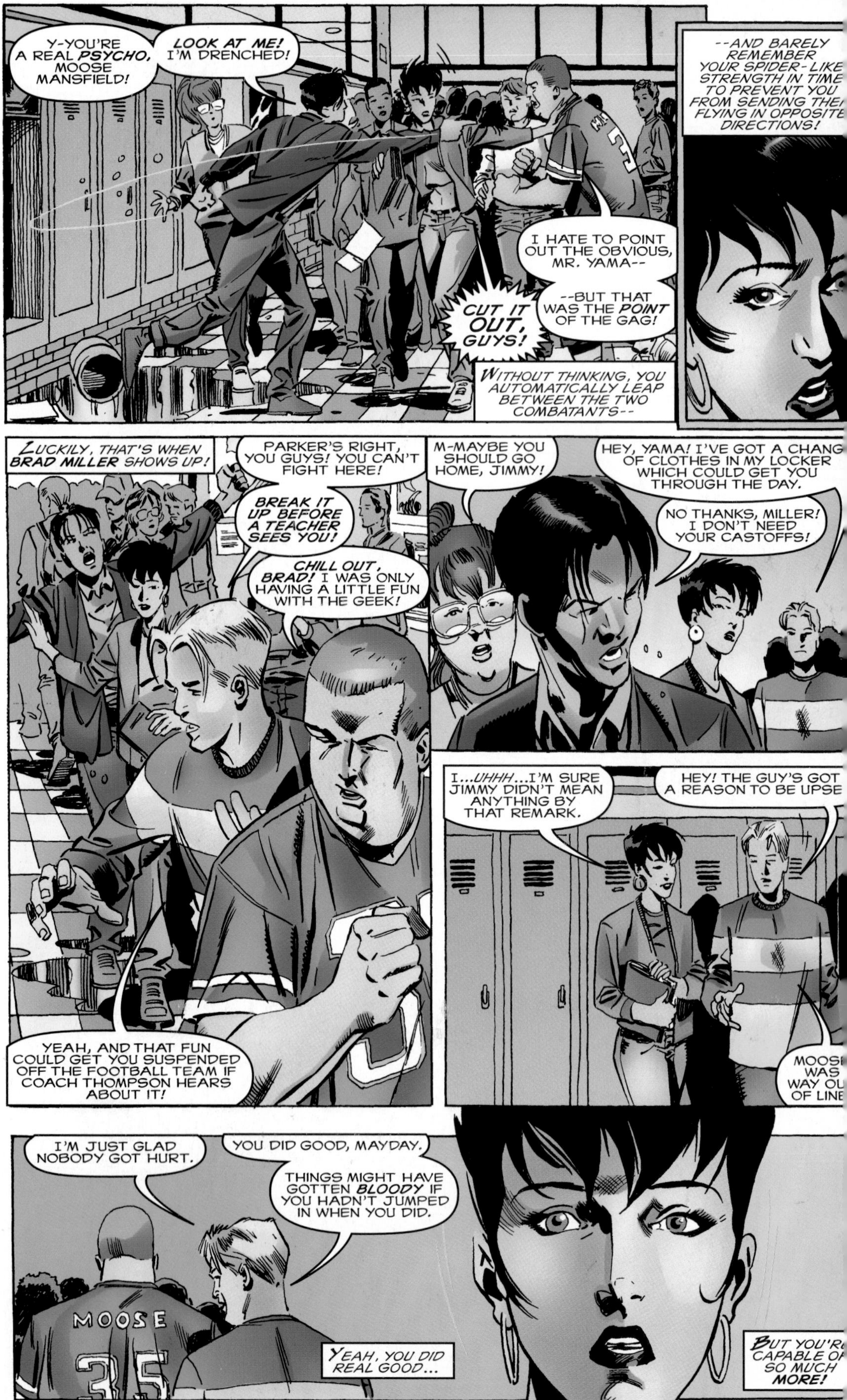

Y-YOU'RE A REAL PSYCHO, MOOSE MANSFIELD!
LOOK AT ME! I'M DRENCHED!
I HATE TO POINT OUT THE OBVIOUS, MR. YAMA--
--BUT THAT WAS THE POINT OF THE GAG!
CUT IT OUT, GUYS!
WITHOUT THINKING, YOU AUTOMATICALLY LEAP BETWEEN THE TWO COMBATANTS--
--AND BARELY REMEMBER YOUR SPIDER-LIKE STRENGTH IN TIME TO PREVENT YOU FROM SENDING THEM FLYING IN OPPOSITE DIRECTIONS!
LUCKILY, THAT'S WHEN BRAD MILLER SHOWS UP!
PARKER'S RIGHT, YOU GUYS! YOU CAN'T FIGHT HERE!
BREAK IT UP BEFORE A TEACHER SEES YOU!
CHILL OUT, BRAD! I WAS ONLY HAVING A LITTLE FUN WITH THE GEEK!
YEAH, AND THAT FUN COULD GET YOU SUSPENDED OFF THE FOOTBALL TEAM IF COACH THOMPSON HEARS ABOUT IT!
M-MAYBE YOU SHOULD GO HOME, JIMMY!
HEY, YAMA! I'VE GOT A CHANG OF CLOTHES IN MY LOCKER WHICH COULD GET YOU THROUGH THE DAY.
NO THANKS, MILLER! I DON'T NEED YOUR CASTOFFS!
I...UHHH...I'M SURE JIMMY DIDN'T MEAN ANYTHING BY THAT REMARK.
HEY! THE GUY'S GOT A REASON TO BE UPSE
MOOS WAS WAY OU OF LINE
I'M JUST GLAD NOBODY GOT HURT.
YOU DID GOOD, MAYDAY.
THINGS MIGHT HAVE GOTTEN BLOODY IF YOU HADN'T JUMPED IN WHEN YOU DID.
MOOSE
35
YEAH, YOU DID REAL GOOD...
BUT YOU'R CAPABLE O SO MUCH MORE!

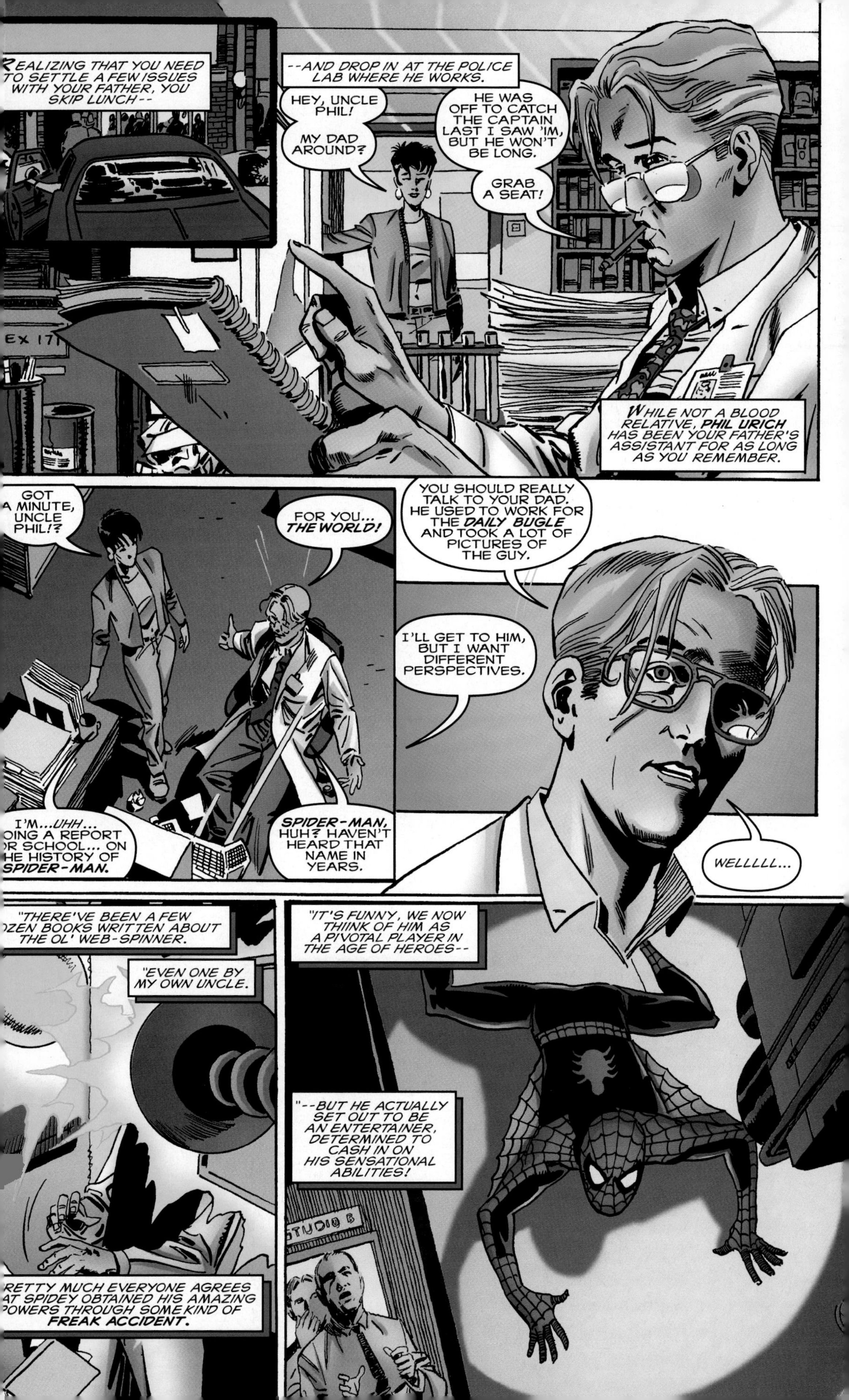
REALIZING THAT YOU NEED TO SETTLE A FEW ISSUES WITH YOUR FATHER, YOU SKIP LUNCH--
--AND DROP IN AT THE POLICE LAB WHERE HE WORKS.
HEY, UNCLE PHIL!
MY DAD AROUND?
HE WAS OFF TO CATCH THE CAPTAIN LAST I SAW 'IM, BUT HE WON'T BE LONG.
GRAB A SEAT!
WHILE NOT A BLOOD RELATIVE, PHIL URICH HAS BEEN YOUR FATHER'S ASSISTANT FOR AS LONG AS YOU REMEMBER.
GOT A MINUTE, UNCLE PHIL!?
FOR YOU... THE WORLD!
I'M...UHH... OING A REPORT OR SCHOOL... ON HE HISTORY OF SPIDER-MAN.
SPIDER-MAN. HUH? HAVEN'T HEARD THAT NAME IN YEARS.
YOU SHOULD REALLY TALK TO YOUR DAD. HE USED TO WORK FOR THE DAILY BUGLE AND TOOK A LOT OF PICTURES OF THE GUY.
I'LL GET TO HIM, BUT I WANT DIFFERENT PERSPECTIVES.
WELLLLL...
"THERE'VE BEEN A FEW OZEN BOOKS WRITTEN ABOUT THE OL' WEB-SPINNER.
"EVEN ONE BY MY OWN UNCLE.
RETTY MUCH EVERYONE AGREES AT SPIDEY OBTAINED HIS AMAZING POWERS THROUGH SOME KIND OF FREAK ACCIDENT.
"IT'S FUNNY, WE NOW THINK OF HIM AS A PIVOTAL PLAYER IN THE AGE OF HEROES--
"--BUT HE ACTUALLY SET OUT TO BE AN ENTERTAINER, DETERMINED TO CASH IN ON HIS SENSATIONAL ABILITIES!
STUDIO B

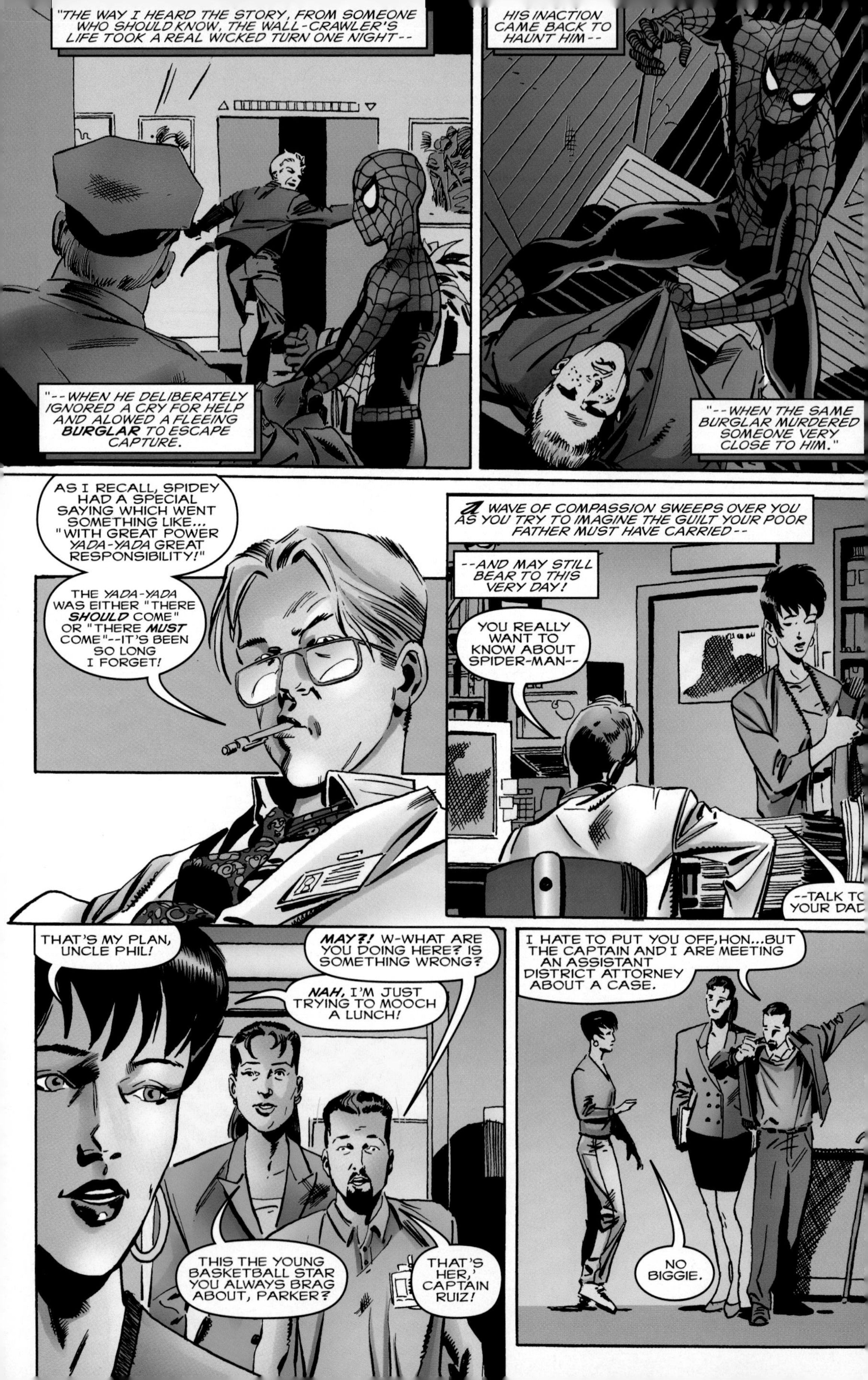
"THE WAY I HEARD THE STORY, FROM SOMEONE WHO SHOULD KNOW, THE WALL-CRAWLER'S LIFE TOOK A REAL WICKED TURN ONE NIGHT--
"--WHEN HE DELIBERATELY IGNORED A CRY FOR HELP AND ALOWED A FLEEING BURGLAR TO ESCAPE CAPTURE.
HIS INACTION CAME BACK TO HAUNT HIM--
"--WHEN THE SAME BURGLAR MURDERED SOMEONE VERY CLOSE TO HIM."
AS I RECALL, SPIDEY HAD A SPECIAL SAYING WHICH WENT SOMETHING LIKE... "WITH GREAT POWER YADA-YADA GREAT RESPONSIBILITY!"
THE YADA-YADA WAS EITHER "THERE SHOULD COME" OR "THERE MUST COME"--IT'S BEEN SO LONG I FORGET!
A WAVE OF COMPASSION SWEEPS OVER YOU AS YOU TRY TO IMAGINE THE GUILT YOUR POOR FATHER MUST HAVE CARRIED--
--AND MAY STILL BEAR TO THIS VERY DAY!
YOU REALLY WANT TO KNOW ABOUT SPIDER-MAN--
--TALK TO YOUR DAD
THAT'S MY PLAN, UNCLE PHIL!
MAY?! W-WHAT ARE YOU DOING HERE? IS SOMETHING WRONG?
NAH, I'M JUST TRYING TO MOOCH A LUNCH!
THIS THE YOUNG BASKETBALL STAR YOU ALWAYS BRAG ABOUT, PARKER?
THAT'S HER, CAPTAIN RUIZ!
I HATE TO PUT YOU OFF, HON...BUT THE CAPTAIN AND I ARE MEETING AN ASSISTANT DISTRICT ATTORNEY ABOUT A CASE.
NO BIGGIE.

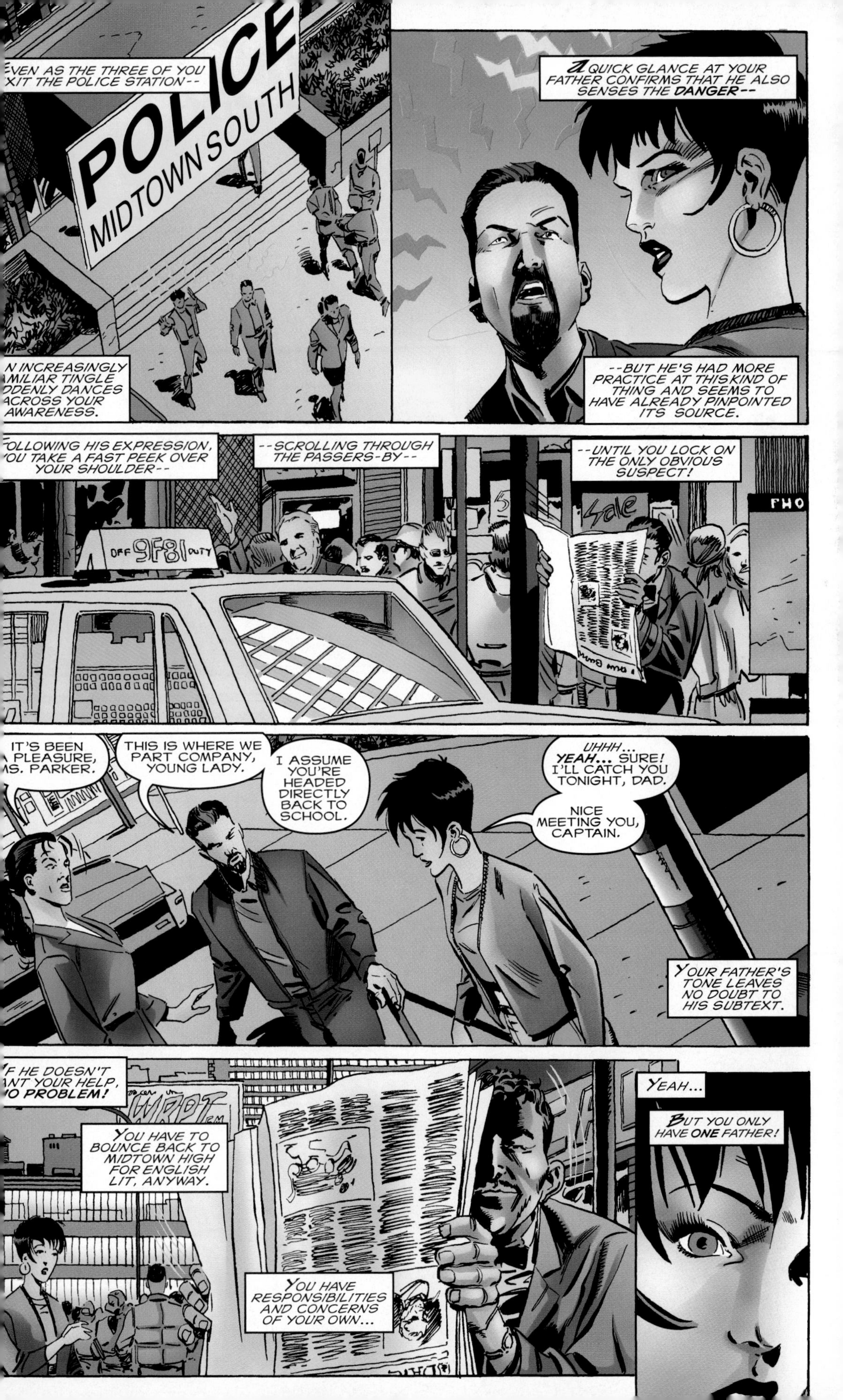
EVEN AS THE THREE OF YOU EXIT THE POLICE STATION--
POLICE
MIDTOWN SOUTH
AN INCREASINGLY FAMILIAR TINGLE SUDDENLY DANCES ACROSS YOUR AWARENESS.
A QUICK GLANCE AT YOUR FATHER CONFIRMS THAT HE ALSO SENSES THE DANGER--
--BUT HE'S HAD MORE PRACTICE AT THIS KIND OF THING AND SEEMS TO HAVE ALREADY PINPOINTED ITS SOURCE.
FOLLOWING HIS EXPRESSION, YOU TAKE A FAST PEEK OVER YOUR SHOULDER--
--SCROLLING THROUGH THE PASSERS-BY--
--UNTIL YOU LOCK ON THE ONLY OBVIOUS SUSPECT!
OFF 9F81 DUTY
Sale
IT'S BEEN A PLEASURE, MS. PARKER.
THIS IS WHERE WE PART COMPANY, YOUNG LADY.
I ASSUME YOU'RE HEADED DIRECTLY BACK TO SCHOOL.
UHHH... YEAH... SURE! I'LL CATCH YOU TONIGHT, DAD.
NICE MEETING YOU, CAPTAIN.
YOUR FATHER'S TONE LEAVES NO DOUBT TO HIS SUBTEXT.
IF HE DOESN'T WANT YOUR HELP, NO PROBLEM!
YOU HAVE TO BOUNCE BACK TO MIDTOWN HIGH FOR ENGLISH LIT, ANYWAY.
YOU HAVE RESPONSIBILITIES AND CONCERNS OF YOUR OWN...
YEAH...
BUT YOU ONLY HAVE ONE FATHER!

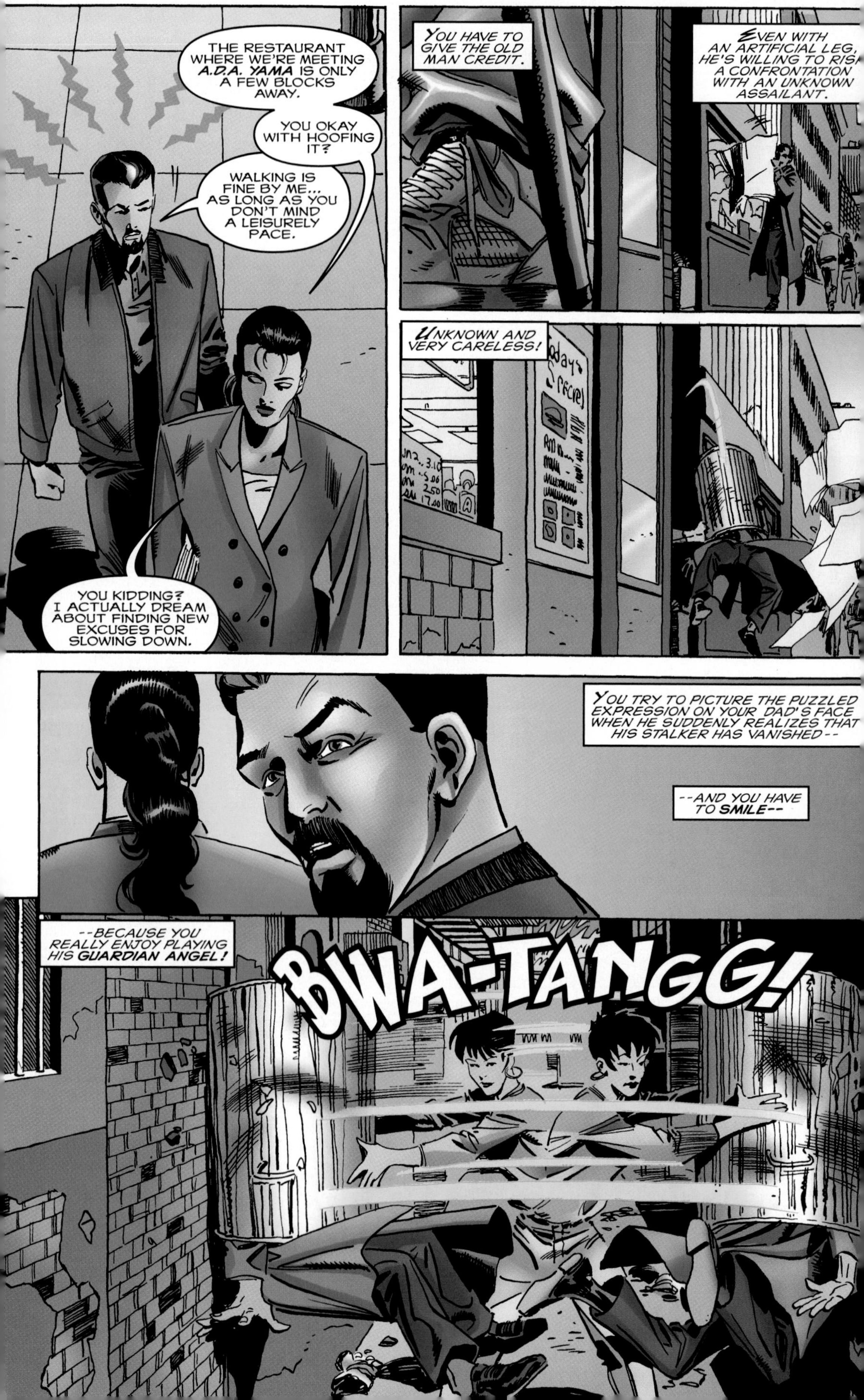
THE RESTAURANT WHERE WE'RE MEETING A.D.A. YAMA IS ONLY A FEW BLOCKS AWAY.
YOU OKAY WITH HOOFING IT?
WALKING IS FINE BY ME... AS LONG AS YOU DON'T MIND A LEISURELY PACE.
YOU KIDDING? I ACTUALLY DREAM ABOUT FINDING NEW EXCUSES FOR SLOWING DOWN.
YOU HAVE TO GIVE THE OLD MAN CREDIT.
EVEN WITH AN ARTIFICIAL LEG, HE'S WILLING TO RISK A CONFRONTATION WITH AN UNKNOWN ASSAILANT.
UNKNOWN AND VERY CARELESS!
YOU TRY TO PICTURE THE PUZZLED EXPRESSION ON YOUR DAD'S FACE WHEN HE SUDDENLY REALIZES THAT HIS STALKER HAS VANISHED--
--AND YOU HAVE TO SMILE--
--BECAUSE YOU REALLY ENJOY PLAYING HIS GUARDIAN ANGEL!
BWA-TANGG!

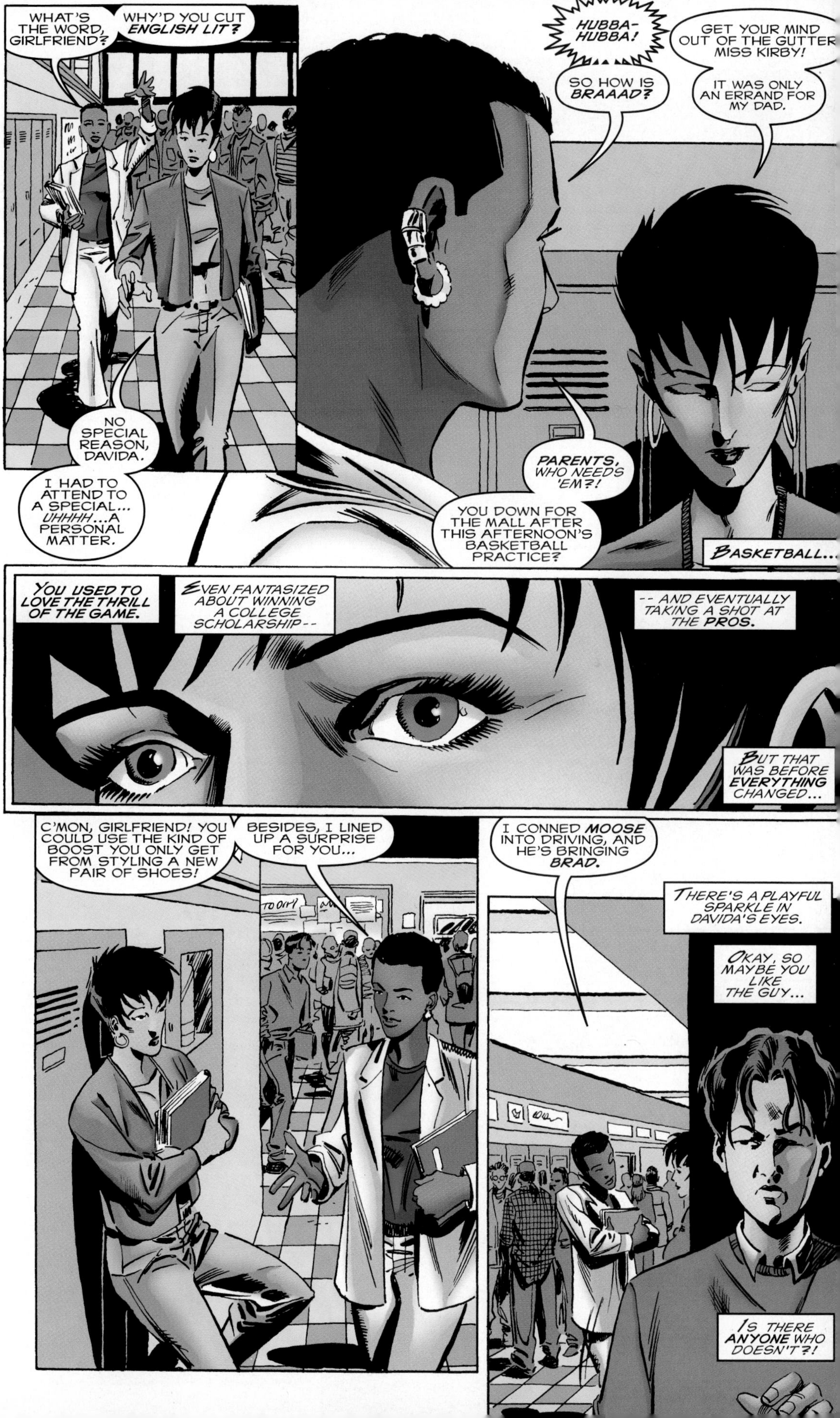
WHAT'S THE WORD, GIRLFRIEND?
WHY'D YOU CUT ENGLISH LIT?
NO SPECIAL REASON, DAVIDA.
I HAD TO ATTEND TO A SPECIAL... UHHHH...A PERSONAL MATTER.
HUBBA-HUBBA!
SO HOW IS BRAAAD?
GET YOUR MIND OUT OF THE GUTTER MISS KIRBY!
IT WAS ONLY AN ERRAND FOR MY DAD.
PARENTS, WHO NEEDS 'EM?!
YOU DOWN FOR THE MALL AFTER THIS AFTERNOON'S BASKETBALL PRACTICE?
BASKETBALL...
YOU USED TO LOVE THE THRILL OF THE GAME.
EVEN FANTASIZED ABOUT WINNING A COLLEGE SCHOLARSHIP--
-- AND EVENTUALLY TAKING A SHOT AT THE PROS.
BUT THAT WAS BEFORE EVERYTHING CHANGED...
C'MON, GIRLFRIEND! YOU COULD USE THE KIND OF BOOST YOU ONLY GET FROM STYLING A NEW PAIR OF SHOES!
BESIDES, I LINED UP A SURPRISE FOR YOU...
I CONNED MOOSE INTO DRIVING, AND HE'S BRINGING BRAD.
THERE'S A PLAYFUL SPARKLE IN DAVIDA'S EYES.
OKAY, SO MAYBE YOU LIKE THE GUY...
IS THERE ANYONE WHO DOESN'T?!

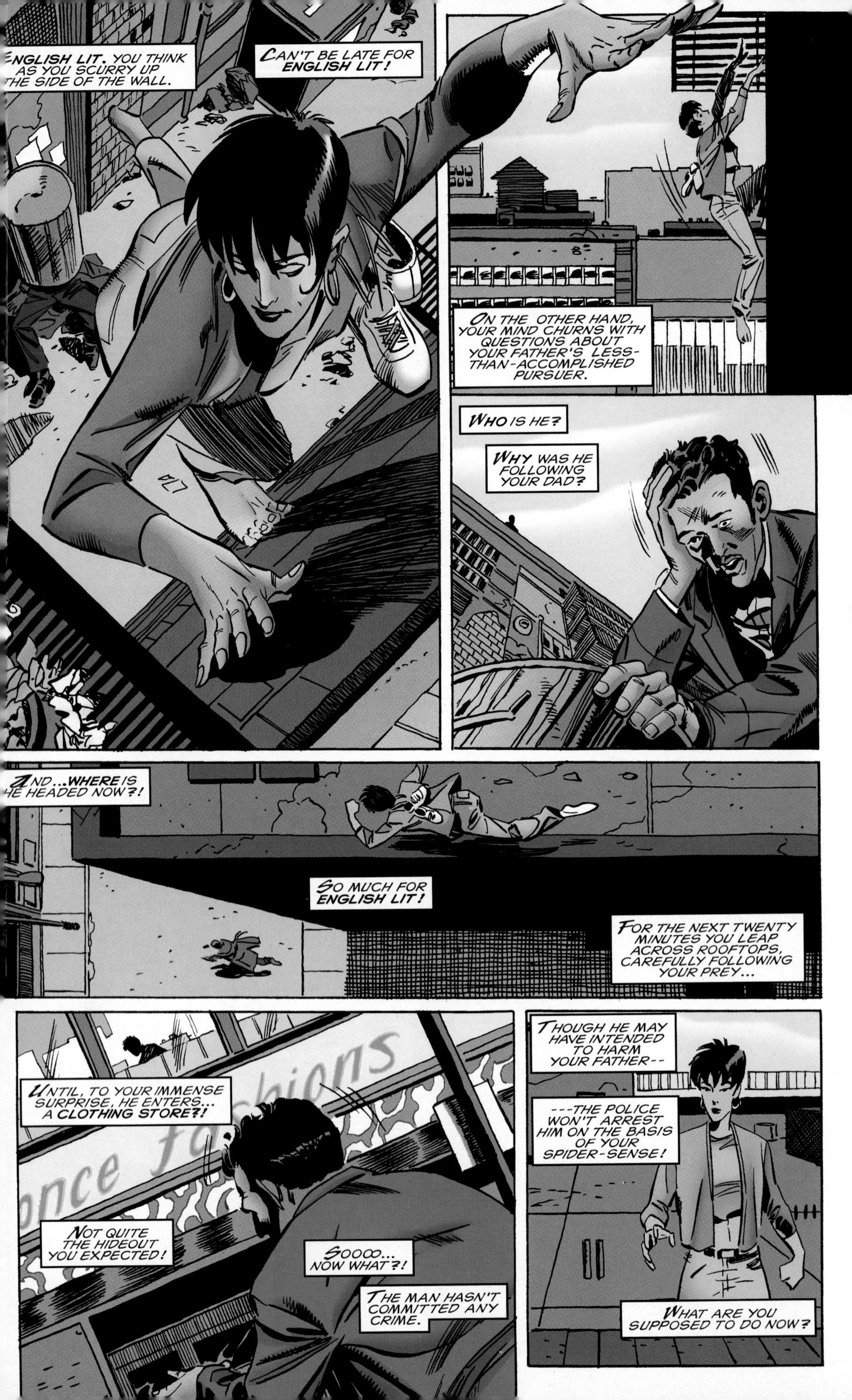
ENGLISH LIT. YOU THINK AS YOU SCURRY UP THE SIDE OF THE WALL.
CAN'T BE LATE FOR ENGLISH LIT!
ON THE OTHER HAND, YOUR MIND CHURNS WITH QUESTIONS ABOUT YOUR FATHER'S LESS-THAN-ACCOMPLISHED PURSUER.
WHO IS HE?
WHY WAS HE FOLLOWING YOUR DAD?
AND...WHERE IS HE HEADED NOW?!
SO MUCH FOR ENGLISH LIT!
FOR THE NEXT TWENTY MINUTES YOU LEAP ACROSS ROOFTOPS, CAREFULLY FOLLOWING YOUR PREY...
UNTIL, TO YOUR IMMENSE SURPRISE, HE ENTERS... A CLOTHING STORE?!
NOT QUITE THE HIDEOUT YOU EXPECTED!
SOOOO... NOW WHAT?!
THE MAN HASN'T COMMITTED ANY CRIME.
THOUGH HE MAY HAVE INTENDED TO HARM YOUR FATHER--
---THE POLICE WON'T ARREST HIM ON THE BASIS OF YOUR SPIDER-SENSE!
WHAT ARE YOU SUPPOSED TO DO NOW?

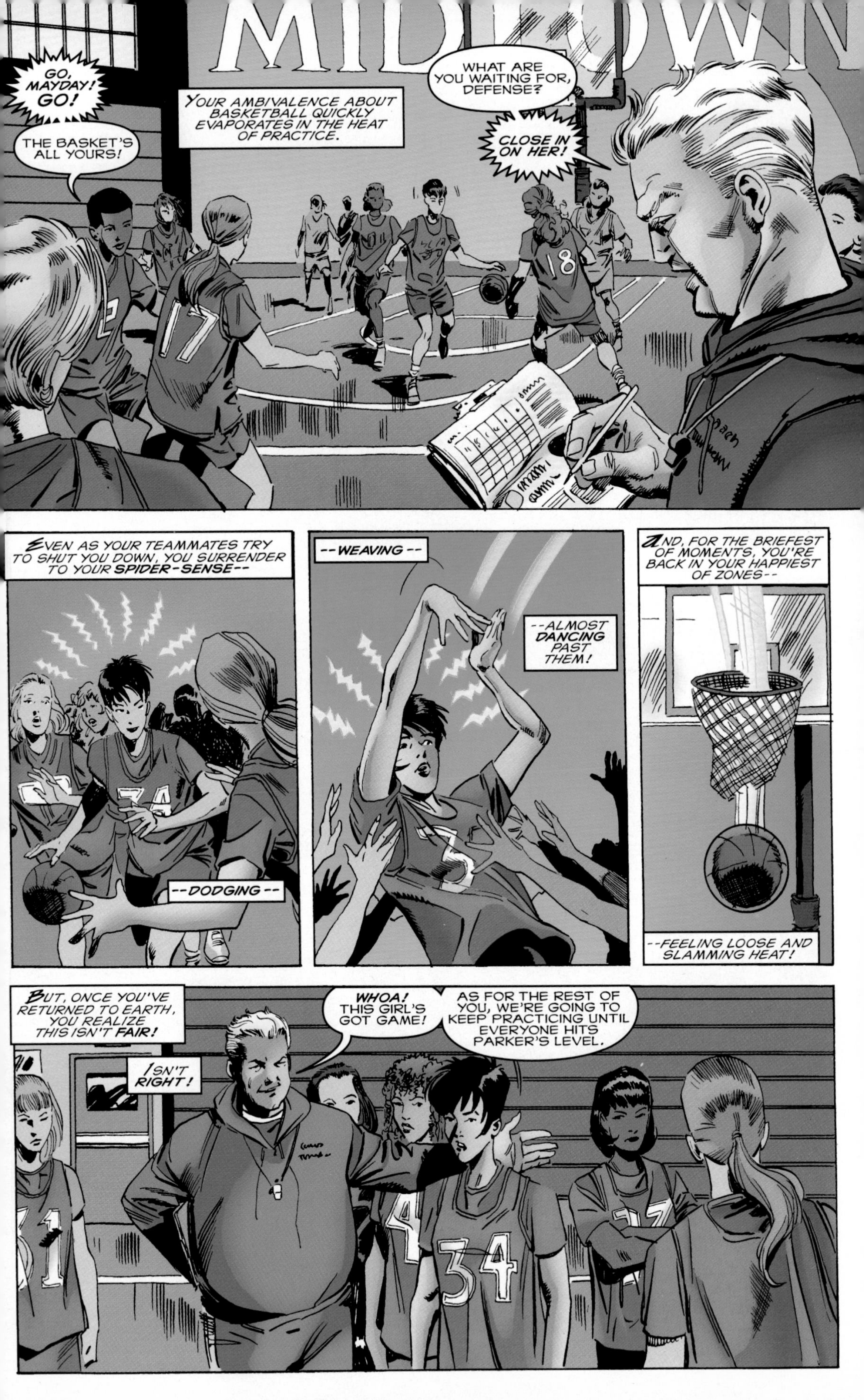
MIDTOWN
GO, MAYDAY! GO!
THE BASKET'S ALL YOURS!
YOUR AMBIVALENCE ABOUT BASKETBALL QUICKLY EVAPORATES IN THE HEAT OF PRACTICE.
WHAT ARE YOU WAITING FOR, DEFENSE?
CLOSE IN ON HER!
EVEN AS YOUR TEAMMATES TRY TO SHUT YOU DOWN, YOU SURRENDER TO YOUR SPIDER-SENSE--
--DODGING--
--WEAVING--
--ALMOST DANCING PAST THEM!
AND, FOR THE BRIEFEST OF MOMENTS, YOU'RE BACK IN YOUR HAPPIEST OF ZONES--
--FEELING LOOSE AND SLAMMING HEAT!
BUT, ONCE YOU'VE RETURNED TO EARTH, YOU REALIZE THIS ISN'T FAIR!
ISN'T RIGHT!
WHOA! THIS GIRL'S GOT GAME!
AS FOR THE REST OF YOU, WE'RE GOING TO KEEP PRACTICING UNTIL EVERYONE HITS PARKER'S LEVEL.

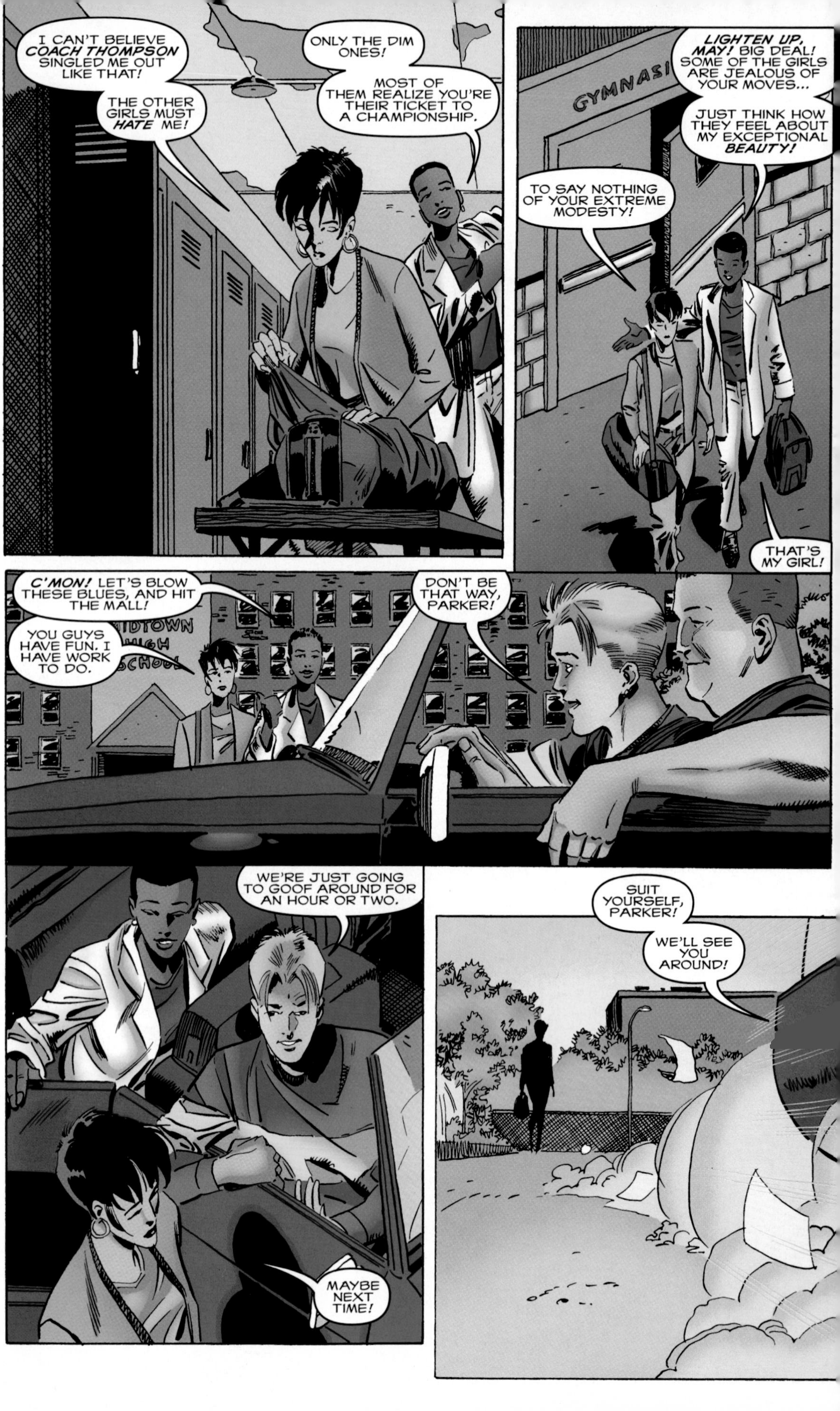
I CAN'T BELIEVE COACH THOMPSON SINGLED ME OUT LIKE THAT!
THE OTHER GIRLS MUST HATE ME!
ONLY THE DIM ONES!
MOST OF THEM REALIZE YOU'RE THEIR TICKET TO A CHAMPIONSHIP.
GYMNASI
LIGHTEN UP, MAY! BIG DEAL! SOME OF THE GIRLS ARE JEALOUS OF YOUR MOVES...
JUST THINK HOW THEY FEEL ABOUT MY EXCEPTIONAL BEAUTY!
TO SAY NOTHING OF YOUR EXTREME MODESTY!
THAT'S MY GIRL!
C'MON! LET'S BLOW THESE BLUES, AND HIT THE MALL!
YOU GUYS HAVE FUN. I HAVE WORK TO DO.
DON'T BE THAT WAY, PARKER!
WE'RE JUST GOING TO GOOF AROUND FOR AN HOUR OR TWO.
MAYBE NEXT TIME!
SUIT YOURSELF, PARKER!
WE'LL SEE YOU AROUND!

SO I HEAR YOU DROPPED IN ON YOUR FATHER AT WORK...

ANY PARTICULAR REASON?

NOT REALLY. I JUST FELT LIKE IT.

ANY OTHER DAY, I WOULD HAVE GRABBED PHIL AND THE THREE OF US WOULD HAVE GONE OUT.

YOU WORKING ON AN IMPORTANT CASE WITH CAPTAIN RUIZ?

SOME LOCAL *MOBSTERS* ARE TRYING TO MUSCLE INTO THE *FASHION INDUSTRY*, AND WE THINK THEY'RE TIED TO A STRING OF UNSOLVED *MURDERS*.

DO WE REALLY NEED TO DISCUSS THIS OVER DINNER?

*THE FASHION INDUSTRY?*

*UNSOLVED MURDERS?*

*WAS THAT WHY YOUR FATHER WAS BEING SHADOWED?*

*IS SOMEONE PLANNING A HIT?*

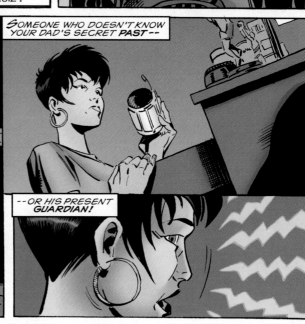

*SOMEONE WHO DOESN'T KNOW YOUR DAD'S SECRET PAST --*

*-- OR HIS PRESENT GUARDIAN!*

ANYTHING GOING ON THAT I SHOULD KNOW, YOUNG LADY?

W-WHAT DO YOU MEAN, MOM?

YOU SUDDENLY SEEM LIKE YOU HAVE A LOT ON YOUR MIND.

I'M HERE IF YOU WANT TO DISCUSS IT.

I-IT'S JUST SCHOOL JUNK.

NOTHING YOU'D UNDERSTAND!

YOU'D BE SURPRISED WHAT I UNDERSTAND, MY DEAR.

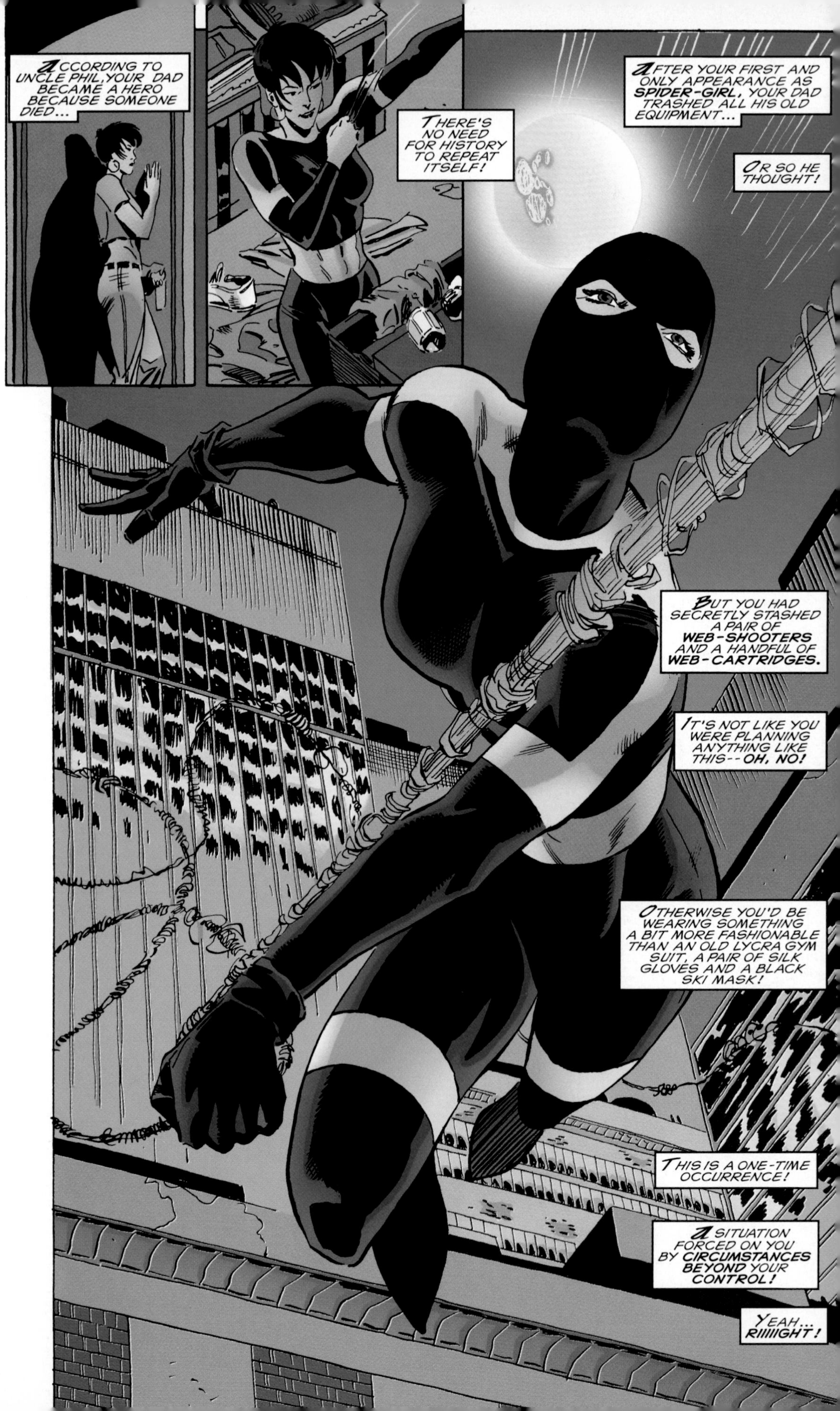
ACCORDING TO UNCLE PHIL, YOUR DAD BECAME A HERO BECAUSE SOMEONE DIED...
THERE'S NO NEED FOR HISTORY TO REPEAT ITSELF!
AFTER YOUR FIRST AND ONLY APPEARANCE AS SPIDER-GIRL, YOUR DAD TRASHED ALL HIS OLD EQUIPMENT...
OR SO HE THOUGHT!
BUT YOU HAD SECRETLY STASHED A PAIR OF WEB-SHOOTERS AND A HANDFUL OF WEB-CARTRIDGES.
IT'S NOT LIKE YOU WERE PLANNING ANYTHING LIKE THIS--OH, NO!
OTHERWISE YOU'D BE WEARING SOMETHING A BIT MORE FASHIONABLE THAN AN OLD LYCRA GYM SUIT, A PAIR OF SILK GLOVES AND A BLACK SKI MASK!
THIS IS A ONE-TIME OCCURRENCE!
A SITUATION FORCED ON YOU BY CIRCUMSTANCES BEYOND YOUR CONTROL!
YEAH... RIIIIGHT!

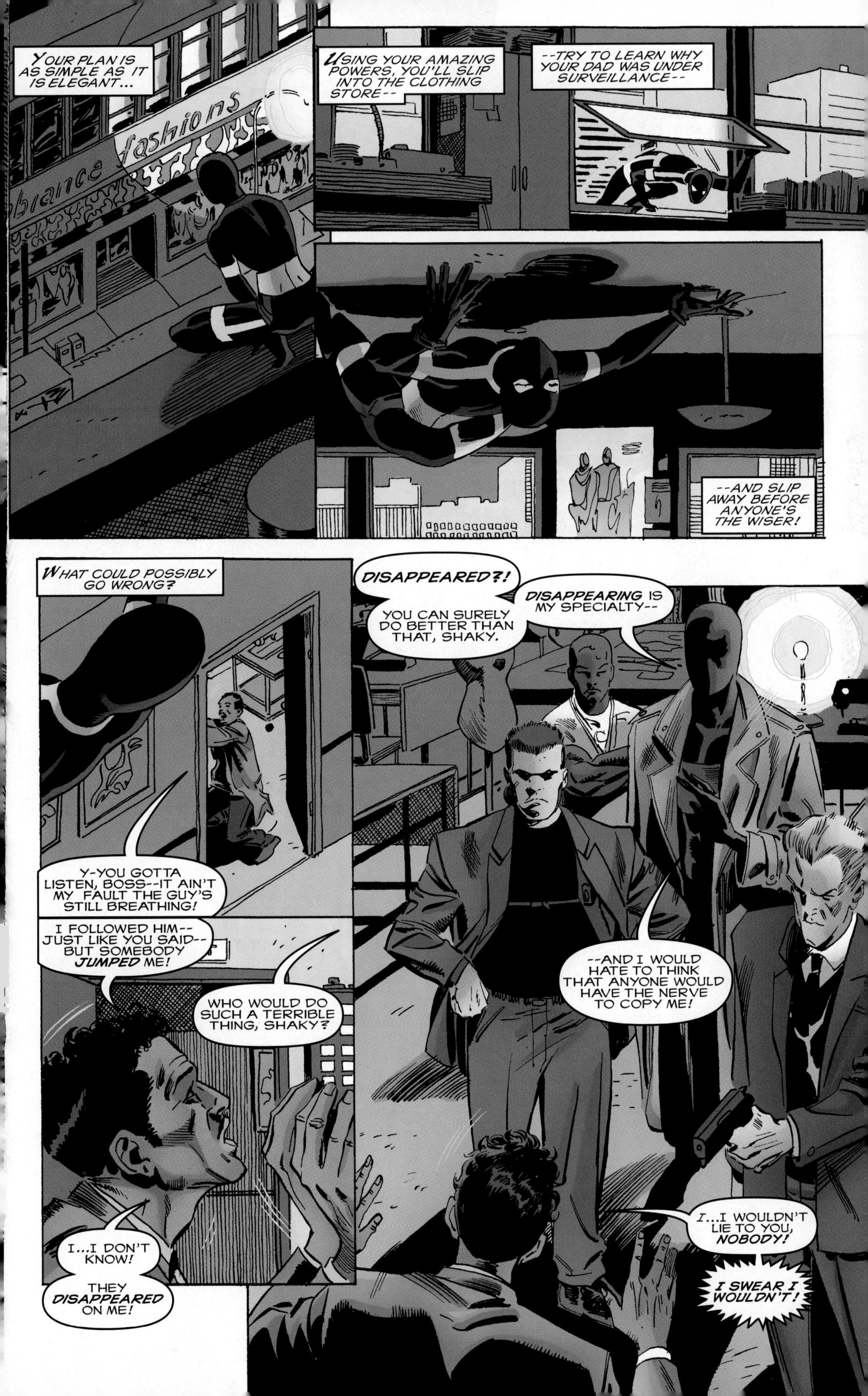
YOUR PLAN IS AS SIMPLE AS IT IS ELEGANT...
fashions
USING YOUR AMAZING POWERS, YOU'LL SLIP INTO THE CLOTHING STORE--
--TRY TO LEARN WHY YOUR DAD WAS UNDER SURVEILLANCE--
--AND SLIP AWAY BEFORE ANYONE'S THE WISER!
WHAT COULD POSSIBLY GO WRONG?
Y-YOU GOTTA LISTEN, BOSS--IT AIN'T MY FAULT THE GUY'S STILL BREATHING!
I FOLLOWED HIM--JUST LIKE YOU SAID--BUT SOMEBODY JUMPED ME!
WHO WOULD DO SUCH A TERRIBLE THING, SHAKY?
I...I DON'T KNOW!
THEY DISAPPEARED ON ME!
DISAPPEARED?!
YOU CAN SURELY DO BETTER THAN THAT, SHAKY.
DISAPPEARING IS MY SPECIALTY--
--AND I WOULD HATE TO THINK THAT ANYONE WOULD HAVE THE NERVE TO COPY ME!
I...I WOULDN'T LIE TO YOU, NOBODY!
I SWEAR I WOULDN'T!

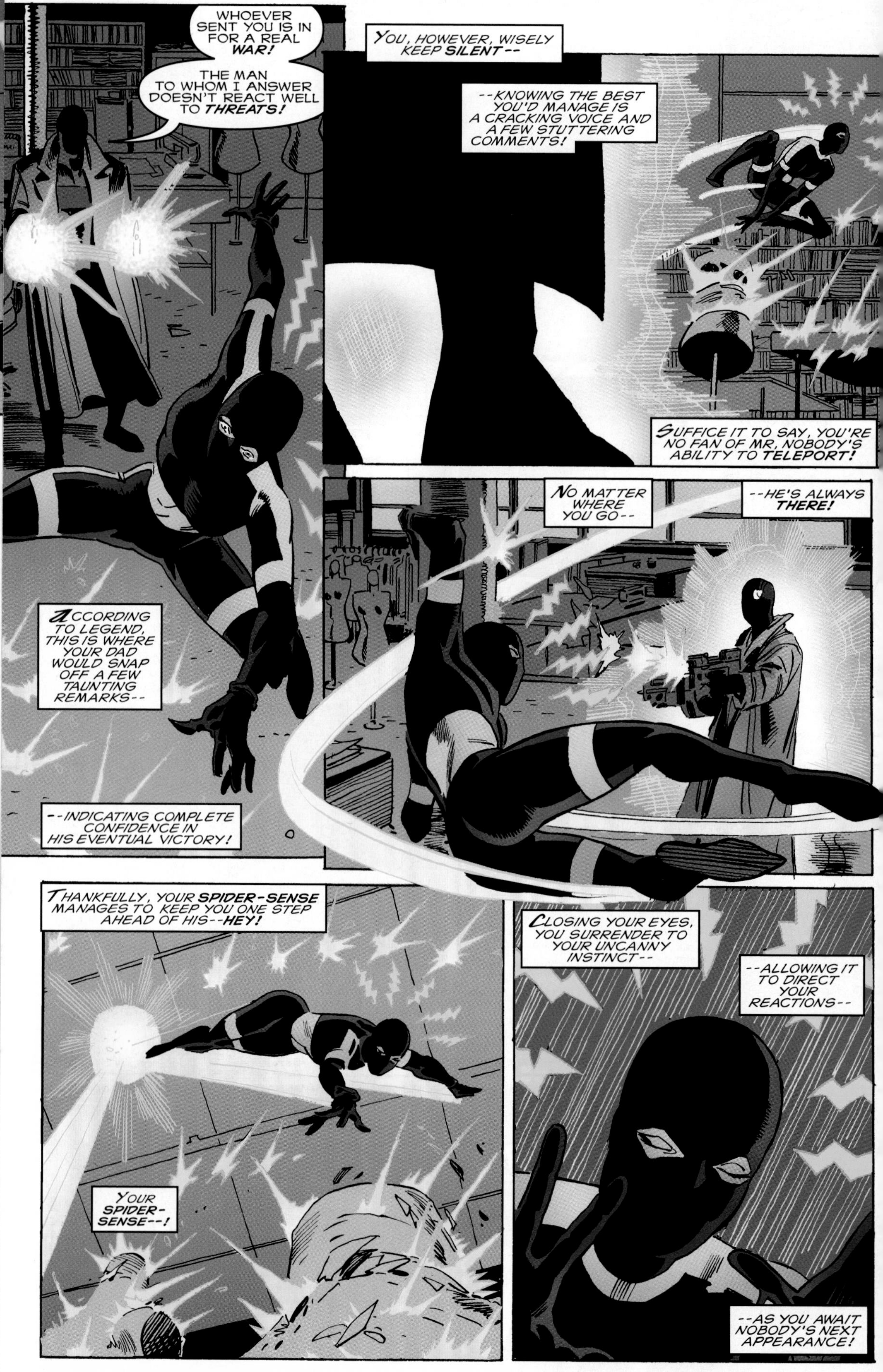
WHOEVER SENT YOU IS IN FOR A REAL WAR!
THE MAN TO WHOM I ANSWER DOESN'T REACT WELL TO THREATS!
ACCORDING TO LEGEND, THIS IS WHERE YOUR DAD WOULD SNAP OFF A FEW TAUNTING REMARKS--
--INDICATING COMPLETE CONFIDENCE IN HIS EVENTUAL VICTORY!
YOU, HOWEVER, WISELY KEEP SILENT--
--KNOWING THE BEST YOU'D MANAGE IS A CRACKING VOICE AND A FEW STUTTERING COMMENTS!
SUFFICE IT TO SAY, YOU'RE NO FAN OF MR. NOBODY'S ABILITY TO TELEPORT!
NO MATTER WHERE YOU GO--
--HE'S ALWAYS THERE!
THANKFULLY, YOUR SPIDER-SENSE MANAGES TO KEEP YOU ONE STEP AHEAD OF HIS--HEY!
YOUR SPIDER-SENSE--!
CLOSING YOUR EYES, YOU SURRENDER TO YOUR UNCANNY INSTINCT--
--ALLOWING IT TO DIRECT YOUR REACTIONS--
--AS YOU AWAIT NOBODY'S NEXT APPEARANCE!

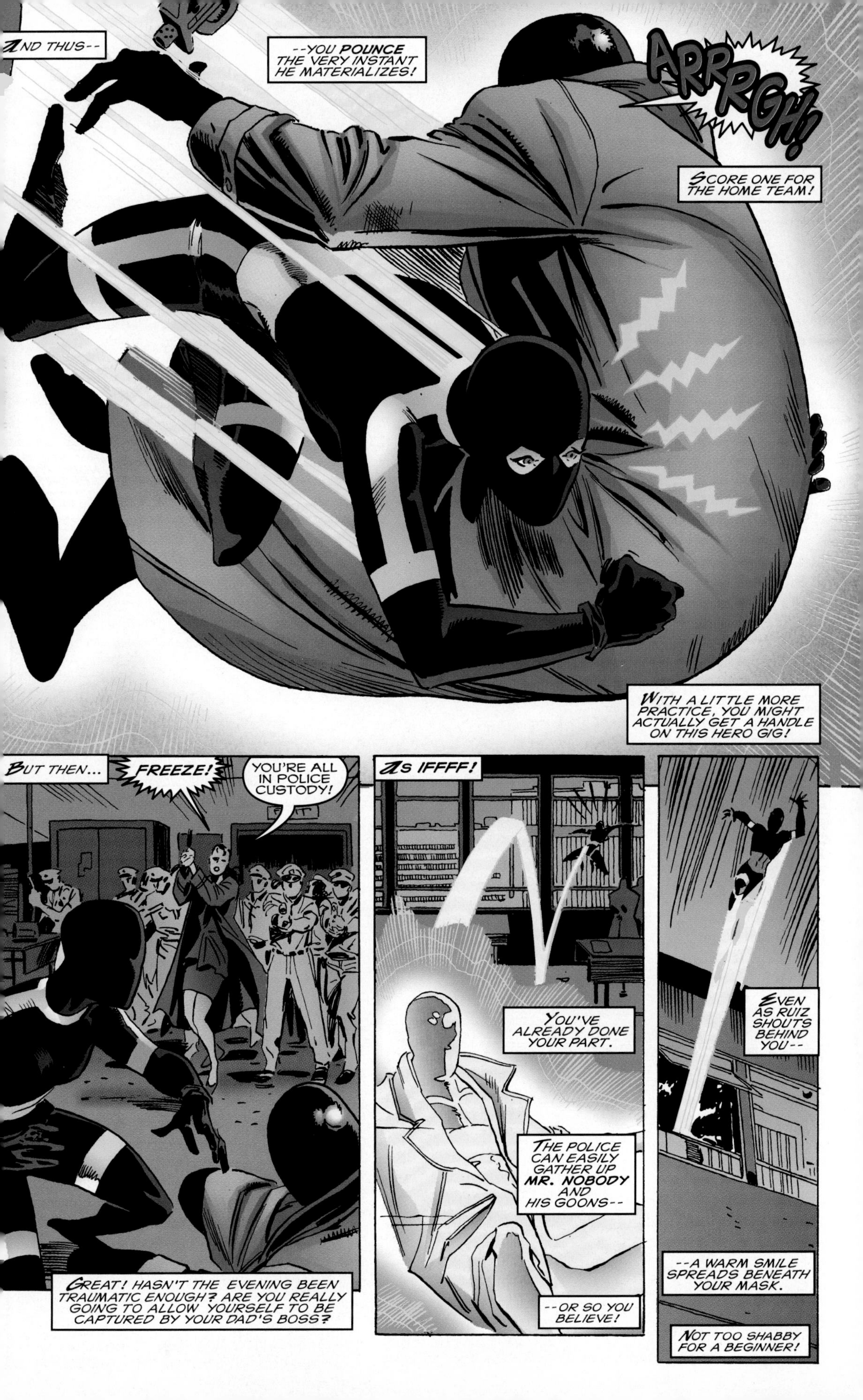
AND THUS--
--YOU **POUNCE** THE VERY INSTANT HE MATERIALIZES!
ARRRGH!!
SCORE ONE FOR THE HOME TEAM!
WITH A LITTLE MORE PRACTICE, YOU MIGHT ACTUALLY GET A HANDLE ON THIS HERO GIG!
BUT THEN...
FREEZE!
YOU'RE ALL IN POLICE CUSTODY!
GREAT! HASN'T THE EVENING BEEN TRAUMATIC ENOUGH? ARE YOU REALLY GOING TO ALLOW YOURSELF TO BE CAPTURED BY YOUR DAD'S BOSS?
AS IFFFF!
YOU'VE ALREADY DONE YOUR PART.
THE POLICE CAN EASILY GATHER UP **MR. NOBODY** AND HIS GOONS--
--OR SO YOU BELIEVE!
EVEN AS RUIZ SHOUTS BEHIND YOU--
--A WARM SMILE SPREADS BENEATH YOUR MASK.
NOT TOO SHABBY FOR A BEGINNER!

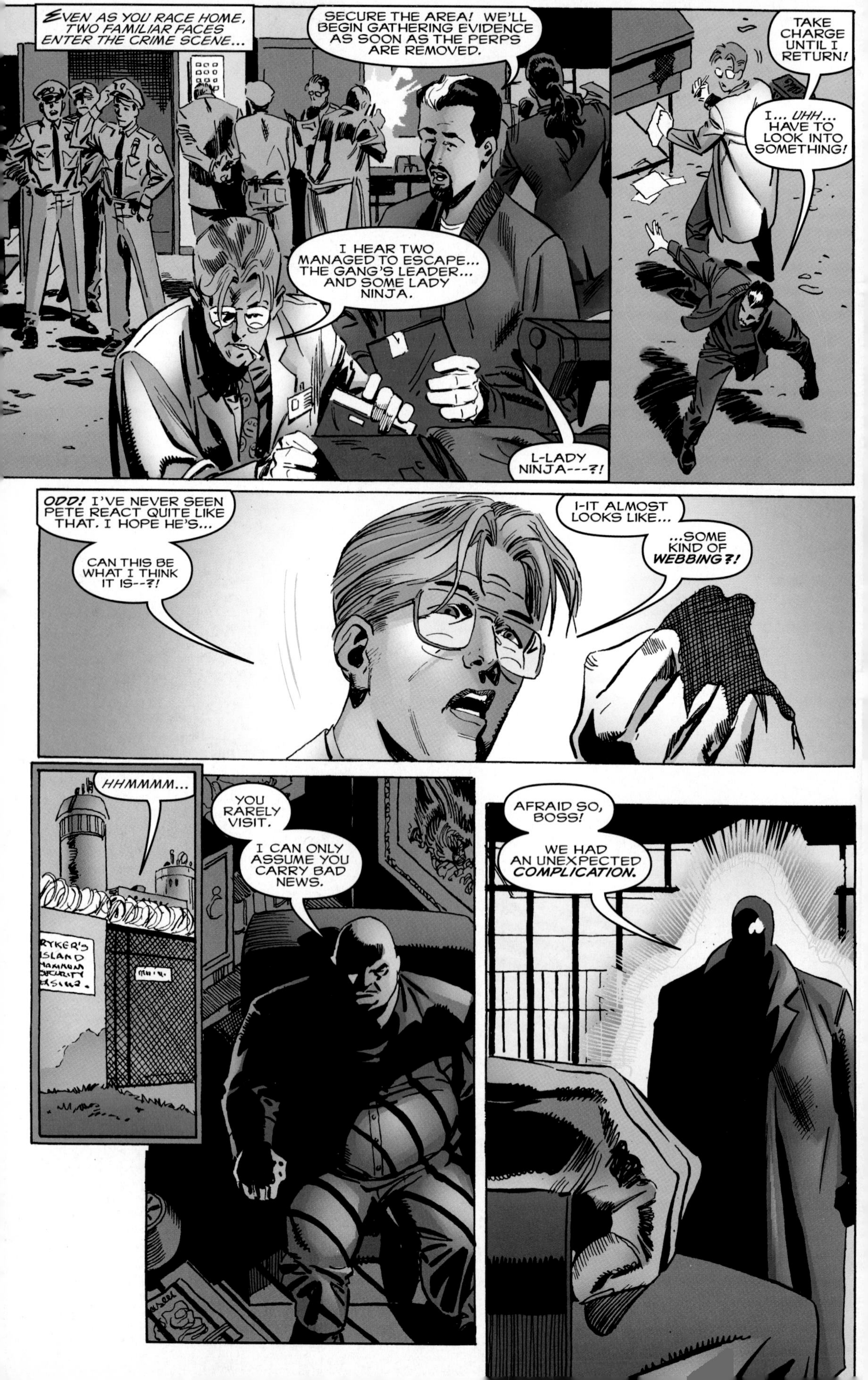
EVEN AS YOU RACE HOME, TWO FAMILIAR FACES ENTER THE CRIME SCENE...
SECURE THE AREA! WE'LL BEGIN GATHERING EVIDENCE AS SOON AS THE PERPS ARE REMOVED.
I HEAR TWO MANAGED TO ESCAPE... THE GANG'S LEADER... AND SOME LADY NINJA.
L-LADY NINJA---?!
TAKE CHARGE UNTIL I RETURN!
I... UHH... HAVE TO LOOK INTO SOMETHING!
ODD! I'VE NEVER SEEN PETE REACT QUITE LIKE THAT. I HOPE HE'S...
CAN THIS BE WHAT I THINK IT IS--?!
I-IT ALMOST LOOKS LIKE...
...SOME KIND OF WEBBING?!
HHMMMM...
YOU RARELY VISIT.
I CAN ONLY ASSUME YOU CARRY BAD NEWS.
AFRAID SO, BOSS!
WE HAD AN UNEXPECTED COMPLICATION.

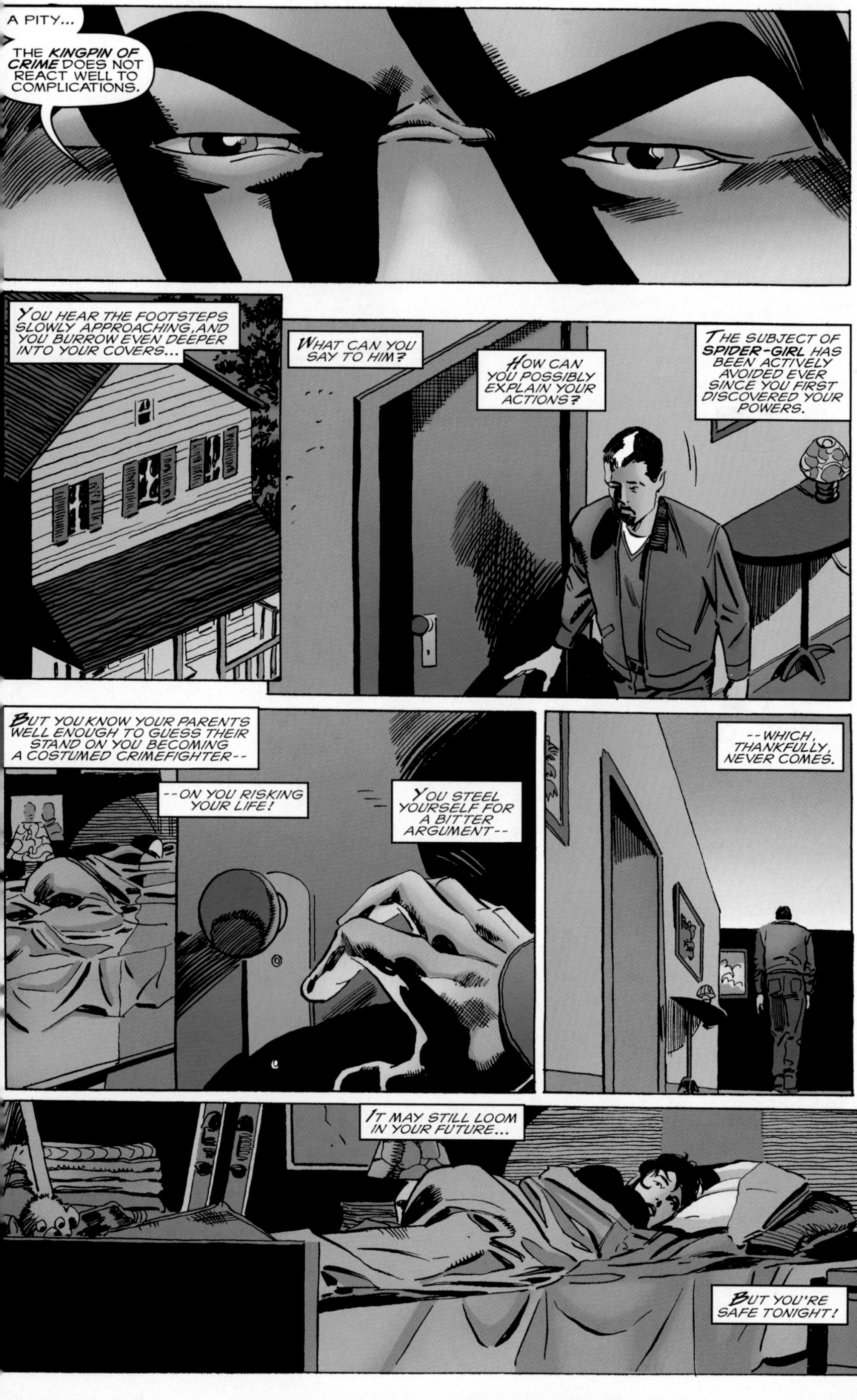
A PITY...
THE KINGPIN OF CRIME DOES NOT REACT WELL TO COMPLICATIONS.
YOU HEAR THE FOOTSTEPS SLOWLY APPROACHING, AND YOU BURROW EVEN DEEPER INTO YOUR COVERS...
WHAT CAN YOU SAY TO HIM?
HOW CAN YOU POSSIBLY EXPLAIN YOUR ACTIONS?
THE SUBJECT OF SPIDER-GIRL HAS BEEN ACTIVELY AVOIDED EVER SINCE YOU FIRST DISCOVERED YOUR POWERS.
BUT YOU KNOW YOUR PARENTS WELL ENOUGH TO GUESS THEIR STAND ON YOU BECOMING A COSTUMED CRIMEFIGHTER--
--ON YOU RISKING YOUR LIFE!
YOU STEEL YOURSELF FOR A BITTER ARGUMENT--
--WHICH, THANKFULLY, NEVER COMES.
IT MAY STILL LOOM IN YOUR FUTURE...
BUT YOU'RE SAFE TONIGHT!

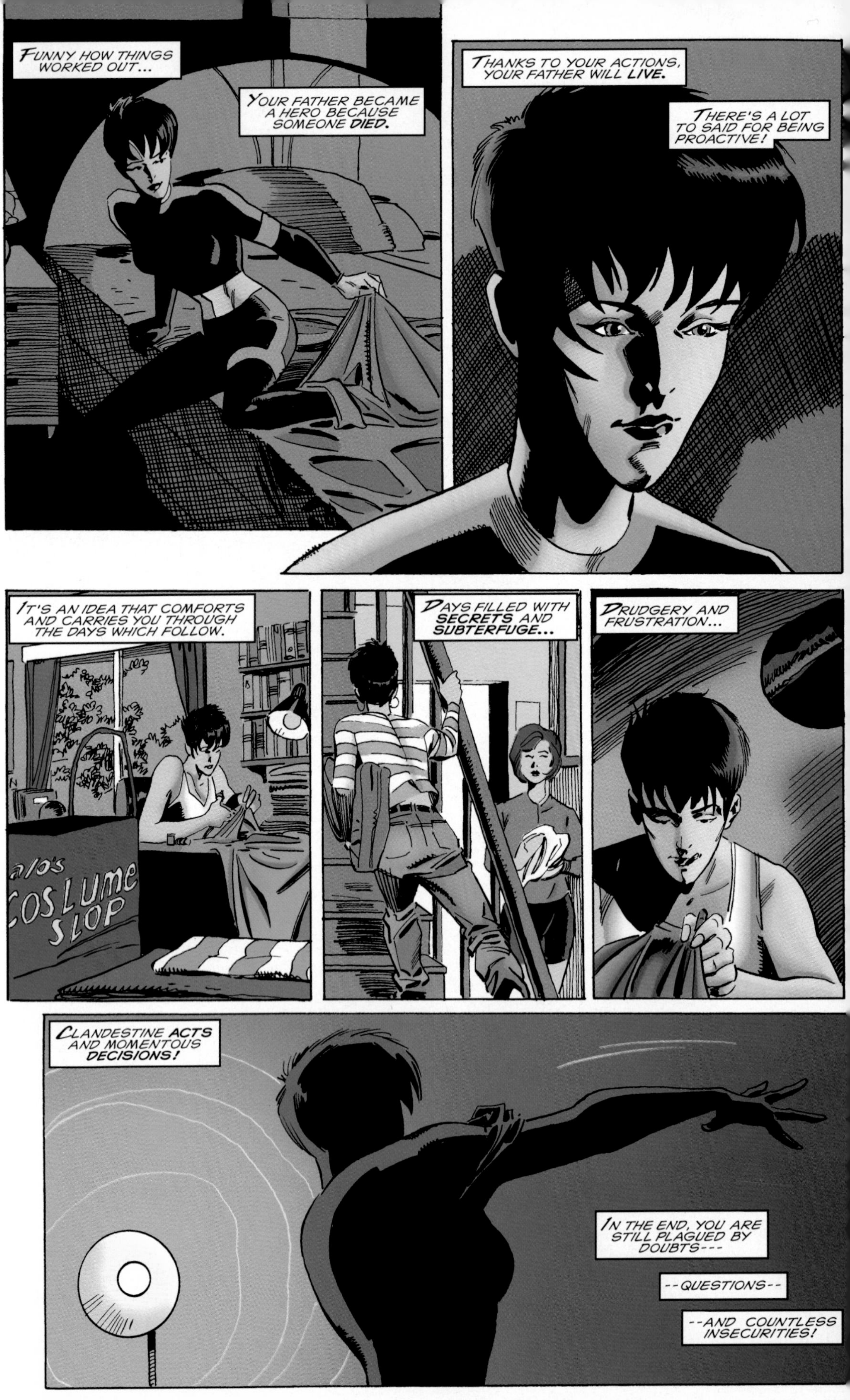
FUNNY HOW THINGS WORKED OUT...
YOUR FATHER BECAME A HERO BECAUSE SOMEONE DIED.
THANKS TO YOUR ACTIONS, YOUR FATHER WILL LIVE.
THERE'S A LOT TO SAID FOR BEING PROACTIVE!
IT'S AN IDEA THAT COMFORTS AND CARRIES YOU THROUGH THE DAYS WHICH FOLLOW.
COSLUME SLOP
DAYS FILLED WITH SECRETS AND SUBTERFUGE...
DRUDGERY AND FRUSTRATION...
CLANDESTINE ACTS AND MOMENTOUS DECISIONS!
IN THE END, YOU ARE STILL PLAGUED BY DOUBTS---
--QUESTIONS--
--AND COUNTLESS INSECURITIES!

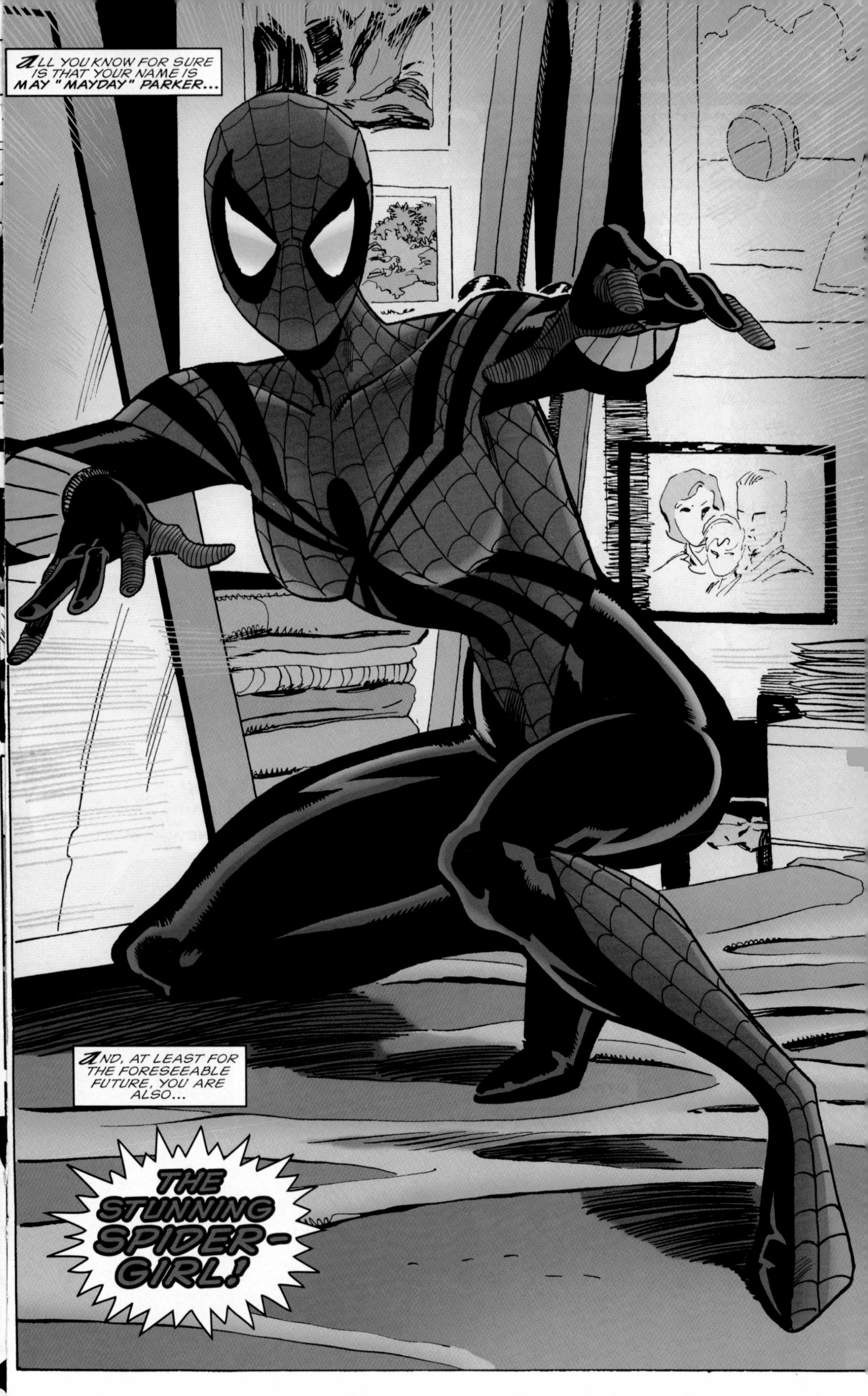
ALL YOU KNOW FOR SURE IS THAT YOUR NAME IS MAY "MAYDAY" PARKER...
AND, AT LEAST FOR THE FORESEEABLE FUTURE, YOU ARE ALSO...
THE STUNNING SPIDER-GIRL!

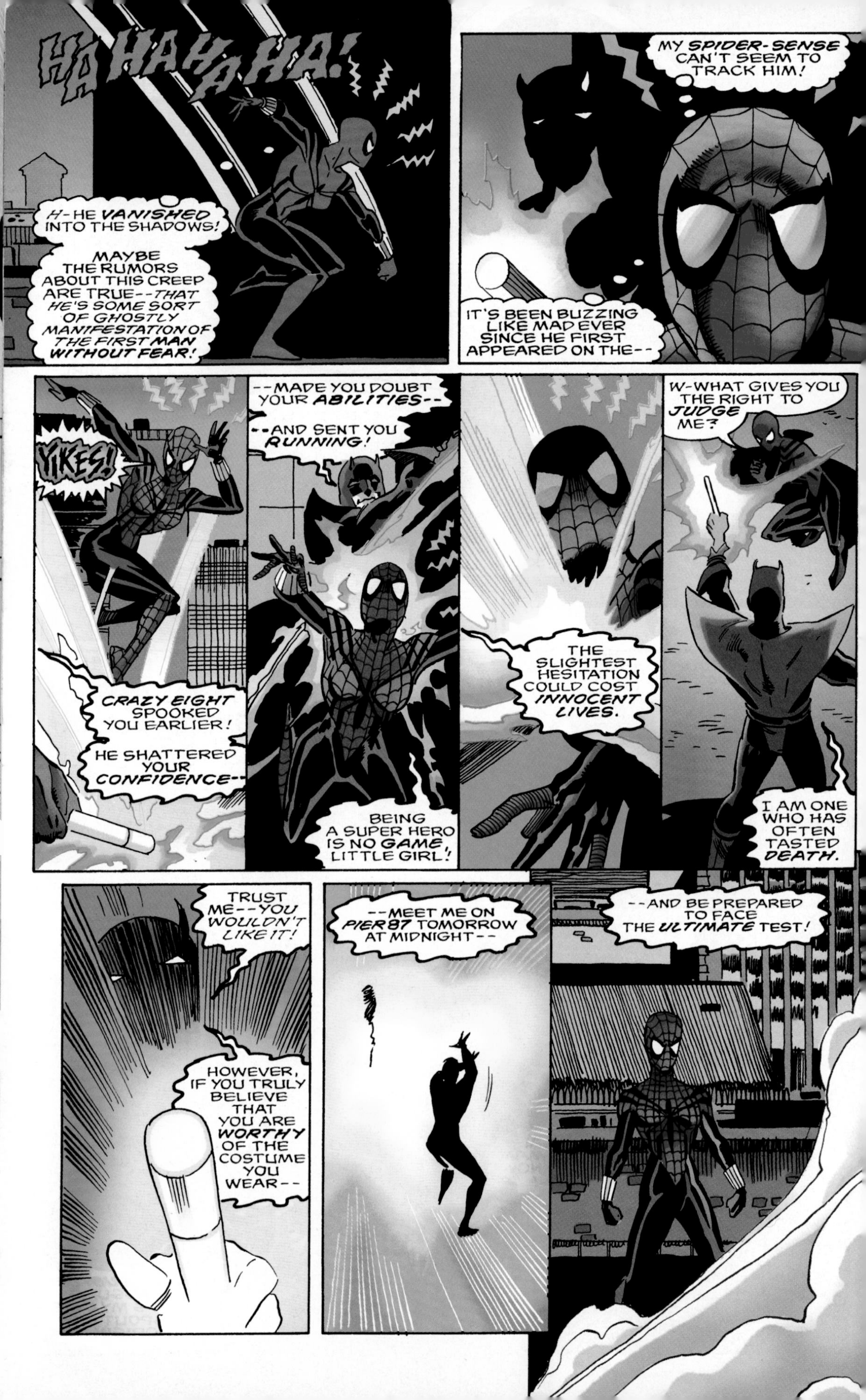

HA HA HA HA!
H-HE VANISHED INTO THE SHADOWS!
MAYBE THE RUMORS ABOUT THIS CREEP ARE TRUE--THAT HE'S SOME SORT OF GHOSTLY MANIFESTATION OF THE FIRST MAN WITHOUT FEAR!
MY SPIDER-SENSE CAN'T SEEM TO TRACK HIM!
IT'S BEEN BUZZING LIKE MAD EVER SINCE HE FIRST APPEARED ON THE--
YIKES!
CRAZY EIGHT SPOOKED YOU EARLIER!
HE SHATTERED YOUR CONFIDENCE--
--MADE YOU DOUBT YOUR ABILITIES--
--AND SENT YOU RUNNING!
BEING A SUPER HERO IS NO GAME, LITTLE GIRL!
THE SLIGHTEST HESITATION COULD COST INNOCENT LIVES.
W-WHAT GIVES YOU THE RIGHT TO JUDGE ME?
I AM ONE WHO HAS OFTEN TASTED DEATH.
TRUST ME--YOU WOULDN'T LIKE IT!
HOWEVER, IF YOU TRULY BELIEVE THAT YOU ARE WORTHY OF THE COSTUME YOU WEAR--
--MEET ME ON PIER 87 TOMORROW AT MIDNIGHT--
--AND BE PREPARED TO FACE THE ULTIMATE TEST!

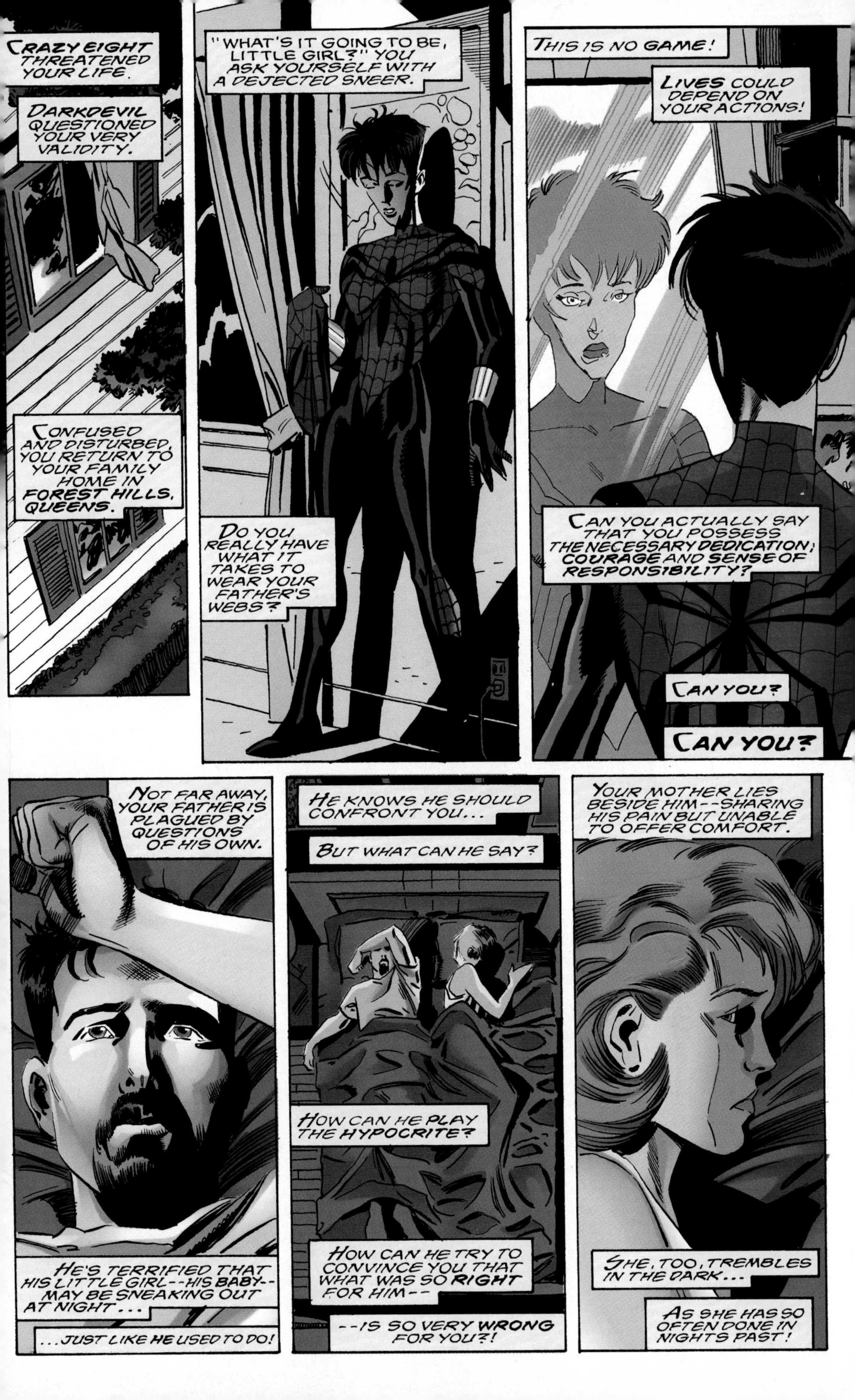

CRAZY EIGHT THREATENED YOUR LIFE.
DARKDEVIL QUESTIONED YOUR VERY VALIDITY.
CONFUSED AND DISTURBED, YOU RETURN TO YOUR FAMILY HOME IN FOREST HILLS, QUEENS.
"WHAT'S IT GOING TO BE, LITTLE GIRL?" YOU ASK YOURSELF WITH A DEJECTED SNEER.
DO YOU REALLY HAVE WHAT IT TAKES TO WEAR YOUR FATHER'S WEBS?
THIS IS NO GAME!
LIVES COULD DEPEND ON YOUR ACTIONS!
CAN YOU ACTUALLY SAY THAT YOU POSSESS THE NECESSARY DEDICATION, COURAGE AND SENSE OF RESPONSIBILITY?
CAN YOU?
CAN YOU?
NOT FAR AWAY, YOUR FATHER IS PLAGUED BY QUESTIONS OF HIS OWN.
HE'S TERRIFIED THAT HIS LITTLE GIRL--HIS BABY--MAY BE SNEAKING OUT AT NIGHT...
...JUST LIKE HE USED TO DO!
HE KNOWS HE SHOULD CONFRONT YOU...
BUT WHAT CAN HE SAY?
HOW CAN HE PLAY THE HYPOCRITE?
HOW CAN HE TRY TO CONVINCE YOU THAT WHAT WAS SO RIGHT FOR HIM--
--IS SO VERY WRONG FOR YOU?!
YOUR MOTHER LIES BESIDE HIM--SHARING HIS PAIN BUT UNABLE TO OFFER COMFORT.
SHE, TOO, TREMBLES IN THE DARK...
AS SHE HAS SO OFTEN DONE IN NIGHTS PAST!

EARLY THE NEXT MORNING, YOU CHANCE TO OVERHEAR A CONVERSATION NOT MEANT FOR YOUR EARS...

WE CAN'T GO ON LIKE THIS, PETER. YOU HAVE TO *TALK* TO YOUR DAUGHTER.

I... I *KNOW*, MARY JANE.

I'M SORRY I PUT IT OFF SO LONG, BUT... WELL... MAY AND I ARE SUPPOSED TO HAVE *LUNCH* TODAY.

YOU'LL FEEL *BETTER* ONCE EVERYTHING'S OUT IN THE OPEN.

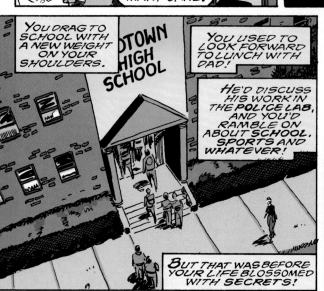

YOU DRAG TO SCHOOL WITH A NEW WEIGHT ON YOUR SHOULDERS.

YOU USED TO LOOK FORWARD TO LUNCH WITH DAD!

HE'D DISCUSS HIS WORK IN THE POLICE LAB, AND YOU'D RAMBLE ON ABOUT SCHOOL, SPORTS AND WHATEVER!

BUT THAT WAS BEFORE YOUR LIFE BLOSSOMED WITH SECRETS!

YO, MAY--! WHERE HAVE YOU BEEN?

I EXPECTED TO SEE YOU AT THE *LIBRARY* LAST NIGHT.

SORRY, JIMMY! SOMETHING ... UNEXPECTED POPPED UP!

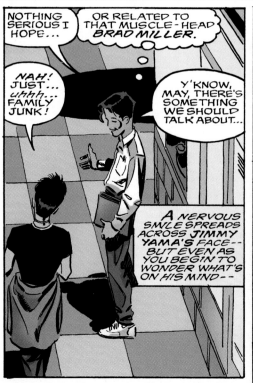

NOTHING SERIOUS I HOPE...

OR RELATED TO THAT MUSCLE-HEAD *BRAD MILLER*.

*NAH!* JUST... UHHH... FAMILY *JUNK!*

Y'KNOW, MAY, THERE'S SOMETHING WE SHOULD TALK ABOUT...

A *NERVOUS SMILE* SPREADS ACROSS *JIMMY YAMA'S* FACE-- BUT EVEN AS YOU BEGIN TO WONDER WHAT'S ON HIS MIND--

--A FAMILIAR TINGLING SUDDENLY WARNS YOU TO FREEZE IN PLACE--

--AND YOU INSTANTLY SEE HOW EVERYONE COULD BENEFIT FROM A *SPIDER-SENSE!*

PWAM!

Ufft

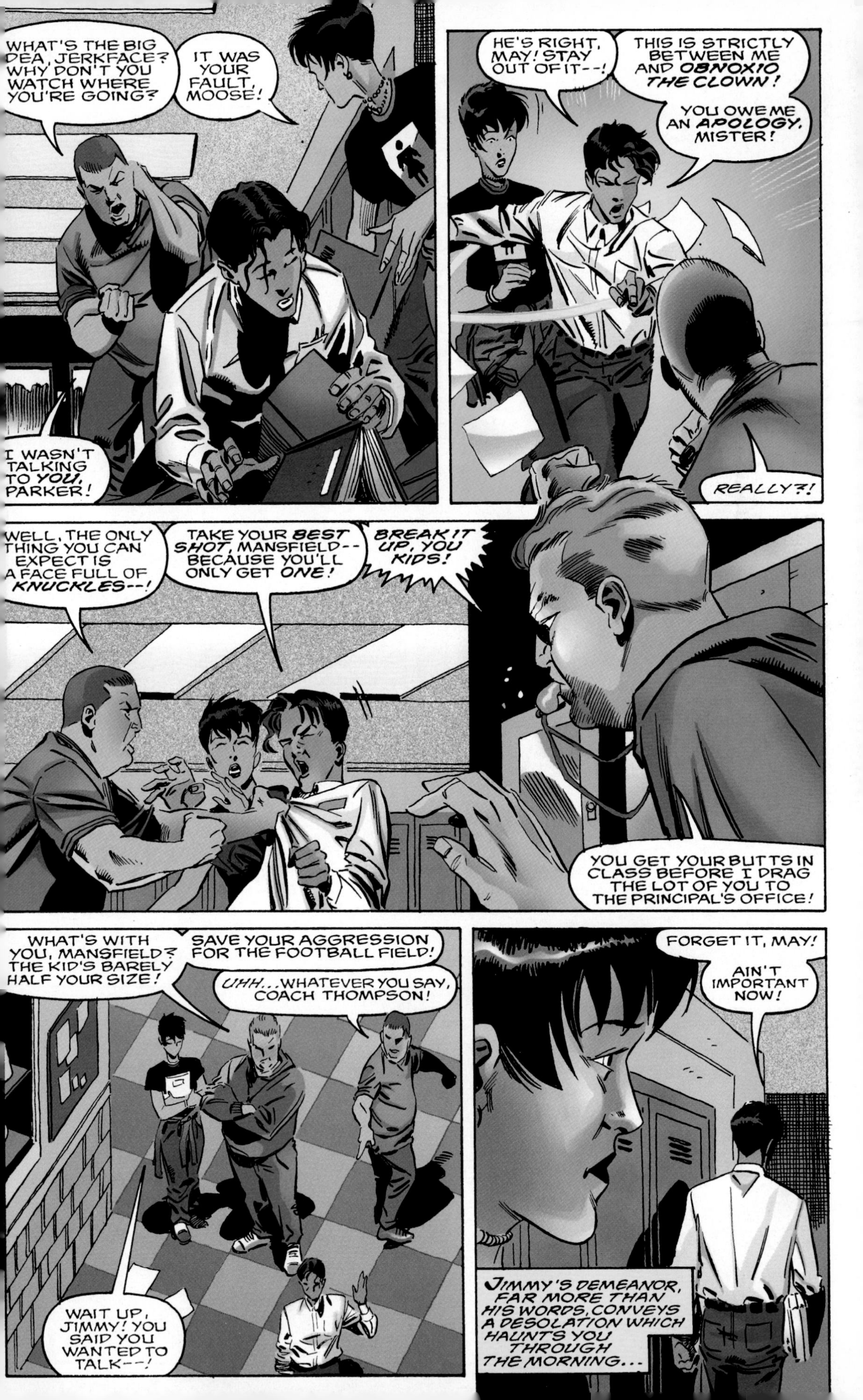

WHAT'S THE BIG IDEA, JERKFACE? WHY DON'T YOU WATCH WHERE YOU'RE GOING?
IT WAS YOUR FAULT, MOOSE!
I WASN'T TALKING TO YOU, PARKER!
HE'S RIGHT, MAY! STAY OUT OF IT--!
THIS IS STRICTLY BETWEEN ME AND OBNOXIO THE CLOWN!
YOU OWE ME AN APOLOGY, MISTER!
REALLY?!
WELL, THE ONLY THING YOU CAN EXPECT IS A FACE FULL OF KNUCKLES--!
TAKE YOUR BEST SHOT, MANSFIELD-- BECAUSE YOU'LL ONLY GET ONE!
BREAK IT UP, YOU KIDS!
YOU GET YOUR BUTTS IN CLASS BEFORE I DRAG THE LOT OF YOU TO THE PRINCIPAL'S OFFICE!
WHAT'S WITH YOU, MANSFIELD? THE KID'S BARELY HALF YOUR SIZE!
SAVE YOUR AGGRESSION FOR THE FOOTBALL FIELD!
UHH... WHATEVER YOU SAY, COACH THOMPSON!
WAIT UP, JIMMY! YOU SAID YOU WANTED TO TALK--!
FORGET IT, MAY!
AIN'T IMPORTANT NOW!
JIMMY'S DEMEANOR, FAR MORE THAN HIS WORDS, CONVEYS A DESOLATION WHICH HAUNTS YOU THROUGH THE MORNING...

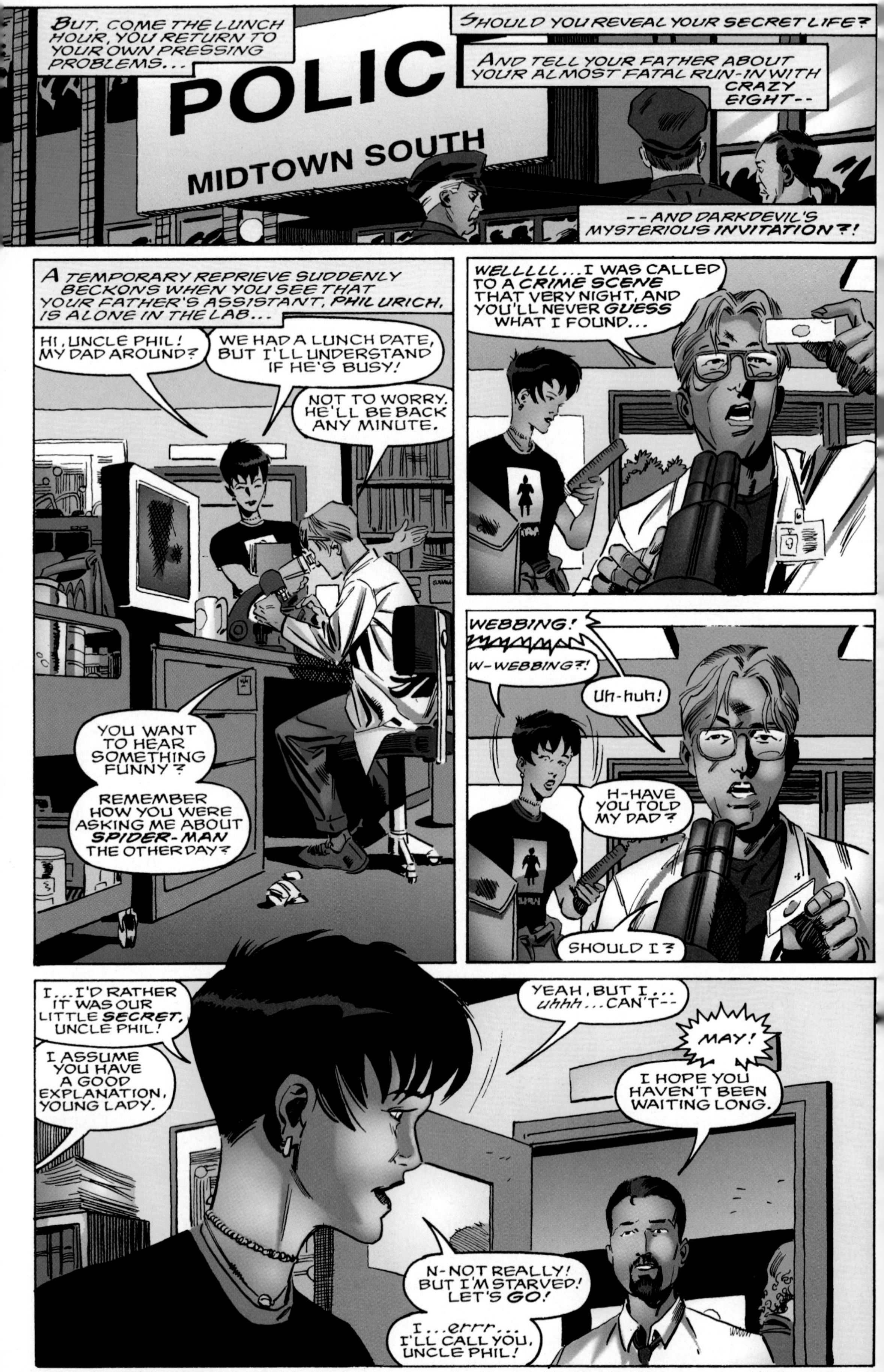
BUT, COME THE LUNCH HOUR, YOU RETURN TO YOUR OWN PRESSING PROBLEMS...
POLIC
MIDTOWN SOUTH
SHOULD YOU REVEAL YOUR SECRET LIFE?
AND TELL YOUR FATHER ABOUT YOUR ALMOST FATAL RUN-IN WITH CRAZY EIGHT--
--AND DARKDEVIL'S MYSTERIOUS INVITATION?!
A TEMPORARY REPRIEVE SUDDENLY BECKONS WHEN YOU SEE THAT YOUR FATHER'S ASSISTANT, PHIL URICH, IS ALONE IN THE LAB...
HI, UNCLE PHIL! MY DAD AROUND?
WE HAD A LUNCH DATE, BUT I'LL UNDERSTAND IF HE'S BUSY!
NOT TO WORRY. HE'LL BE BACK ANY MINUTE.
YOU WANT TO HEAR SOMETHING FUNNY?
REMEMBER HOW YOU WERE ASKING ME ABOUT SPIDER-MAN THE OTHER DAY?
WELLLLL...I WAS CALLED TO A CRIME SCENE THAT VERY NIGHT, AND YOU'LL NEVER GUESS WHAT I FOUND...
WEBBING!
W-WEBBING?!
Uh-huh!
H-HAVE YOU TOLD MY DAD?
SHOULD I?
I...I'D RATHER IT WAS OUR LITTLE SECRET, UNCLE PHIL!
YEAH, BUT I... uhhh...CAN'T--
MAY!
I HOPE YOU HAVEN'T BEEN WAITING LONG.
I ASSUME YOU HAVE A GOOD EXPLANATION, YOUNG LADY.
N-NOT REALLY! BUT I'M STARVED! LET'S GO!
I...errr... I'LL CALL YOU, UNCLE PHIL!

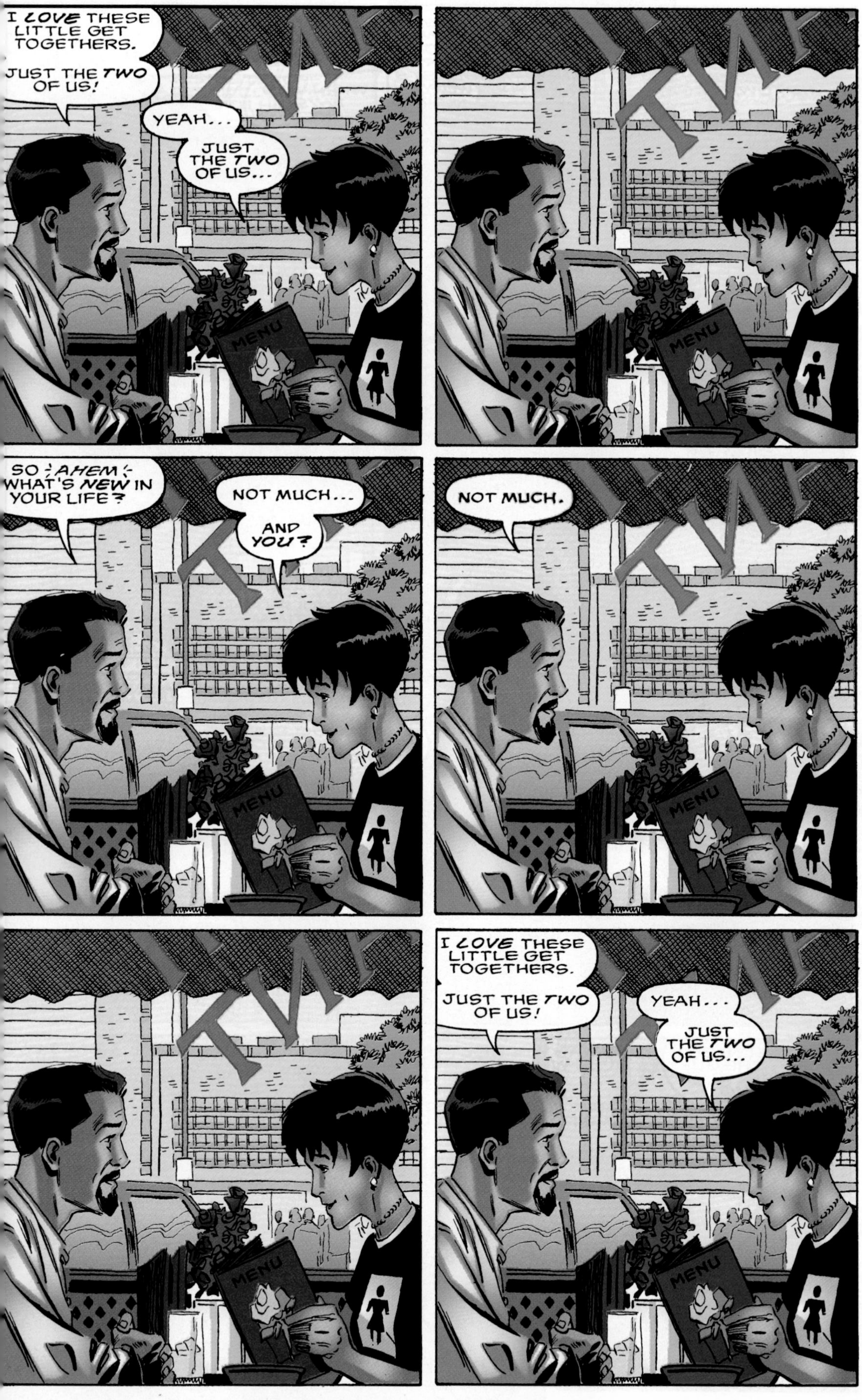
I LOVE THESE LITTLE GET TOGETHERS.
JUST THE TWO OF US!
YEAH...
JUST THE TWO OF US...
SO -AHEM- WHAT'S NEW IN YOUR LIFE?
NOT MUCH...
AND YOU?
NOT MUCH.
MENU
I LOVE THESE LITTLE GET TOGETHERS.
JUST THE TWO OF US!
YEAH...
JUST THE TWO OF US...

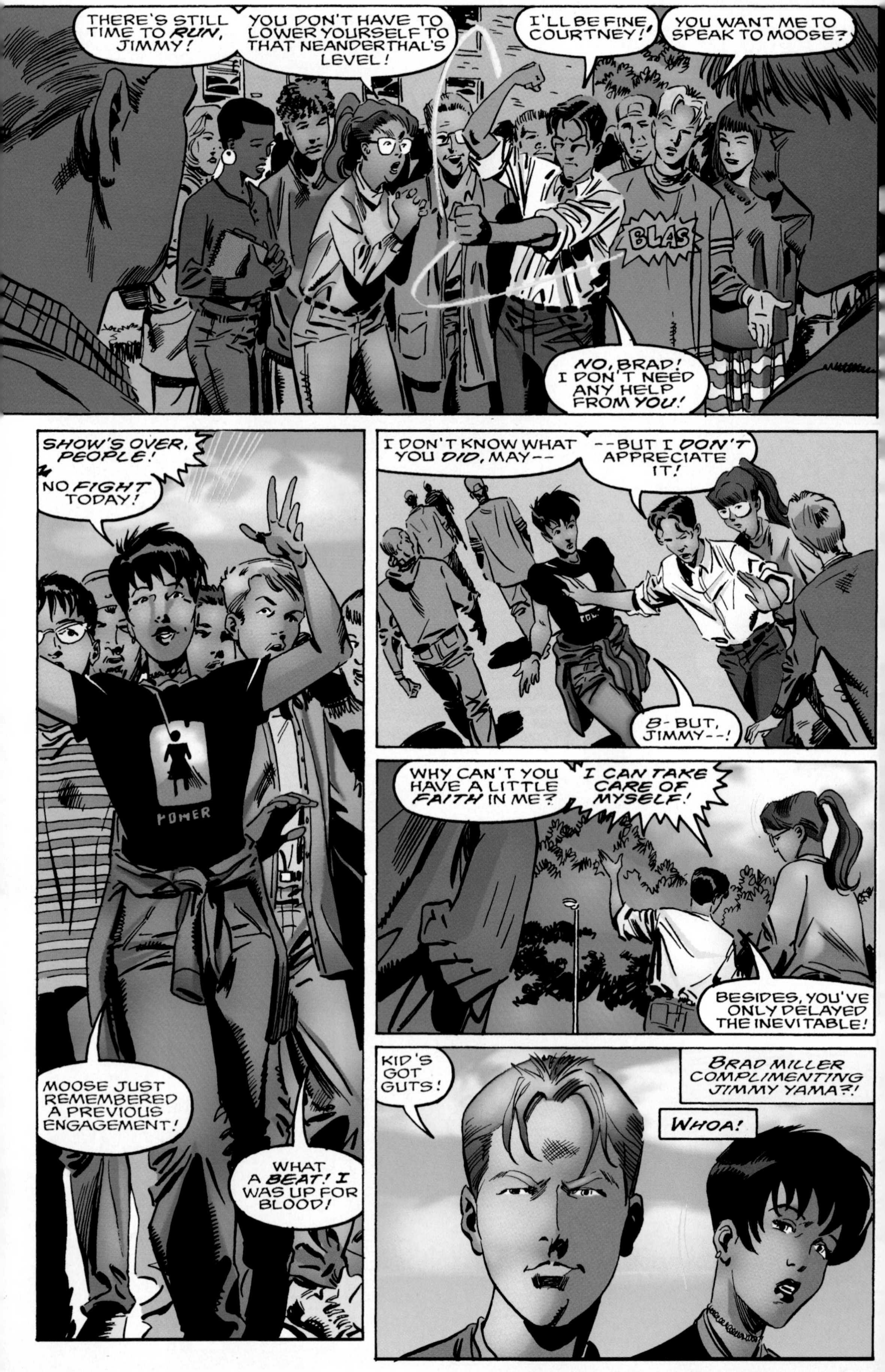
THERE'S STILL TIME TO RUN, JIMMY!
YOU DON'T HAVE TO LOWER YOURSELF TO THAT NEANDERTHAL'S LEVEL!
I'LL BE FINE, COURTNEY!
YOU WANT ME TO SPEAK TO MOOSE?
BLAS
NO, BRAD! I DON'T NEED ANY HELP FROM YOU!
SHOW'S OVER, PEOPLE!
NO FIGHT TODAY!
POWER
MOOSE JUST REMEMBERED A PREVIOUS ENGAGEMENT!
WHAT A BEAT! I WAS UP FOR BLOOD!
I DON'T KNOW WHAT YOU DID, MAY--
--BUT I DON'T APPRECIATE IT!
B-BUT, JIMMY--!
WHY CAN'T YOU HAVE A LITTLE FAITH IN ME?
I CAN TAKE CARE OF MYSELF!
BESIDES, YOU'VE ONLY DELAYED THE INEVITABLE!
KID'S GOT GUTS!
BRAD MILLER COMPLIMENTING JIMMY YAMA?!
WHOA!

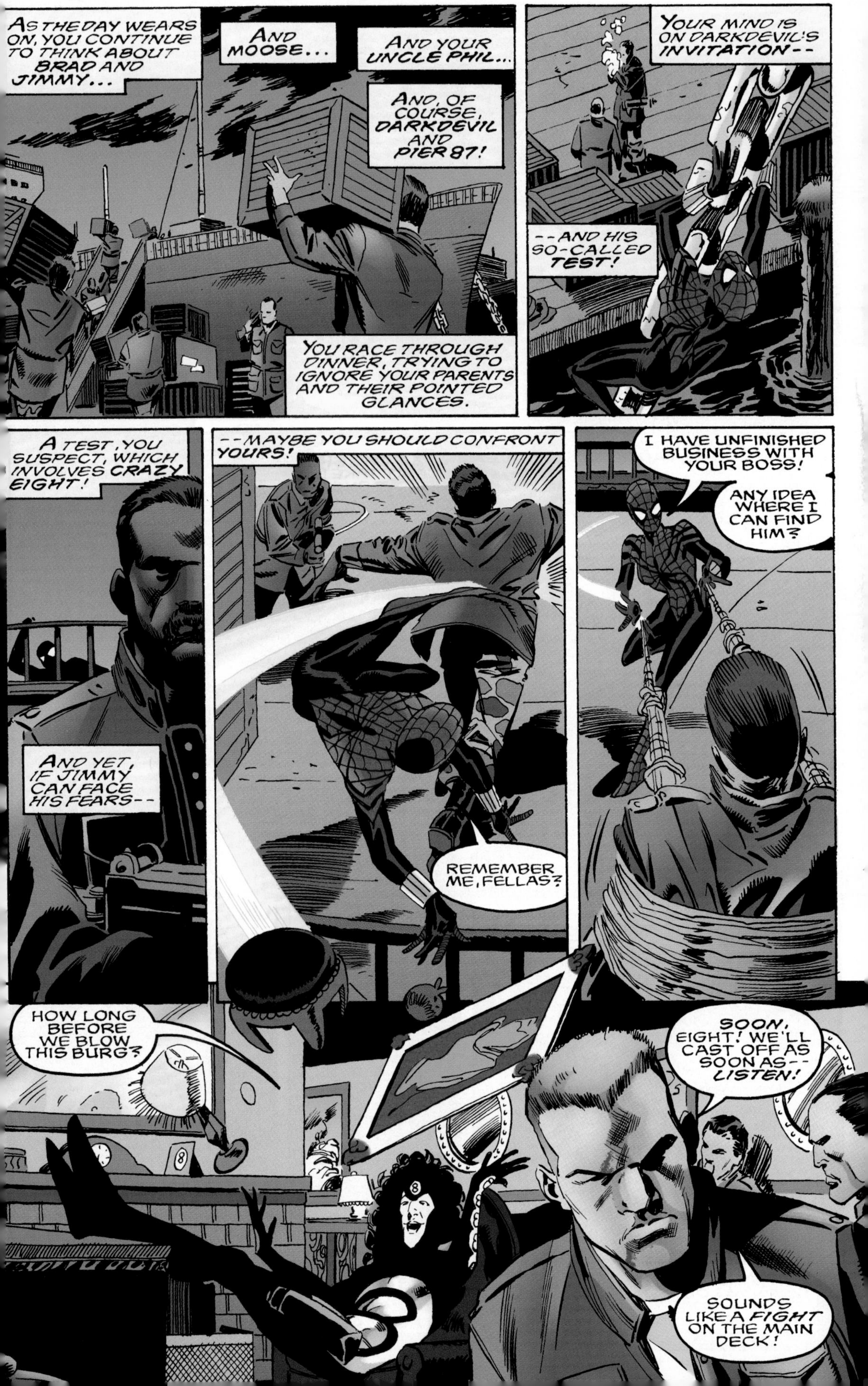
AS THE DAY WEARS ON, YOU CONTINUE TO THINK ABOUT BRAD AND JIMMY...
AND MOOSE...
AND YOUR UNCLE PHIL...
AND, OF COURSE, DARKDEVIL AND PIER 87!
YOU RACE THROUGH DINNER, TRYING TO IGNORE YOUR PARENTS AND THEIR POINTED GLANCES.
YOUR MIND IS ON DARKDEVIL'S INVITATION--
--AND HIS SO-CALLED TEST!
A TEST, YOU SUSPECT, WHICH INVOLVES CRAZY EIGHT!
AND YET, IF JIMMY CAN FACE HIS FEARS--
--MAYBE YOU SHOULD CONFRONT YOURS!
REMEMBER ME, FELLAS?
I HAVE UNFINISHED BUSINESS WITH YOUR BOSS!
ANY IDEA WHERE I CAN FIND HIM?
HOW LONG BEFORE WE BLOW THIS BURG?
SOON, EIGHT! WE'LL CAST OFF AS SOON AS-- LISTEN!
SOUNDS LIKE A FIGHT ON THE MAIN DECK!

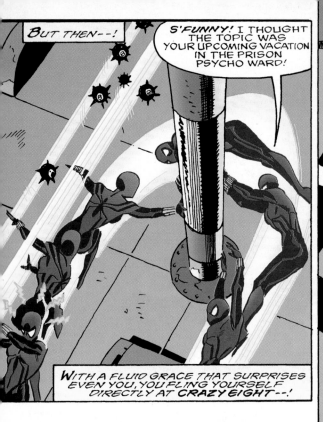

BUT THEN--!

S'FUNNY! I THOUGHT THE TOPIC WAS YOUR UPCOMING VACATION IN THE PRISON PSYCHO WARD!

WITH A FLUID GRACE THAT SURPRISES EVEN YOU, YOU FLING YOURSELF DIRECTLY AT *CRAZY EIGHT*--!

VERY IMPRESSIVE, MY SWEET--

--BUT, AS YOU SEE, I'M ALSO A TRAINED ACROBAT!

NOT ONLY AM I ABLE TO DODGE YOUR ATTACK, BUT I CAN ALSO PREPARE A WARM RECEPTION FOR YOU--

HE RELEASES A HANDFUL OF *EIGHT BALLS*--

--WHICH PERFECTLY MATCH YOUR *SPEED* AND *TRAJECTORY*!

UNABLE TO HALT YOUR FORWARD MOMENTUM, YOU IMMEDIATELY ATTEMPT TO *MINIMIZE* THE INEVITABLE COLLISION--

--WITH A HASTILY CONSTRUCTED *WEB-COCOON!*

KAWA-TWOOM!

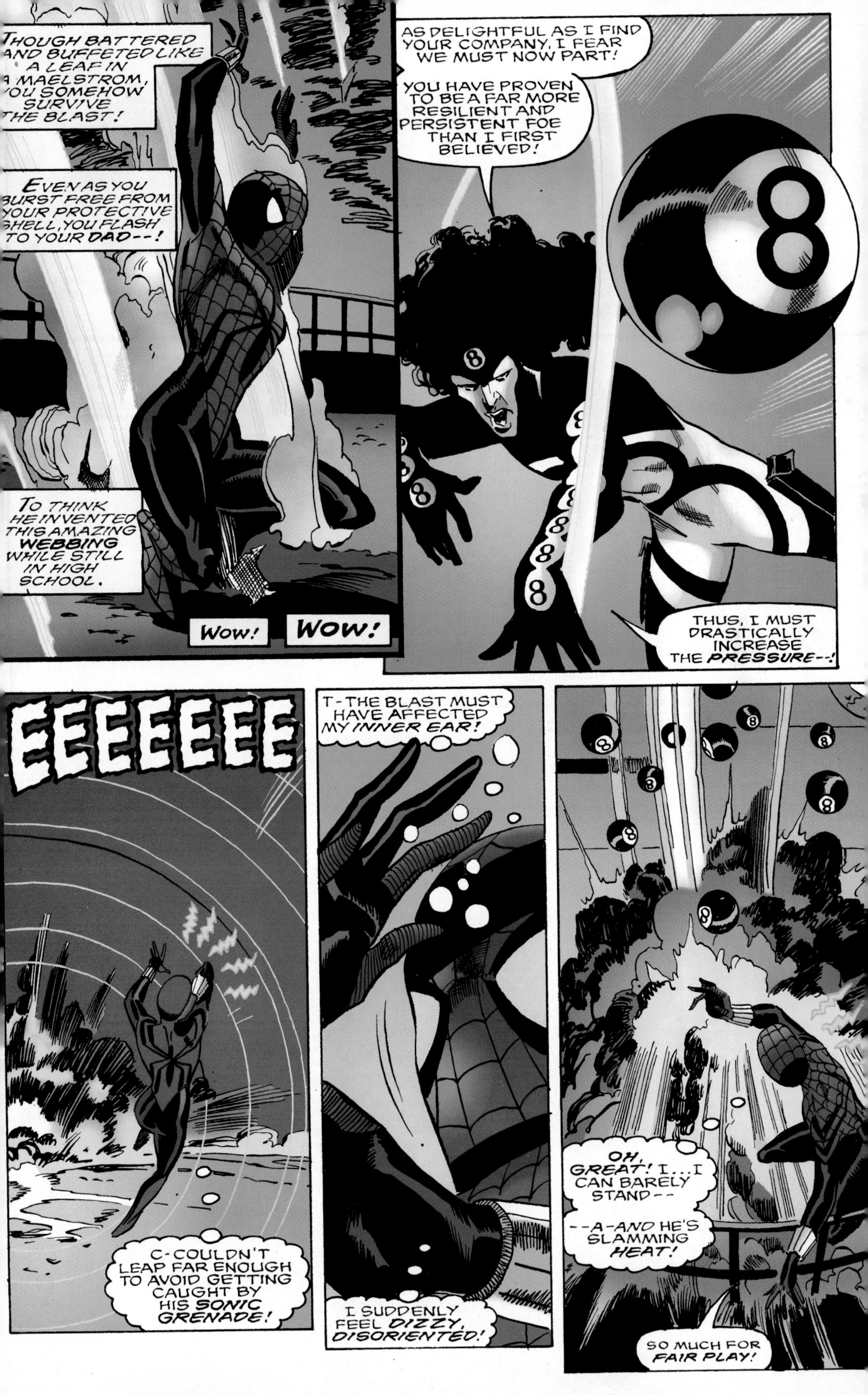
THOUGH BATTERED AND BUFFETED LIKE A LEAF IN A MAELSTROM, YOU SOMEHOW SURVIVE THE BLAST!
EVEN AS YOU BURST FREE FROM YOUR PROTECTIVE SHELL, YOU FLASH TO YOUR DAD--!
TO THINK HE INVENTED THIS AMAZING WEBBING WHILE STILL IN HIGH SCHOOL.
WOW!
WOW!
AS DELIGHTFUL AS I FIND YOUR COMPANY, I FEAR WE MUST NOW PART!
YOU HAVE PROVEN TO BE A FAR MORE RESILIENT AND PERSISTENT FOE THAN I FIRST BELIEVED!
THUS, I MUST DRASTICALLY INCREASE THE PRESSURE--!
EEEEEEE
C-COULDN'T LEAP FAR ENOUGH TO AVOID GETTING CAUGHT BY HIS SONIC GRENADE!
T-THE BLAST MUST HAVE AFFECTED MY INNER EAR!
I SUDDENLY FEEL DIZZY, DISORIENTED!
OH, GREAT! I...I CAN BARELY STAND--
--A-AND HE'S SLAMMING HEAT!
SO MUCH FOR FAIR PLAY!

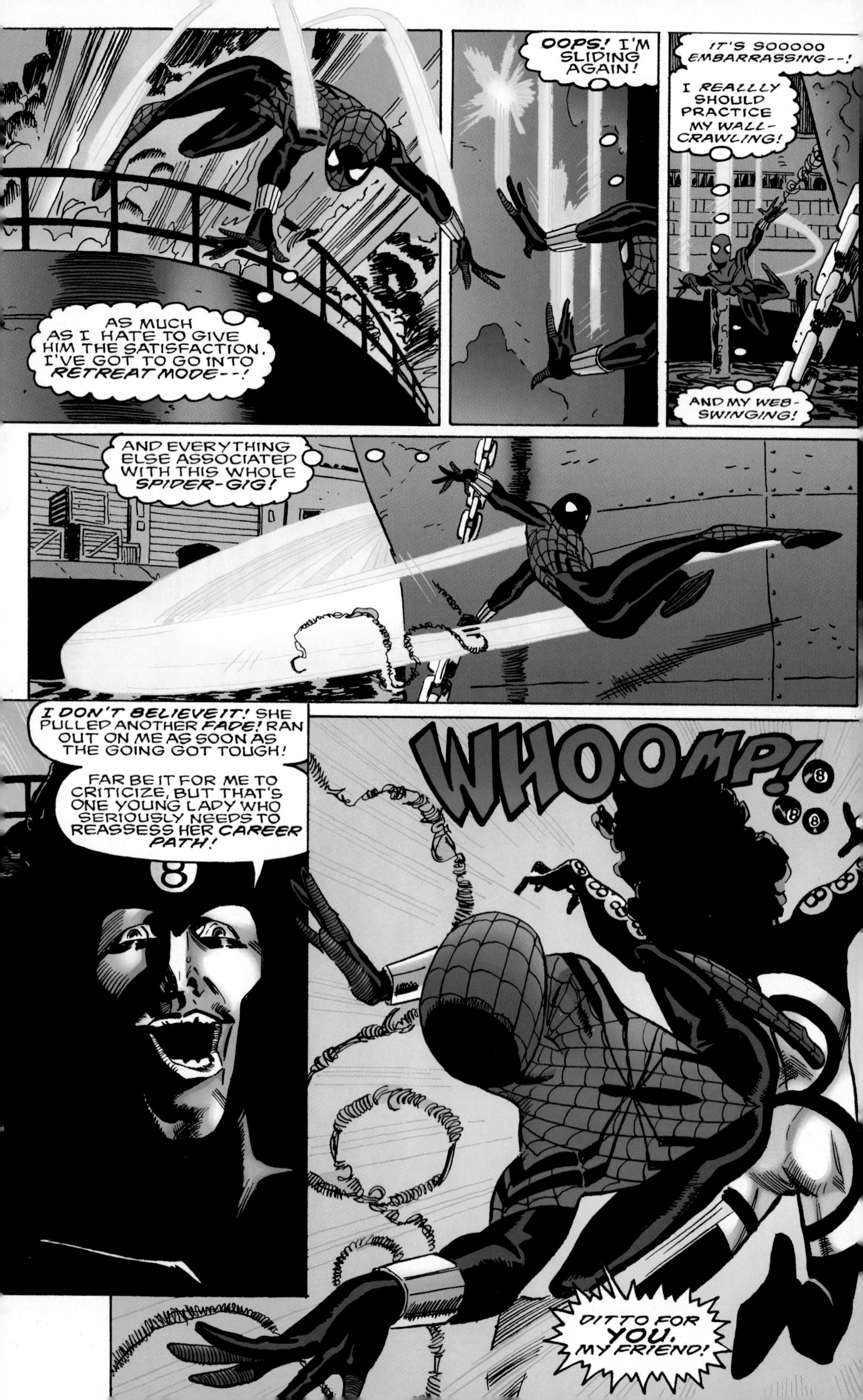
AS MUCH AS I HATE TO GIVE HIM THE SATISFACTION, I'VE GOT TO GO INTO RETREAT MODE--!
OOPS! I'M SLIDING AGAIN!
IT'S SOOOOO EMBARRASSING--!
I REALLLY SHOULD PRACTICE MY WALL-CRAWLING!
AND MY WEB-SWINGING!
AND EVERYTHING ELSE ASSOCIATED WITH THIS WHOLE SPIDER-GIG!
I DON'T BELIEVE IT! SHE PULLED ANOTHER FADE! RAN OUT ON ME AS SOON AS THE GOING GOT TOUGH!
FAR BE IT FOR ME TO CRITICIZE, BUT THAT'S ONE YOUNG LADY WHO SERIOUSLY NEEDS TO REASSESS HER CAREER PATH!
WHOOMP!
DITTO FOR YOU, MY FRIEND!

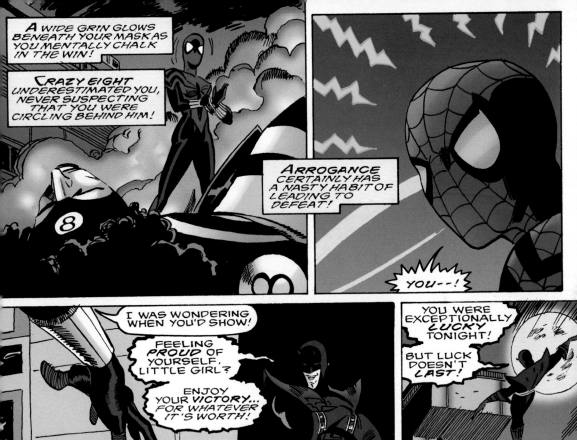

A WIDE GRIN GLOWS BENEATH YOUR MASK AS YOU MENTALLY CHALK IN THE WIN!

CRAZY EIGHT UNDERESTIMATED YOU, NEVER SUSPECTING THAT YOU WERE CIRCLING BEHIND HIM!

ARROGANCE CERTAINLY HAS A NASTY HABIT OF LEADING TO DEFEAT!

YOU--!

I WAS WONDERING WHEN YOU'D SHOW!

FEELING PROUD OF YOURSELF, LITTLE GIRL?

ENJOY YOUR VICTORY... FOR WHATEVER IT'S WORTH!

WHAT'S YOUR DEAL, ANYWAY? WHY ARE YOU HASSLING ME?

I'M MERELY TRYING TO FORESTALL AN UNNECESSARY FUNERAL, KID!

YOU WERE EXCEPTIONALLY LUCKY TONIGHT!

BUT LUCK DOESN'T LAST!

NEITHER DO THOSE WHO PLAY AT BEING A HERO!

IT'S ALMOST FUNNY...

CRAZY EIGHT TREATS YOU WITH RESPECT, AND TRIES TO KILL YOU...

DARKDEVIL MOCKS YOU, AND TRIES TO SAVE YOU.

YOUR LIFE IS SUDDENLY BRIMMING WITH LITTLE IRONIES...

LIKE JIMMY YAMA ASKING YOU OUT!

LIKE YOUR UNCLE PHIL FINDING YOUR WEBBING!

LIKE YOUR WRETCHED ATTEMPT TO BE WORTHY OF YOUR FATHER'S WEBS!

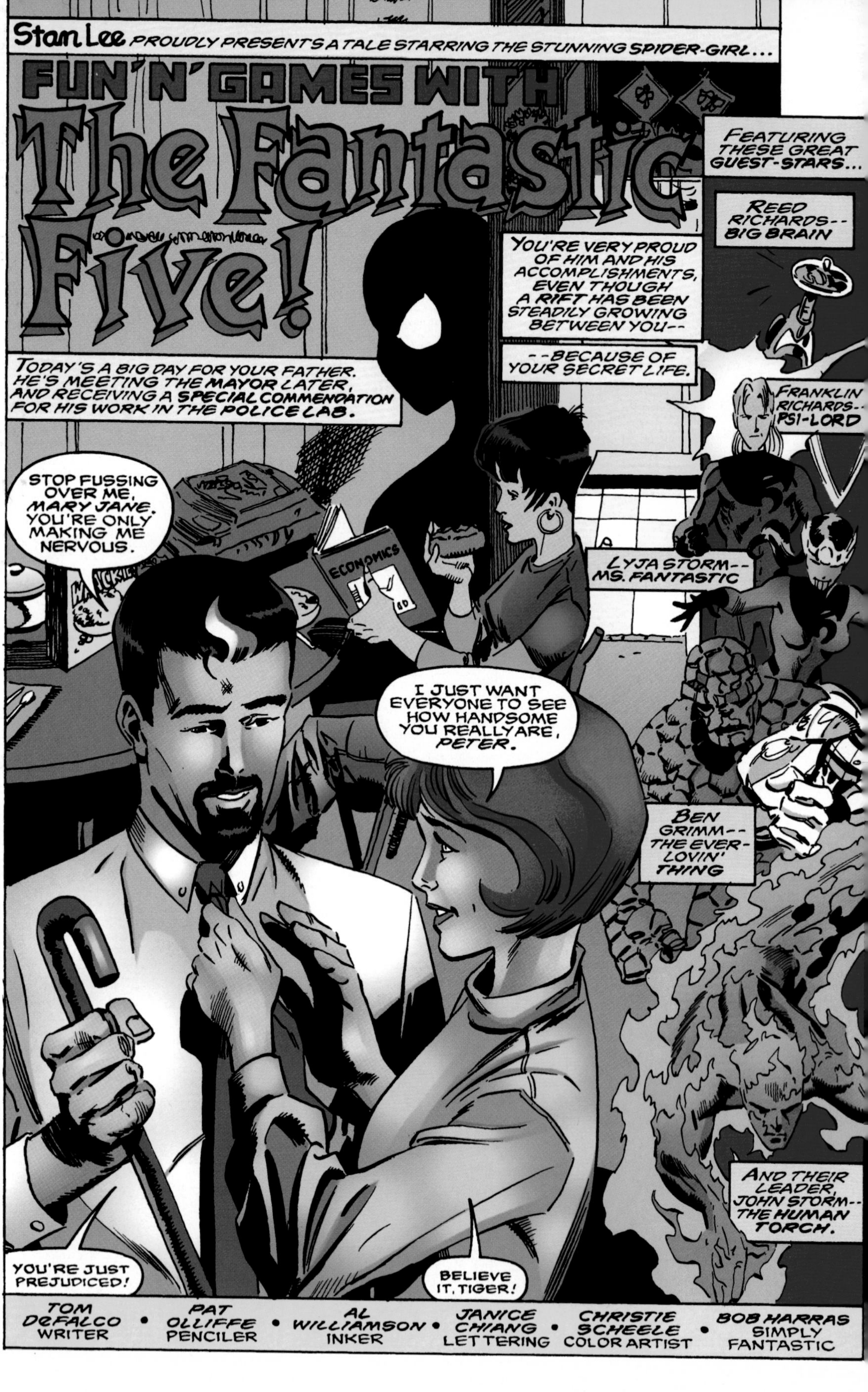

Stan Lee PROUDLY PRESENTS A TALE STARRING THE STUNNING SPIDER-GIRL...
FUN 'N' GAMES WITH The Fantastic Five!
TODAY'S A BIG DAY FOR YOUR FATHER. HE'S MEETING THE MAYOR LATER, AND RECEIVING A SPECIAL COMMENDATION FOR HIS WORK IN THE POLICE LAB.
YOU'RE VERY PROUD OF HIM AND HIS ACCOMPLISHMENTS, EVEN THOUGH A RIFT HAS BEEN STEADILY GROWING BETWEEN YOU--
--BECAUSE OF YOUR SECRET LIFE.
STOP FUSSING OVER ME, MARY JANE. YOU'RE ONLY MAKING ME NERVOUS.
I JUST WANT EVERYONE TO SEE HOW HANDSOME YOU REALLY ARE, PETER.
YOU'RE JUST PREJUDICED!
BELIEVE IT, TIGER!
ECONOMICS
FEATURING THESE GREAT GUEST-STARS...
REED RICHARDS-- BIG BRAIN
FRANKLIN RICHARDS-- PSI-LORD
LYJA STORM-- MS. FANTASTIC
BEN GRIMM-- THE EVER-LOVIN' THING
AND THEIR LEADER, JOHN STORM-- THE HUMAN TORCH.
TOM DeFALCO WRITER • PAT OLLIFFE PENCILER • AL WILLIAMSON INKER • JANICE CHIANG LETTERING • CHRISTIE SCHEELE COLOR ARTIST • BOB HARRAS SIMPLY FANTASTIC

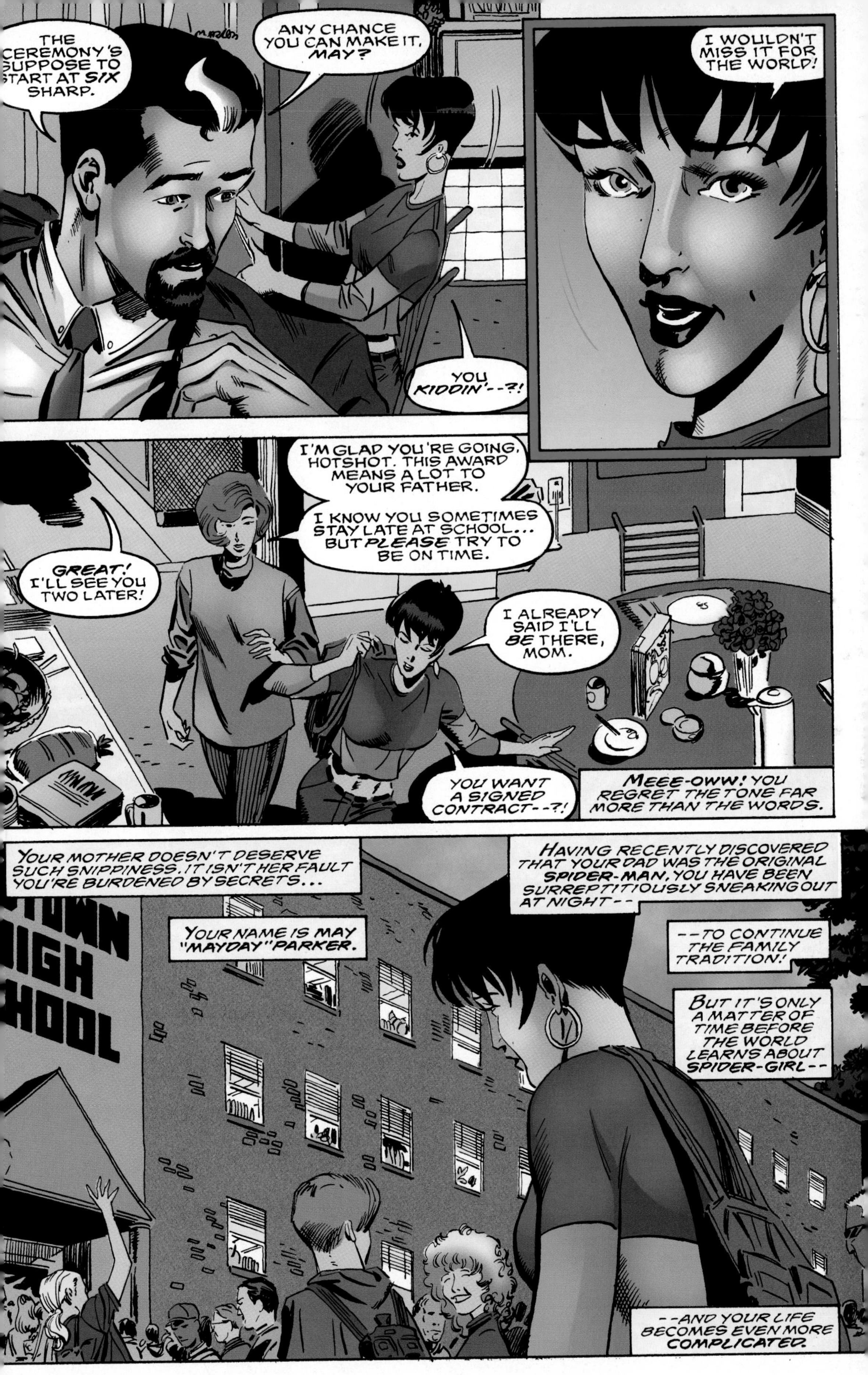
THE CEREMONY'S SUPPOSE TO START AT SIX SHARP.
ANY CHANCE YOU CAN MAKE IT, MAY?
YOU KIDDIN'--?!
I WOULDN'T MISS IT FOR THE WORLD!
GREAT! I'LL SEE YOU TWO LATER!
I'M GLAD YOU'RE GOING, HOTSHOT. THIS AWARD MEANS A LOT TO YOUR FATHER.
I KNOW YOU SOMETIMES STAY LATE AT SCHOOL... BUT PLEASE TRY TO BE ON TIME.
I ALREADY SAID I'LL BE THERE, MOM.
YOU WANT A SIGNED CONTRACT--?!
MEEE-OWW! YOU REGRET THE TONE FAR MORE THAN THE WORDS.
YOUR MOTHER DOESN'T DESERVE SUCH SNIPPINESS. IT ISN'T HER FAULT YOU'RE BURDENED BY SECRETS...
YOUR NAME IS MAY "MAYDAY" PARKER.
HAVING RECENTLY DISCOVERED THAT YOUR DAD WAS THE ORIGINAL SPIDER-MAN, YOU HAVE BEEN SURREPTITIOUSLY SNEAKING OUT AT NIGHT--
--TO CONTINUE THE FAMILY TRADITION!
BUT IT'S ONLY A MATTER OF TIME BEFORE THE WORLD LEARNS ABOUT SPIDER-GIRL--
--AND YOUR LIFE BECOMES EVEN MORE COMPLICATED.

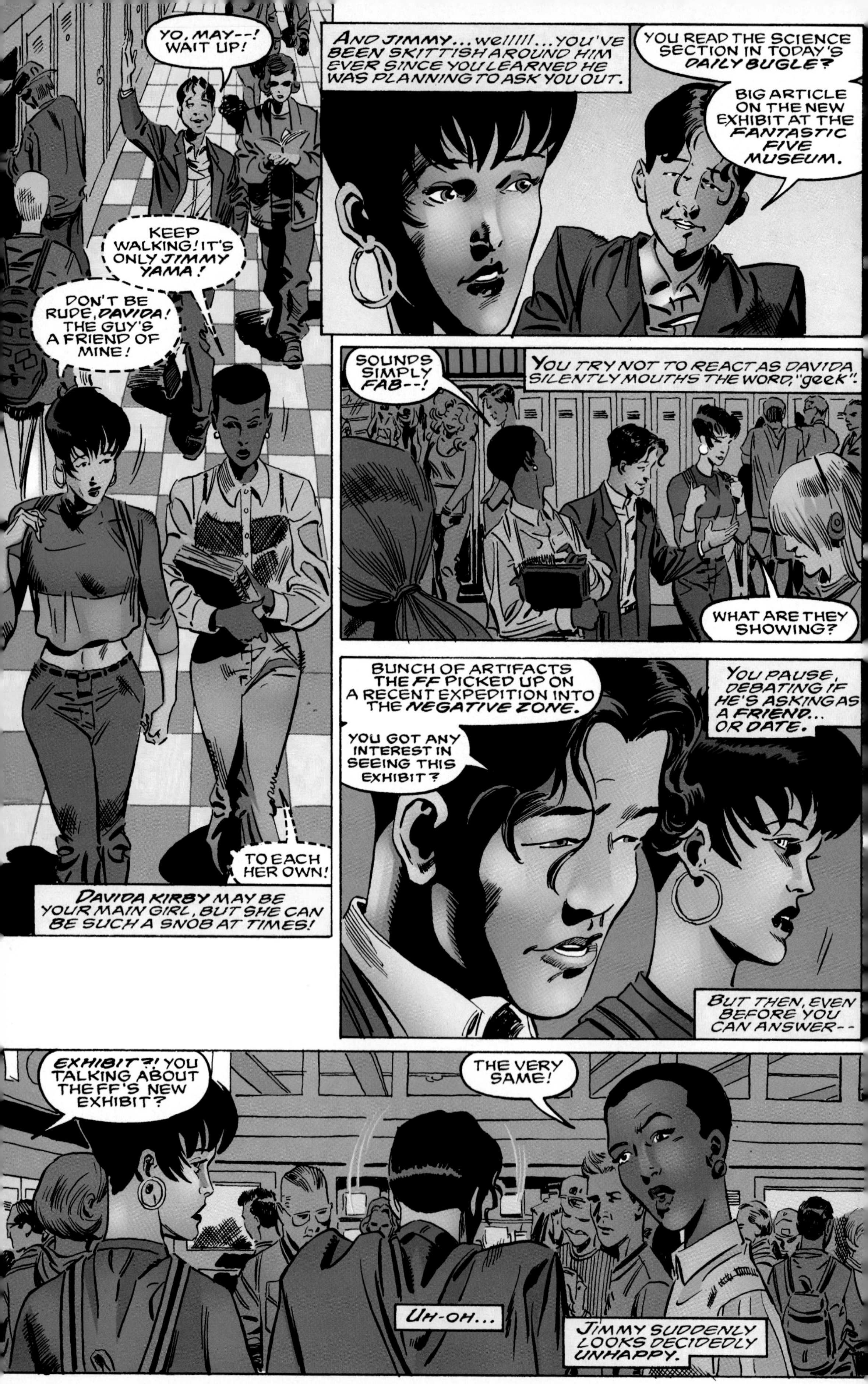
YO, MAY--! WAIT UP!
KEEP WALKING! IT'S ONLY JIMMY YAMA!
DON'T BE RUDE, DAVIDA! THE GUY'S A FRIEND OF MINE!
TO EACH HER OWN!
DAVIDA KIRBY MAY BE YOUR MAIN GIRL, BUT SHE CAN BE SUCH A SNOB AT TIMES!
AND JIMMY... wellll... YOU'VE BEEN SKITTISH AROUND HIM EVER SINCE YOU LEARNED HE WAS PLANNING TO ASK YOU OUT.
YOU READ THE SCIENCE SECTION IN TODAY'S DAILY BUGLE?
BIG ARTICLE ON THE NEW EXHIBIT AT THE FANTASTIC FIVE MUSEUM.
SOUNDS SIMPLY FAB--!
YOU TRY NOT TO REACT AS DAVIDA SILENTLY MOUTHS THE WORD, "geek".
WHAT ARE THEY SHOWING?
BUNCH OF ARTIFACTS THE FF PICKED UP ON A RECENT EXPEDITION INTO THE NEGATIVE ZONE.
YOU GOT ANY INTEREST IN SEEING THIS EXHIBIT?
YOU PAUSE, DEBATING IF HE'S ASKING AS A FRIEND... OR DATE.
BUT THEN, EVEN BEFORE YOU CAN ANSWER--
EXHIBIT?! YOU TALKING ABOUT THE FF'S NEW EXHIBIT?
THE VERY SAME!
UH-OH...
JIMMY SUDDENLY LOOKS DECIDEDLY UNHAPPY.

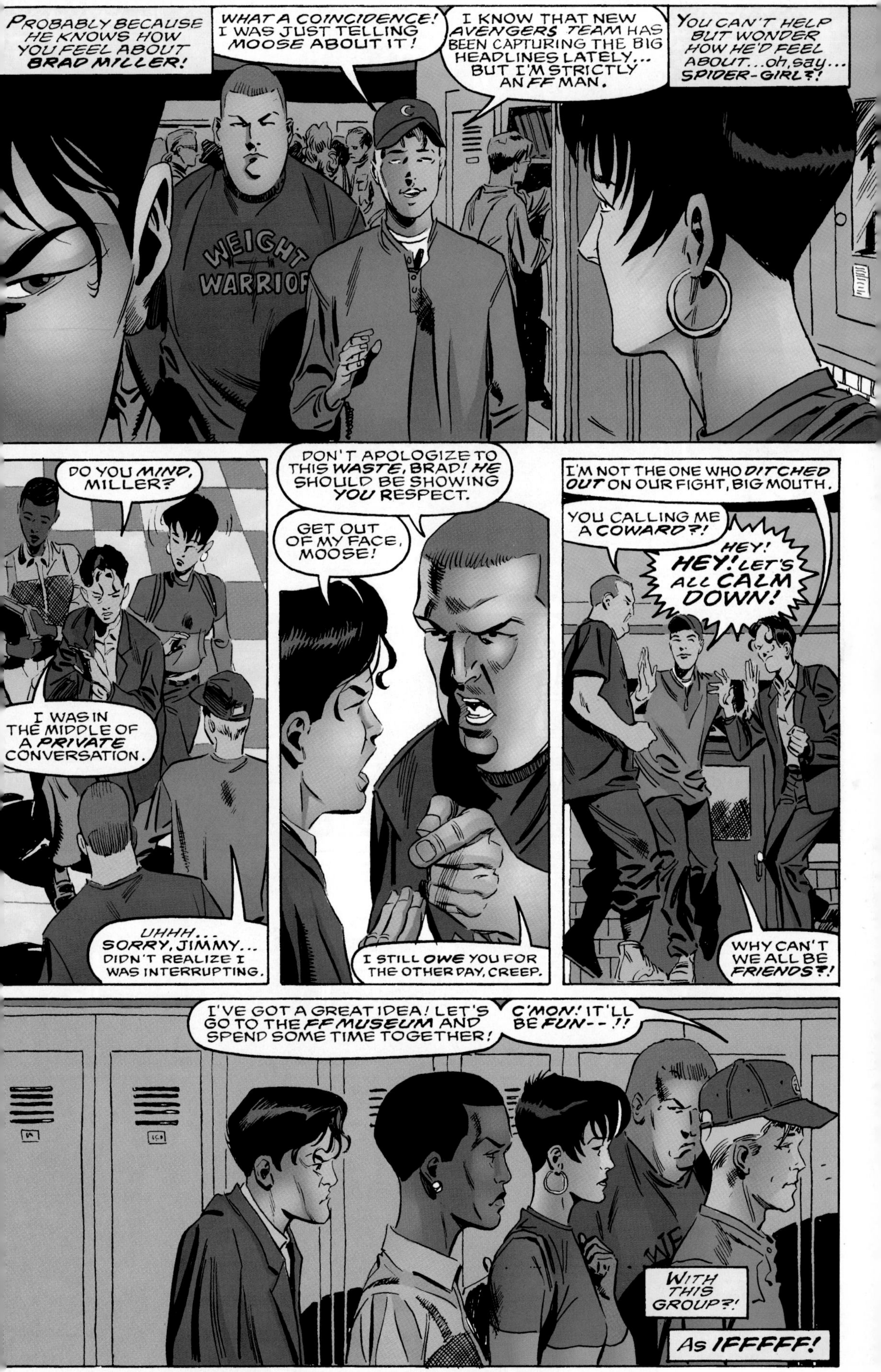
PROBABLY BECAUSE HE KNOWS HOW YOU FEEL ABOUT BRAD MILLER!
WHAT A COINCIDENCE! I WAS JUST TELLING MOOSE ABOUT IT!
I KNOW THAT NEW AVENGERS TEAM HAS BEEN CAPTURING THE BIG HEADLINES LATELY... BUT I'M STRICTLY AN FF MAN.
YOU CAN'T HELP BUT WONDER HOW HE'D FEEL ABOUT...oh, say... SPIDER-GIRL?!
WEIGHT WARRIOR
DO YOU MIND, MILLER?
I WAS IN THE MIDDLE OF A PRIVATE CONVERSATION.
UHHH... SORRY, JIMMY... DIDN'T REALIZE I WAS INTERRUPTING.
DON'T APOLOGIZE TO THIS WASTE, BRAD! HE SHOULD BE SHOWING YOU RESPECT.
GET OUT OF MY FACE, MOOSE!
I STILL OWE YOU FOR THE OTHER DAY, CREEP.
I'M NOT THE ONE WHO DITCHED OUT ON OUR FIGHT, BIG MOUTH.
YOU CALLING ME A COWARD?!
HEY! HEY! LET'S ALL CALM DOWN!
WHY CAN'T WE ALL BE FRIENDS?!
I'VE GOT A GREAT IDEA! LET'S GO TO THE FF MUSEUM AND SPEND SOME TIME TOGETHER!
C'MON! IT'LL BE FUN--!!
WITH THIS GROUP?!
As IFFFFF!

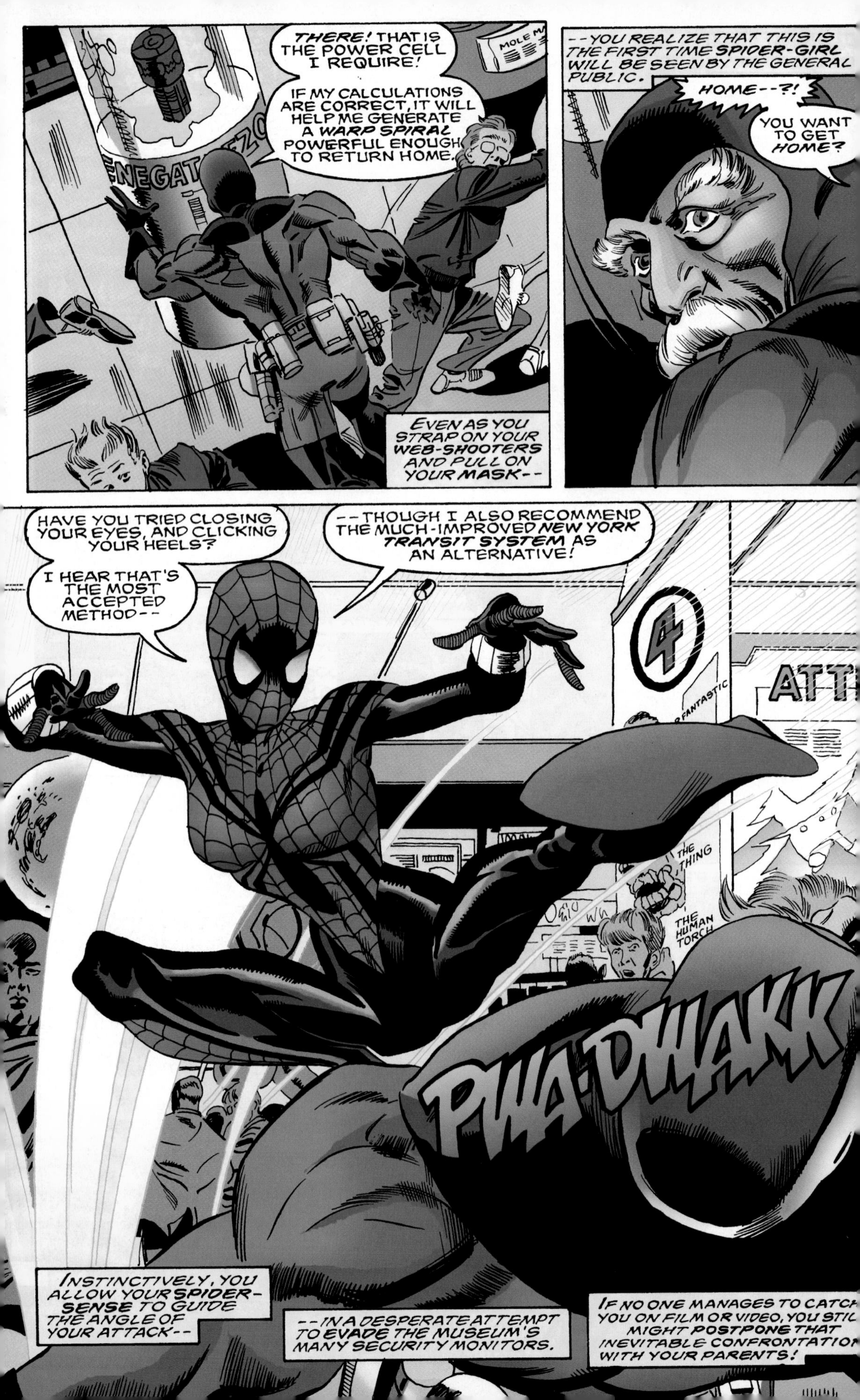
THERE! THAT IS THE POWER CELL I REQUIRE!
IF MY CALCULATIONS ARE CORRECT, IT WILL HELP ME GENERATE A WARP SPIRAL POWERFUL ENOUGH TO RETURN HOME.
ENEGAT
EVEN AS YOU STRAP ON YOUR WEB-SHOOTERS AND PULL ON YOUR MASK--
--YOU REALIZE THAT THIS IS THE FIRST TIME SPIDER-GIRL WILL BE SEEN BY THE GENERAL PUBLIC.
HOME--?!
YOU WANT TO GET HOME?
HAVE YOU TRIED CLOSING YOUR EYES, AND CLICKING YOUR HEELS?
I HEAR THAT'S THE MOST ACCEPTED METHOD--
--THOUGH I ALSO RECOMMEND THE MUCH-IMPROVED NEW YORK TRANSIT SYSTEM AS AN ALTERNATIVE!
4
THE THING
THE HUMAN TORCH
PWA-DWAKK
INSTINCTIVELY, YOU ALLOW YOUR SPIDER-SENSE TO GUIDE THE ANGLE OF YOUR ATTACK--
--IN A DESPERATE ATTEMPT TO EVADE THE MUSEUM'S MANY SECURITY MONITORS.
IF NO ONE MANAGES TO CATCH YOU ON FILM OR VIDEO, YOU STILL MIGHT POSTPONE THAT INEVITABLE CONFRONTATION WITH YOUR PARENTS!

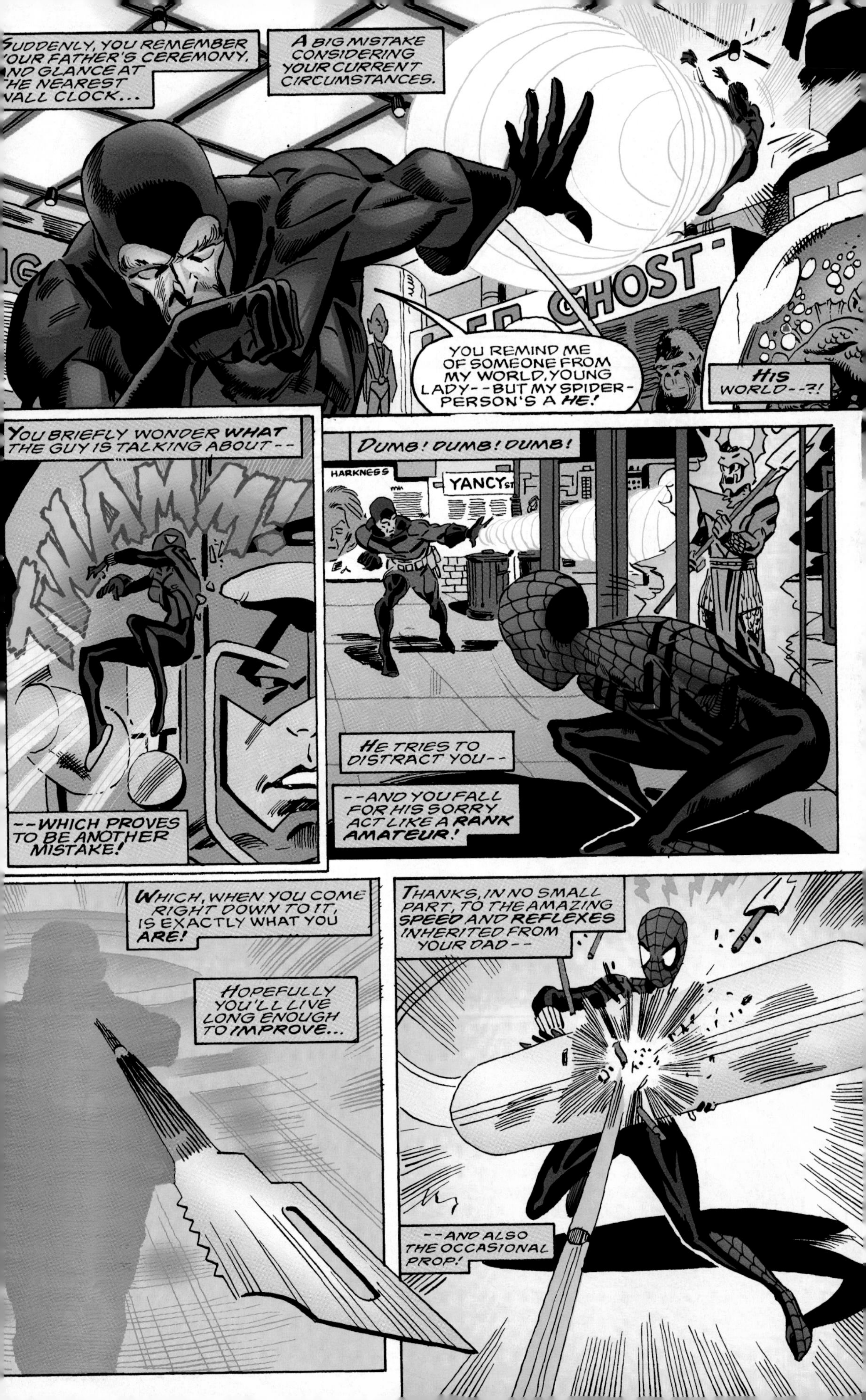

SUDDENLY, YOU REMEMBER
OUR FATHER'S CEREMONY,
ND GLANCE AT
HE NEAREST
ALL CLOCK...
A BIG MISTAKE CONSIDERING YOUR CURRENT CIRCUMSTANCES.
GHOST
YOU REMIND ME OF SOMEONE FROM MY WORLD, YOUNG LADY--BUT MY SPIDER-PERSON'S A HE!
HIS WORLD--?!
YOU BRIEFLY WONDER WHAT THE GUY IS TALKING ABOUT--
--WHICH PROVES TO BE ANOTHER MISTAKE!
DUMB! DUMB! DUMB!
HARKNESS
YANCY ST
HE TRIES TO DISTRACT YOU--
--AND YOU FALL FOR HIS SORRY ACT LIKE A RANK AMATEUR!
WHICH, WHEN YOU COME RIGHT DOWN TO IT, IS EXACTLY WHAT YOU ARE!
HOPEFULLY YOU'LL LIVE LONG ENOUGH TO IMPROVE...
THANKS, IN NO SMALL PART, TO THE AMAZING SPEED AND REFLEXES INHERITED FROM YOUR DAD--
--AND ALSO THE OCCASIONAL PROP!

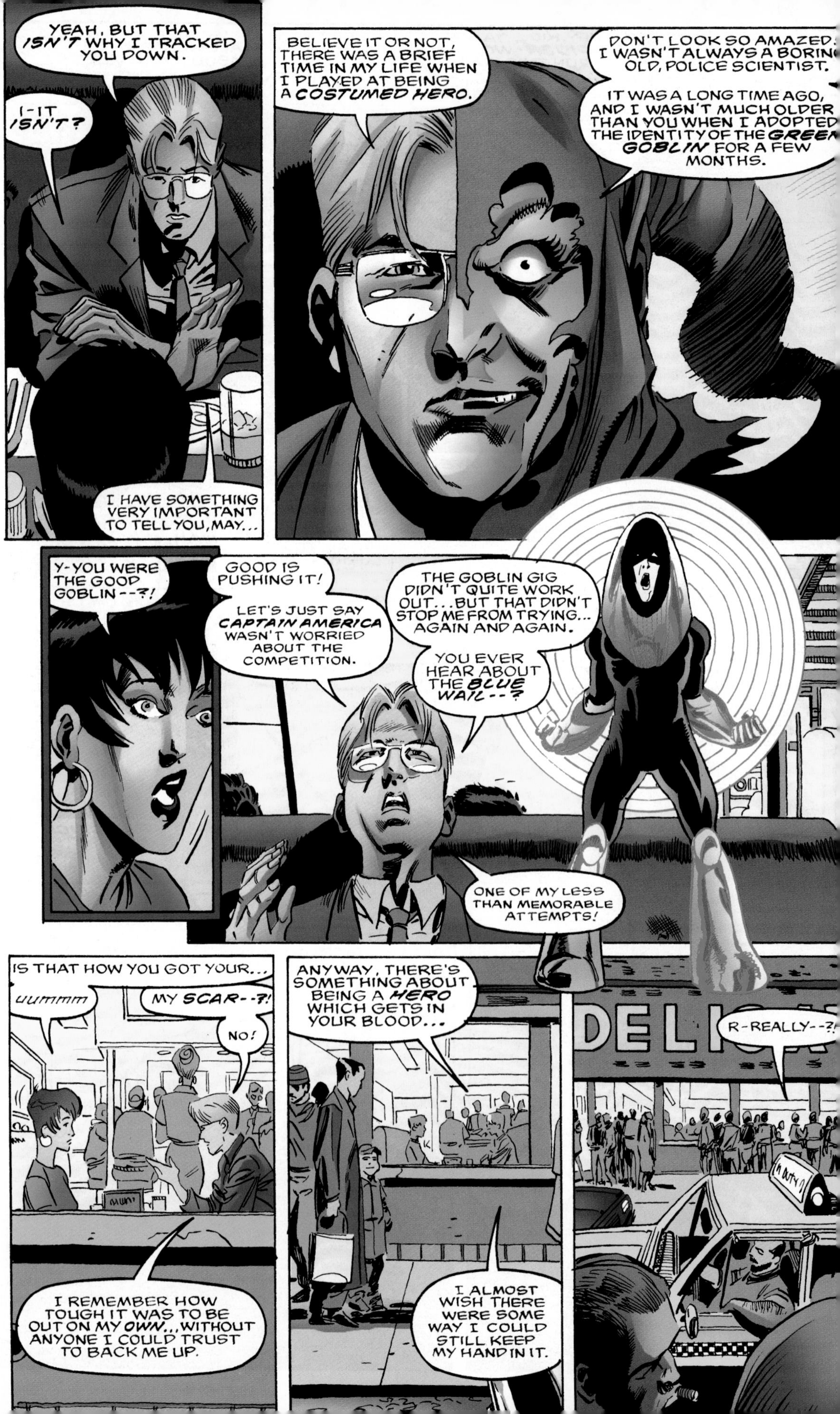
YEAH, BUT THAT ISN'T WHY I TRACKED YOU DOWN.
I-IT ISN'T?
I HAVE SOMETHING VERY IMPORTANT TO TELL YOU, MAY...
BELIEVE IT OR NOT, THERE WAS A BRIEF TIME IN MY LIFE WHEN I PLAYED AT BEING A COSTUMED HERO.
DON'T LOOK SO AMAZED! I WASN'T ALWAYS A BORING OLD, POLICE SCIENTIST.
IT WAS A LONG TIME AGO, AND I WASN'T MUCH OLDER THAN YOU WHEN I ADOPTED THE IDENTITY OF THE GREEN GOBLIN FOR A FEW MONTHS.
Y-YOU WERE THE GOOD GOBLIN--?!
GOOD IS PUSHING IT!
LET'S JUST SAY CAPTAIN AMERICA WASN'T WORRIED ABOUT THE COMPETITION.
THE GOBLIN GIG DIDN'T QUITE WORK OUT...BUT THAT DIDN'T STOP ME FROM TRYING... AGAIN AND AGAIN.
YOU EVER HEAR ABOUT THE BLUE WAIL--?
ONE OF MY LESS THAN MEMORABLE ATTEMPTS!
IS THAT HOW YOU GOT YOUR...
UUMMMM
MY SCAR--?!
NO!
I REMEMBER HOW TOUGH IT WAS TO BE OUT ON MY OWN... WITHOUT ANYONE I COULD TRUST TO BACK ME UP.
ANYWAY, THERE'S SOMETHING ABOUT BEING A HERO WHICH GETS IN YOUR BLOOD...
I ALMOST WISH THERE WERE SOME WAY I COULD STILL KEEP MY HAND IN IT.
DELI
R-REALLY--?!

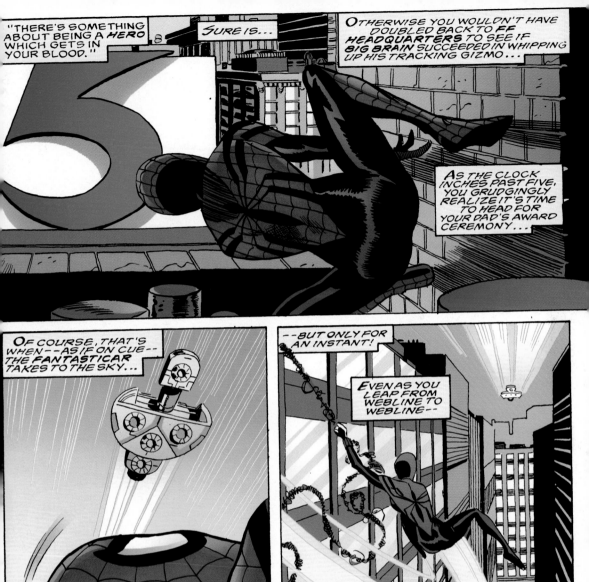

"THERE'S SOMETHING ABOUT BEING A *HERO* WHICH GETS IN YOUR BLOOD."

SURE IS...

OTHERWISE YOU WOULDN'T HAVE DOUBLED BACK TO *FF HEADQUARTERS* TO SEE IF *BIG BRAIN* SUCCEEDED IN WHIPPING UP HIS TRACKING GIZMO...

AS THE CLOCK INCHES PAST FIVE, YOU GRUDGINGLY REALIZE IT'S TIME TO HEAD FOR YOUR DAD'S AWARD CEREMONY...

OF COURSE, THAT'S WHEN --AS IF ON CUE-- THE *FANTASTICAR* TAKES TO THE SKY...

YOU DEBATE THE MERITS OF FOLLOWING IT...

--BUT ONLY FOR AN INSTANT!

EVEN AS YOU LEAP FROM WEBLINE TO WEBLINE--

--YOUR MIND DRIFTS BACK TO UNCLE PHIL.

ON THE VERY DAY YOU QUESTION HIM ABOUT *SPIDER-MAN,* HE DISCOVERS WEBBING AT A CRIME SITE.

ONE PLUS ONE EQUALS THE OBVIOUS REASON FOR TODAY'S REVELATION.

EVEN AS YOU TOY WITH THE IDEA OF ACCEPTING HIS NOT SO VEILED OFFER, THE *FF* VEER TOWARD STANDARD VILLAIN HIDEOUT #3...

...THE SEEMINGLY DESERTED WAREHOUSE.

317

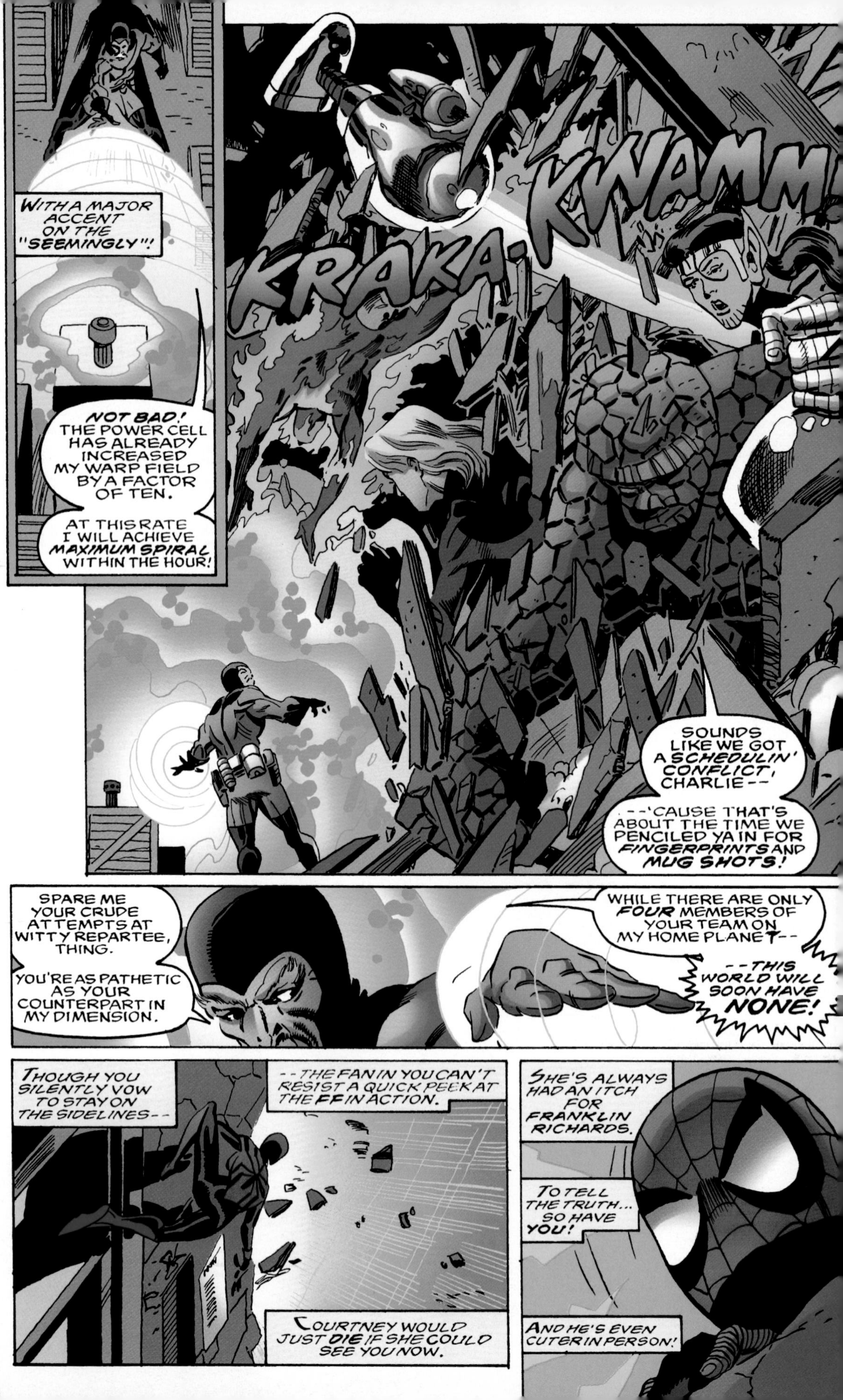
WITH A MAJOR ACCENT ON THE "SEEMINGLY"!
NOT BAD! THE POWER CELL HAS ALREADY INCREASED MY WARP FIELD BY A FACTOR OF TEN.
AT THIS RATE I WILL ACHIEVE MAXIMUM SPIRAL WITHIN THE HOUR!
KRAKA-KWAMM
SOUNDS LIKE WE GOT A SCHEDULIN' CONFLICT, CHARLIE--
--'CAUSE THAT'S ABOUT THE TIME WE PENCILED YA IN FOR FINGERPRINTS AND MUG SHOTS!
SPARE ME YOUR CRUDE ATTEMPTS AT WITTY REPARTEE, THING.
YOU'RE AS PATHETIC AS YOUR COUNTERPART IN MY DIMENSION.
WHILE THERE ARE ONLY FOUR MEMBERS OF YOUR TEAM ON MY HOME PLANET--
--THIS WORLD WILL SOON HAVE NONE!
THOUGH YOU SILENTLY VOW TO STAY ON THE SIDELINES--
--THE FAN IN YOU CAN'T RESIST A QUICK PEEK AT THE FF IN ACTION.
COURTNEY WOULD JUST DIE IF SHE COULD SEE YOU NOW.
SHE'S ALWAYS HAD AN ITCH FOR FRANKLIN RICHARDS.
TO TELL THE TRUTH... SO HAVE YOU!
AND HE'S EVEN CUTER IN PERSON!

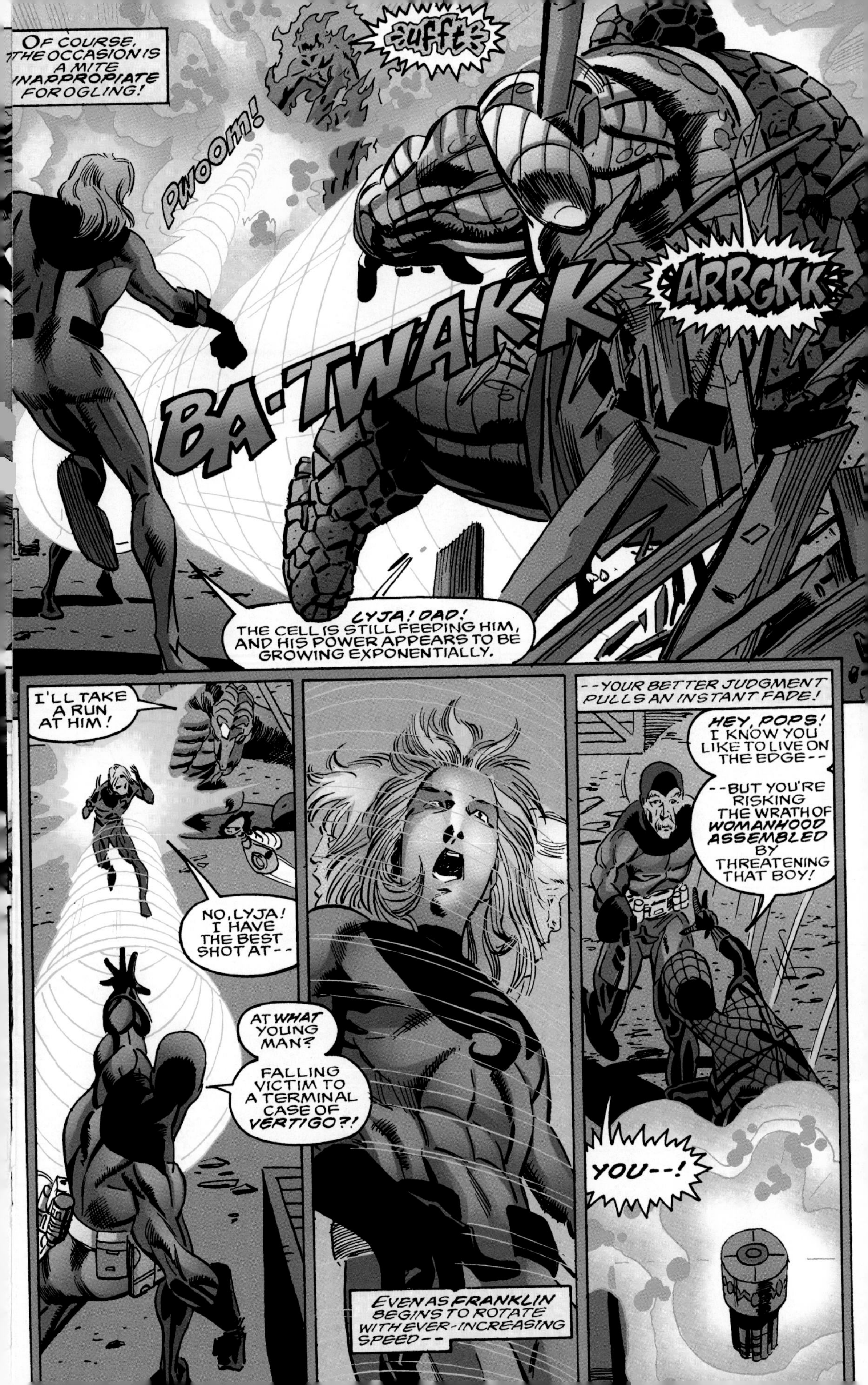
OF COURSE, THE OCCASION IS A MITE INAPPROPIATE FOR OGLING!
-UFFT-
PWOOMM!
ARRGKK
BA-TWAKK
LYJA! DAD! THE CELL IS STILL FEEDING HIM, AND HIS POWER APPEARS TO BE GROWING EXPONENTIALLY.
I'LL TAKE A RUN AT HIM!
NO, LYJA! I HAVE THE BEST SHOT AT--
AT WHAT YOUNG MAN?
FALLING VICTIM TO A TERMINAL CASE OF VERTIGO?!
EVEN AS FRANKLIN BEGINS TO ROTATE WITH EVER-INCREASING SPEED--
--YOUR BETTER JUDGMENT PULLS AN INSTANT FADE!
HEY, POPS! I KNOW YOU LIKE TO LIVE ON THE EDGE--
--BUT YOU'RE RISKING THE WRATH OF WOMANHOOD ASSEMBLED BY THREATENING THAT BOY!
YOU--!

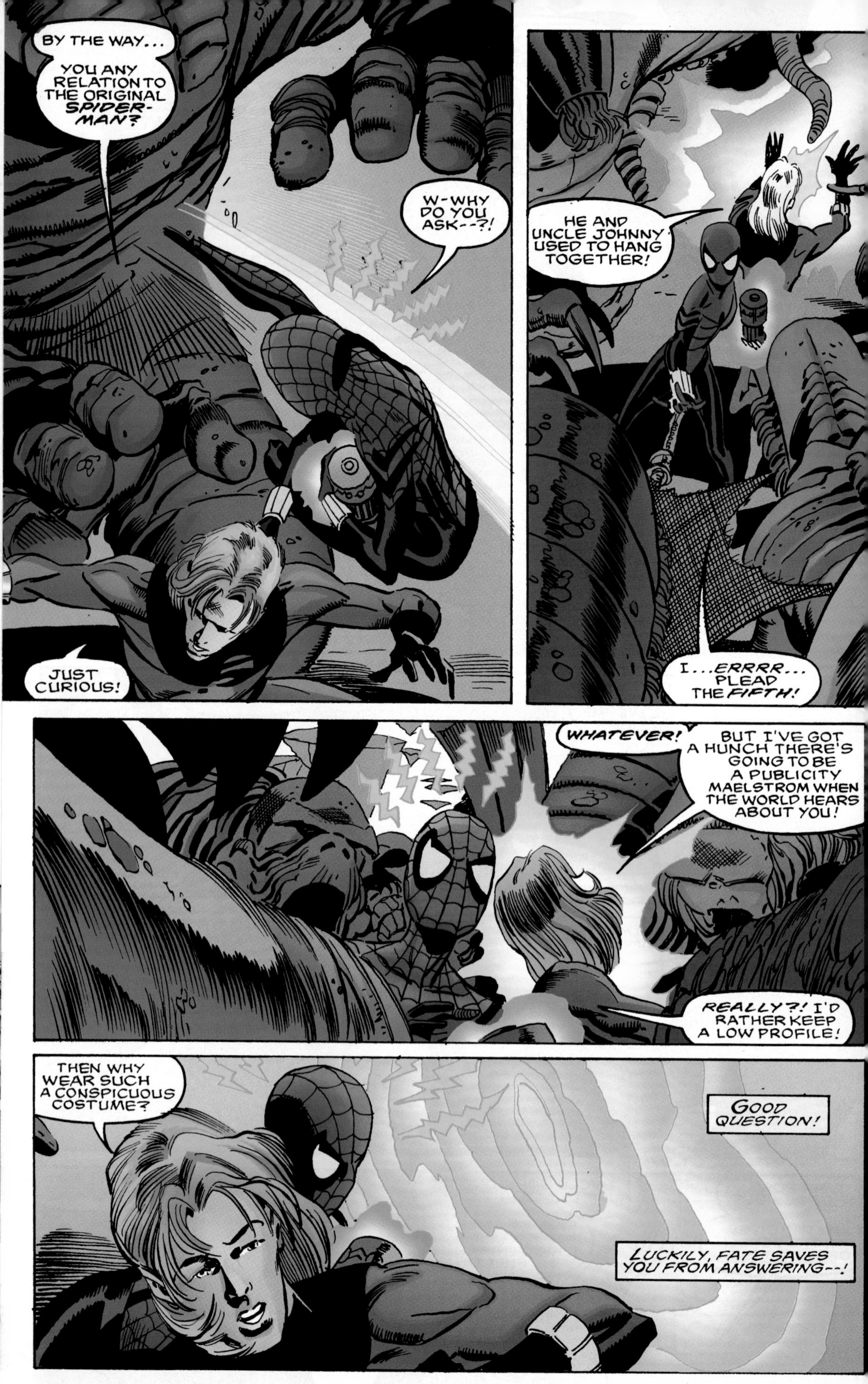
BY THE WAY...
YOU ANY RELATION TO THE ORIGINAL SPIDER-MAN?
W-WHY DO YOU ASK--?!
JUST CURIOUS!
HE AND UNCLE JOHNNY USED TO HANG TOGETHER!
I...ERRRR... PLEAD THE FIFTH!
WHATEVER!
BUT I'VE GOT A HUNCH THERE'S GOING TO BE A PUBLICITY MAELSTROM WHEN THE WORLD HEARS ABOUT YOU!
REALLY?! I'D RATHER KEEP A LOW PROFILE!
THEN WHY WEAR SUCH A CONSPICUOUS COSTUME?
GOOD QUESTION!
LUCKILY, FATE SAVES YOU FROM ANSWERING--!

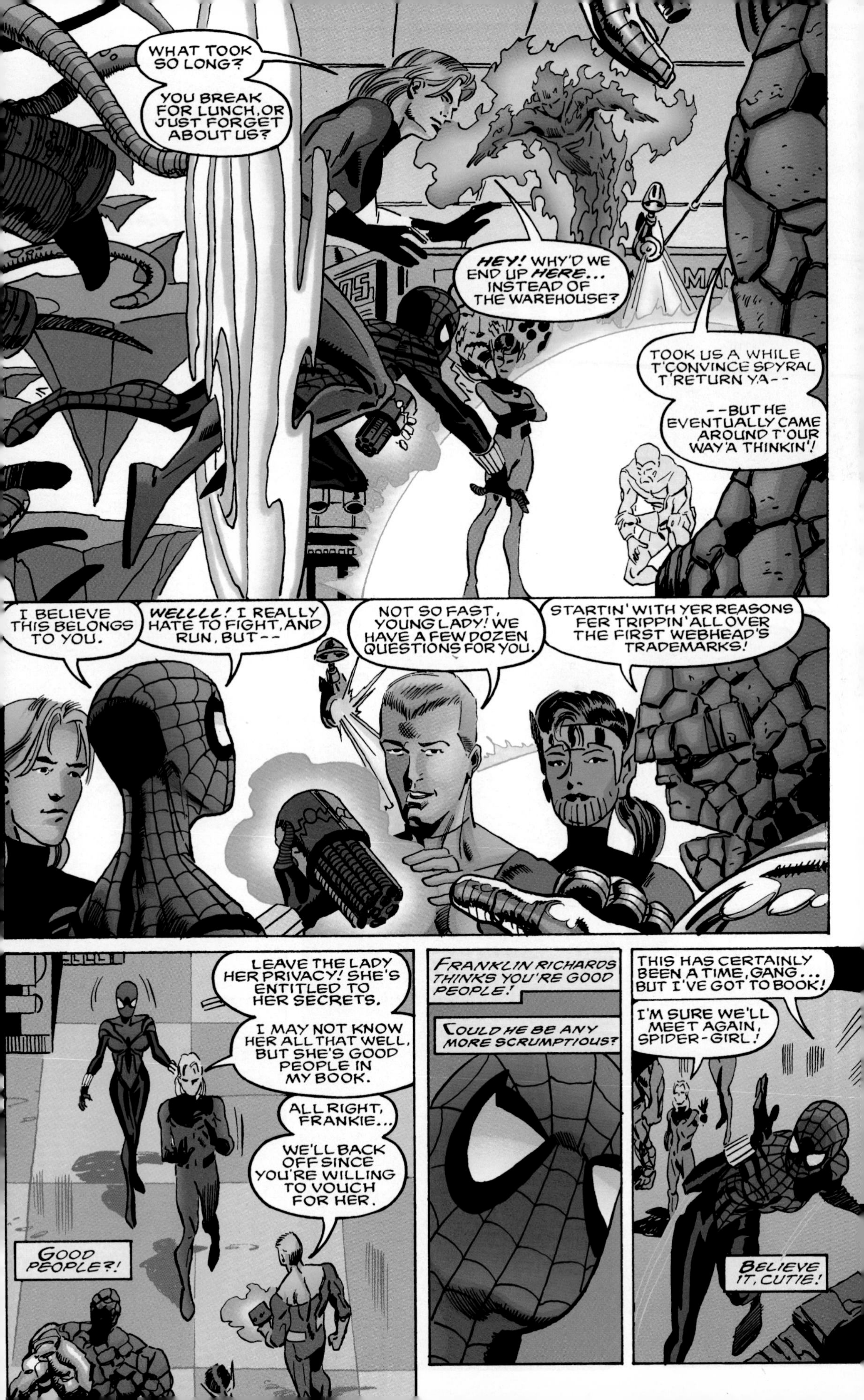
WHAT TOOK SO LONG?
YOU BREAK FOR LUNCH, OR JUST FORGET ABOUT US?
HEY! WHY'D WE END UP HERE... INSTEAD OF THE WAREHOUSE?
TOOK US A WHILE T'CONVINCE SPYRAL T'RETURN YA--
--BUT HE EVENTUALLY CAME AROUND T'OUR WAY'A THINKIN'!
I BELIEVE THIS BELONGS TO YOU.
WELLLL! I REALLY HATE TO FIGHT, AND RUN, BUT--
NOT SO FAST, YOUNG LADY! WE HAVE A FEW DOZEN QUESTIONS FOR YOU.
STARTIN' WITH YER REASONS FER TRIPPIN' ALL OVER THE FIRST WEBHEAD'S TRADEMARKS!
LEAVE THE LADY HER PRIVACY! SHE'S ENTITLED TO HER SECRETS.
I MAY NOT KNOW HER ALL THAT WELL, BUT SHE'S GOOD PEOPLE IN MY BOOK.
ALL RIGHT, FRANKIE...
WE'LL BACK OFF SINCE YOU'RE WILLING TO VOUCH FOR HER.
GOOD PEOPLE?!
FRANKLIN RICHARDS THINKS YOU'RE GOOD PEOPLE!
COULD HE BE ANY MORE SCRUMPTIOUS?
THIS HAS CERTAINLY BEEN A TIME, GANG... BUT I'VE GOT TO BOOK!
I'M SURE WE'LL MEET AGAIN, SPIDER-GIRL!
BELIEVE IT, CUTIE!

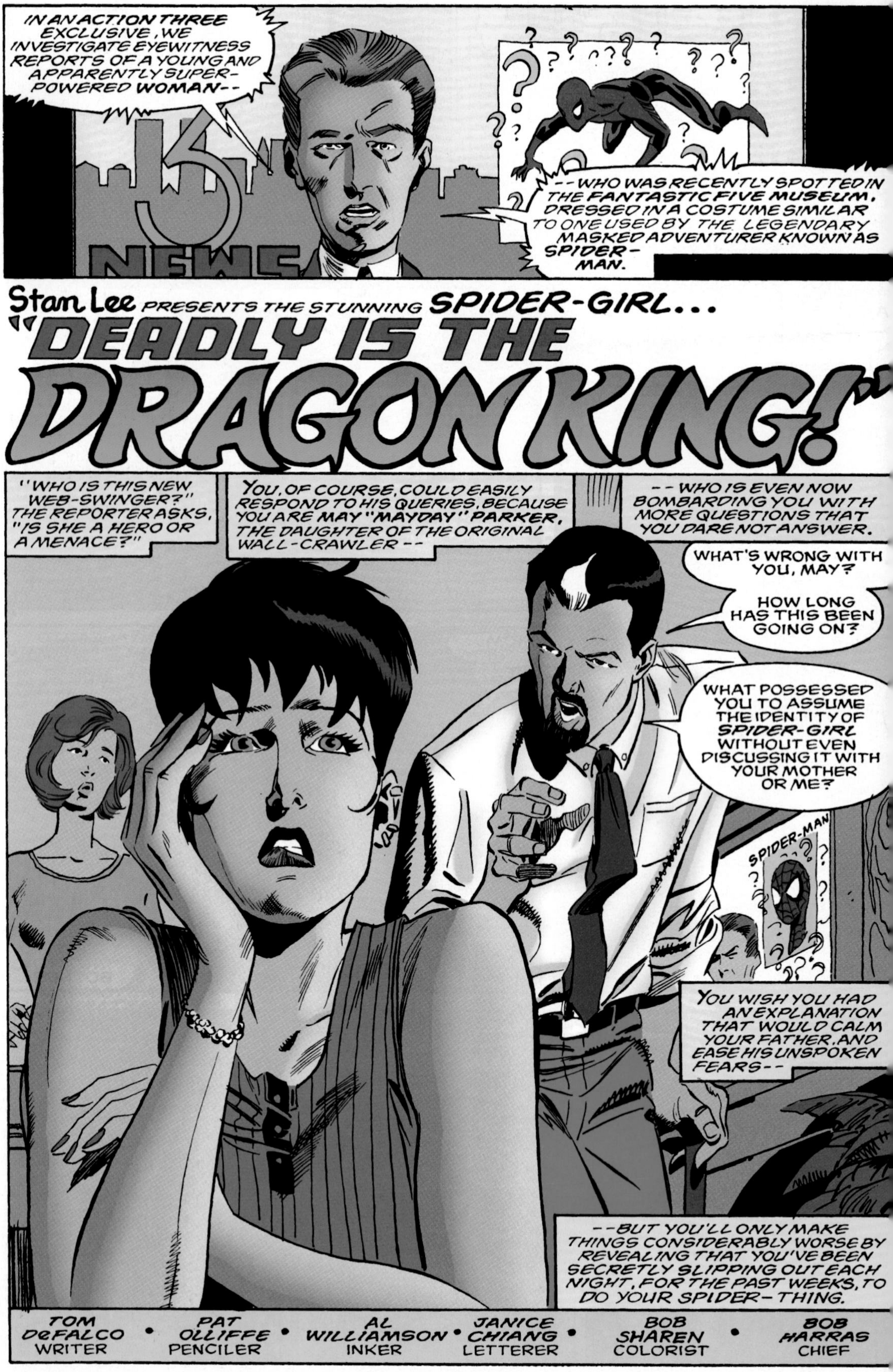
IN AN ACTION THREE EXCLUSIVE, WE INVESTIGATE EYEWITNESS REPORTS OF A YOUNG AND APPARENTLY SUPER-POWERED WOMAN--
13 NEWS
--WHO WAS RECENTLY SPOTTED IN THE FANTASTIC FIVE MUSEUM, DRESSED IN A COSTUME SIMILAR TO ONE USED BY THE LEGENDARY MASKED ADVENTURER KNOWN AS SPIDER-MAN.
Stan Lee PRESENTS THE STUNNING SPIDER-GIRL...
"DEADLY IS THE DRAGON KING!"
"WHO IS THIS NEW WEB-SWINGER?" THE REPORTER ASKS, "IS SHE A HERO OR A MENACE?"
YOU, OF COURSE, COULD EASILY RESPOND TO HIS QUERIES, BECAUSE YOU ARE MAY "MAYDAY" PARKER, THE DAUGHTER OF THE ORIGINAL WALL-CRAWLER--
--WHO IS EVEN NOW BOMBARDING YOU WITH MORE QUESTIONS THAT YOU DARE NOT ANSWER.
WHAT'S WRONG WITH YOU, MAY?
HOW LONG HAS THIS BEEN GOING ON?
WHAT POSSESSED YOU TO ASSUME THE IDENTITY OF SPIDER-GIRL WITHOUT EVEN DISCUSSING IT WITH YOUR MOTHER OR ME?
SPIDER-MAN
YOU WISH YOU HAD AN EXPLANATION THAT WOULD CALM YOUR FATHER, AND EASE HIS UNSPOKEN FEARS--
--BUT YOU'LL ONLY MAKE THINGS CONSIDERABLY WORSE BY REVEALING THAT YOU'VE BEEN SECRETLY SLIPPING OUT EACH NIGHT, FOR THE PAST WEEKS, TO DO YOUR SPIDER-THING.
TOM DeFALCO WRITER • PAT OLLIFFE PENCILER • AL WILLIAMSON INKER • JANICE CHIANG LETTERER • BOB SHAREN COLORIST • BOB HARRAS CHIEF

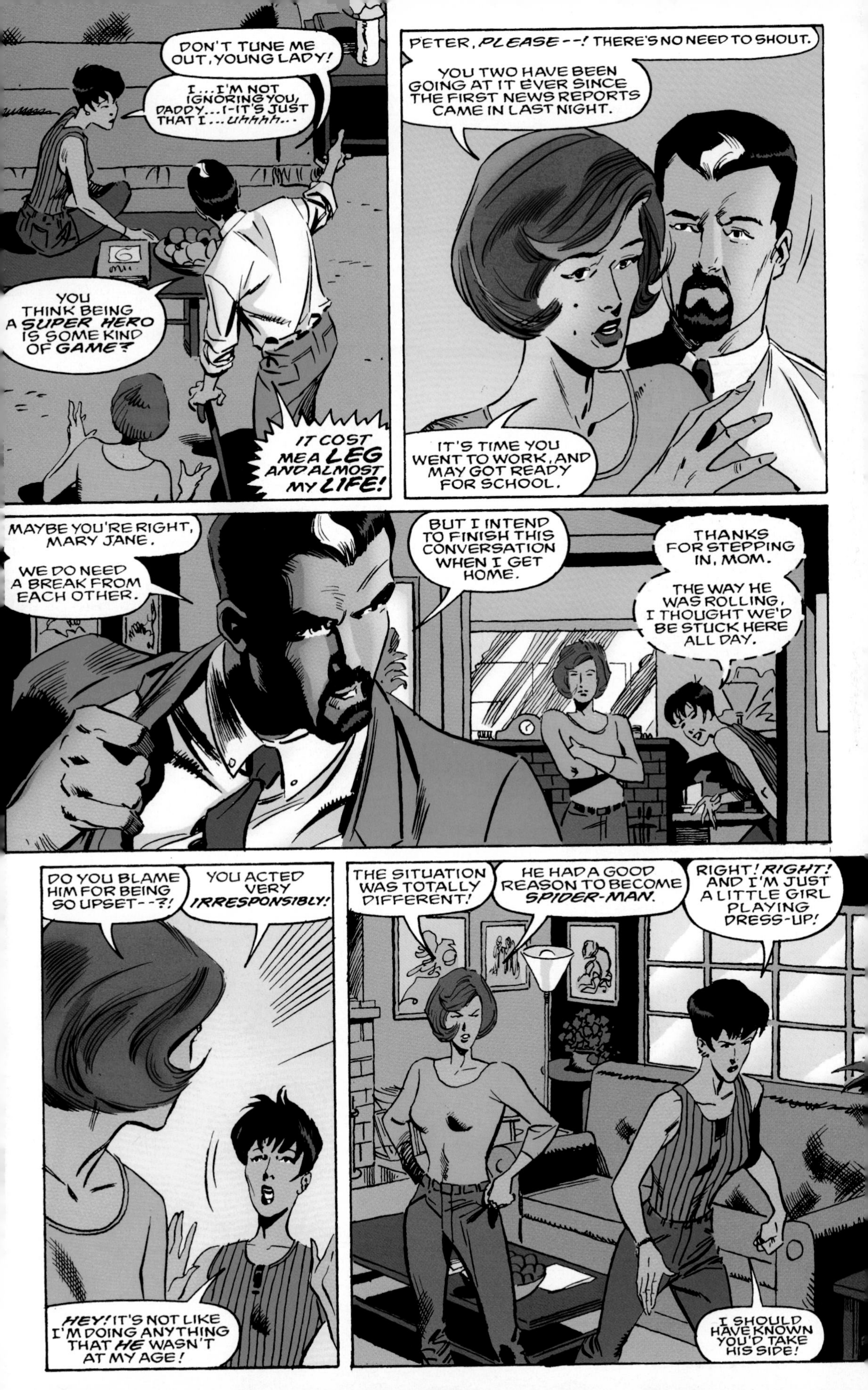

DON'T TUNE ME OUT, YOUNG LADY!
I...I'M NOT IGNORING YOU, DADDY...I-IT'S JUST THAT I...uhhhh...
YOU THINK BEING A SUPER HERO IS SOME KIND OF GAME?
IT COST ME A LEG AND ALMOST MY LIFE!
PETER, PLEASE--! THERE'S NO NEED TO SHOUT.
YOU TWO HAVE BEEN GOING AT IT EVER SINCE THE FIRST NEWS REPORTS CAME IN LAST NIGHT.
IT'S TIME YOU WENT TO WORK, AND MAY GOT READY FOR SCHOOL.
MAYBE YOU'RE RIGHT, MARY JANE.
WE DO NEED A BREAK FROM EACH OTHER.
BUT I INTEND TO FINISH THIS CONVERSATION WHEN I GET HOME.
THANKS FOR STEPPING IN, MOM.
THE WAY HE WAS ROLLING, I THOUGHT WE'D BE STUCK HERE ALL DAY.
DO YOU BLAME HIM FOR BEING SO UPSET--?!
YOU ACTED VERY IRRESPONSIBLY!
HEY! IT'S NOT LIKE I'M DOING ANYTHING THAT HE WASN'T AT MY AGE!
THE SITUATION WAS TOTALLY DIFFERENT!
HE HAD A GOOD REASON TO BECOME SPIDER-MAN.
RIGHT! RIGHT! AND I'M JUST A LITTLE GIRL PLAYING DRESS-UP!
I SHOULD HAVE KNOWN YOU'D TAKE HIS SIDE!

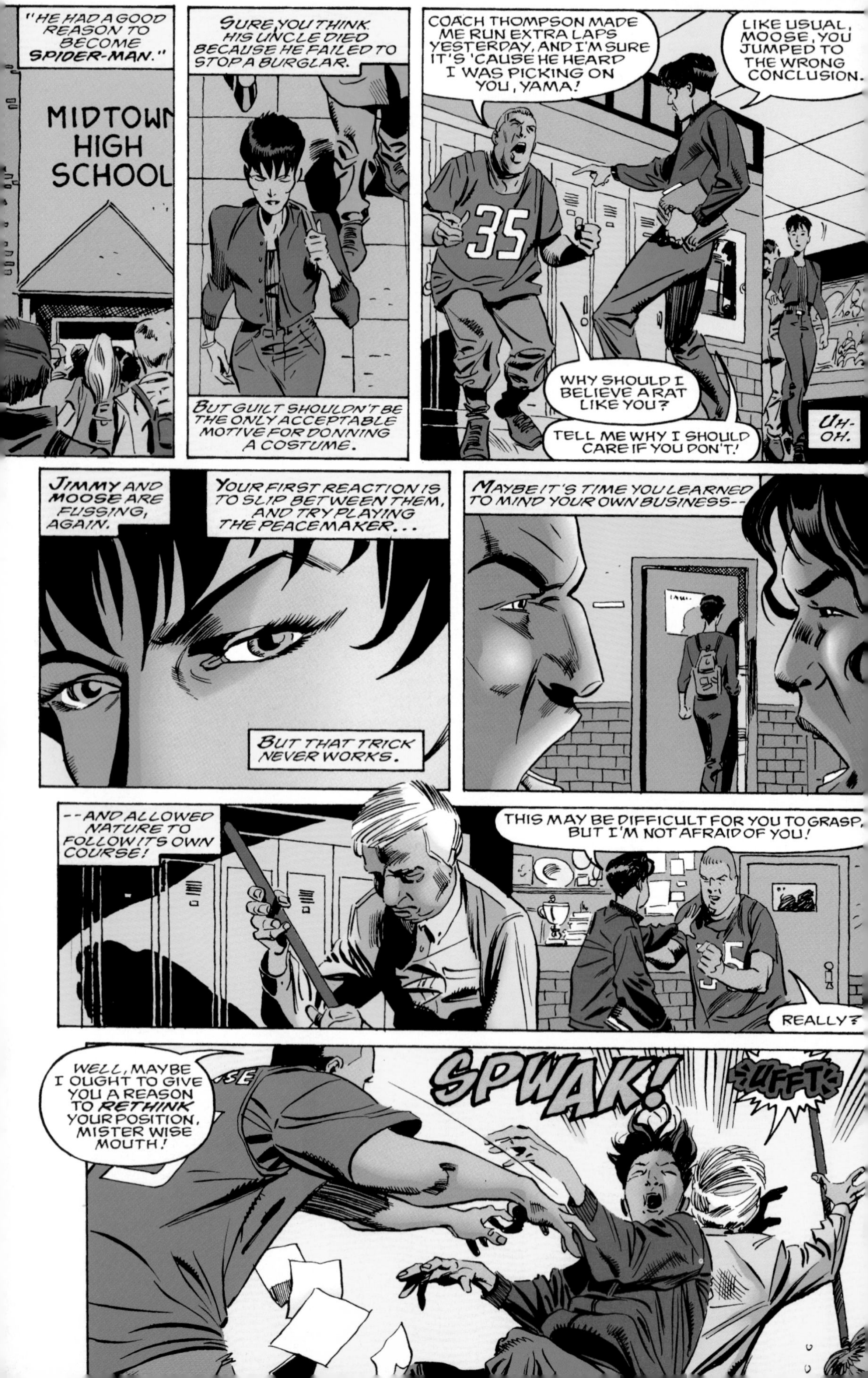
"HE HAD A GOOD REASON TO BECOME SPIDER-MAN."
MIDTOWN HIGH SCHOOL
SURE YOU THINK HIS UNCLE DIED BECAUSE HE FAILED TO STOP A BURGLAR.
BUT GUILT SHOULDN'T BE THE ONLY ACCEPTABLE MOTIVE FOR DONNING A COSTUME.
COACH THOMPSON MADE ME RUN EXTRA LAPS YESTERDAY, AND I'M SURE IT'S 'CAUSE HE HEARD I WAS PICKING ON YOU, YAMA!
LIKE USUAL, MOOSE, YOU JUMPED TO THE WRONG CONCLUSION.
35
WHY SHOULD I BELIEVE A RAT LIKE YOU?
TELL ME WHY I SHOULD CARE IF YOU DON'T!
UH-OH.
JIMMY AND MOOSE ARE FUSSING, AGAIN.
YOUR FIRST REACTION IS TO SLIP BETWEEN THEM, AND TRY PLAYING THE PEACEMAKER...
BUT THAT TRICK NEVER WORKS.
MAYBE IT'S TIME YOU LEARNED TO MIND YOUR OWN BUSINESS--
--AND ALLOWED NATURE TO FOLLOW ITS OWN COURSE!
THIS MAY BE DIFFICULT FOR YOU TO GRASP, BUT I'M NOT AFRAID OF YOU!
REALLY?
WELL, MAYBE I OUGHT TO GIVE YOU A REASON TO RETHINK YOUR POSITION, MISTER WISE MOUTH!
SPWAK!
UFFT!

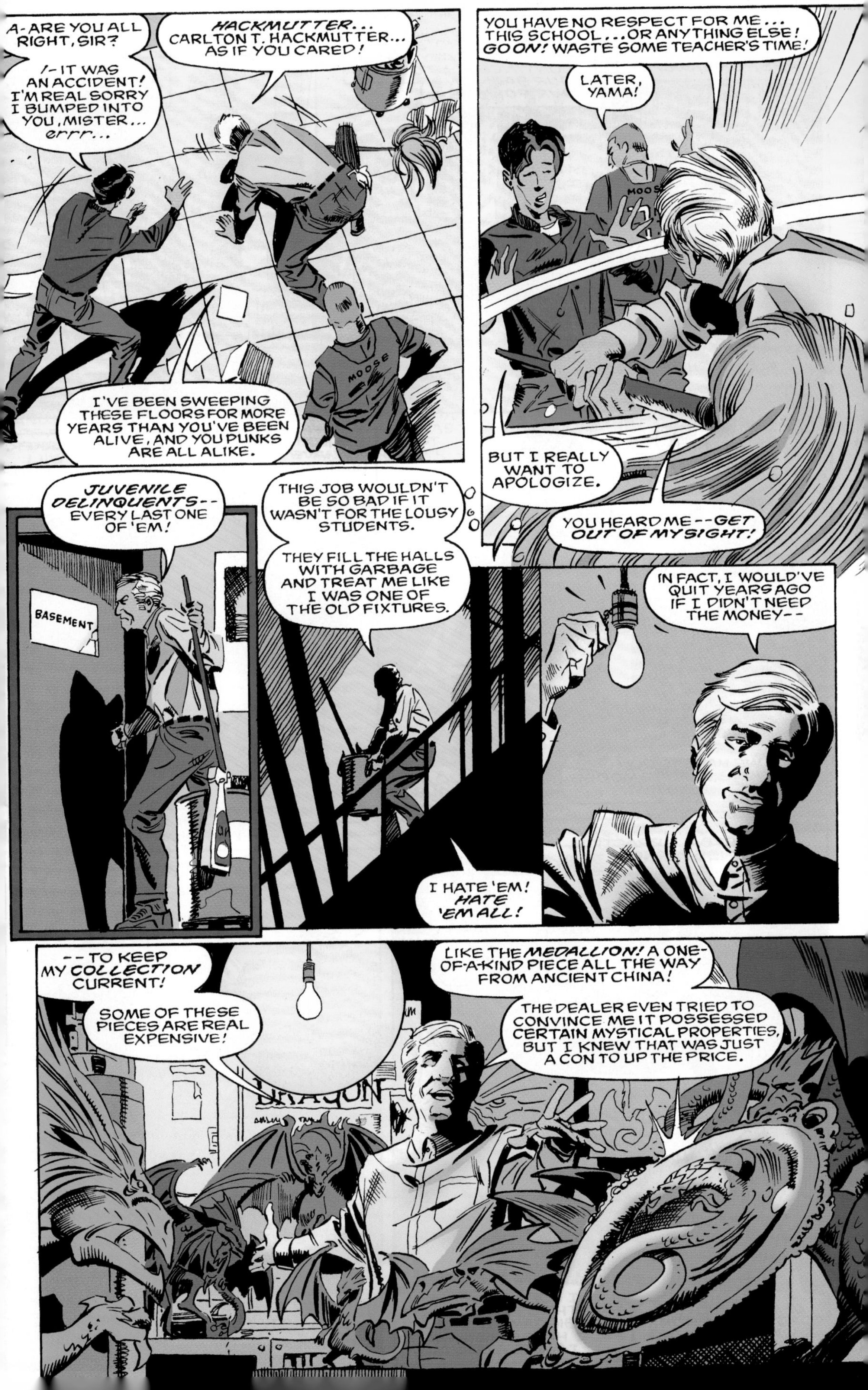
A-ARE YOU ALL RIGHT, SIR?
I-IT WAS AN ACCIDENT! I'M REAL SORRY I BUMPED INTO YOU, MISTER... errr...
HACKMUTTER... CARLTON T. HACKMUTTER... AS IF YOU CARED!
I'VE BEEN SWEEPING THESE FLOORS FOR MORE YEARS THAN YOU'VE BEEN ALIVE, AND YOU PUNKS ARE ALL ALIKE.
MOOSE
YOU HAVE NO RESPECT FOR ME... THIS SCHOOL... OR ANYTHING ELSE! GO ON! WASTE SOME TEACHER'S TIME!
LATER, YAMA!
BUT I REALLY WANT TO APOLOGIZE.
YOU HEARD ME--GET OUT OF MY SIGHT!
JUVENILE DELINQUENTS-- EVERY LAST ONE OF 'EM!
BASEMENT
THIS JOB WOULDN'T BE SO BAD IF IT WASN'T FOR THE LOUSY STUDENTS.
THEY FILL THE HALLS WITH GARBAGE AND TREAT ME LIKE I WAS ONE OF THE OLD FIXTURES.
IN FACT, I WOULD'VE QUIT YEARS AGO IF I DIDN'T NEED THE MONEY--
I HATE 'EM! HATE 'EM ALL!
--TO KEEP MY COLLECTION CURRENT!
SOME OF THESE PIECES ARE REAL EXPENSIVE!
LIKE THE MEDALLION! A ONE-OF-A-KIND PIECE ALL THE WAY FROM ANCIENT CHINA!
THE DEALER EVEN TRIED TO CONVINCE ME IT POSSESSED CERTAIN MYSTICAL PROPERTIES, BUT I KNEW THAT WAS JUST A CON TO UP THE PRICE.

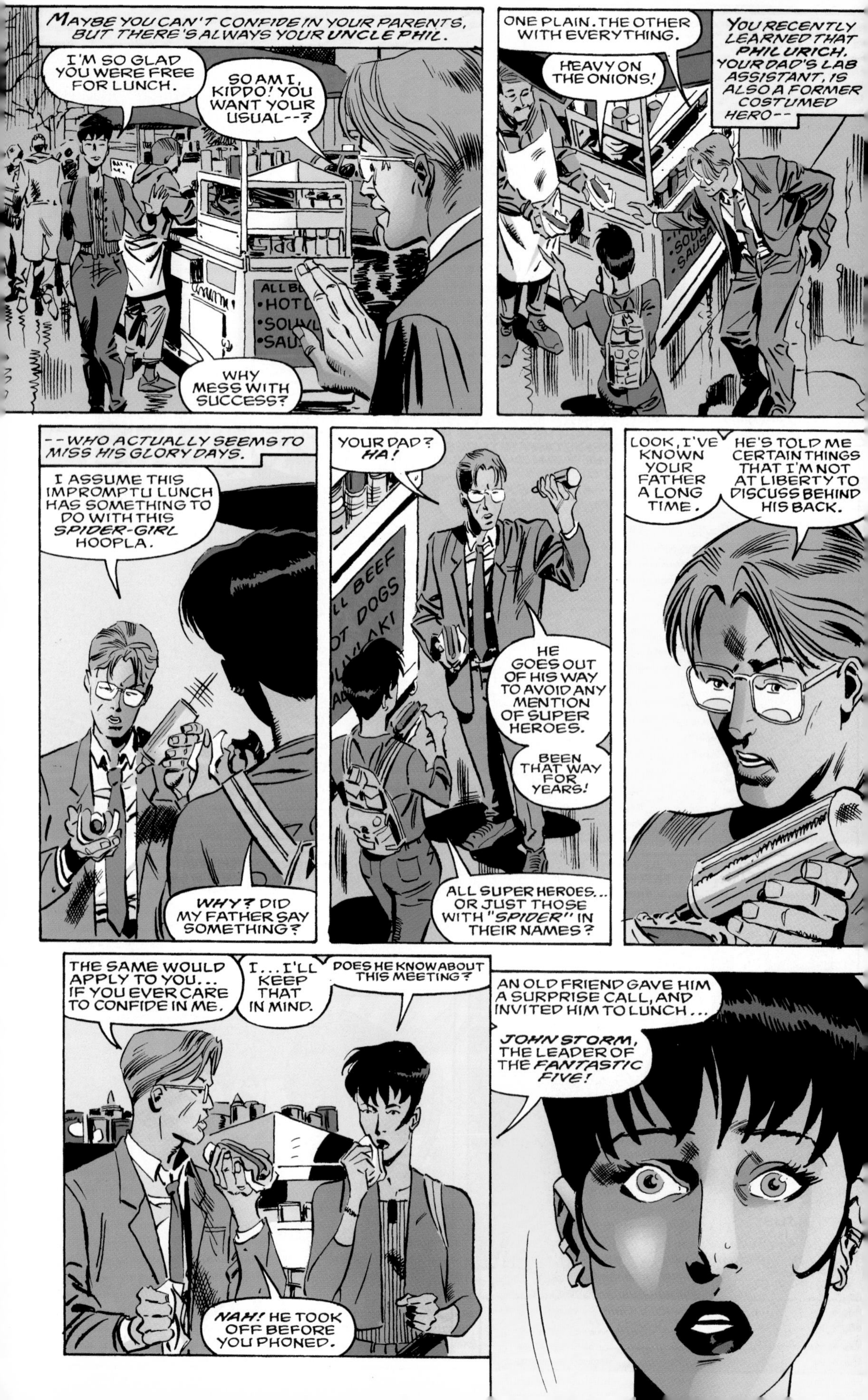
MAYBE YOU CAN'T CONFIDE IN YOUR PARENTS, BUT THERE'S ALWAYS YOUR UNCLE PHIL.
I'M SO GLAD YOU WERE FREE FOR LUNCH.
SO AM I, KIDDO! YOU WANT YOUR USUAL--?
WHY MESS WITH SUCCESS?
ONE PLAIN. THE OTHER WITH EVERYTHING.
HEAVY ON THE ONIONS!
YOU RECENTLY LEARNED THAT PHIL URICH, YOUR DAD'S LAB ASSISTANT, IS ALSO A FORMER COSTUMED HERO--
--WHO ACTUALLY SEEMS TO MISS HIS GLORY DAYS.
I ASSUME THIS IMPROMPTU LUNCH HAS SOMETHING TO DO WITH THIS SPIDER-GIRL HOOPLA.
WHY? DID MY FATHER SAY SOMETHING?
YOUR DAD? HA!
HE GOES OUT OF HIS WAY TO AVOID ANY MENTION OF SUPER HEROES.
BEEN THAT WAY FOR YEARS!
ALL SUPER HEROES... OR JUST THOSE WITH "SPIDER" IN THEIR NAMES?
LOOK, I'VE KNOWN YOUR FATHER A LONG TIME.
HE'S TOLD ME CERTAIN THINGS THAT I'M NOT AT LIBERTY TO DISCUSS BEHIND HIS BACK.
THE SAME WOULD APPLY TO YOU... IF YOU EVER CARE TO CONFIDE IN ME.
I... I'LL KEEP THAT IN MIND.
DOES HE KNOW ABOUT THIS MEETING?
NAH! HE TOOK OFF BEFORE YOU PHONED.
AN OLD FRIEND GAVE HIM A SURPRISE CALL, AND INVITED HIM TO LUNCH...
JOHN STORM, THE LEADER OF THE FANTASTIC FIVE!

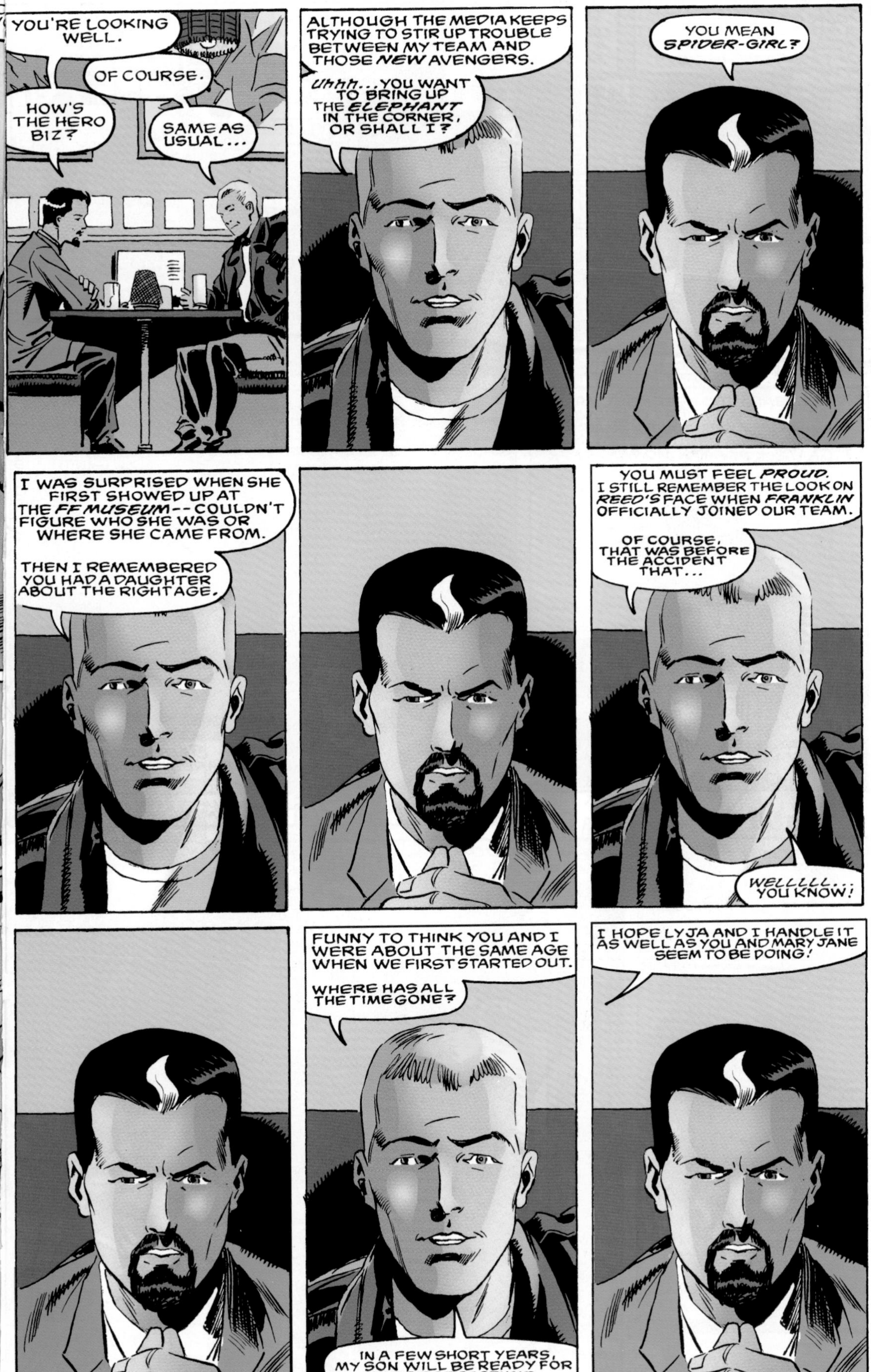

YOU'RE LOOKING WELL.
OF COURSE.
HOW'S THE HERO BIZ?
SAME AS USUAL...
ALTHOUGH THE MEDIA KEEPS TRYING TO STIR UP TROUBLE BETWEEN MY TEAM AND THOSE NEW AVENGERS.
UHHH... YOU WANT TO BRING UP THE ELEPHANT IN THE CORNER, OR SHALL I?
YOU MEAN SPIDER-GIRL?
I WAS SURPRISED WHEN SHE FIRST SHOWED UP AT THE FF MUSEUM--COULDN'T FIGURE WHO SHE WAS OR WHERE SHE CAME FROM.
THEN I REMEMBERED YOU HAD A DAUGHTER ABOUT THE RIGHT AGE.
YOU MUST FEEL PROUD. I STILL REMEMBER THE LOOK ON REED'S FACE WHEN FRANKLIN OFFICIALLY JOINED OUR TEAM.
OF COURSE, THAT WAS BEFORE THE ACCIDENT THAT...
WELLLLL... YOU KNOW!
FUNNY TO THINK YOU AND I WERE ABOUT THE SAME AGE WHEN WE FIRST STARTED OUT.
WHERE HAS ALL THE TIME GONE?
IN A FEW SHORT YEARS, MY SON WILL BE READY FOR HIS FIRST COSTUME...
I HOPE LYJA AND I HANDLE IT AS WELL AS YOU AND MARY JANE SEEM TO BE DOING!

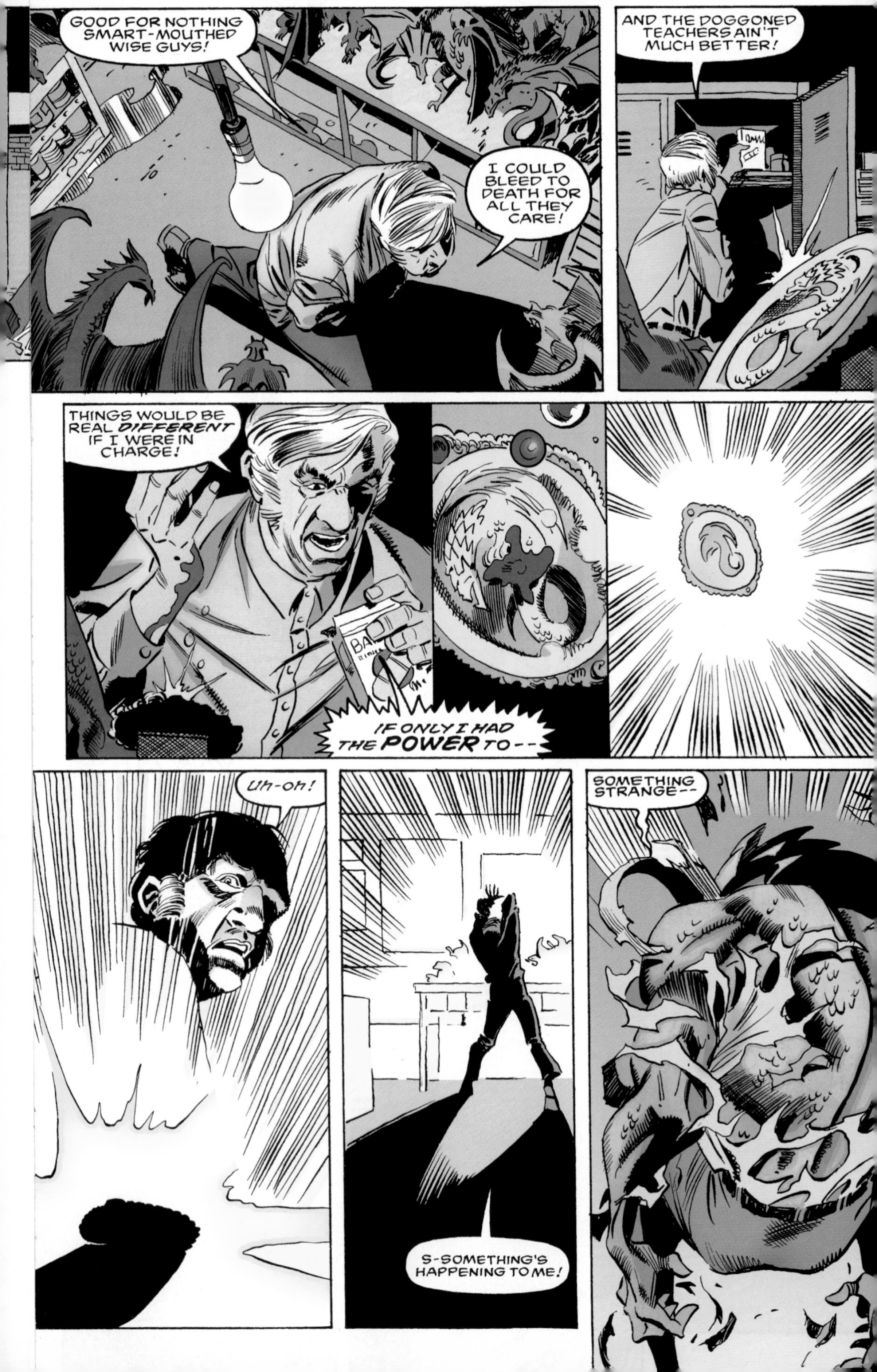

GOOD FOR NOTHING SMART-MOUTHED WISE GUYS!
I COULD BLEED TO DEATH FOR ALL THEY CARE!
AND THE DOGGONED TEACHERS AIN'T MUCH BETTER!
THINGS WOULD BE REAL DIFFERENT IF I WERE IN CHARGE!
IF ONLY I HAD THE POWER TO--
UH-OH!
S-SOMETHING'S HAPPENING TO ME!
SOMETHING STRANGE--

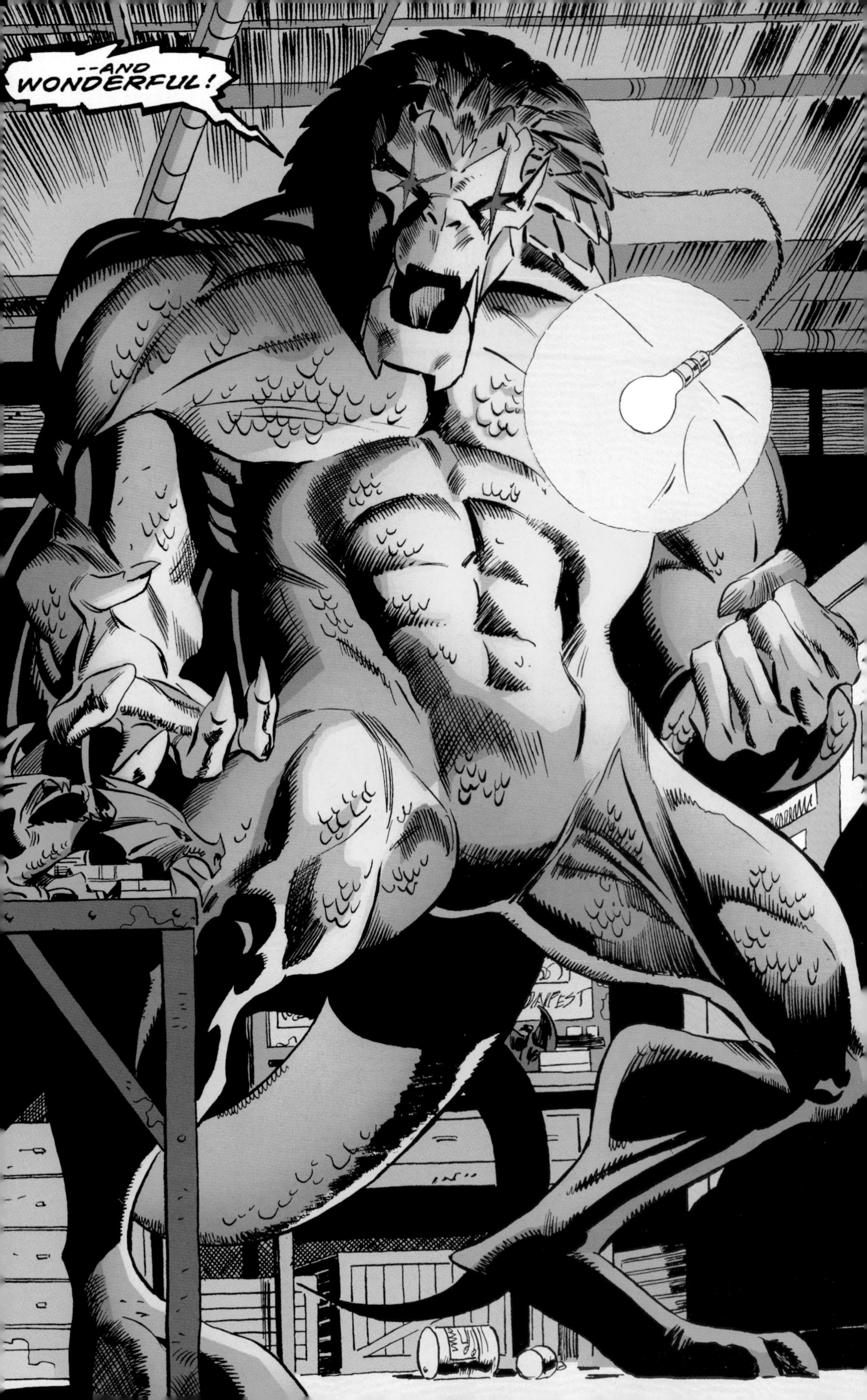
--AND WONDERFUL!

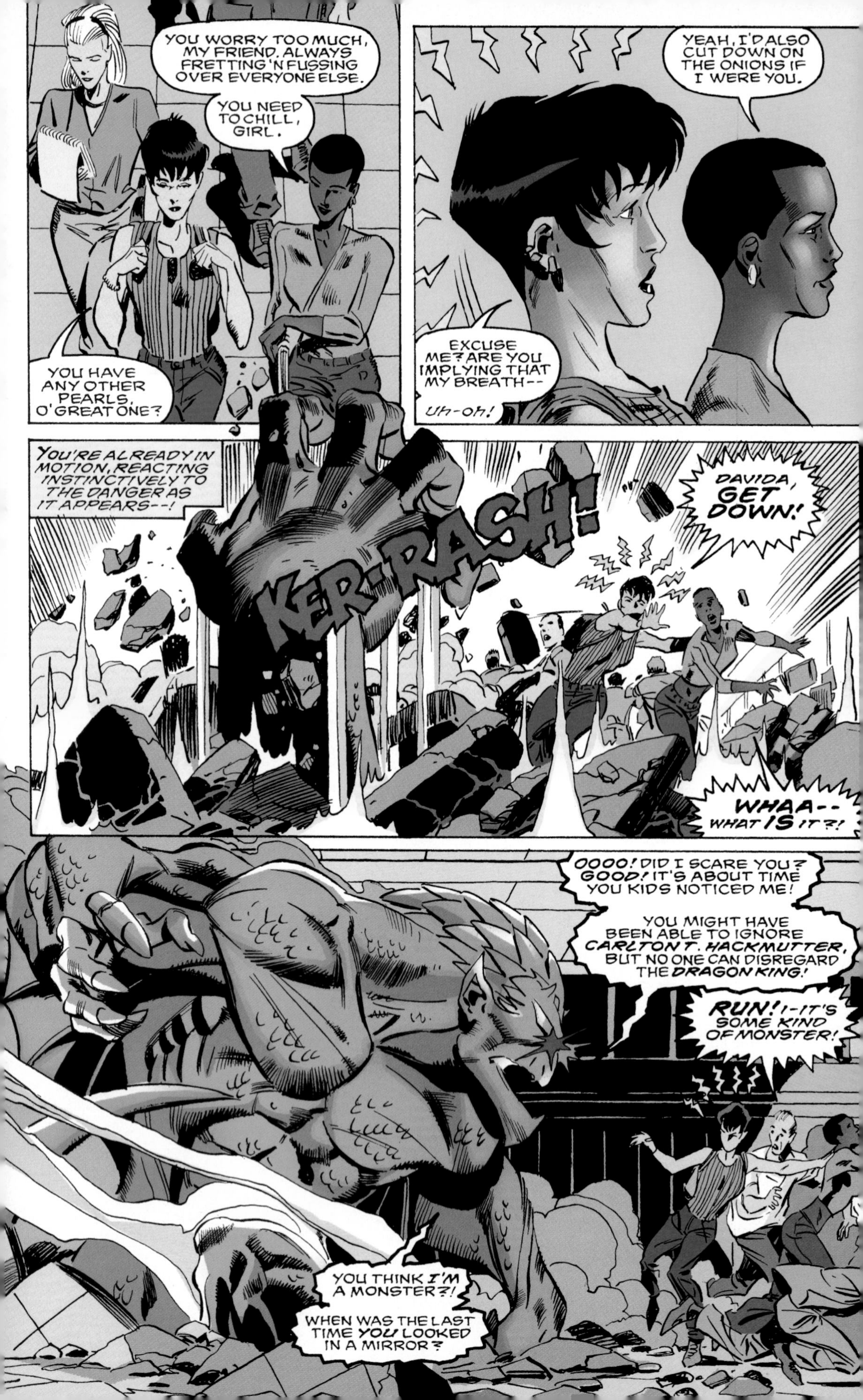

YOU WORRY TOO MUCH, MY FRIEND. ALWAYS FRETTING 'N FUSSING OVER EVERYONE ELSE.
YOU NEED TO CHILL, GIRL.
YOU HAVE ANY OTHER PEARLS, O' GREAT ONE?
YEAH, I'D ALSO CUT DOWN ON THE ONIONS IF I WERE YOU.
EXCUSE ME? ARE YOU IMPLYING THAT MY BREATH--
UH-OH!
YOU'RE ALREADY IN MOTION, REACTING INSTINCTIVELY TO THE DANGER AS IT APPEARS--!
KER-RASH!
DAVIDA, GET DOWN!
WHAA-- WHAT IS IT?!
OOOO! DID I SCARE YOU? GOOD! IT'S ABOUT TIME YOU KIDS NOTICED ME!
YOU MIGHT HAVE BEEN ABLE TO IGNORE CARLTON T. HACKMUTTER, BUT NO ONE CAN DISREGARD THE DRAGON KING!
RUN! I-IT'S SOME KIND OF MONSTER!
YOU THINK I'M A MONSTER?!
WHEN WAS THE LAST TIME YOU LOOKED IN A MIRROR?

YOU KIDS ARE LIKE *LOCUSTS!* ALL YOU DO IS EAT... ANNOY PEOPLE... AND LEAVE A BIG MESS!

YOU DON'T KNOW *WHERE* THIS CREATURE CAME FROM OR *WHAT* IT WANTS--

--AND YOU REALLY *DON'T CARE* AT THIS POINT!

YOUR FIRST PRIORITY IS TO ASSURE THE *SAFETY* OF YOUR FELLOW STUDENTS.

ONCE THEY'VE REACHED THE NEAREST EXIT, YOU TURN YOUR MIND TO MORE MUNDANE MATTERS--

--LIKE FINDING A LITTLE PRIVACY.

SINCE THE DRAGON-THINGEE IS BETWEEN YOU AND THE NEAREST LADIES ROOM, YOU'RE FORCED TO AD-LIB--!

YOU'RE HALFWAY IN YOUR COSTUME BEFORE YOU REMEMBER THIS WHOLE SPIDER-THING IS STILL UNDER DISCUSSION!

*OOPS!*

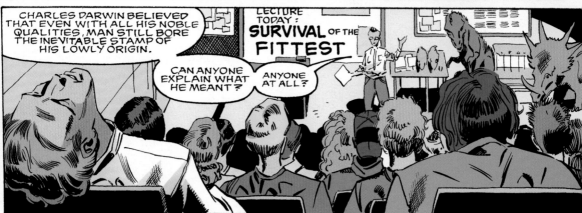

CHARLES DARWIN BELIEVED THAT EVEN WITH ALL HIS NOBLE QUALITIES, MAN STILL BORE THE INEVITABLE STAMP OF HIS LOWLY ORIGIN.

CAN ANYONE EXPLAIN WHAT HE MEANT?

ANYONE AT ALL?

LECTURE TODAY: **SURVIVAL** OF THE **FITTEST**

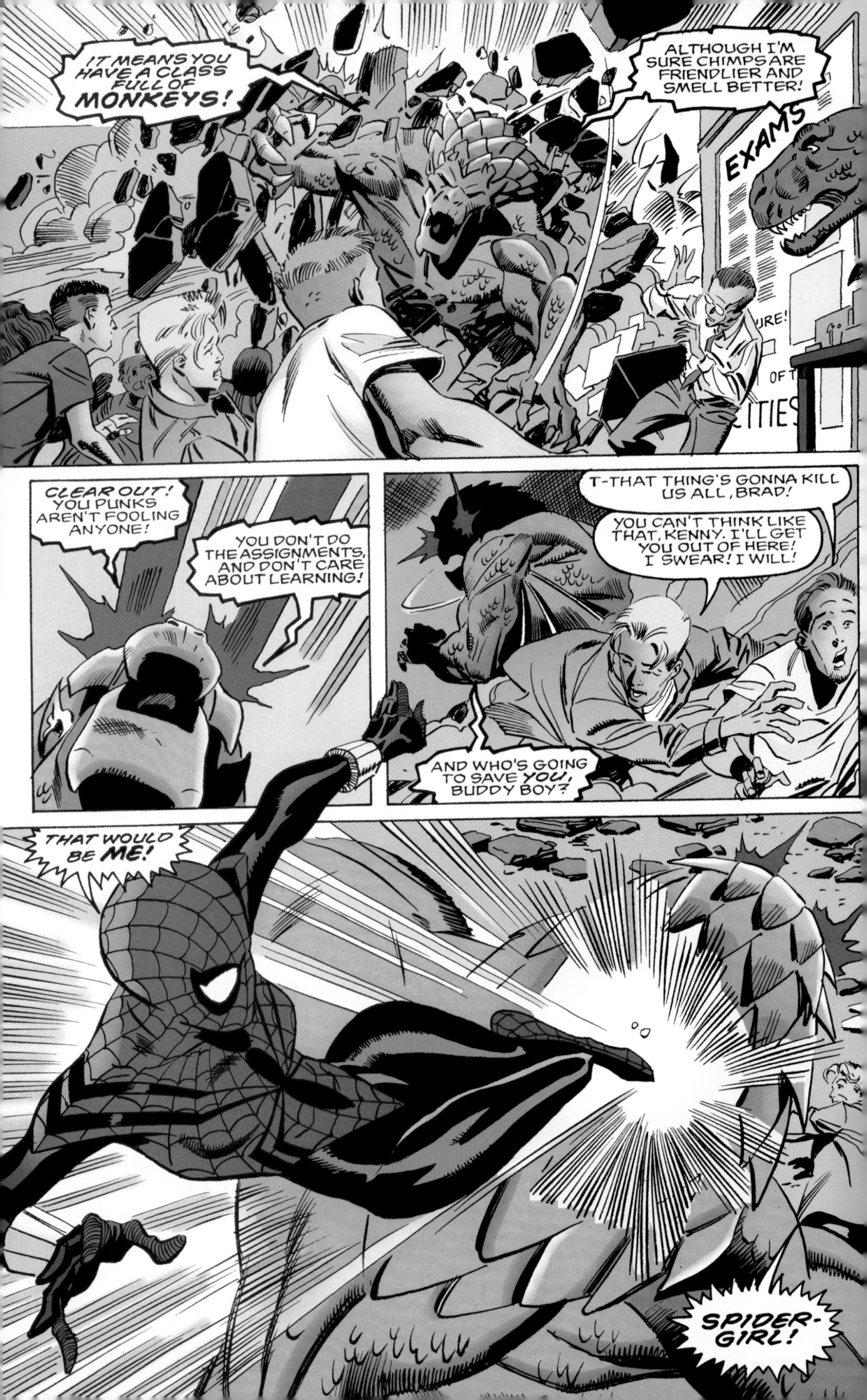
IT MEANS YOU HAVE A CLASS FULL OF MONKEYS!
ALTHOUGH I'M SURE CHIMPS ARE FRIENDLIER AND SMELL BETTER!
EXAMS
CLEAR OUT! YOU PUNKS AREN'T FOOLING ANYONE!
YOU DON'T DO THE ASSIGNMENTS, AND DON'T CARE ABOUT LEARNING!
T-THAT THING'S GONNA KILL US ALL, BRAD!
YOU CAN'T THINK LIKE THAT, KENNY. I'LL GET YOU OUT OF HERE! I SWEAR! I WILL!
AND WHO'S GOING TO SAVE YOU, BUDDY BOY?
THAT WOULD BE ME!
SPIDER-GIRL!

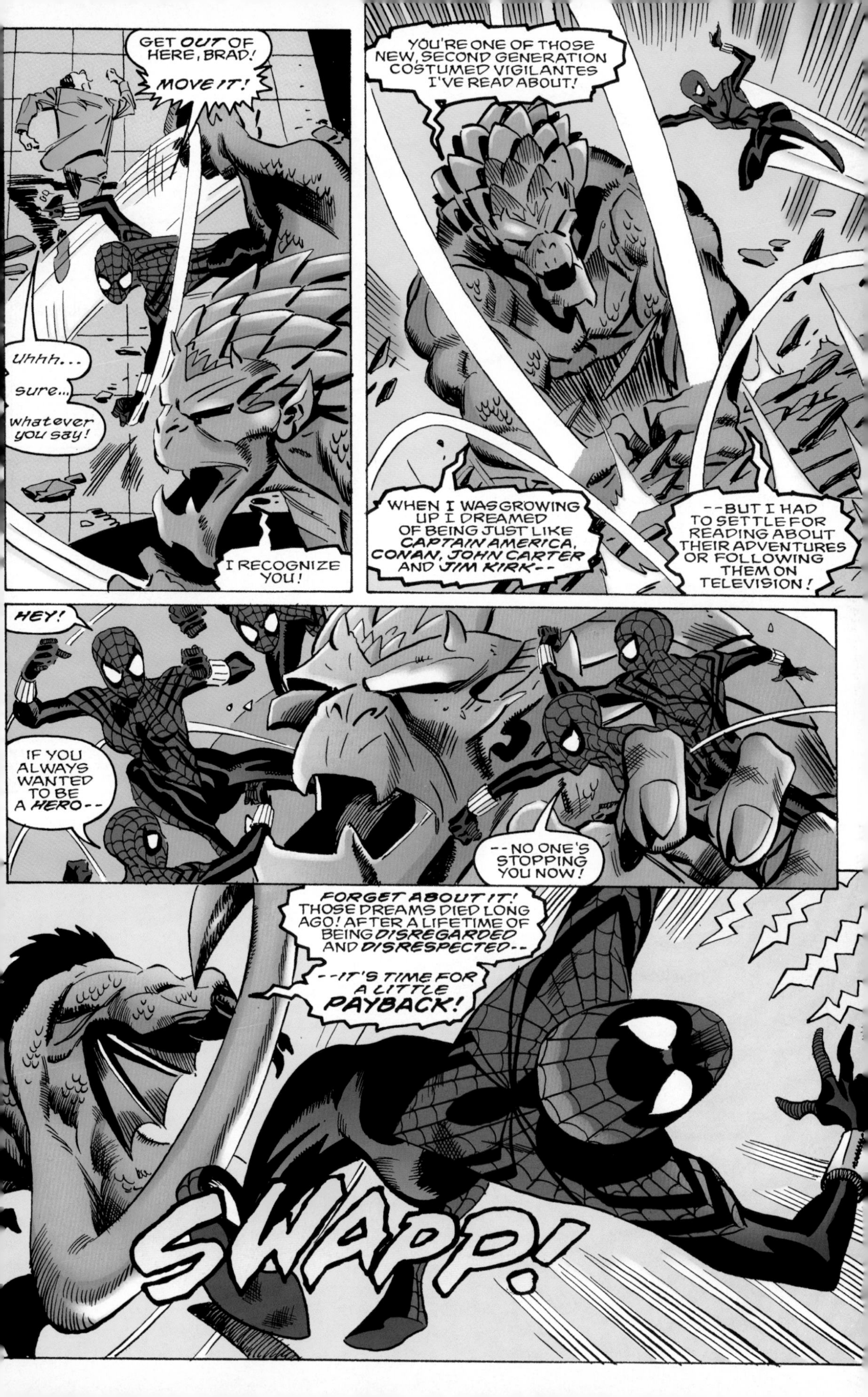
GET OUT OF HERE, BRAD!
MOVE IT!
Uhhh... sure... whatever you say!
I RECOGNIZE YOU!
YOU'RE ONE OF THOSE NEW, SECOND GENERATION COSTUMED VIGILANTES I'VE READ ABOUT!
WHEN I WAS GROWING UP I DREAMED OF BEING JUST LIKE CAPTAIN AMERICA, CONAN, JOHN CARTER AND JIM KIRK--
--BUT I HAD TO SETTLE FOR READING ABOUT THEIR ADVENTURES OR FOLLOWING THEM ON TELEVISION!
HEY!
IF YOU ALWAYS WANTED TO BE A HERO--
--NO ONE'S STOPPING YOU NOW!
FORGET ABOUT IT! THOSE DREAMS DIED LONG AGO! AFTER A LIFETIME OF BEING DISREGARDED AND DISRESPECTED--
--IT'S TIME FOR A LITTLE PAYBACK!
SWAPP!

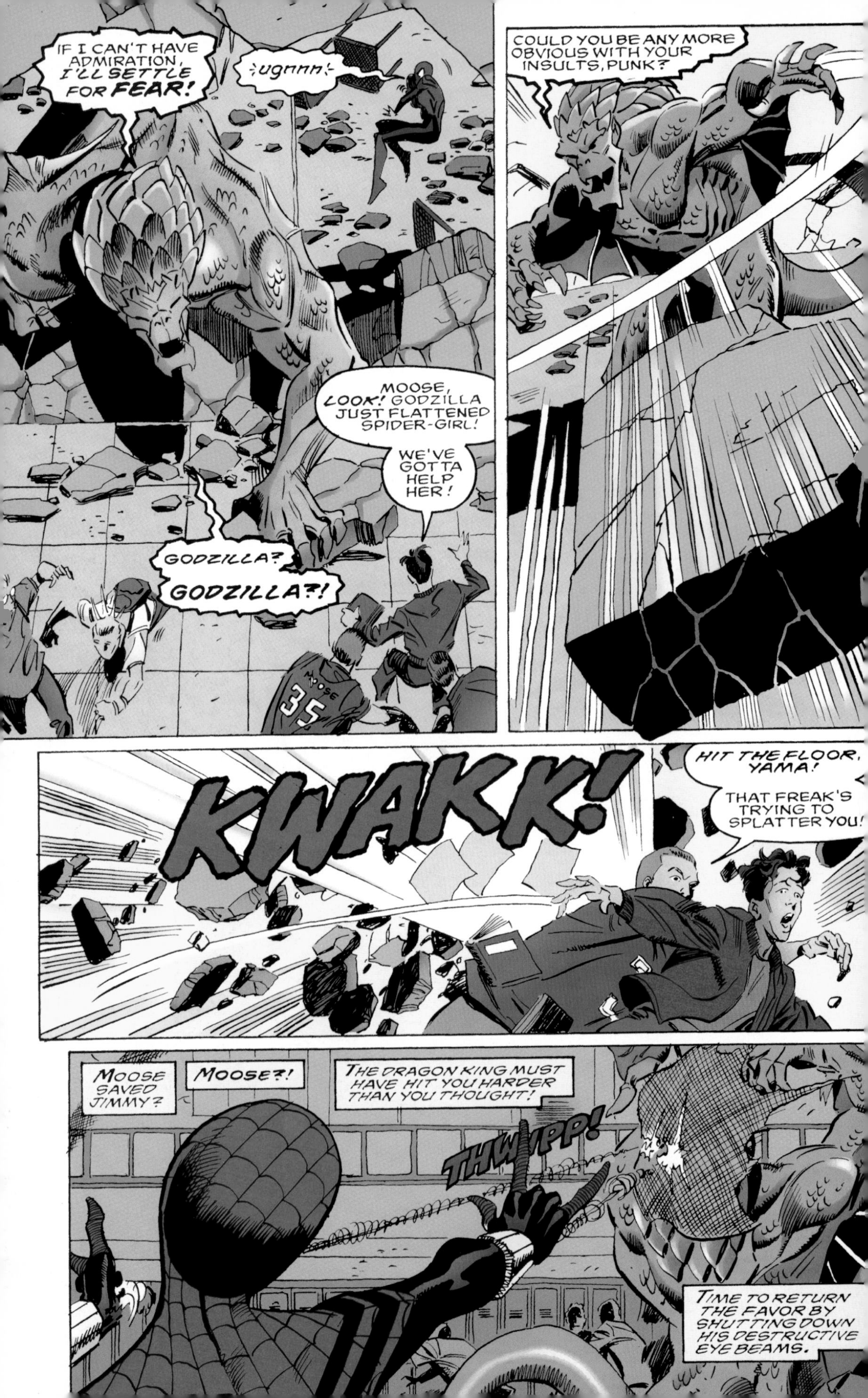
IF I CAN'T HAVE ADMIRATION, I'LL SETTLE FOR FEAR!
ugnnn
COULD YOU BE ANY MORE OBVIOUS WITH YOUR INSULTS, PUNK?
MOOSE, LOOK! GODZILLA JUST FLATTENED SPIDER-GIRL!
WE'VE GOTTA HELP HER!
GODZILLA?
GODZILLA?!
MOOSE
35
KWAKK!
HIT THE FLOOR, YAMA!
THAT FREAK'S TRYING TO SPLATTER YOU!
MOOSE SAVED JIMMY?
MOOSE?!
THE DRAGON KING MUST HAVE HIT YOU HARDER THAN YOU THOUGHT!
THWIPP!
TIME TO RETURN THE FAVOR BY SHUTTING DOWN HIS DESTRUCTIVE EYE BEAMS.

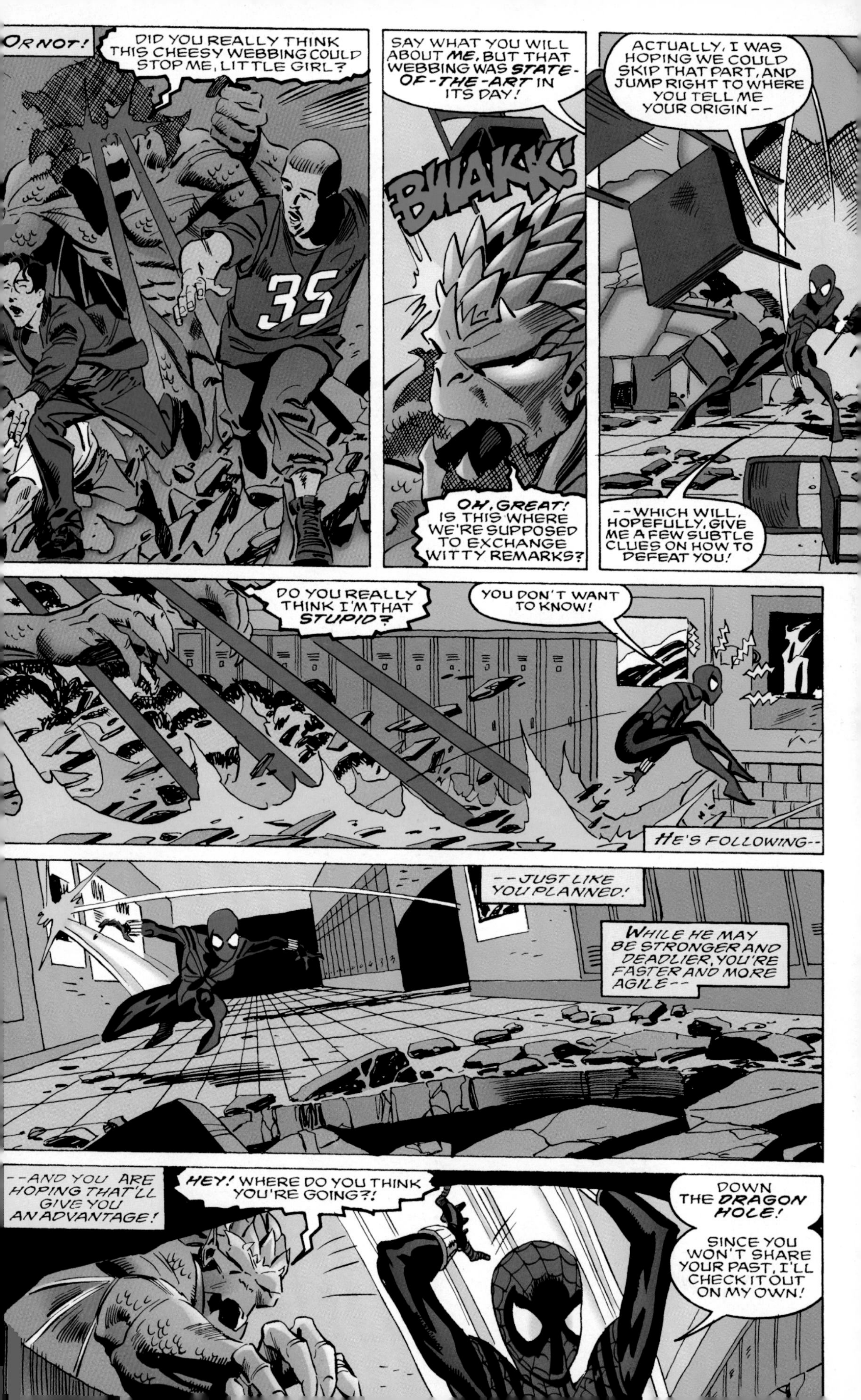
OR NOT!
DID YOU REALLY THINK THIS CHEESY WEBBING COULD STOP ME, LITTLE GIRL?
SAY WHAT YOU WILL ABOUT ME, BUT THAT WEBBING WAS STATE-OF-THE-ART IN ITS DAY!
BWAKK!
OH, GREAT! IS THIS WHERE WE'RE SUPPOSED TO EXCHANGE WITTY REMARKS?
ACTUALLY, I WAS HOPING WE COULD SKIP THAT PART, AND JUMP RIGHT TO WHERE YOU TELL ME YOUR ORIGIN --
--WHICH WILL, HOPEFULLY, GIVE ME A FEW SUBTLE CLUES ON HOW TO DEFEAT YOU!
DO YOU REALLY THINK I'M THAT STUPID?
YOU DON'T WANT TO KNOW!
HE'S FOLLOWING--
--JUST LIKE YOU PLANNED!
WHILE HE MAY BE STRONGER AND DEADLIER, YOU'RE FASTER AND MORE AGILE--
--AND YOU ARE HOPING THAT'LL GIVE YOU AN ADVANTAGE!
HEY! WHERE DO YOU THINK YOU'RE GOING?!
DOWN THE DRAGON HOLE!
SINCE YOU WON'T SHARE YOUR PAST, I'LL CHECK IT OUT ON MY OWN!

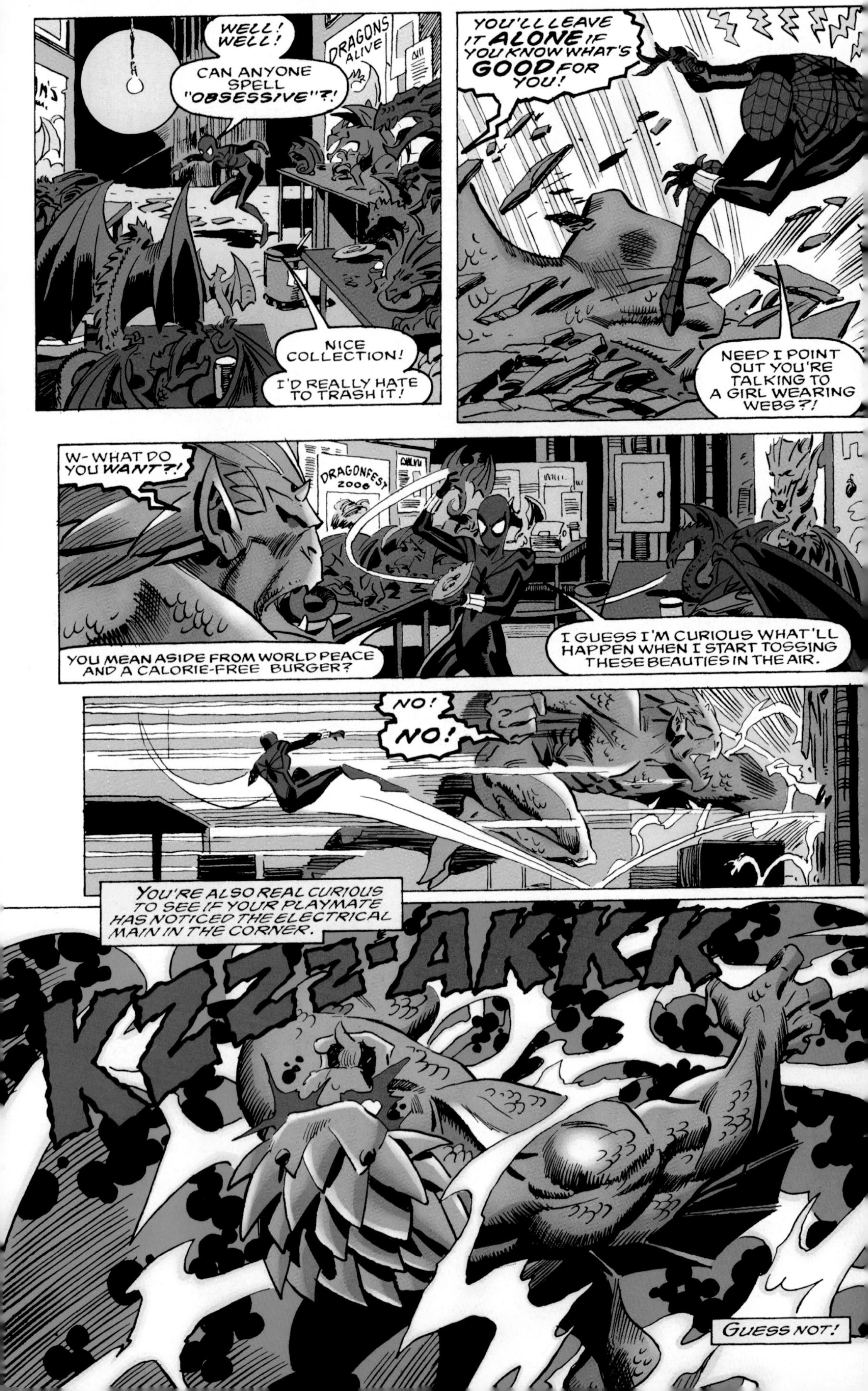

WELL! WELL!
CAN ANYONE SPELL "OBSESSIVE"?!
DRAGONS ALIVE
NICE COLLECTION!
I'D REALLY HATE TO TRASH IT!
YOU'LL LEAVE IT ALONE IF YOU KNOW WHAT'S GOOD FOR YOU!
NEED I POINT OUT YOU'RE TALKING TO A GIRL WEARING WEBS?!
W-WHAT DO YOU WANT?!
DRAGONFEST 2006
YOU MEAN ASIDE FROM WORLD PEACE AND A CALORIE-FREE BURGER?
I GUESS I'M CURIOUS WHAT'LL HAPPEN WHEN I START TOSSING THESE BEAUTIES IN THE AIR.
NO!
NO!
YOU'RE ALSO REAL CURIOUS TO SEE IF YOUR PLAYMATE HAS NOTICED THE ELECTRICAL MAIN IN THE CORNER.
KZZZ-AKKK
GUESS NOT!

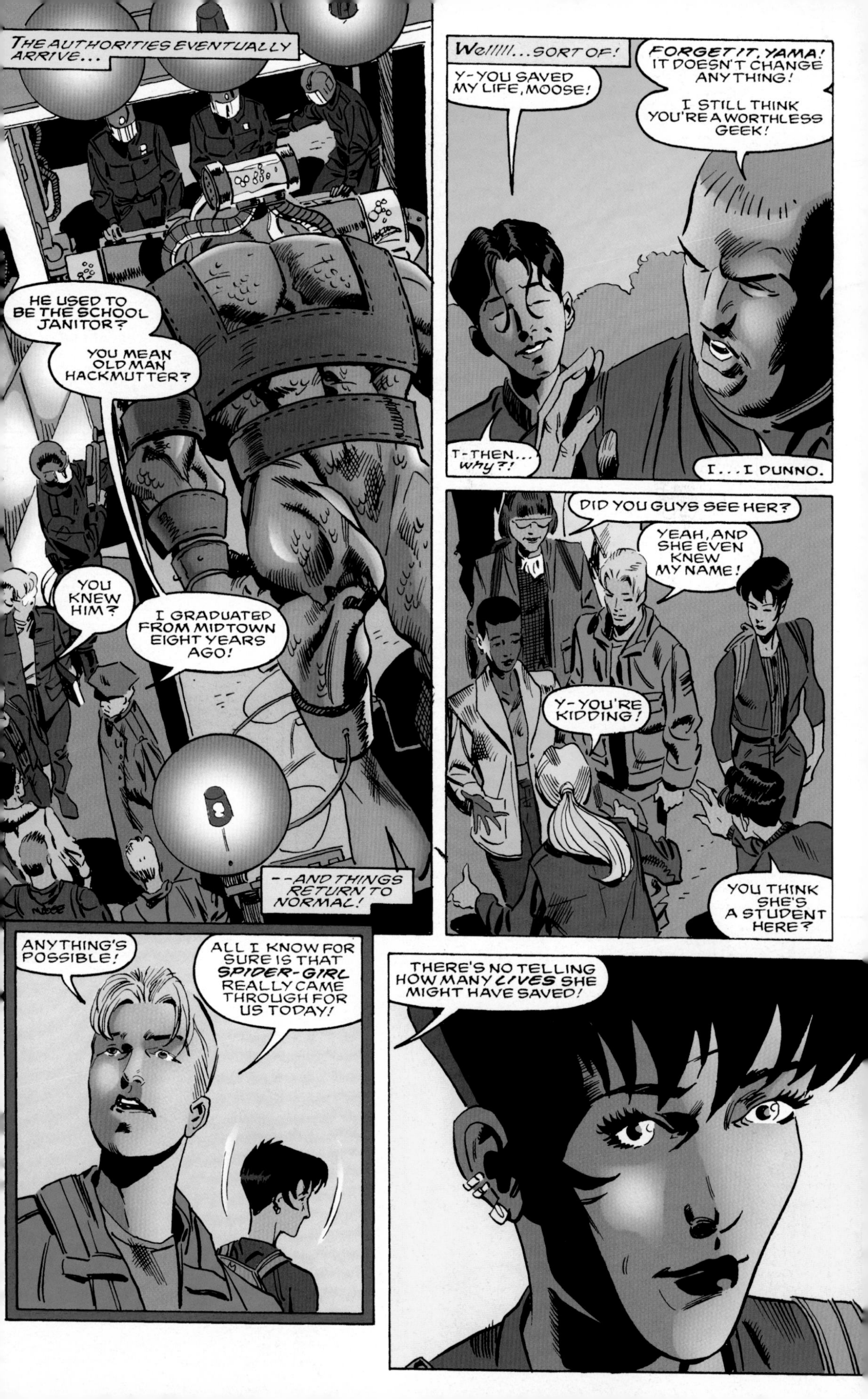
THE AUTHORITIES EVENTUALLY ARRIVE...
HE USED TO BE THE SCHOOL JANITOR?
YOU MEAN OLD MAN HACKMUTTER?
YOU KNEW HIM?
I GRADUATED FROM MIDTOWN EIGHT YEARS AGO!
--AND THINGS RETURN TO NORMAL!
Wellll... SORT OF!
Y-YOU SAVED MY LIFE, MOOSE!
FORGET IT, YAMA! IT DOESN'T CHANGE ANYTHING!
I STILL THINK YOU'RE A WORTHLESS GEEK!
T-THEN... why?!
I... I DUNNO.
DID YOU GUYS SEE HER?
YEAH, AND SHE EVEN KNEW MY NAME!
Y-YOU'RE KIDDING!
YOU THINK SHE'S A STUDENT HERE?
ANYTHING'S POSSIBLE!
ALL I KNOW FOR SURE IS THAT SPIDER-GIRL REALLY CAME THROUGH FOR US TODAY!
THERE'S NO TELLING HOW MANY LIVES SHE MIGHT HAVE SAVED!

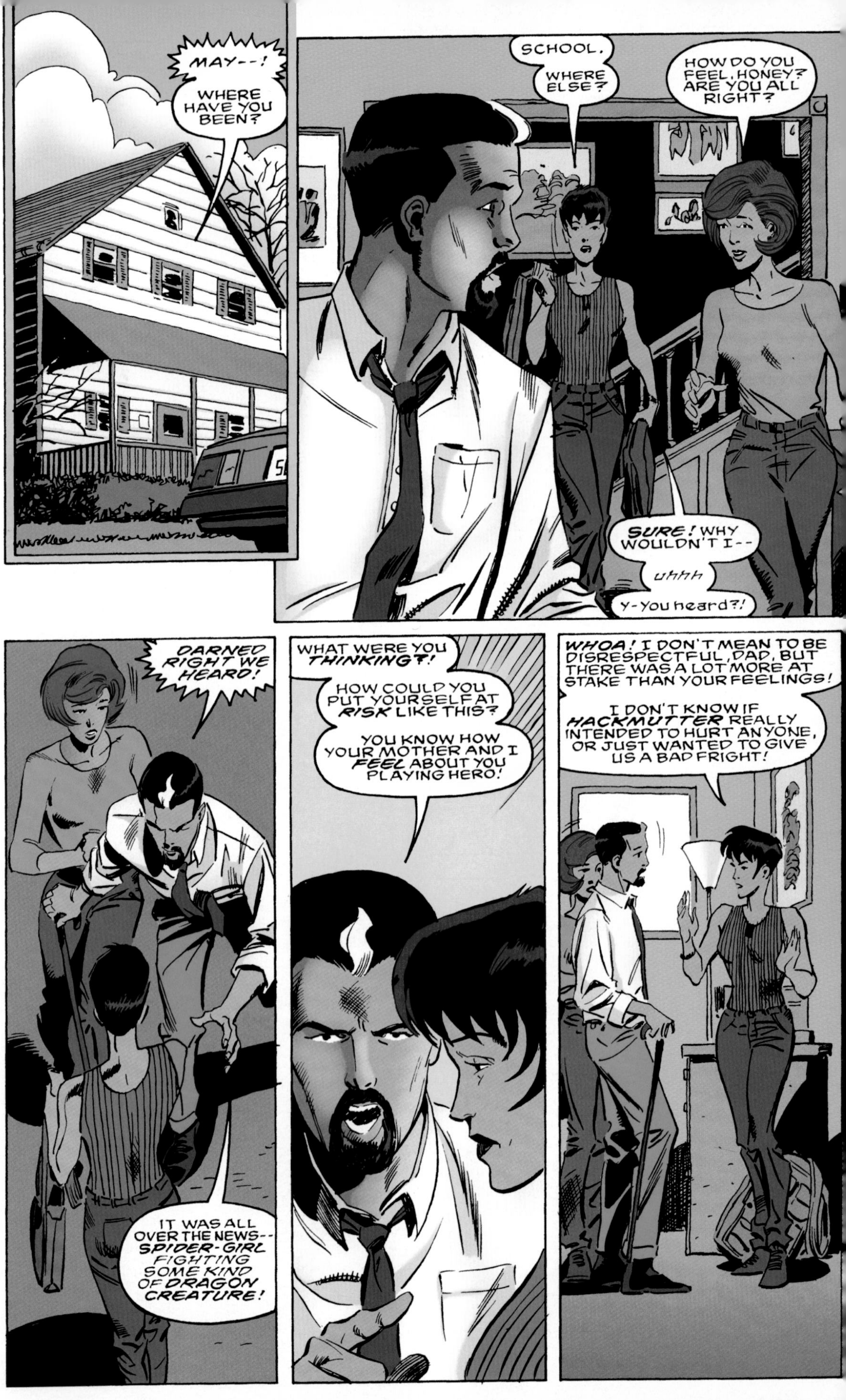
MAY--!
WHERE HAVE YOU BEEN?
SCHOOL.
WHERE ELSE?
HOW DO YOU FEEL, HONEY? ARE YOU ALL RIGHT?
SURE! WHY WOULDN'T I--
uhhh
Y-You heard?!
DARNED RIGHT WE HEARD!
IT WAS ALL OVER THE NEWS-- SPIDER-GIRL FIGHTING SOME KIND OF DRAGON CREATURE!
WHAT WERE YOU THINKING?!
HOW COULD YOU PUT YOURSELF AT RISK LIKE THIS?
YOU KNOW HOW YOUR MOTHER AND I FEEL ABOUT YOU PLAYING HERO!
WHOA! I DON'T MEAN TO BE DISRESPECTFUL, DAD, BUT THERE WAS A LOT MORE AT STAKE THAN YOUR FEELINGS!
I DON'T KNOW IF HACKMUTTER REALLY INTENDED TO HURT ANYONE, OR JUST WANTED TO GIVE US A BAD FRIGHT!

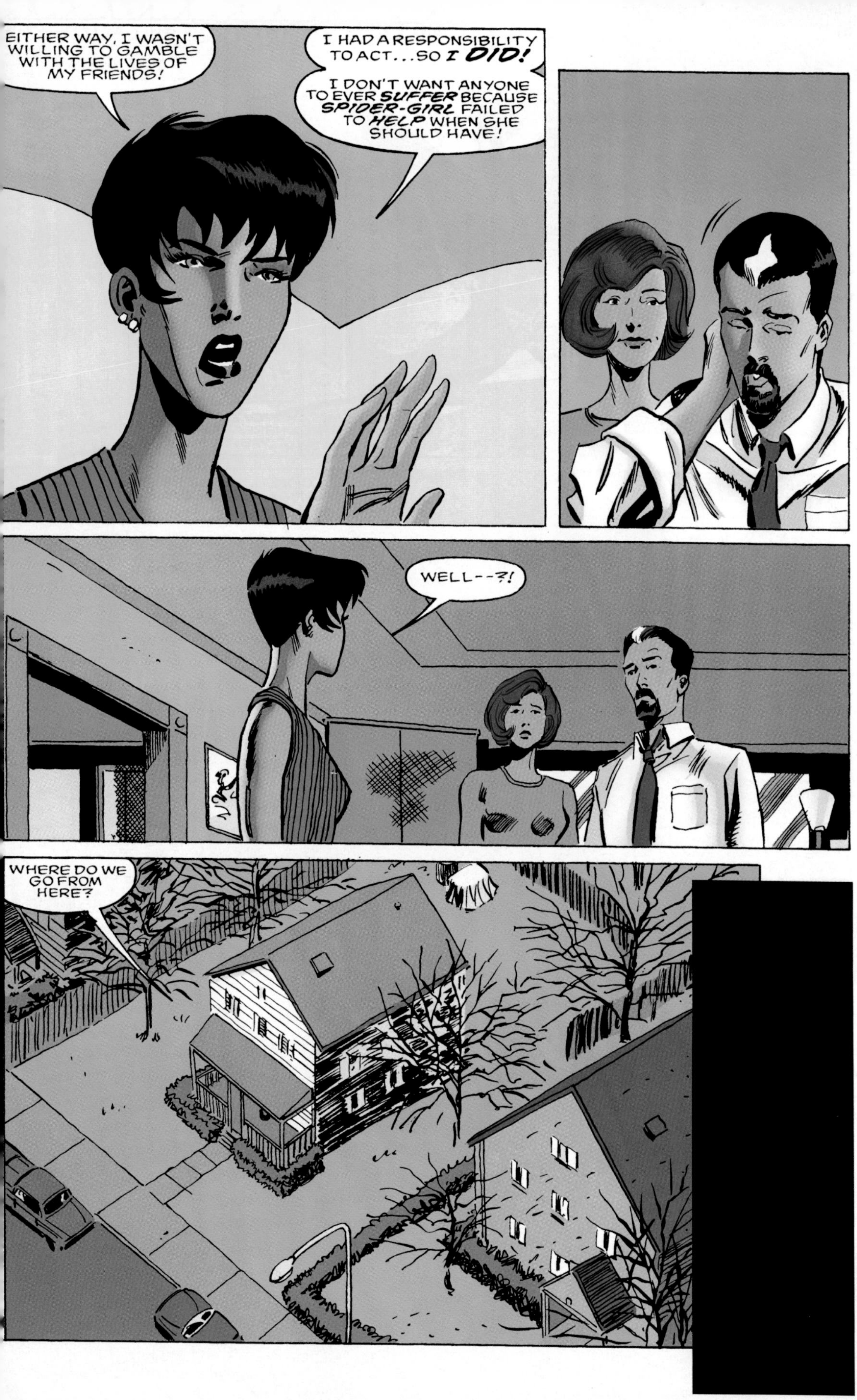
EITHER WAY, I WASN'T WILLING TO GAMBLE WITH THE LIVES OF MY FRIENDS!
I HAD A RESPONSIBILITY TO ACT... SO I DID!
I DON'T WANT ANYONE TO EVER SUFFER BECAUSE SPIDER-GIRL FAILED TO HELP WHEN SHE SHOULD HAVE!
WELL--?!
WHERE DO WE GO FROM HERE?

[redacted]

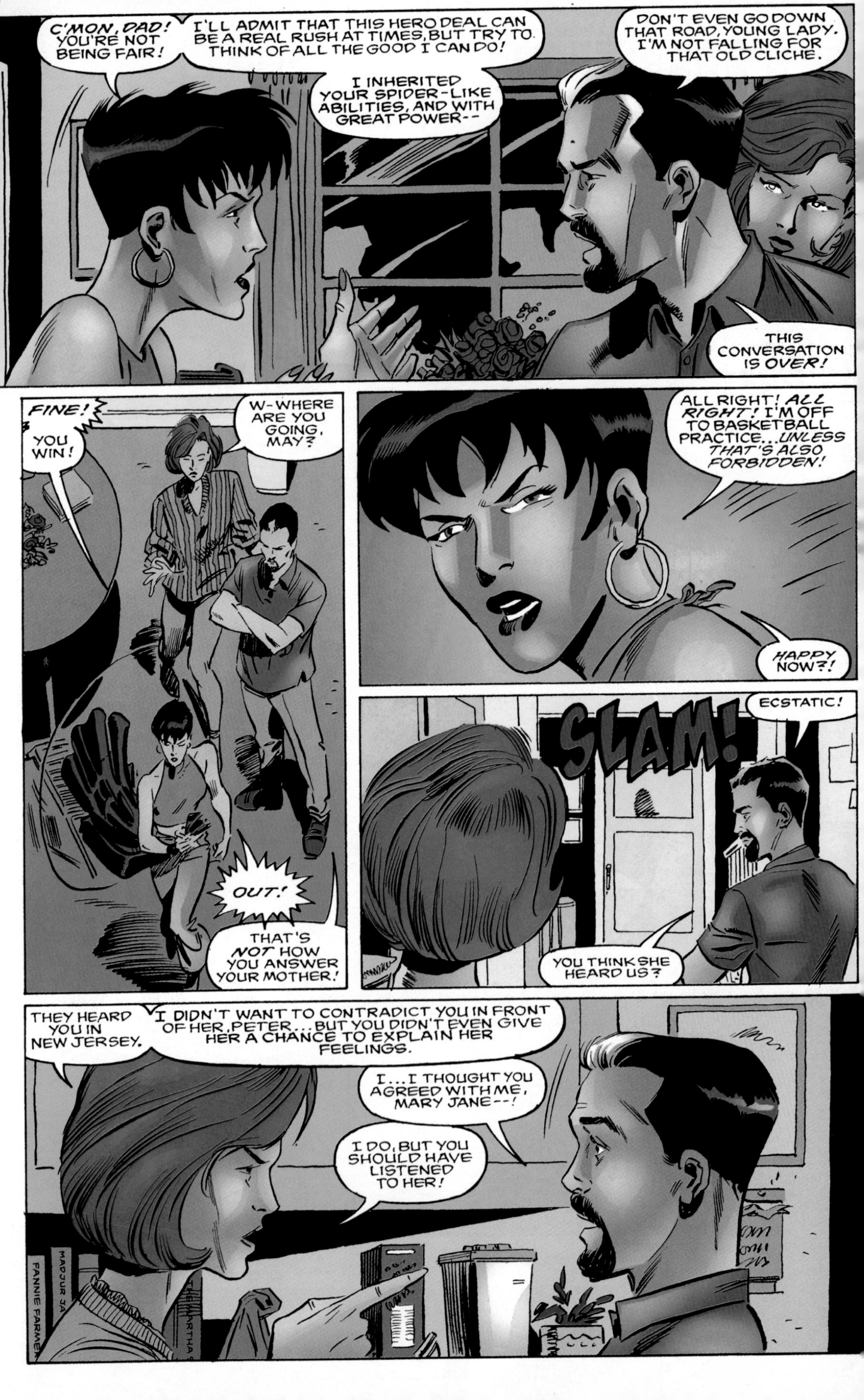
C'MON, DAD! YOU'RE NOT BEING FAIR!
I'LL ADMIT THAT THIS HERO DEAL CAN BE A REAL RUSH AT TIMES, BUT TRY TO THINK OF ALL THE GOOD I CAN DO!
I INHERITED YOUR SPIDER-LIKE ABILITIES, AND WITH GREAT POWER--
DON'T EVEN GO DOWN THAT ROAD, YOUNG LADY. I'M NOT FALLING FOR THAT OLD CLICHE.
THIS CONVERSATION IS OVER!
FINE!
YOU WIN!
W-WHERE ARE YOU GOING, MAY?
OUT!
THAT'S NOT HOW YOU ANSWER YOUR MOTHER!
ALL RIGHT! ALL RIGHT! I'M OFF TO BASKETBALL PRACTICE... UNLESS THAT'S ALSO FORBIDDEN!
HAPPY NOW?!
SLAM!
ECSTATIC!
YOU THINK SHE HEARD US?
THEY HEARD YOU IN NEW JERSEY.
I DIDN'T WANT TO CONTRADICT YOU IN FRONT OF HER, PETER... BUT YOU DIDN'T EVEN GIVE HER A CHANCE TO EXPLAIN HER FEELINGS.
I... I THOUGHT YOU AGREED WITH ME, MARY JANE--!
I DO, BUT YOU SHOULD HAVE LISTENED TO HER!
FANNIE FARMER
MADJUR JA
THE MARTHA

FUN'N'GAMES, HUH?

ONLY A FEW WEEKS AGO, YOU WERE AN AVERAGE ALL-AMERICAN TEENAGER.

(OKAY, MAYBE AVERAGE IS STRETCHING IT FOR A GIRL WHO'S A STRAIGHT-A STUDENT, AND A STARTER FOR THE MIDTOWN HIGH GIRLS' BASKETBALL TEAM.)

ANYWAY, THAT'S WHEN YOU FIRST LEARNED ABOUT YOUR DAD'S SECRET LIFE.

HE USED TO BE THE ORIGINAL SPIDER-MAN...

(UNTIL A BATTLE WITH A SUPER-VILLAIN RESULTED IN THE LOSS OF HIS RIGHT LEG.)

HAVING RECENTLY DISCOVERED THAT YOU ALSO HAD SPIDER-LIKE POWERS, YOU ATTEMPTED TO CONTINUE THE FAMILY TRADITION.

BUT YOUR PARENTS AREN'T PLEASED.

IN FACT, YOUR ONLY SUPPORTER IS YOUR UNCLE PHIL--

--WHO, SURPRISE, SURPRISE, WAS ONCE THE COSTUMED HERO KNOWN AS THE GREEN GOBLIN!

¿Sheesh!- Is it any wonder you're so drawn to the spandex life?!

YOU'RE AT A CROSSROAD MISS PARKER...

DO YOU OBEY YOUR PARENTS, AND HANG UP YOUR WEBS LIKE A GOOD LITTLE GIRL?

OR--?!

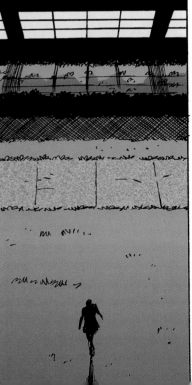

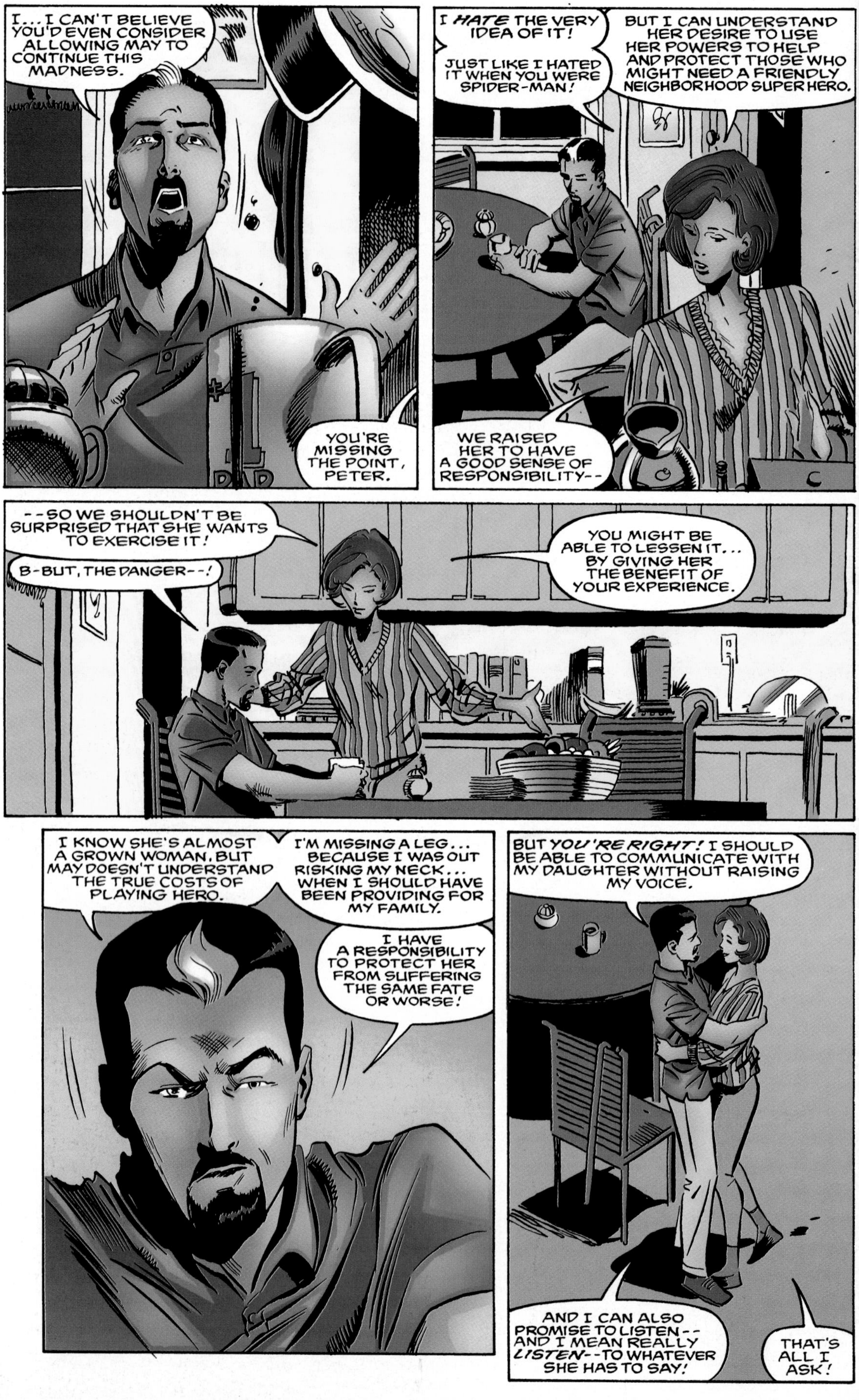
I... I CAN'T BELIEVE YOU'D EVEN CONSIDER ALLOWING MAY TO CONTINUE THIS MADNESS.
YOU'RE MISSING THE POINT, PETER.
I HATE THE VERY IDEA OF IT!
JUST LIKE I HATED IT WHEN YOU WERE SPIDER-MAN!
BUT I CAN UNDERSTAND HER DESIRE TO USE HER POWERS TO HELP AND PROTECT THOSE WHO MIGHT NEED A FRIENDLY NEIGHBORHOOD SUPER HERO.
WE RAISED HER TO HAVE A GOOD SENSE OF RESPONSIBILITY--
--SO WE SHOULDN'T BE SURPRISED THAT SHE WANTS TO EXERCISE IT!
B-BUT, THE DANGER--!
YOU MIGHT BE ABLE TO LESSEN IT... BY GIVING HER THE BENEFIT OF YOUR EXPERIENCE.
I KNOW SHE'S ALMOST A GROWN WOMAN, BUT MAY DOESN'T UNDERSTAND THE TRUE COSTS OF PLAYING HERO.
I'M MISSING A LEG... BECAUSE I WAS OUT RISKING MY NECK... WHEN I SHOULD HAVE BEEN PROVIDING FOR MY FAMILY.
I HAVE A RESPONSIBILITY TO PROTECT HER FROM SUFFERING THE SAME FATE OR WORSE!
BUT YOU'RE RIGHT! I SHOULD BE ABLE TO COMMUNICATE WITH MY DAUGHTER WITHOUT RAISING MY VOICE.
AND I CAN ALSO PROMISE TO LISTEN-- AND I MEAN REALLY LISTEN--TO WHATEVER SHE HAS TO SAY!
THAT'S ALL I ASK!

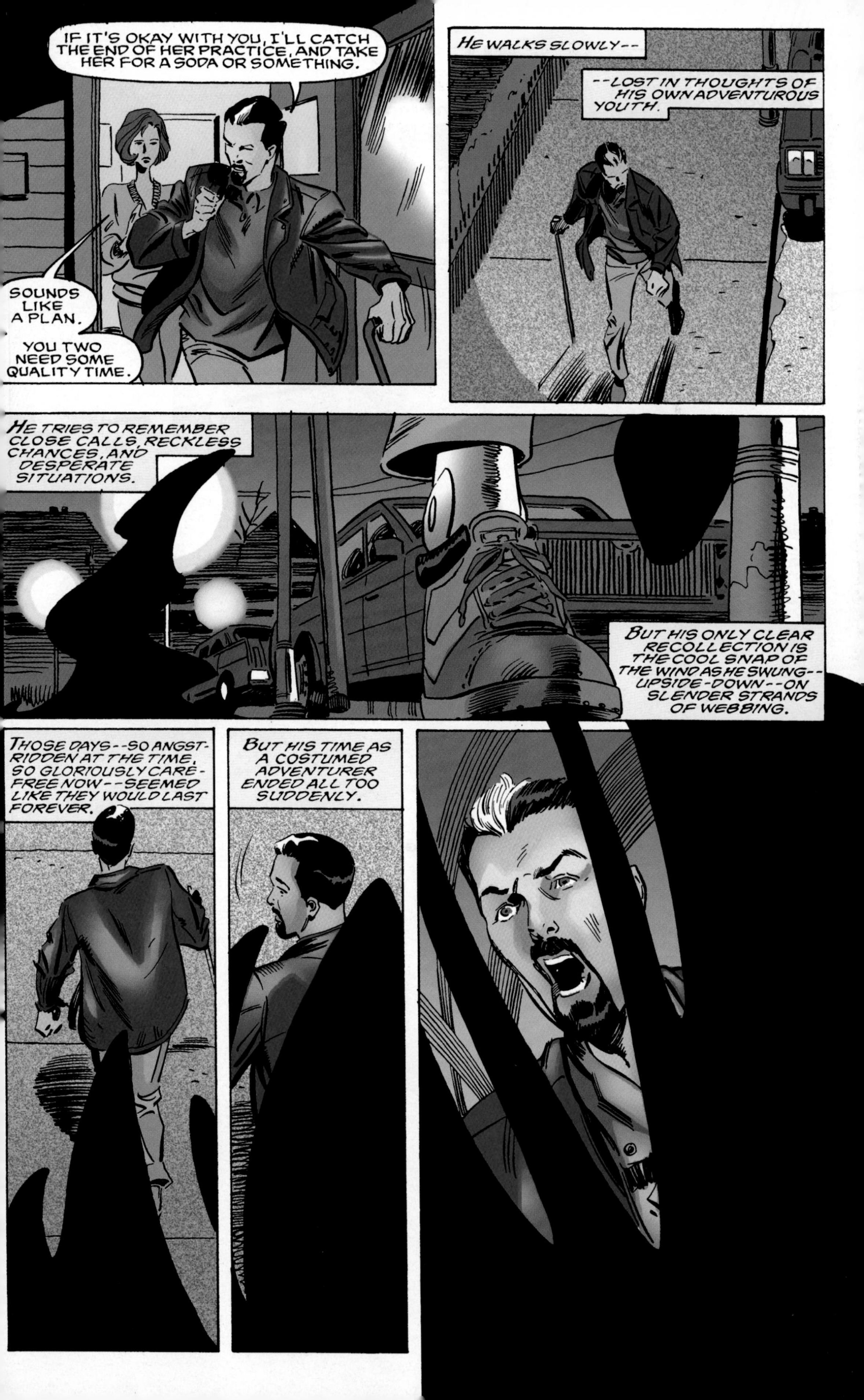
IF IT'S OKAY WITH YOU, I'LL CATCH THE END OF HER PRACTICE, AND TAKE HER FOR A SODA OR SOMETHING.
SOUNDS LIKE A PLAN.
YOU TWO NEED SOME QUALITY TIME.
HE WALKS SLOWLY--
--LOST IN THOUGHTS OF HIS OWN ADVENTUROUS YOUTH.
HE TRIES TO REMEMBER CLOSE CALLS, RECKLESS CHANCES, AND DESPERATE SITUATIONS.
BUT HIS ONLY CLEAR RECOLLECTION IS THE COOL SNAP OF THE WIND AS HE SWUNG--UPSIDE-DOWN--ON SLENDER STRANDS OF WEBBING.
THOSE DAYS--SO ANGST-RIDDEN AT THE TIME, SO GLORIOUSLY CARE-FREE NOW--SEEMED LIKE THEY WOULD LAST FOREVER.
BUT HIS TIME AS A COSTUMED ADVENTURER ENDED ALL TOO SUDDENLY.

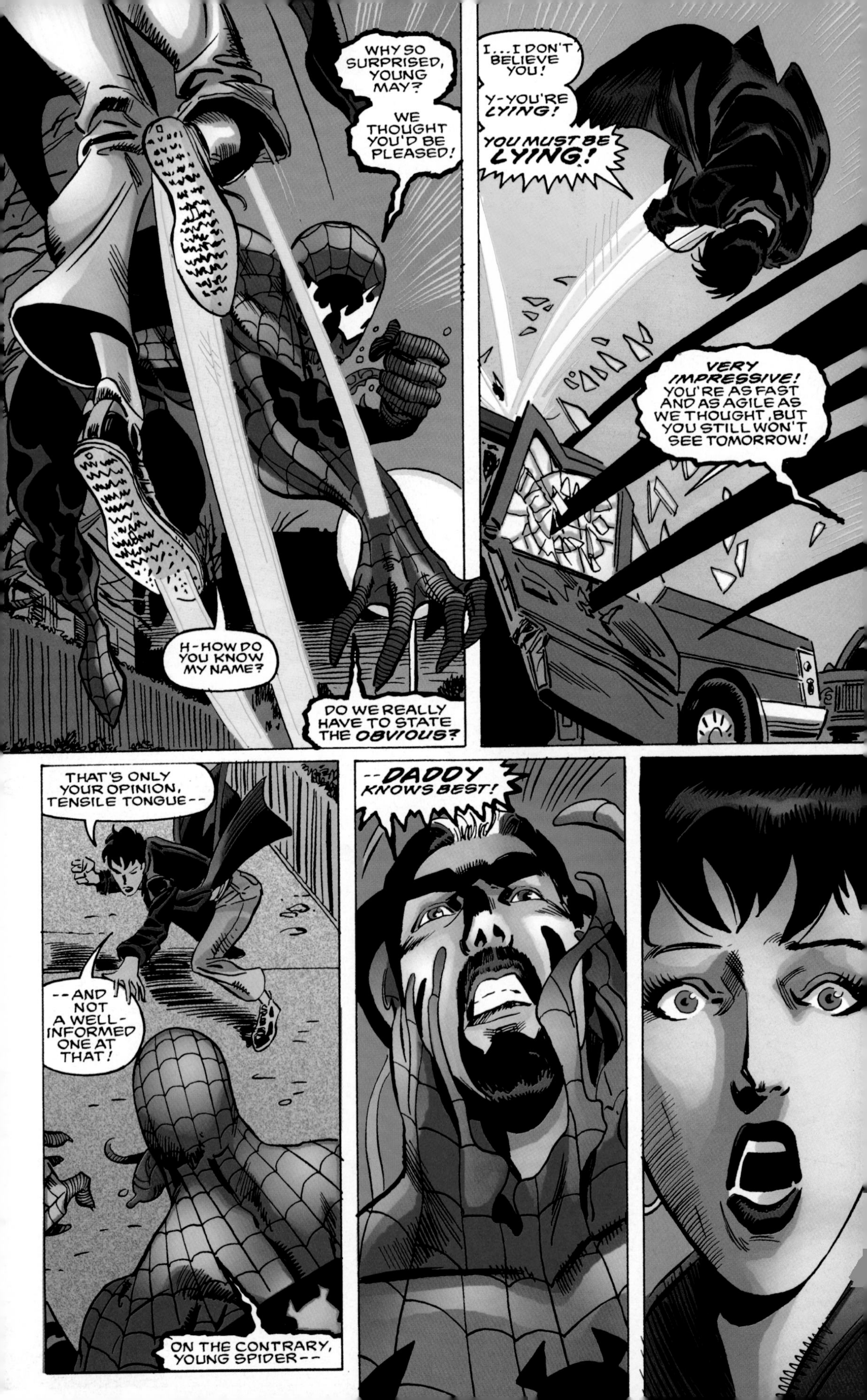
WHY SO SURPRISED, YOUNG MAY?
WE THOUGHT YOU'D BE PLEASED!
H-HOW DO YOU KNOW MY NAME?
DO WE REALLY HAVE TO STATE THE OBVIOUS?
I...I DON'T BELIEVE YOU!
Y-YOU'RE LYING!
YOU MUST BE LYING!
VERY IMPRESSIVE! YOU'RE AS FAST AND AS AGILE AS WE THOUGHT, BUT YOU STILL WON'T SEE TOMORROW!
THAT'S ONLY YOUR OPINION, TENSILE TONGUE--
--AND NOT A WELL-INFORMED ONE AT THAT!
ON THE CONTRARY, YOUNG SPIDER--
--DADDY KNOWS BEST!

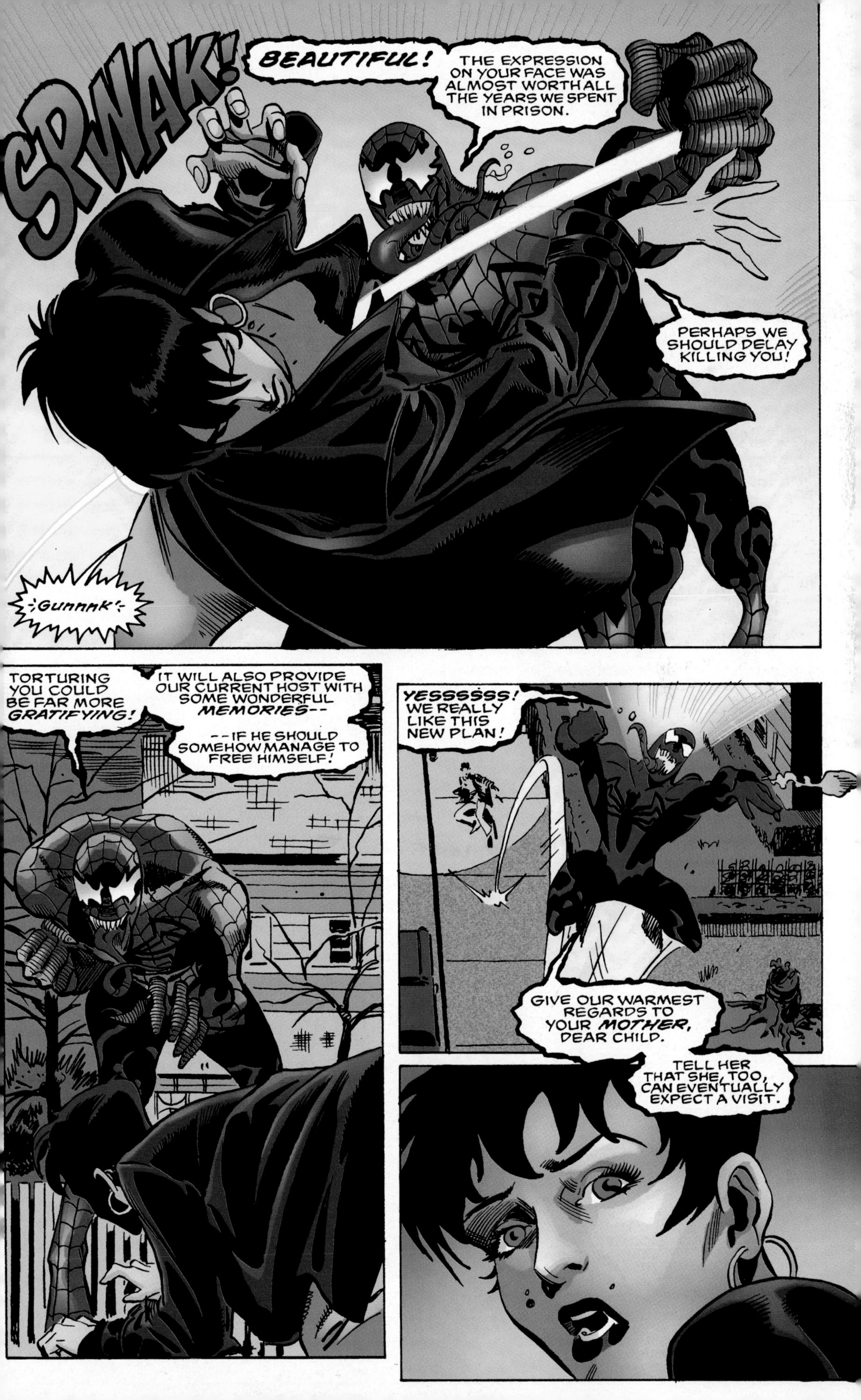
SPWAK!
BEAUTIFUL!
THE EXPRESSION ON YOUR FACE WAS ALMOST WORTH ALL THE YEARS WE SPENT IN PRISON.
PERHAPS WE SHOULD DELAY KILLING YOU!
:Gunnnk:
TORTURING YOU COULD BE FAR MORE GRATIFYING!
IT WILL ALSO PROVIDE OUR CURRENT HOST WITH SOME WONDERFUL MEMORIES--
--IF HE SHOULD SOMEHOW MANAGE TO FREE HIMSELF!
YESSSSSS! WE REALLY LIKE THIS NEW PLAN!
GIVE OUR WARMEST REGARDS TO YOUR MOTHER, DEAR CHILD.
TELL HER THAT SHE, TOO, CAN EVENTUALLY EXPECT A VISIT.

AS YOUR HEART TRIES TO PUNCH AN ESCAPE ROUTE THROUGH YOUR CHEST, YOU FRANTICALLY RACE HOME.

MOM! MOM! THANK GOD YOU'RE ALL RIGHT!

W- WHAT'S HAPPENED, HOTSHOT?

WHERE'S YOUR FATHER?!

PLEASE DON'T TELL ME THAT HORRIBLE CREATURE IS--

WE HAVE NO TIME FOR THE HYSTERICAL THING, MOM!

I NEED YOU TO TELL ME EVERYTHING YOU KNOW ABOUT A CREATURE CALLED VENOM!

WHAAA--?!

I NEED MAJOR BACK STORY-- AND FAST!

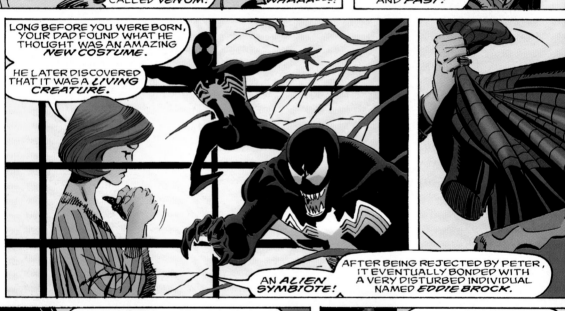

LONG BEFORE YOU WERE BORN, YOUR DAD FOUND WHAT HE THOUGHT WAS AN AMAZING NEW COSTUME.

HE LATER DISCOVERED THAT IT WAS A LIVING CREATURE.

AN ALIEN SYMBIOTE!

AFTER BEING REJECTED BY PETER, IT EVENTUALLY BONDED WITH A VERY DISTURBED INDIVIDUAL NAMED EDDIE BROCK.

FOR REASONS THAT DON'T REALLY MATTER NOW, VENOM HATED YOUR FATHER AND KEPT TRYING TO KILL SPIDER-MAN!

IF VENOM'S REALLY BACK WE SHOULD ALERT THE FANTASTIC FIVE AND--

FINE! THAT'S YOUR JOB!

IT POSSESSES ALL OF PETER'S SPIDER-LIKE POWERS ALONG WITH THE SYMBIOTE'S UNCANNY ABILITY TO MORPH ITS SHAPE AND APPEARANCE--

--BUT IT IS VULNERABLE TO HIGH-FREQUENCY SOUNDS.

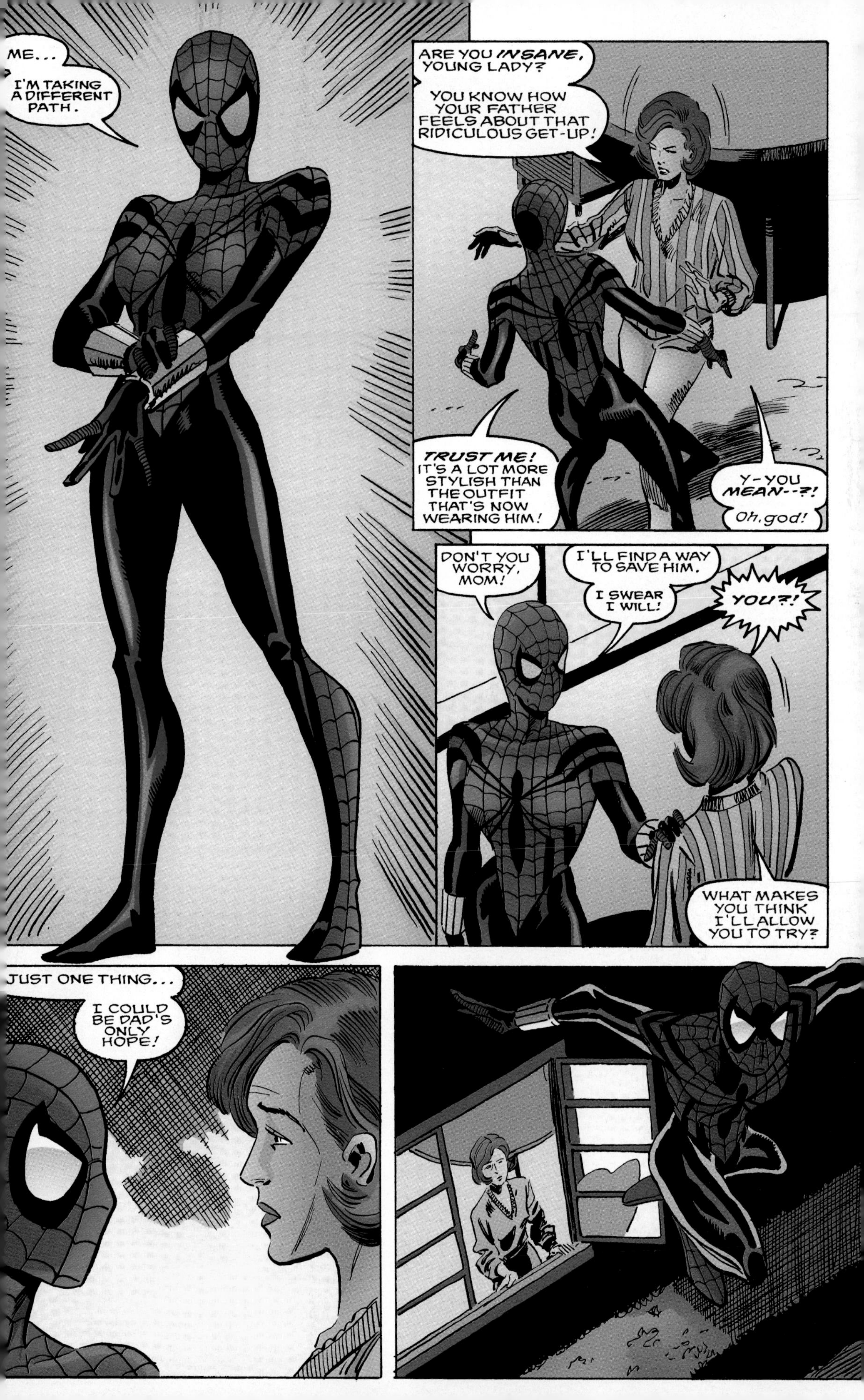
ME...
I'M TAKING A DIFFERENT PATH.
ARE YOU INSANE, YOUNG LADY?
YOU KNOW HOW YOUR FATHER FEELS ABOUT THAT RIDICULOUS GET-UP!
TRUST ME! IT'S A LOT MORE STYLISH THAN THE OUTFIT THAT'S NOW WEARING HIM!
Y-YOU MEAN--?!
Oh, god!
DON'T YOU WORRY, MOM!
I'LL FIND A WAY TO SAVE HIM.
I SWEAR I WILL!
YOU?!
WHAT MAKES YOU THINK I'LL ALLOW YOU TO TRY?
JUST ONE THING...
I COULD BE DAD'S ONLY HOPE!

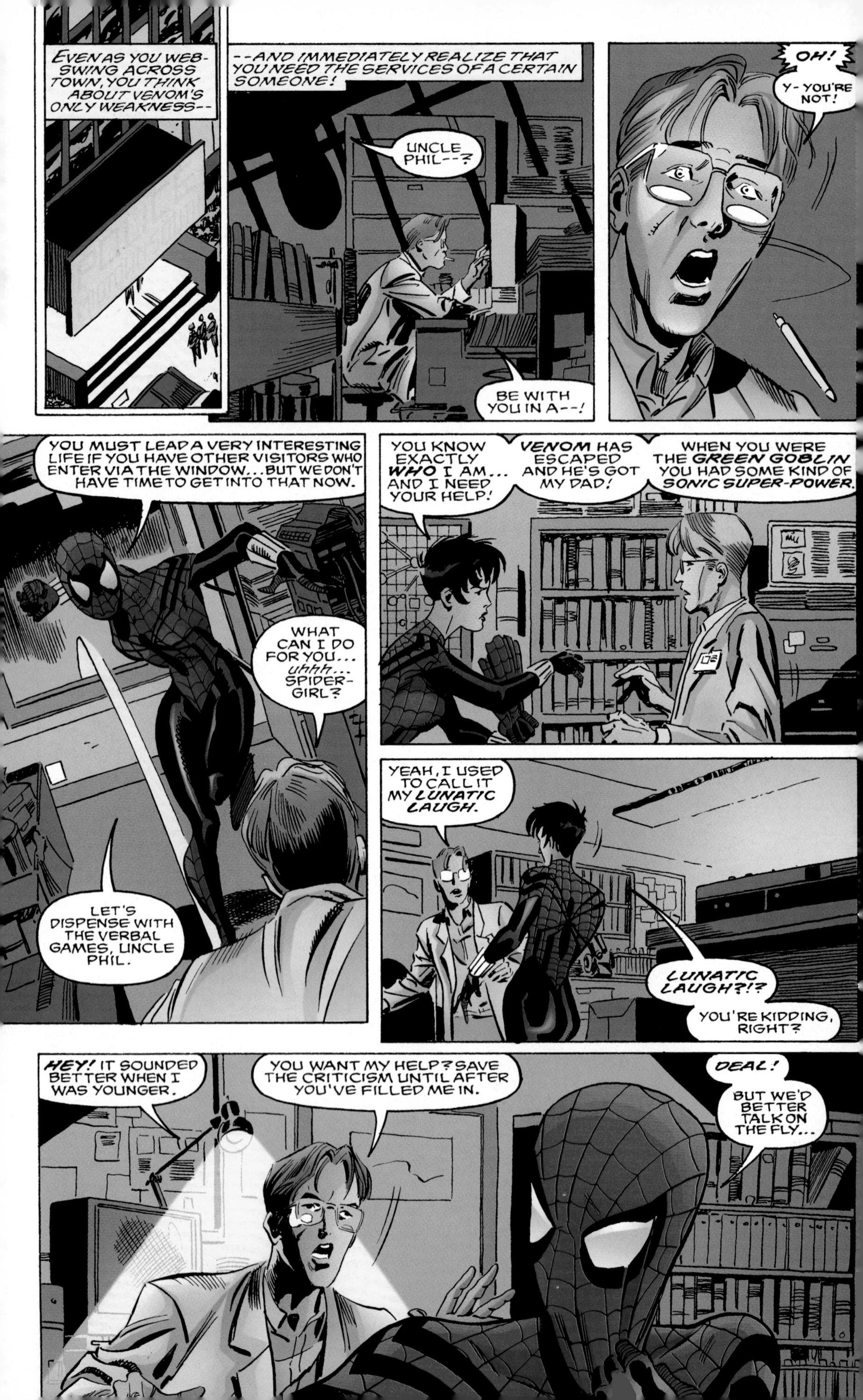
EVEN AS YOU WEB-SWING ACROSS TOWN, YOU THINK ABOUT VENOM'S ONLY WEAKNESS--
--AND IMMEDIATELY REALIZE THAT YOU NEED THE SERVICES OF A CERTAIN SOMEONE!
UNCLE PHIL--?
BE WITH YOU IN A--!
OH!
Y-YOU'RE NOT!
YOU MUST LEAD A VERY INTERESTING LIFE IF YOU HAVE OTHER VISITORS WHO ENTER VIA THE WINDOW... BUT WE DON'T HAVE TIME TO GET INTO THAT NOW.
WHAT CAN I DO FOR YOU... uhhh... SPIDER-GIRL?
LET'S DISPENSE WITH THE VERBAL GAMES, UNCLE PHIL.
YOU KNOW EXACTLY WHO I AM... AND I NEED YOUR HELP!
VENOM HAS ESCAPED AND HE'S GOT MY DAD!
WHEN YOU WERE THE GREEN GOBLIN YOU HAD SOME KIND OF SONIC SUPER-POWER.
YEAH, I USED TO CALL IT MY LUNATIC LAUGH.
LUNATIC LAUGH?!?
YOU'RE KIDDING, RIGHT?
HEY! IT SOUNDED BETTER WHEN I WAS YOUNGER.
YOU WANT MY HELP? SAVE THE CRITICISM UNTIL AFTER YOU'VE FILLED ME IN.
DEAL!
BUT WE'D BETTER TALK ON THE FLY...

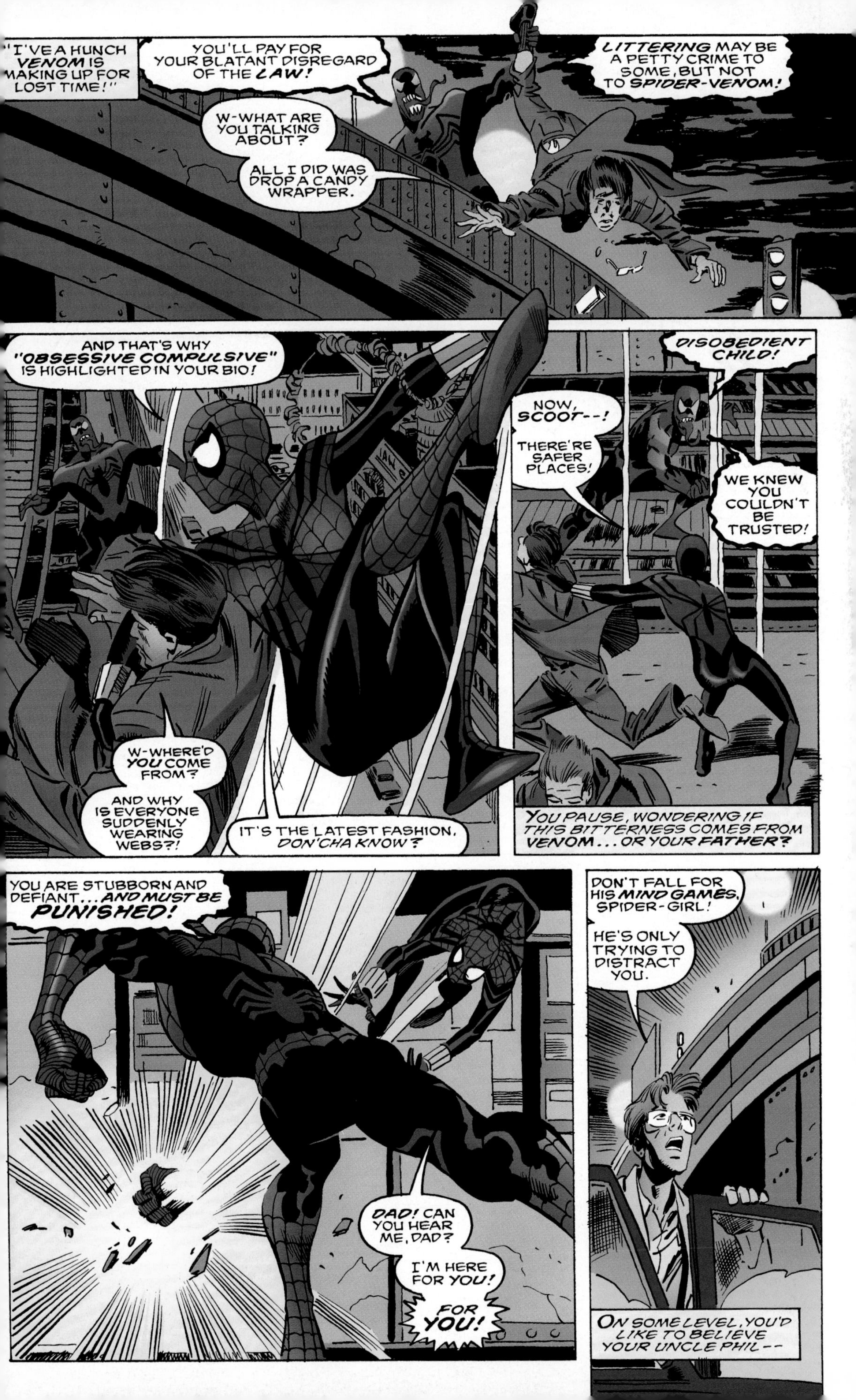

"I'VE A HUNCH VENOM IS MAKING UP FOR LOST TIME!"
YOU'LL PAY FOR YOUR BLATANT DISREGARD OF THE LAW!
LITTERING MAY BE A PETTY CRIME TO SOME, BUT NOT TO SPIDER-VENOM!
W-WHAT ARE YOU TALKING ABOUT?
ALL I DID WAS DROP A CANDY WRAPPER.
AND THAT'S WHY "OBSESSIVE COMPULSIVE" IS HIGHLIGHTED IN YOUR BIO!
W-WHERE'D YOU COME FROM?
AND WHY IS EVERYONE SUDDENLY WEARING WEBS?!
IT'S THE LATEST FASHION, DON'CHA KNOW?
DISOBEDIENT CHILD!
NOW, SCOOT--!
THERE'RE SAFER PLACES!
WE KNEW YOU COULDN'T BE TRUSTED!
YOU PAUSE, WONDERING IF THIS BITTERNESS COMES FROM VENOM... OR YOUR FATHER?
YOU ARE STUBBORN AND DEFIANT... AND MUST BE PUNISHED!
DAD! CAN YOU HEAR ME, DAD?
I'M HERE FOR YOU!
FOR YOU!
DON'T FALL FOR HIS MIND GAMES, SPIDER-GIRL!
HE'S ONLY TRYING TO DISTRACT YOU.
ON SOME LEVEL, YOU'D LIKE TO BELIEVE YOUR UNCLE PHIL--

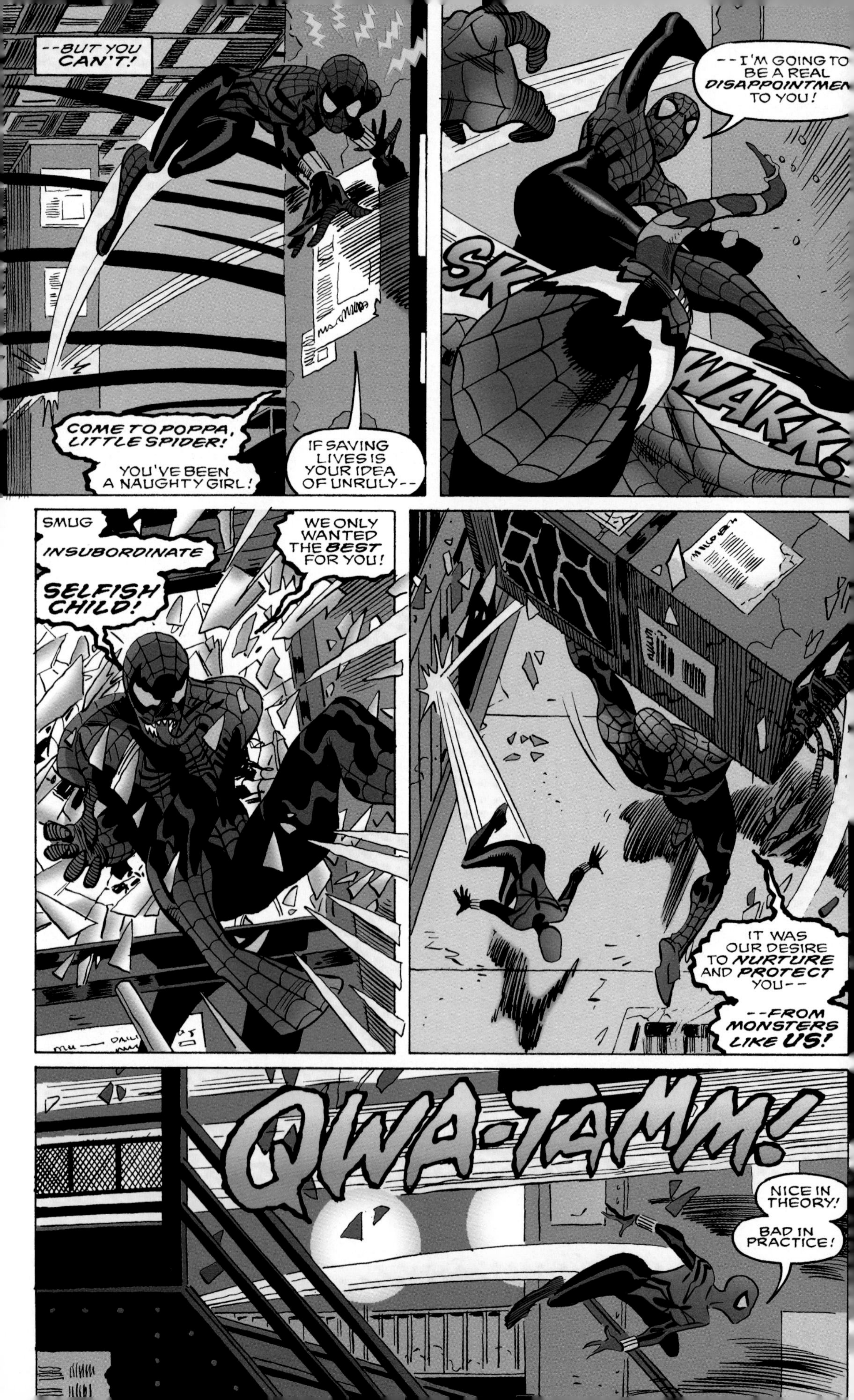
--BUT YOU CAN'T!
COME TO POPPA, LITTLE SPIDER!
YOU'VE BEEN A NAUGHTY GIRL!
IF SAVING LIVES IS YOUR IDEA OF UNRULY--
--I'M GOING TO BE A REAL DISAPPOINTMEN TO YOU!
SKWAKK!
SMUG
INSUBORDINATE
SELFISH CHILD!
WE ONLY WANTED THE BEST FOR YOU!
IT WAS OUR DESIRE TO NURTURE AND PROTECT YOU--
--FROM MONSTERS LIKE US!
QWA-TAMM!
NICE IN THEORY!
BAD IN PRACTICE!

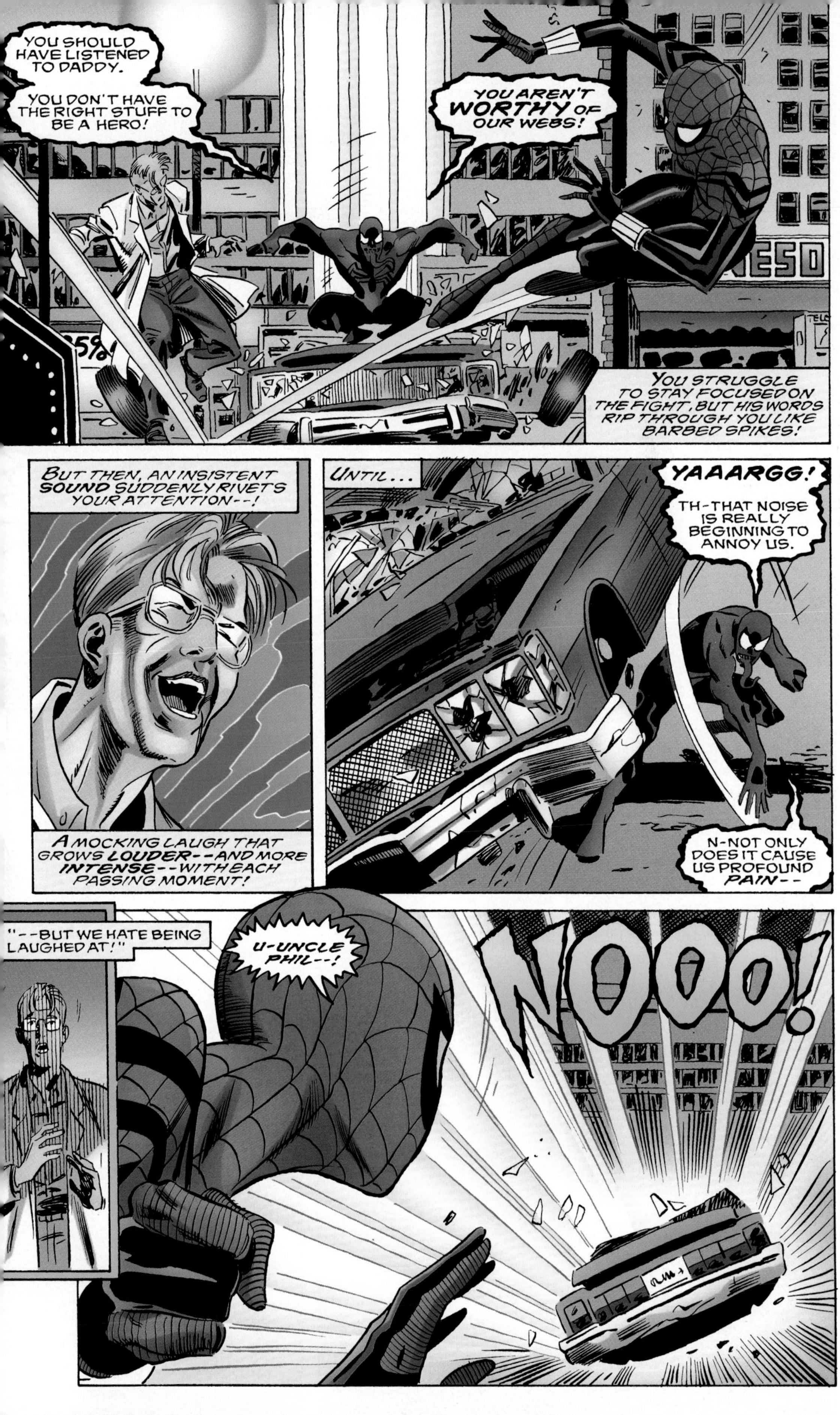
YOU SHOULD HAVE LISTENED TO DADDY.
YOU DON'T HAVE THE RIGHT STUFF TO BE A HERO!
YOU AREN'T WORTHY OF OUR WEBS!
YOU STRUGGLE TO STAY FOCUSED ON THE FIGHT, BUT HIS WORDS RIP THROUGH YOU LIKE BARBED SPIKES!
BUT THEN, AN INSISTENT SOUND SUDDENLY RIVETS YOUR ATTENTION--!
A MOCKING LAUGH THAT GROWS LOUDER--AND MORE INTENSE--WITH EACH PASSING MOMENT!
UNTIL...
YAAARGG!
TH-THAT NOISE IS REALLY BEGINNING TO ANNOY US.
N-NOT ONLY DOES IT CAUSE US PROFOUND PAIN--
"--BUT WE HATE BEING LAUGHED AT!"
U-UNCLE PHIL--!
NOOO!

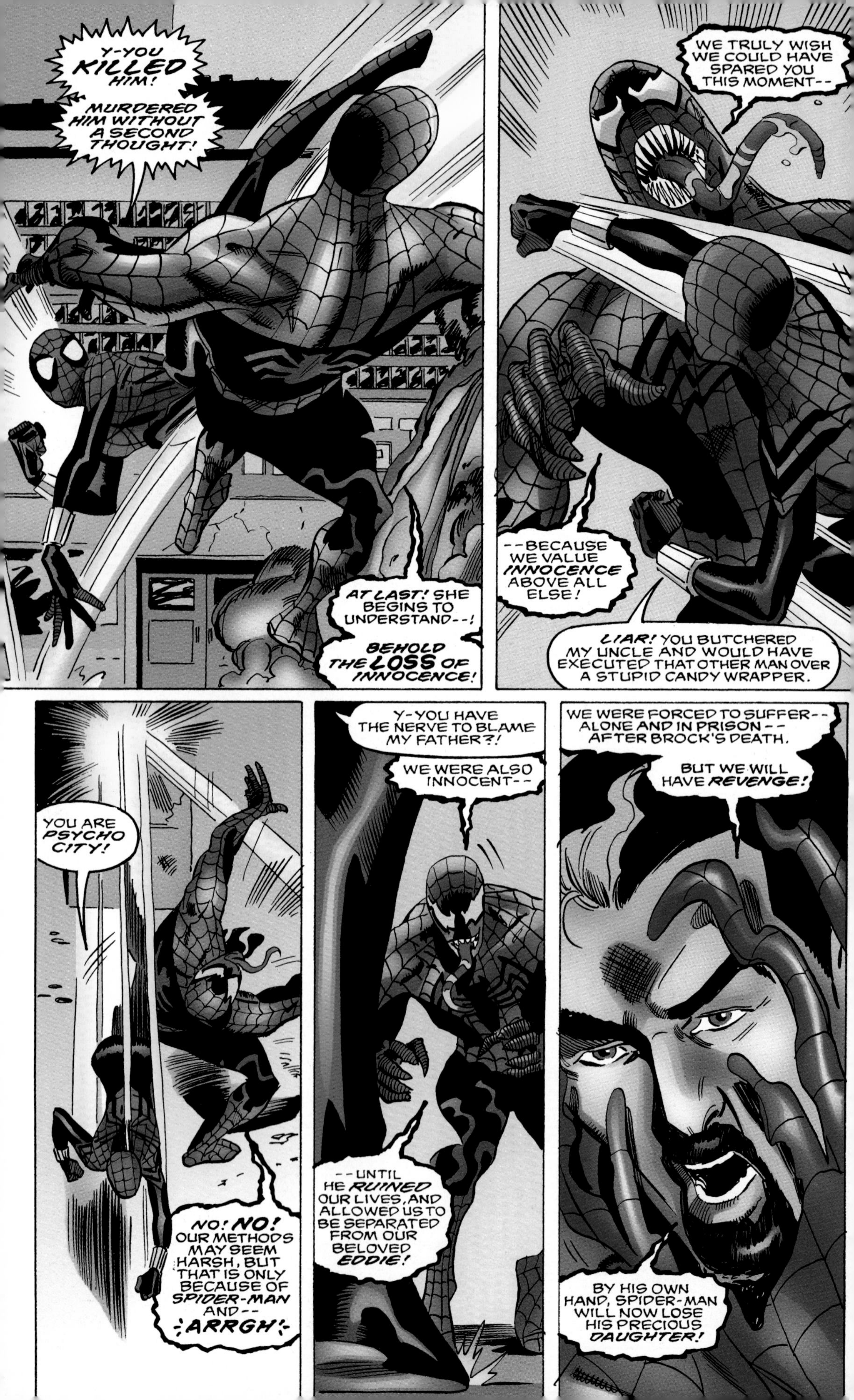

Y-YOU KILLED HIM! MURDERED HIM WITHOUT A SECOND THOUGHT!
AT LAST! SHE BEGINS TO UNDERSTAND--!
BEHOLD THE LOSS OF INNOCENCE!
WE TRULY WISH WE COULD HAVE SPARED YOU THIS MOMENT--
--BECAUSE WE VALUE INNOCENCE ABOVE ALL ELSE!
LIAR! YOU BUTCHERED MY UNCLE AND WOULD HAVE EXECUTED THAT OTHER MAN OVER A STUPID CANDY WRAPPER.
YOU ARE PSYCHO CITY!
NO! NO! OUR METHODS MAY SEEM HARSH, BUT THAT IS ONLY BECAUSE OF SPIDER-MAN AND-- -ARRGH-
Y-YOU HAVE THE NERVE TO BLAME MY FATHER?!
WE WERE ALSO INNOCENT--
--UNTIL HE RUINED OUR LIVES, AND ALLOWED US TO BE SEPARATED FROM OUR BELOVED EDDIE!
WE WERE FORCED TO SUFFER-- ALONE AND IN PRISON-- AFTER BROCK'S DEATH.
BUT WE WILL HAVE REVENGE!
BY HIS OWN HAND, SPIDER-MAN WILL NOW LOSE HIS PRECIOUS DAUGHTER!

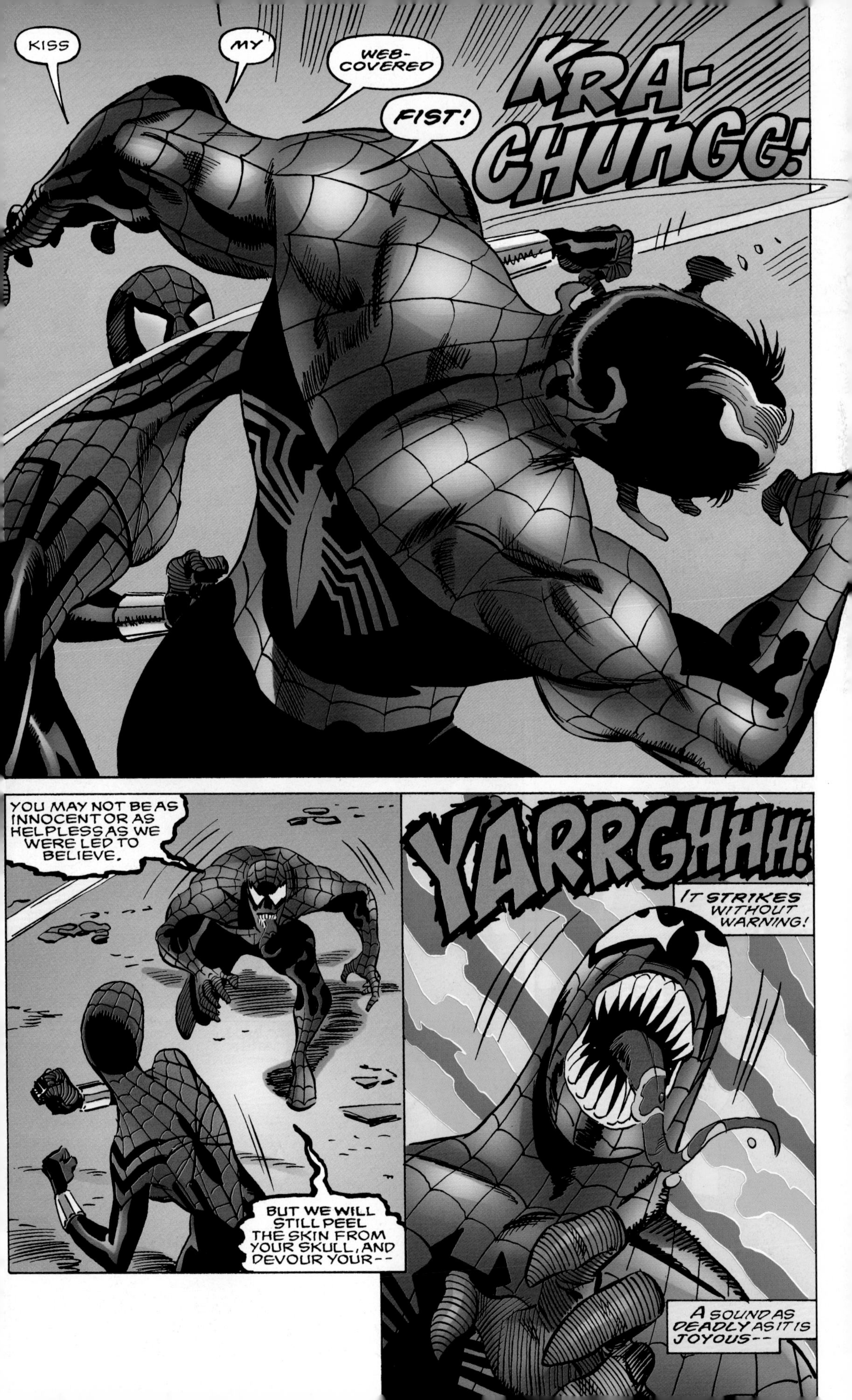
KISS
MY
WEB-COVERED
FIST!
KRA-CHUNGG!
YOU MAY NOT BE AS INNOCENT OR AS HELPLESS AS WE WERE LED TO BELIEVE.
BUT WE WILL STILL PEEL THE SKIN FROM YOUR SKULL, AND DEVOUR YOUR--
YARRGHHH!
IT STRIKES WITHOUT WARNING!
A SOUND AS DEADLY AS IT IS JOYOUS--

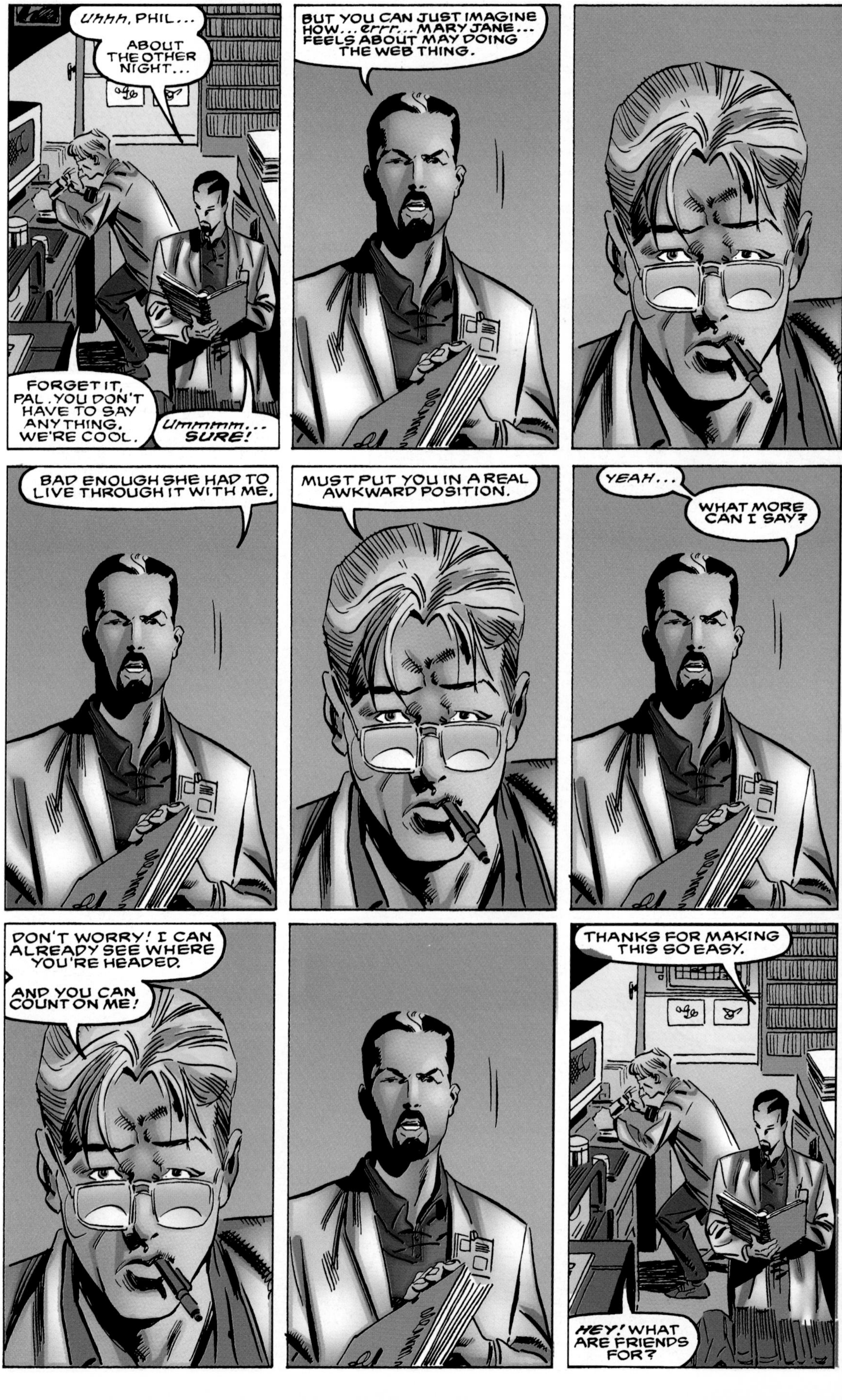

UHHH, PHIL...
ABOUT THE OTHER NIGHT...
FORGET IT, PAL. YOU DON'T HAVE TO SAY ANYTHING. WE'RE COOL.
UMMMM... SURE!
BUT YOU CAN JUST IMAGINE HOW... ERRR... MARY JANE... FEELS ABOUT MAY DOING THE WEB THING.
BAD ENOUGH SHE HAD TO LIVE THROUGH IT WITH ME.
MUST PUT YOU IN A REAL AWKWARD POSITION.
YEAH...
WHAT MORE CAN I SAY?
DON'T WORRY! I CAN ALREADY SEE WHERE YOU'RE HEADED.
AND YOU CAN COUNT ON ME!
THANKS FOR MAKING THIS SO EASY.
HEY! WHAT ARE FRIENDS FOR?

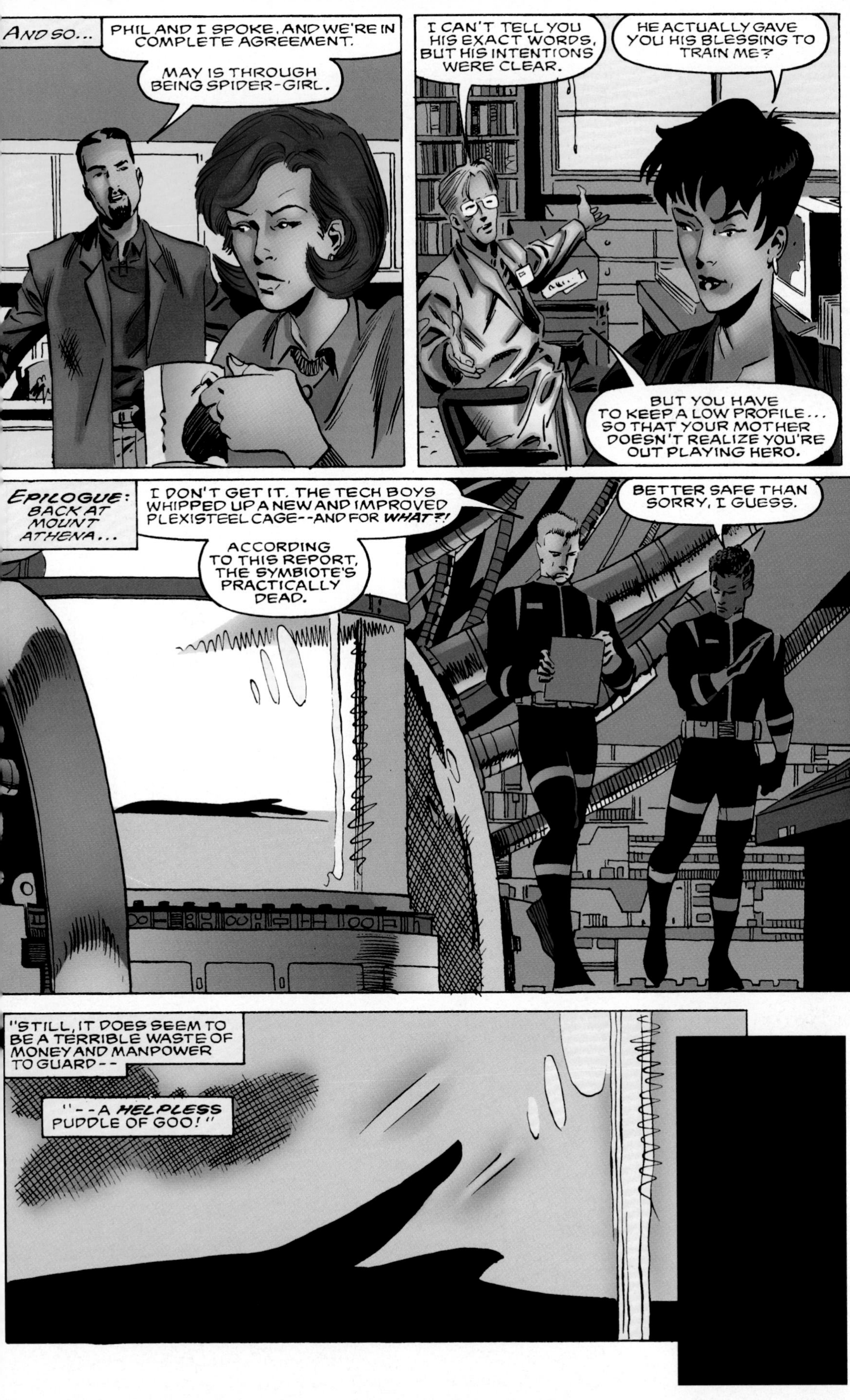

AND SO...
PHIL AND I SPOKE, AND WE'RE IN COMPLETE AGREEMENT.
MAY IS THROUGH BEING SPIDER-GIRL.
I CAN'T TELL YOU HIS EXACT WORDS, BUT HIS INTENTIONS WERE CLEAR.
HE ACTUALLY GAVE YOU HIS BLESSING TO TRAIN ME?
BUT YOU HAVE TO KEEP A LOW PROFILE... SO THAT YOUR MOTHER DOESN'T REALIZE YOU'RE OUT PLAYING HERO.
EPILOGUE: BACK AT MOUNT ATHENA...
I DON'T GET IT. THE TECH BOYS WHIPPED UP A NEW AND IMPROVED PLEXISTEEL CAGE--AND FOR WHAT?!
ACCORDING TO THIS REPORT, THE SYMBIOTE'S PRACTICALLY DEAD.
BETTER SAFE THAN SORRY, I GUESS.
"STILL, IT DOES SEEM TO BE A TERRIBLE WASTE OF MONEY AND MANPOWER TO GUARD--
"--A HELPLESS PUDDLE OF GOO!"

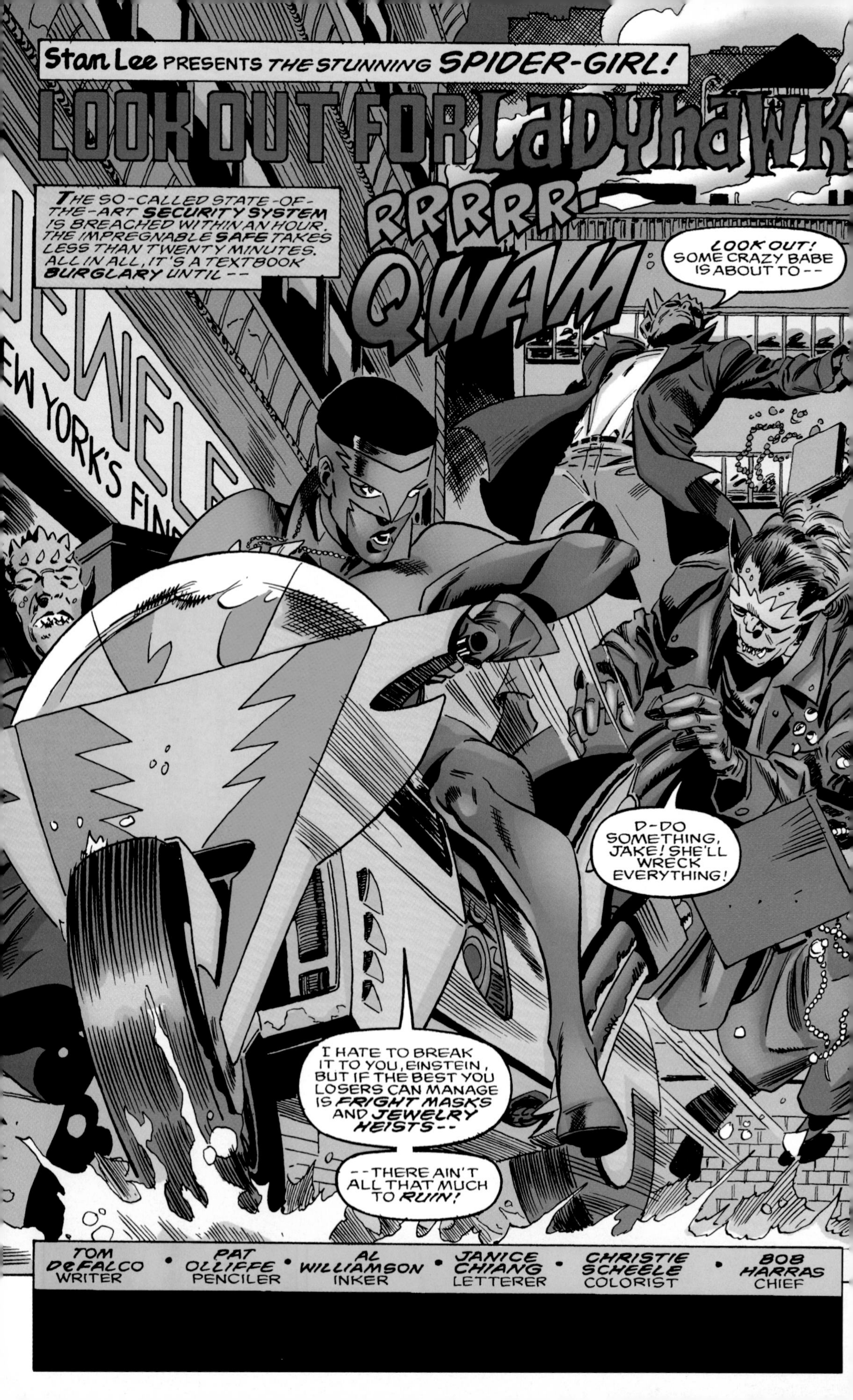

Stan Lee PRESENTS THE STUNNING SPIDER-GIRL!
LOOK OUT FOR LADYHAWK
THE SO-CALLED STATE-OF-THE-ART SECURITY SYSTEM IS BREACHED WITHIN AN HOUR. THE IMPREGNABLE SAFE TAKES LESS THAN TWENTY MINUTES. ALL IN ALL, IT'S A TEXTBOOK BURGLARY UNTIL--
RRRRR-QWAM
LOOK OUT! SOME CRAZY BABE IS ABOUT TO--
JEWEL
NEW YORK'S FIN
D-DO SOMETHING, JAKE! SHE'LL WRECK EVERYTHING!
I HATE TO BREAK IT TO YOU, EINSTEIN, BUT IF THE BEST YOU LOSERS CAN MANAGE IS FRIGHT MASKS AND JEWELRY HEISTS--
--THERE AIN'T ALL THAT MUCH TO RUIN!
TOM DEFALCO WRITER • PAT OLLIFFE PENCILER • AL WILLIAMSON INKER • JANICE CHIANG LETTERER • CHRISTIE SCHEELE COLORIST • BOB HARRAS CHIEF

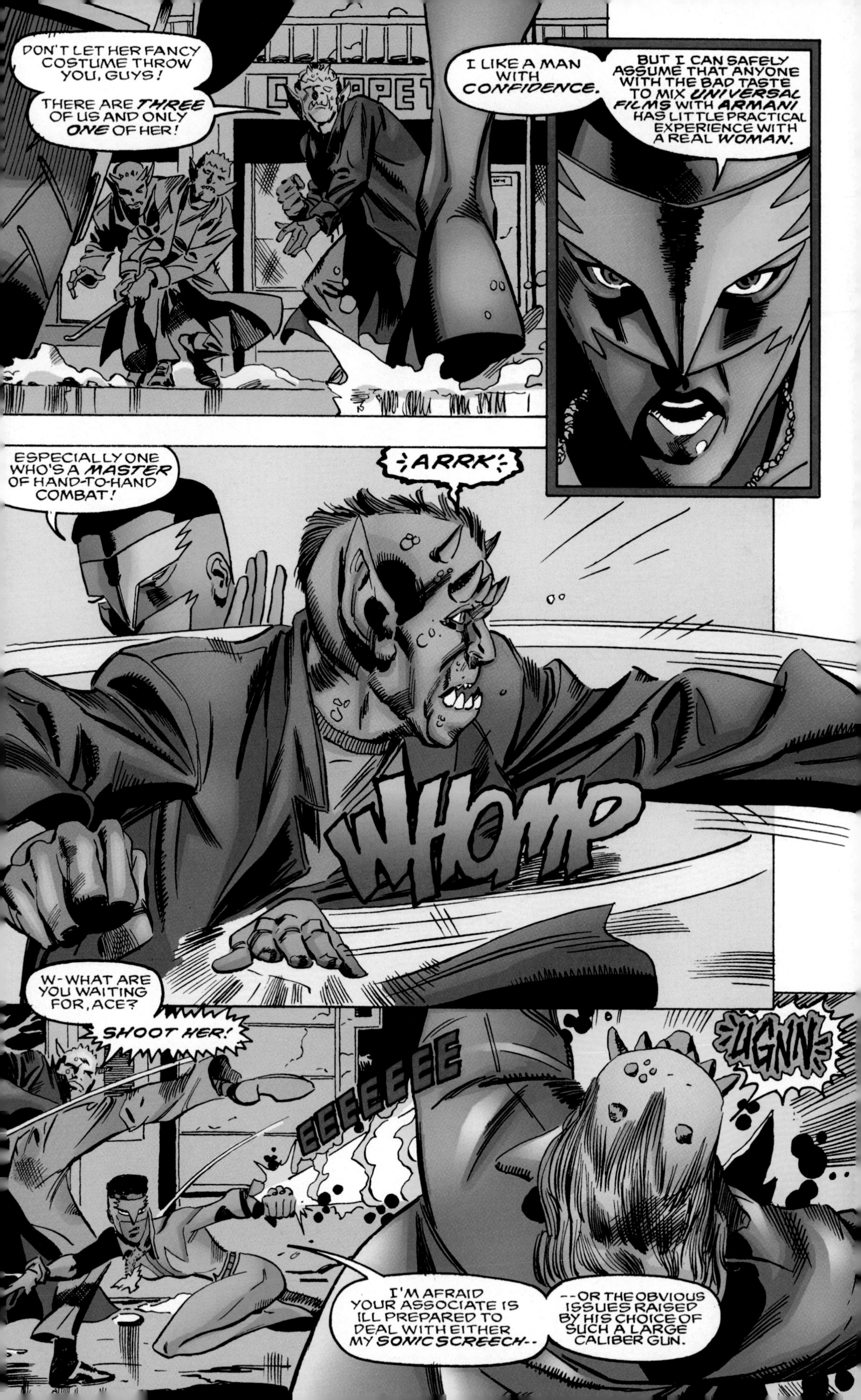

DON'T LET HER FANCY COSTUME THROW YOU, GUYS!
THERE ARE THREE OF US AND ONLY ONE OF HER!
I LIKE A MAN WITH CONFIDENCE.
BUT I CAN SAFELY ASSUME THAT ANYONE WITH THE BAD TASTE TO MIX UNIVERSAL FILMS WITH ARMANI HAS LITTLE PRACTICAL EXPERIENCE WITH A REAL WOMAN.
ESPECIALLY ONE WHO'S A MASTER OF HAND-TO-HAND COMBAT!
ARRK
WHOMP
W-WHAT ARE YOU WAITING FOR, ACE?
SHOOT HER!
EEEEEEEE
UGNN
I'M AFRAID YOUR ASSOCIATE IS ILL PREPARED TO DEAL WITH EITHER MY SONIC SCREECH--
--OR THE OBVIOUS ISSUES RAISED BY HIS CHOICE OF SUCH A LARGE CALIBER GUN.

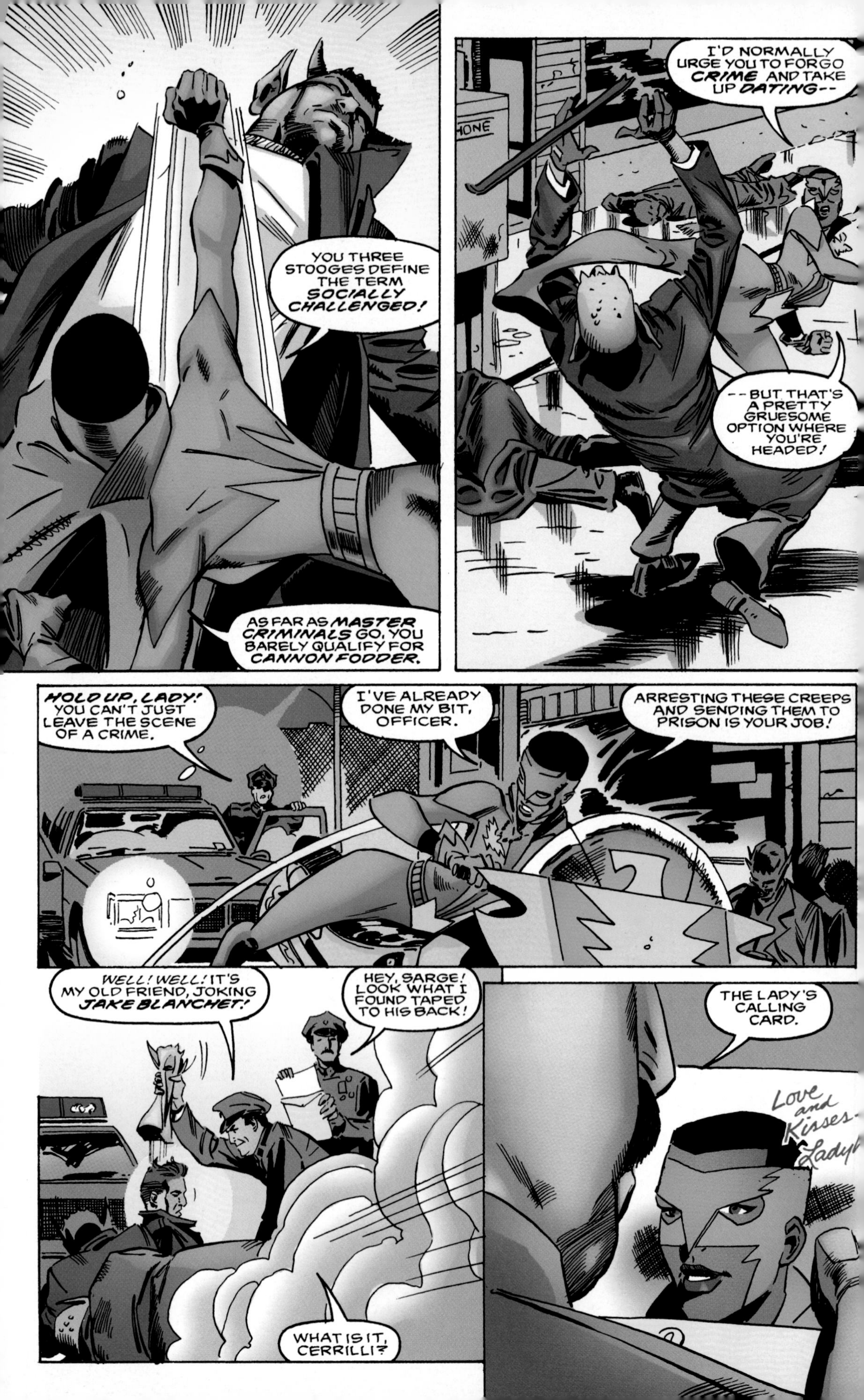
YOU THREE STOOGES DEFINE THE TERM SOCIALLY CHALLENGED!
AS FAR AS MASTER CRIMINALS GO, YOU BARELY QUALIFY FOR CANNON FODDER.
I'D NORMALLY URGE YOU TO FORGO CRIME AND TAKE UP DATING--
--BUT THAT'S A PRETTY GRUESOME OPTION WHERE YOU'RE HEADED!
HOLD UP, LADY! YOU CAN'T JUST LEAVE THE SCENE OF A CRIME.
I'VE ALREADY DONE MY BIT, OFFICER.
ARRESTING THESE CREEPS AND SENDING THEM TO PRISON IS YOUR JOB!
WELL! WELL! IT'S MY OLD FRIEND, JOKING JAKE BLANCHET!
HEY, SARGE! LOOK WHAT I FOUND TAPED TO HIS BACK!
WHAT IS IT, CERRILLI?
THE LADY'S CALLING CARD.
Love and Kisses. Lady

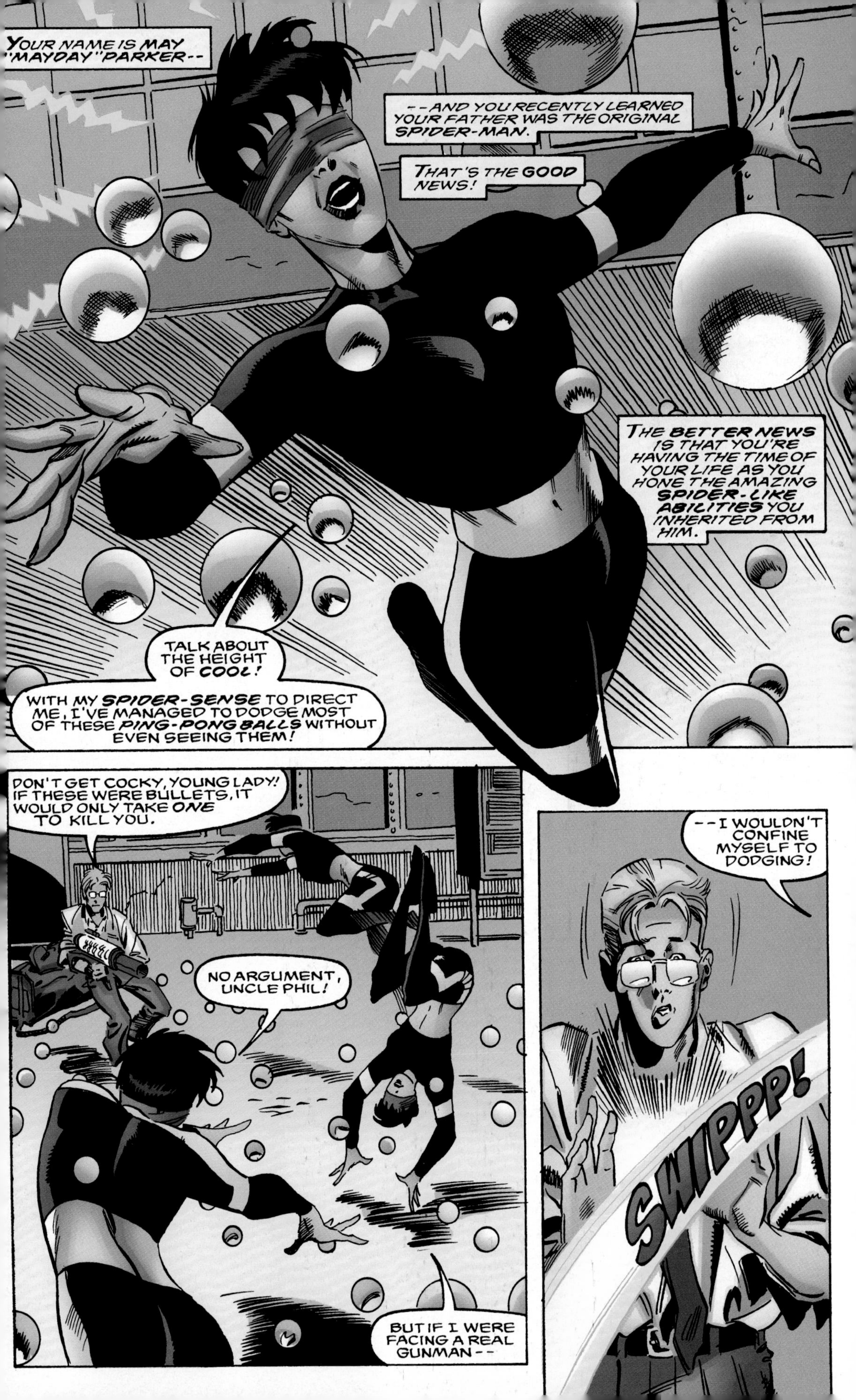
YOUR NAME IS MAY "MAYDAY" PARKER--
--AND YOU RECENTLY LEARNED YOUR FATHER WAS THE ORIGINAL SPIDER-MAN.
THAT'S THE GOOD NEWS!
THE BETTER NEWS IS THAT YOU'RE HAVING THE TIME OF YOUR LIFE AS YOU HONE THE AMAZING SPIDER-LIKE ABILITIES YOU INHERITED FROM HIM.
TALK ABOUT THE HEIGHT OF COOL!
WITH MY SPIDER-SENSE TO DIRECT ME, I'VE MANAGED TO DODGE MOST OF THESE PING-PONG BALLS WITHOUT EVEN SEEING THEM!
DON'T GET COCKY, YOUNG LADY! IF THESE WERE BULLETS, IT WOULD ONLY TAKE ONE TO KILL YOU.
NO ARGUMENT, UNCLE PHIL!
BUT IF I WERE FACING A REAL GUNMAN--
--I WOULDN'T CONFINE MYSELF TO DODGING!
SWIPPP!

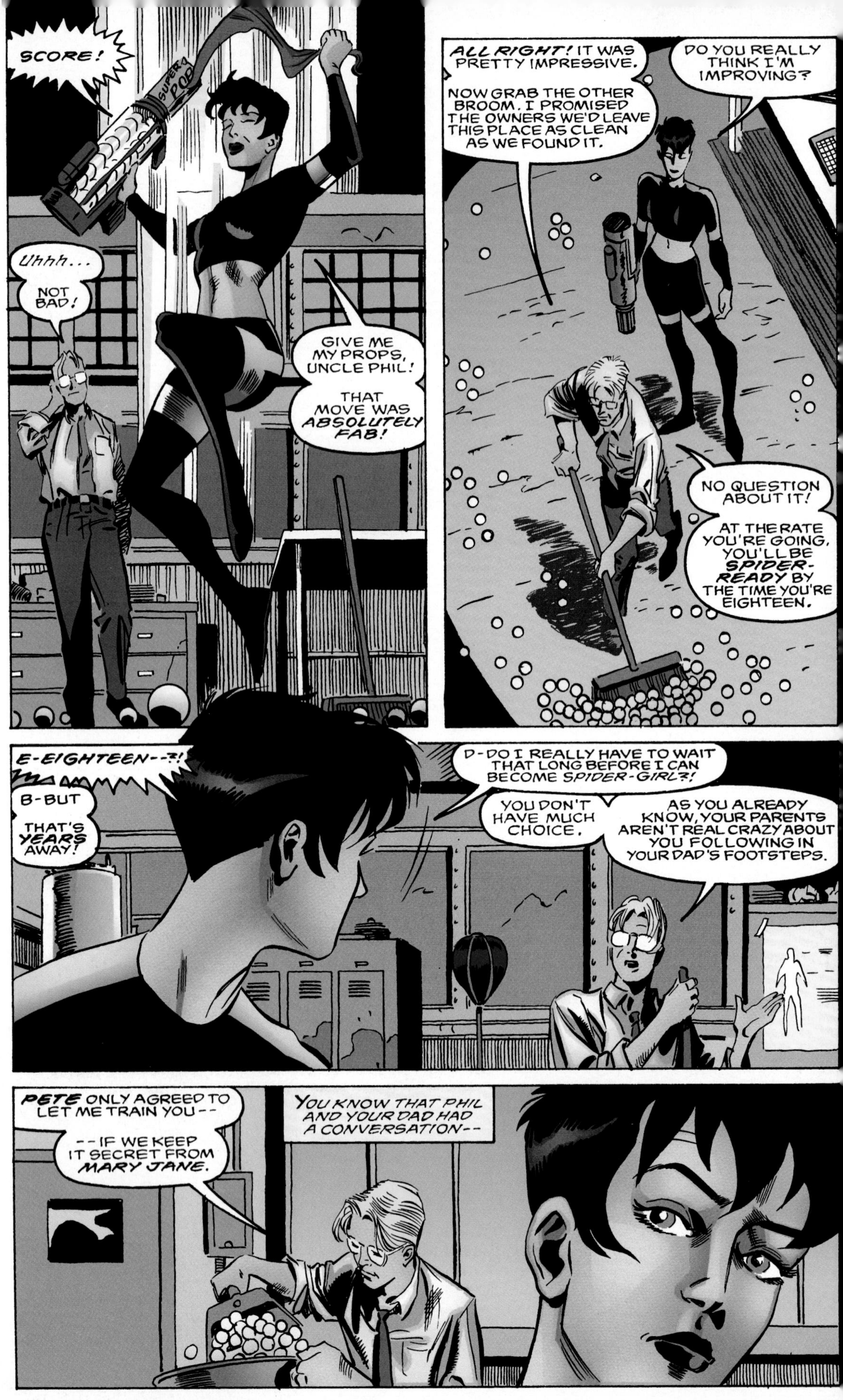
SCORE!
SUPER POP
Uhhh...
NOT BAD!
GIVE ME MY PROPS, UNCLE PHIL!
THAT MOVE WAS ABSOLUTELY FAB!
ALL RIGHT! IT WAS PRETTY IMPRESSIVE.
NOW GRAB THE OTHER BROOM. I PROMISED THE OWNERS WE'D LEAVE THIS PLACE AS CLEAN AS WE FOUND IT.
DO YOU REALLY THINK I'M IMPROVING?
NO QUESTION ABOUT IT!
AT THE RATE YOU'RE GOING, YOU'LL BE SPIDER-READY BY THE TIME YOU'RE EIGHTEEN.
E-EIGHTEEN--?!
B-BUT
THAT'S YEARS AWAY!
D-DO I REALLY HAVE TO WAIT THAT LONG BEFORE I CAN BECOME SPIDER-GIRL?!
YOU DON'T HAVE MUCH CHOICE.
AS YOU ALREADY KNOW, YOUR PARENTS AREN'T REAL CRAZY ABOUT YOU FOLLOWING IN YOUR DAD'S FOOTSTEPS.
PETE ONLY AGREED TO LET ME TRAIN YOU--
--IF WE KEEP IT SECRET FROM MARY JANE.
YOU KNOW THAT PHIL AND YOUR DAD HAD A CONVERSATION--

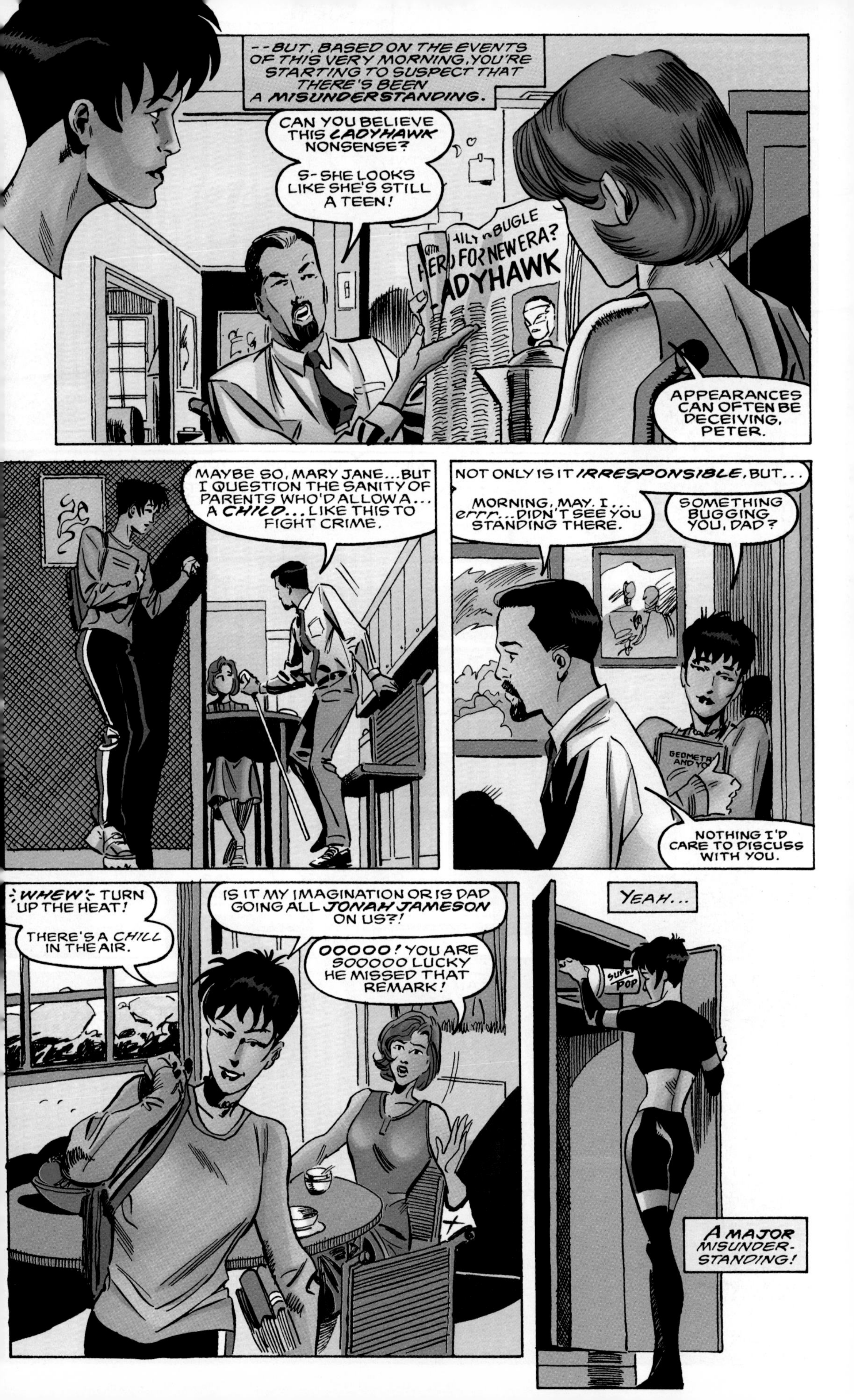
--BUT, BASED ON THE EVENTS OF THIS VERY MORNING, YOU'RE STARTING TO SUSPECT THAT THERE'S BEEN A MISUNDERSTANDING.
CAN YOU BELIEVE THIS LADYHAWK NONSENSE?
S-SHE LOOKS LIKE SHE'S STILL A TEEN!
HERO FOR NEW ERA? LADYHAWK
APPEARANCES CAN OFTEN BE DECEIVING, PETER.
MAYBE SO, MARY JANE... BUT I QUESTION THE SANITY OF PARENTS WHO'D ALLOW A... A CHILD... LIKE THIS TO FIGHT CRIME.
NOT ONLY IS IT IRRESPONSIBLE, BUT...
MORNING, MAY. I... errr... DIDN'T SEE YOU STANDING THERE.
SOMETHING BUGGING YOU, DAD?
GEOMETRY AND YOU
NOTHING I'D CARE TO DISCUSS WITH YOU.
WHEW-- TURN UP THE HEAT!
THERE'S A CHILL IN THE AIR.
IS IT MY IMAGINATION OR IS DAD GOING ALL JONAH JAMESON ON US?!
OOOOO! YOU ARE SOOOOO LUCKY HE MISSED THAT REMARK!
YEAH...
SUPER POP
A MAJOR MISUNDER-STANDING!

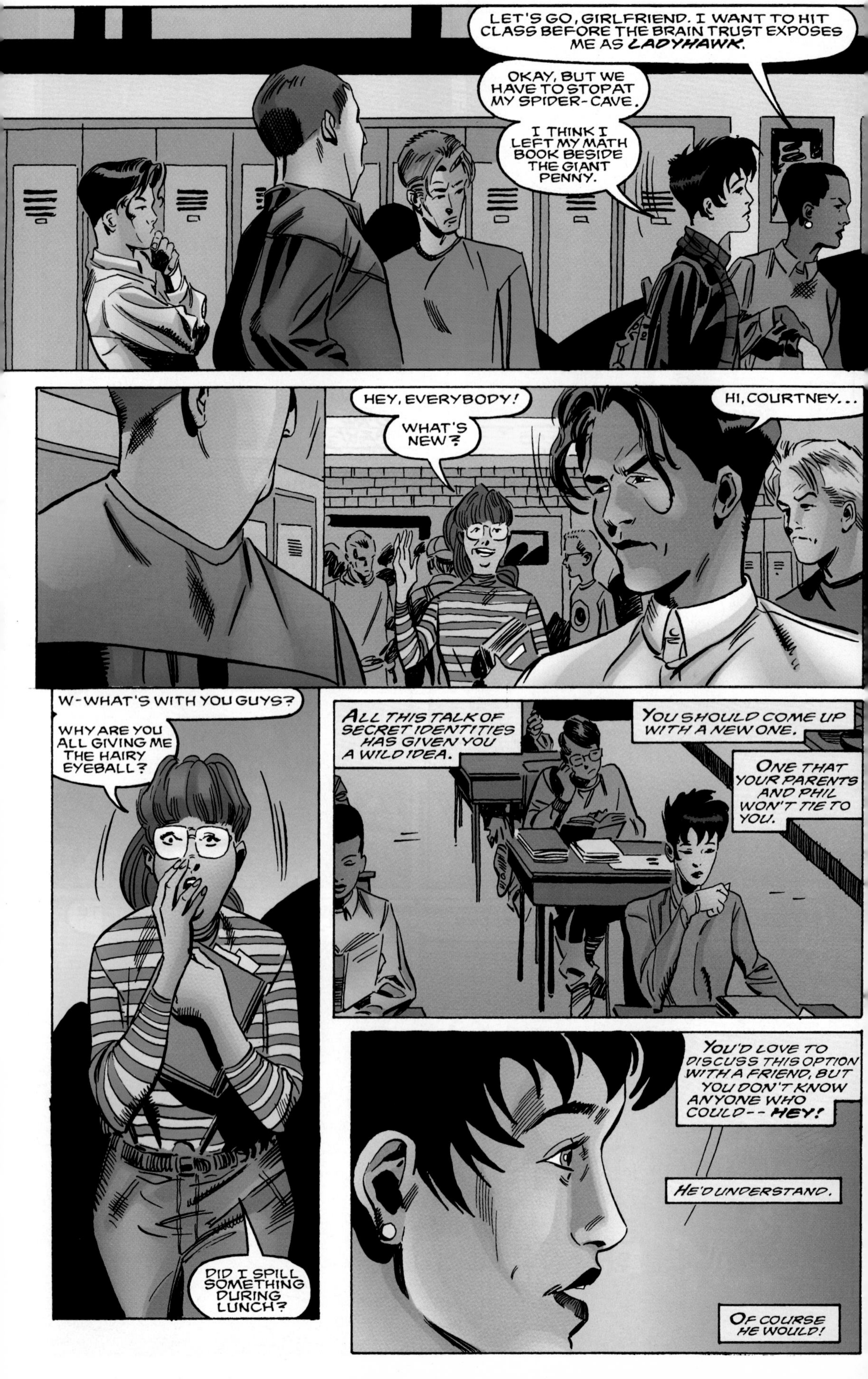

LET'S GO, GIRLFRIEND. I WANT TO HIT CLASS BEFORE THE BRAIN TRUST EXPOSES ME AS LADYHAWK.
OKAY, BUT WE HAVE TO STOP AT MY SPIDER-CAVE.
I THINK I LEFT MY MATH BOOK BESIDE THE GIANT PENNY.
HEY, EVERYBODY!
WHAT'S NEW?
HI, COURTNEY...
W-WHAT'S WITH YOU GUYS?
WHY ARE YOU ALL GIVING ME THE HAIRY EYEBALL?
DID I SPILL SOMETHING DURING LUNCH?
ALL THIS TALK OF SECRET IDENTITIES HAS GIVEN YOU A WILD IDEA.
YOU SHOULD COME UP WITH A NEW ONE.
ONE THAT YOUR PARENTS AND PHIL WON'T TIE TO YOU.
YOU'D LOVE TO DISCUSS THIS OPTION WITH A FRIEND, BUT YOU DON'T KNOW ANYONE WHO COULD-- HEY!
HE'D UNDERSTAND.
OF COURSE HE WOULD!

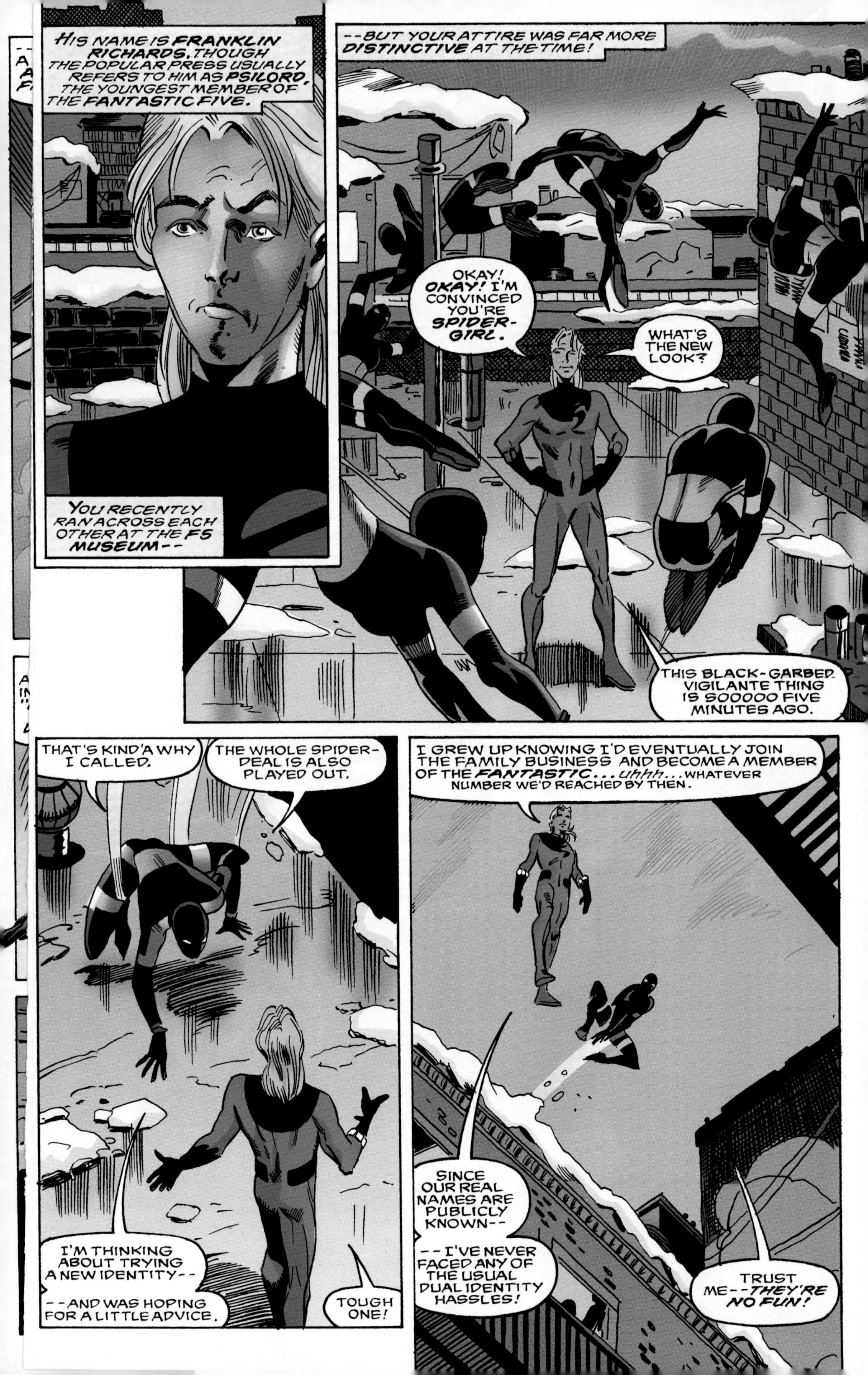
HIS NAME IS FRANKLIN RICHARDS, THOUGH THE POPULAR PRESS USUALLY REFERS TO HIM AS PSILORD, THE YOUNGEST MEMBER OF THE FANTASTIC FIVE.
YOU RECENTLY RAN ACROSS EACH OTHER AT THE F5 MUSEUM--
--BUT YOUR ATTIRE WAS FAR MORE DISTINCTIVE AT THE TIME!
OKAY! OKAY! I'M CONVINCED YOU'RE SPIDER-GIRL.
WHAT'S THE NEW LOOK?
THIS BLACK-GARBED VIGILANTE THING IS SOOOOO FIVE MINUTES AGO.
THAT'S KIND'A WHY I CALLED.
THE WHOLE SPIDER-DEAL IS ALSO PLAYED OUT.
I'M THINKING ABOUT TRYING A NEW IDENTITY--
--AND WAS HOPING FOR A LITTLE ADVICE.
TOUGH ONE!
I GREW UP KNOWING I'D EVENTUALLY JOIN THE FAMILY BUSINESS AND BECOME A MEMBER OF THE FANTASTIC... uhhh... WHATEVER NUMBER WE'D REACHED BY THEN.
SINCE OUR REAL NAMES ARE PUBLICLY KNOWN--
--I'VE NEVER FACED ANY OF THE USUAL DUAL IDENTITY HASSLES!
TRUST ME--THEY'RE NO FUN!

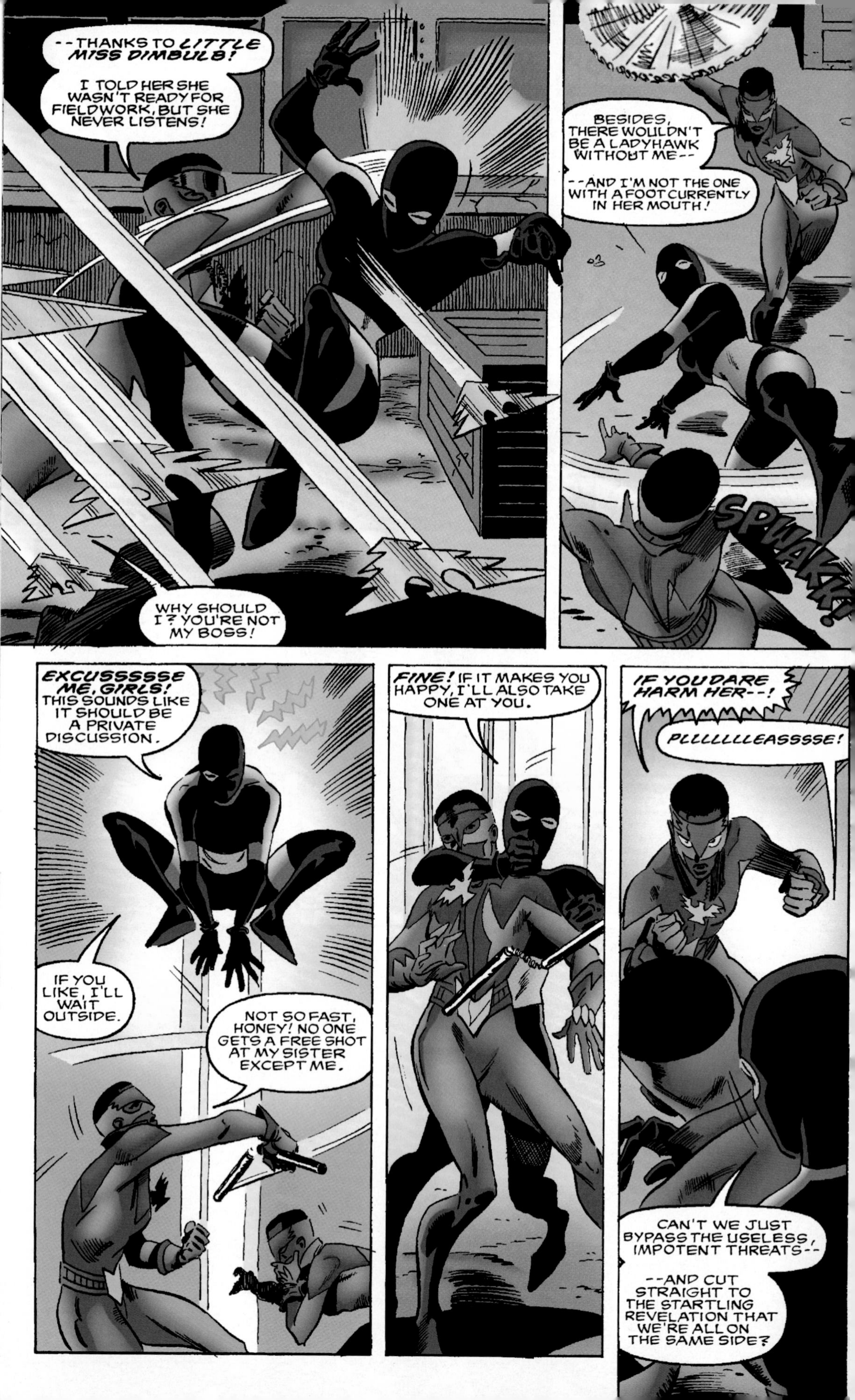
--THANKS TO LITTLE MISS DIMBULB!
I TOLD HER SHE WASN'T READY FOR FIELDWORK, BUT SHE NEVER LISTENS!
WHY SHOULD I? YOU'RE NOT MY BOSS!
BESIDES, THERE WOULDN'T BE A LADYHAWK WITHOUT ME--
--AND I'M NOT THE ONE WITH A FOOT CURRENTLY IN HER MOUTH!
SPWAKK!
EXCUSSSSSE ME, GIRLS! THIS SOUNDS LIKE IT SHOULD BE A PRIVATE DISCUSSION.
IF YOU LIKE, I'LL WAIT OUTSIDE.
NOT SO FAST, HONEY! NO ONE GETS A FREE SHOT AT MY SISTER EXCEPT ME.
FINE! IF IT MAKES YOU HAPPY, I'LL ALSO TAKE ONE AT YOU.
IF YOU DARE HARM HER--!
MMMMMM
PLLLLLLLEASSSSE!
CAN'T WE JUST BYPASS THE USELESS, IMPOTENT THREATS--
--AND CUT STRAIGHT TO THE STARTLING REVELATION THAT WE'RE ALL ON THE SAME SIDE?

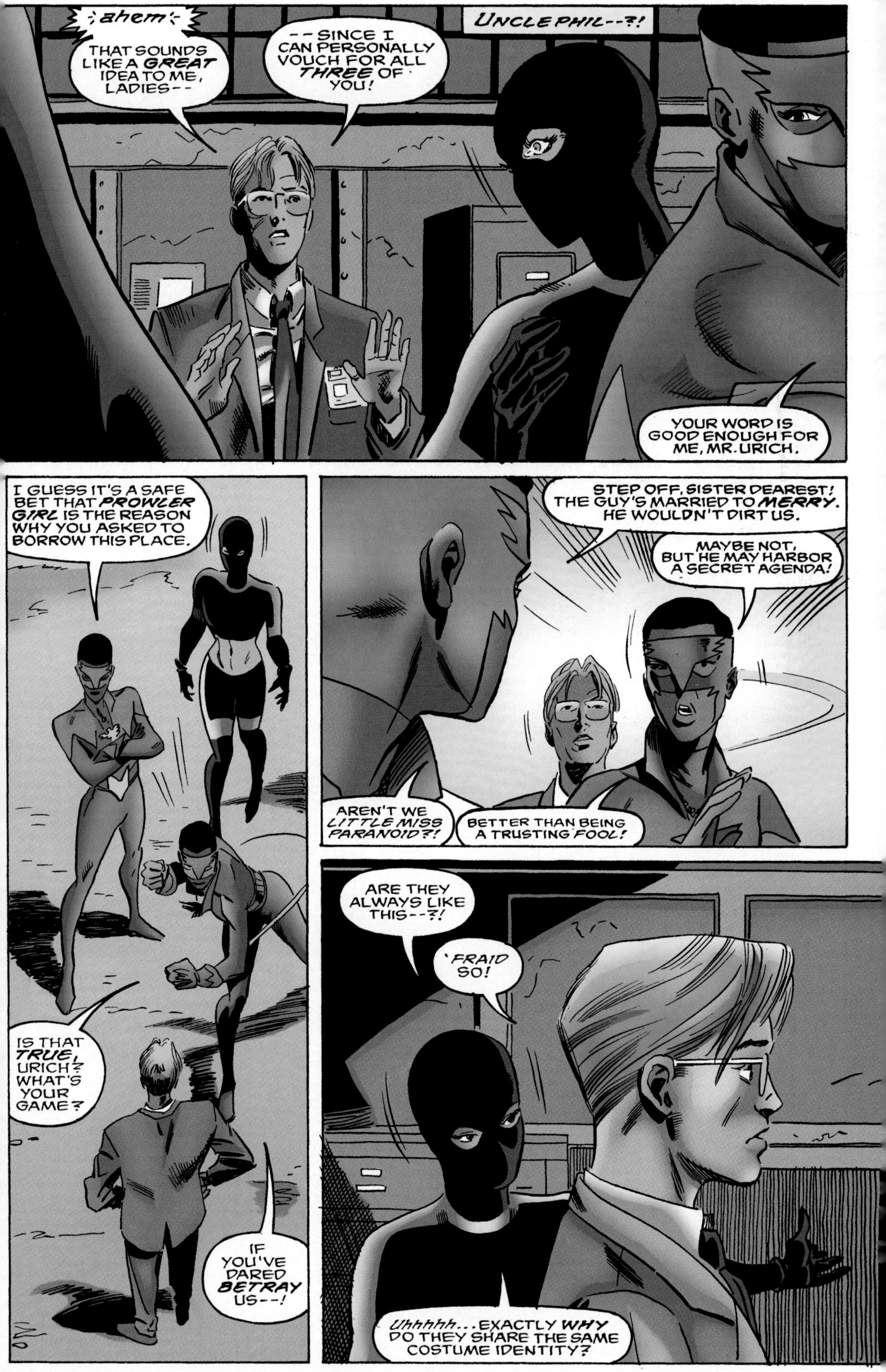

:ahem:
THAT SOUNDS LIKE A GREAT IDEA TO ME, LADIES--
--SINCE I CAN PERSONALLY VOUCH FOR ALL THREE OF YOU!
UNCLE PHIL--?!
YOUR WORD IS GOOD ENOUGH FOR ME, MR. URICH.
I GUESS IT'S A SAFE BET THAT PROWLER GIRL IS THE REASON WHY YOU ASKED TO BORROW THIS PLACE.
IS THAT TRUE, URICH? WHAT'S YOUR GAME?
IF YOU'VE DARED BETRAY US--!
STEP OFF, SISTER DEAREST! THE GUY'S MARRIED TO MERRY. HE WOULDN'T DIRT US.
MAYBE NOT, BUT HE MAY HARBOR A SECRET AGENDA!
AREN'T WE LITTLE MISS PARANOID?!
BETTER THAN BEING A TRUSTING FOOL!
ARE THEY ALWAYS LIKE THIS--?!
'FRAID SO!
Uhhhhh...EXACTLY WHY DO THEY SHARE THE SAME COSTUME IDENTITY?

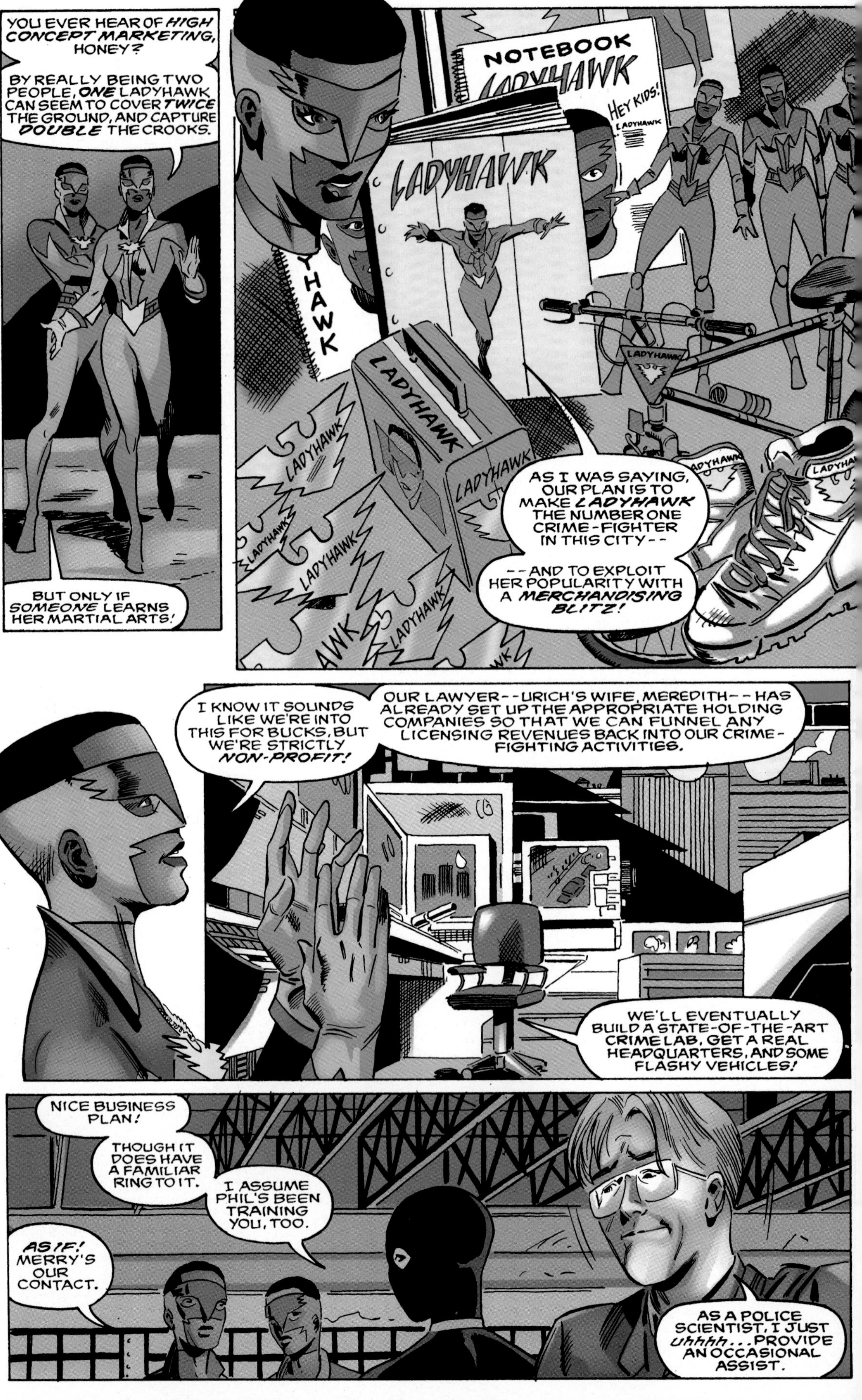
YOU EVER HEAR OF HIGH CONCEPT MARKETING, HONEY?
BY REALLY BEING TWO PEOPLE, ONE LADYHAWK CAN SEEM TO COVER TWICE THE GROUND, AND CAPTURE DOUBLE THE CROOKS.
BUT ONLY IF SOMEONE LEARNS HER MARTIAL ARTS!
NOTEBOOK LADYHAWK
HEY KIDS! LADYHAWK
LADYHAWK
LADYHAWK
AS I WAS SAYING, OUR PLAN IS TO MAKE LADYHAWK THE NUMBER ONE CRIME-FIGHTER IN THIS CITY--
--AND TO EXPLOIT HER POPULARITY WITH A MERCHANDISING BLITZ!
I KNOW IT SOUNDS LIKE WE'RE INTO THIS FOR BUCKS, BUT WE'RE STRICTLY NON-PROFIT!
OUR LAWYER--URICH'S WIFE, MEREDITH--HAS ALREADY SET UP THE APPROPRIATE HOLDING COMPANIES SO THAT WE CAN FUNNEL ANY LICENSING REVENUES BACK INTO OUR CRIME-FIGHTING ACTIVITIES.
WE'LL EVENTUALLY BUILD A STATE-OF-THE-ART CRIME LAB, GET A REAL HEADQUARTERS, AND SOME FLASHY VEHICLES!
NICE BUSINESS PLAN!
THOUGH IT DOES HAVE A FAMILIAR RING TO IT.
I ASSUME PHIL'S BEEN TRAINING YOU, TOO.
AS IF! MERRY'S OUR CONTACT.
AS A POLICE SCIENTIST, I JUST uhhhh... PROVIDE AN OCCASIONAL ASSIST.

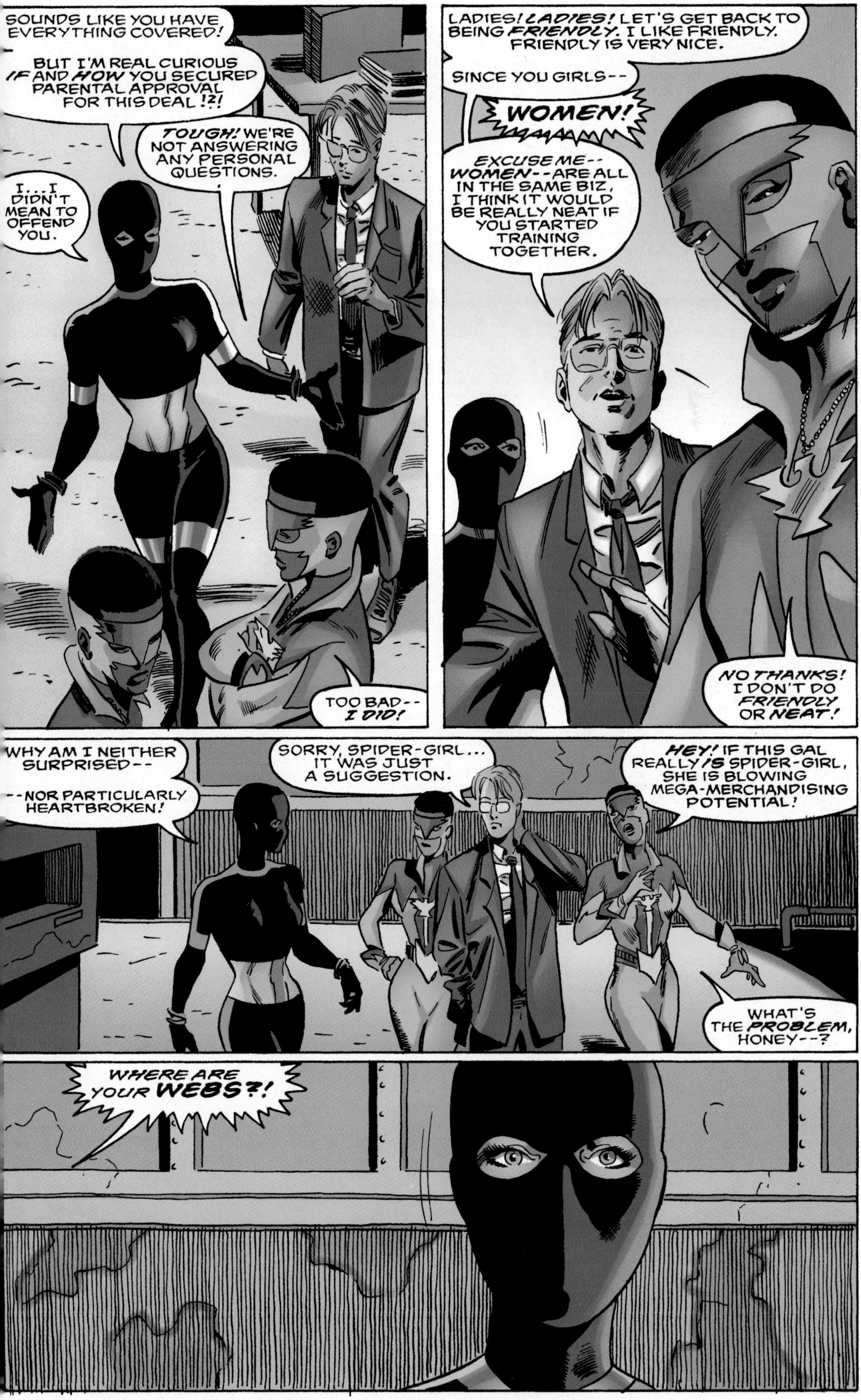
SOUNDS LIKE YOU HAVE EVERYTHING COVERED!
BUT I'M REAL CURIOUS IF AND HOW YOU SECURED PARENTAL APPROVAL FOR THIS DEAL !?!
TOUGH! WE'RE NOT ANSWERING ANY PERSONAL QUESTIONS.
I... I DIDN'T MEAN TO OFFEND YOU.
TOO BAD-- I DID!
LADIES! LADIES! LET'S GET BACK TO BEING FRIENDLY. I LIKE FRIENDLY. FRIENDLY IS VERY NICE.
SINCE YOU GIRLS--
WOMEN!
EXCUSE ME-- WOMEN--ARE ALL IN THE SAME BIZ, I THINK IT WOULD BE REALLY NEAT IF YOU STARTED TRAINING TOGETHER.
NO THANKS! I DON'T DO FRIENDLY OR NEAT!
WHY AM I NEITHER SURPRISED--
--NOR PARTICULARLY HEARTBROKEN!
SORRY, SPIDER-GIRL... IT WAS JUST A SUGGESTION.
HEY! IF THIS GAL REALLY IS SPIDER-GIRL, SHE IS BLOWING MEGA-MERCHANDISING POTENTIAL!
WHAT'S THE PROBLEM, HONEY--?
WHERE ARE YOUR WEBS?!

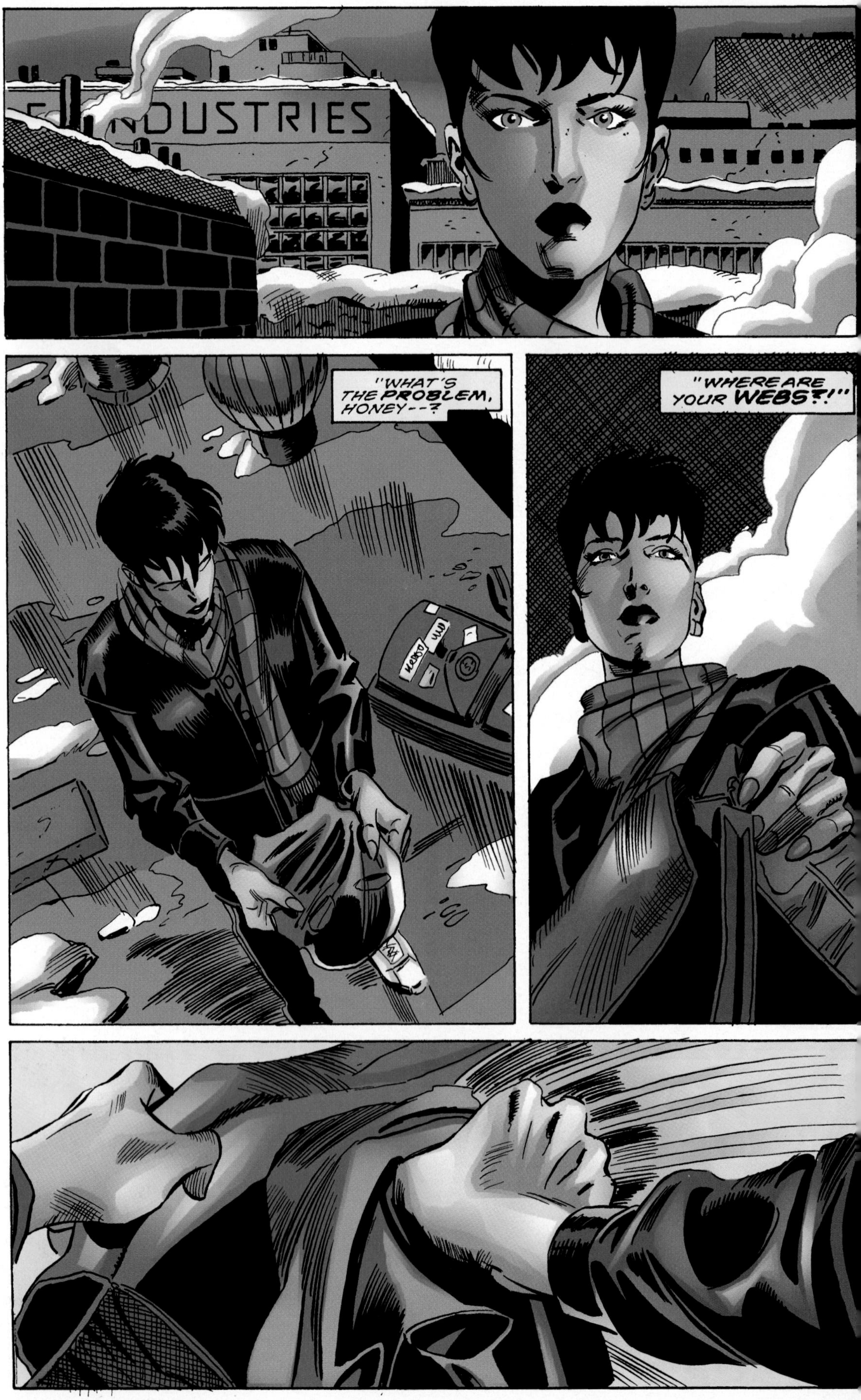
INDUSTRIES
"WHAT'S THE PROBLEM, HONEY--?
"WHERE ARE YOUR WEBS?!"

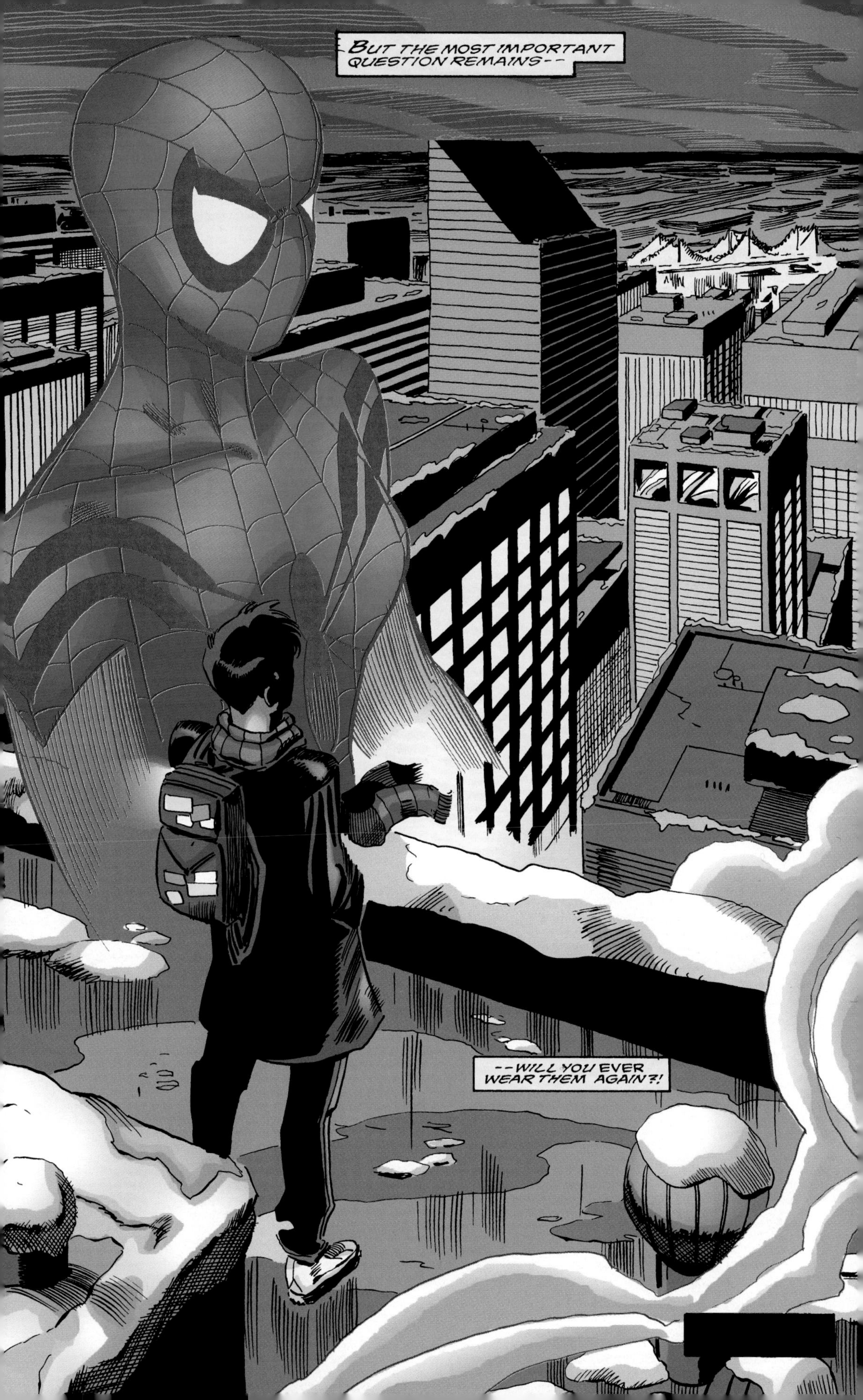
BUT THE MOST IMPORTANT QUESTION REMAINS--
--WILL YOU EVER WEAR THEM AGAIN?!
[redacted]

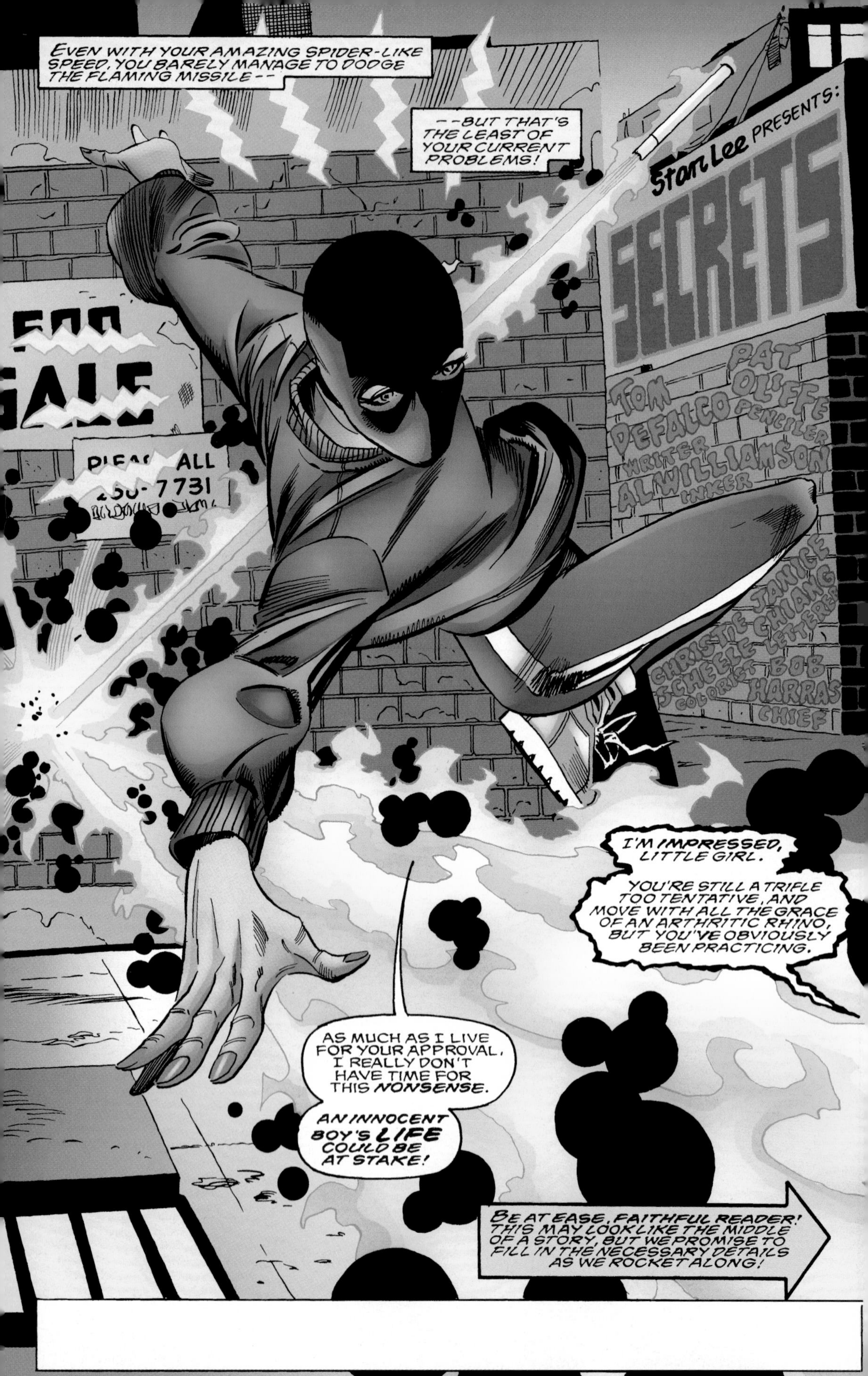
EVEN WITH YOUR AMAZING SPIDER-LIKE SPEED, YOU BARELY MANAGE TO DODGE THE FLAMING MISSILE--
--BUT THAT'S THE LEAST OF YOUR CURRENT PROBLEMS!
Stan Lee PRESENTS: SECRETS
TOM DEFALCO WRITER
PAT OLIFFE PENCILER
AL WILLIAMSON INKER
CHRISTIE J. SCHEELE COLORIST
JANICE CHIANG LETTERER
BOB HARRAS CHIEF
FOR SALE
250-7731
I'M IMPRESSED, LITTLE GIRL.
YOU'RE STILL A TRIFLE TOO TENTATIVE, AND MOVE WITH ALL THE GRACE OF AN ARTHRITIC RHINO, BUT YOU'VE OBVIOUSLY BEEN PRACTICING.
AS MUCH AS I LIVE FOR YOUR APPROVAL, I REALLY DON'T HAVE TIME FOR THIS NONSENSE.
AN INNOCENT BOY'S LIFE COULD BE AT STAKE!
BE AT EASE, FAITHFUL READER! THIS MAY LOOK LIKE THE MIDDLE OF A STORY, BUT WE PROMISE TO FILL IN THE NECESSARY DETAILS AS WE ROCKET ALONG!

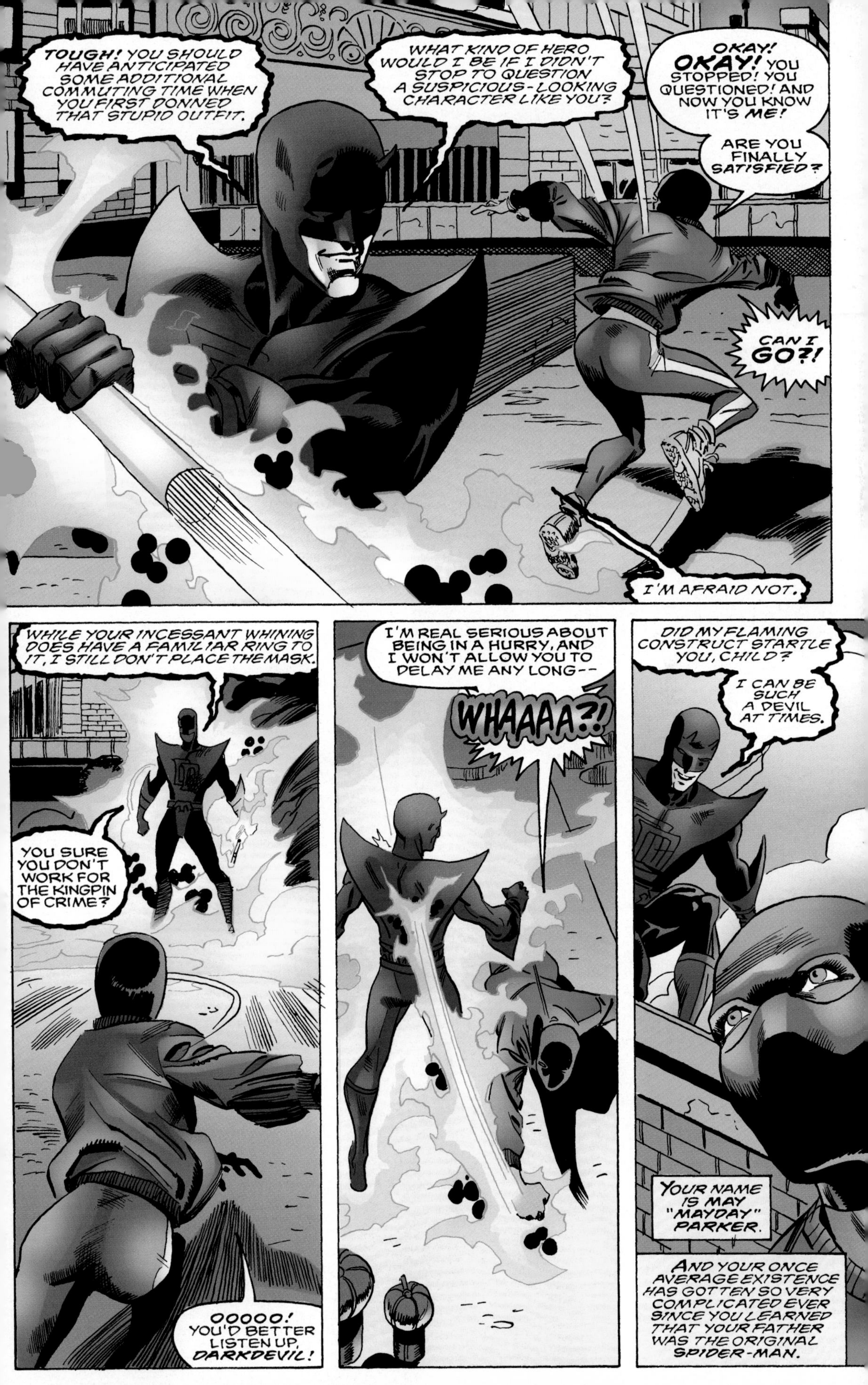

TOUGH! YOU SHOULD HAVE ANTICIPATED SOME ADDITIONAL COMMUTING TIME WHEN YOU FIRST DONNED THAT STUPID OUTFIT.
WHAT KIND OF HERO WOULD I BE IF I DIDN'T STOP TO QUESTION A SUSPICIOUS-LOOKING CHARACTER LIKE YOU?
OKAY! OKAY! YOU STOPPED! YOU QUESTIONED! AND NOW YOU KNOW IT'S ME!
ARE YOU FINALLY SATISFIED?
CAN I GO?!
I'M AFRAID NOT.
WHILE YOUR INCESSANT WHINING DOES HAVE A FAMILIAR RING TO IT, I STILL DON'T PLACE THE MASK.
YOU SURE YOU DON'T WORK FOR THE KINGPIN OF CRIME?
OOOOO! YOU'D BETTER LISTEN UP, DARKDEVIL!
I'M REAL SERIOUS ABOUT BEING IN A HURRY, AND I WON'T ALLOW YOU TO DELAY ME ANY LONG--
WHAAAA?!
DID MY FLAMING CONSTRUCT STARTLE YOU, CHILD?
I CAN BE SUCH A DEVIL AT TIMES.
YOUR NAME IS MAY "MAYDAY" PARKER.
AND YOUR ONCE AVERAGE EXISTENCE HAS GOTTEN SO VERY COMPLICATED EVER SINCE YOU LEARNED THAT YOUR FATHER WAS THE ORIGINAL SPIDER-MAN.

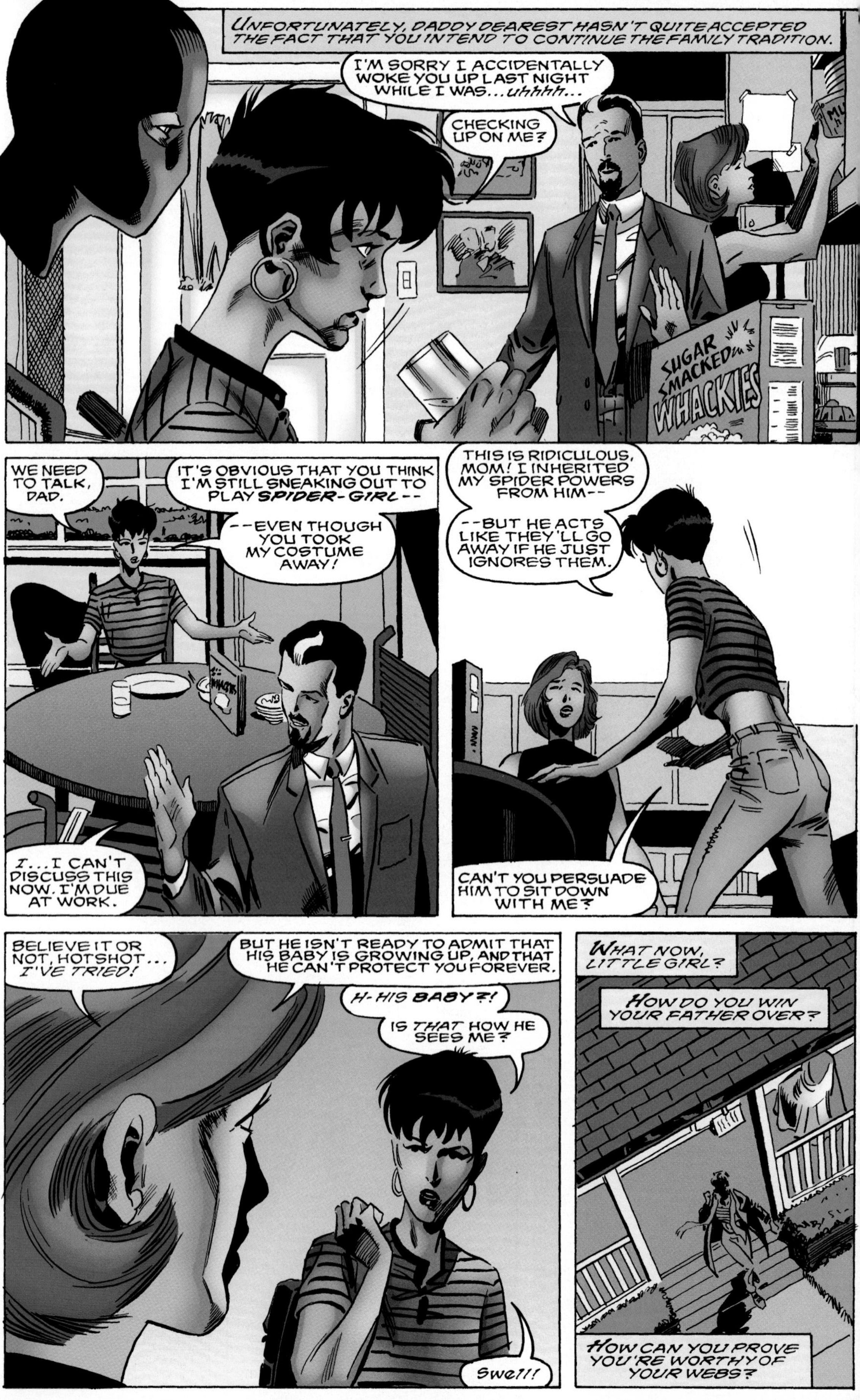
UNFORTUNATELY, DADDY DEAREST HASN'T QUITE ACCEPTED THE FACT THAT YOU INTEND TO CONTINUE THE FAMILY TRADITION.
I'M SORRY I ACCIDENTALLY WOKE YOU UP LAST NIGHT WHILE I WAS... uhhhh...
CHECKING UP ON ME?
SUGAR SMACKED WHACKIES
WE NEED TO TALK, DAD.
IT'S OBVIOUS THAT YOU THINK I'M STILL SNEAKING OUT TO PLAY SPIDER-GIRL--
--EVEN THOUGH YOU TOOK MY COSTUME AWAY!
I... I CAN'T DISCUSS THIS NOW. I'M DUE AT WORK.
THIS IS RIDICULOUS, MOM! I INHERITED MY SPIDER POWERS FROM HIM--
--BUT HE ACTS LIKE THEY'LL GO AWAY IF HE JUST IGNORES THEM.
CAN'T YOU PERSUADE HIM TO SIT DOWN WITH ME?
BELIEVE IT OR NOT, HOTSHOT... I'VE TRIED!
BUT HE ISN'T READY TO ADMIT THAT HIS BABY IS GROWING UP, AND THAT HE CAN'T PROTECT YOU FOREVER.
H-HIS BABY?!
IS THAT HOW HE SEES ME?
Swell!
WHAT NOW, LITTLE GIRL?
HOW DO YOU WIN YOUR FATHER OVER?
HOW CAN YOU PROVE YOU'RE WORTHY OF YOUR WEBS?

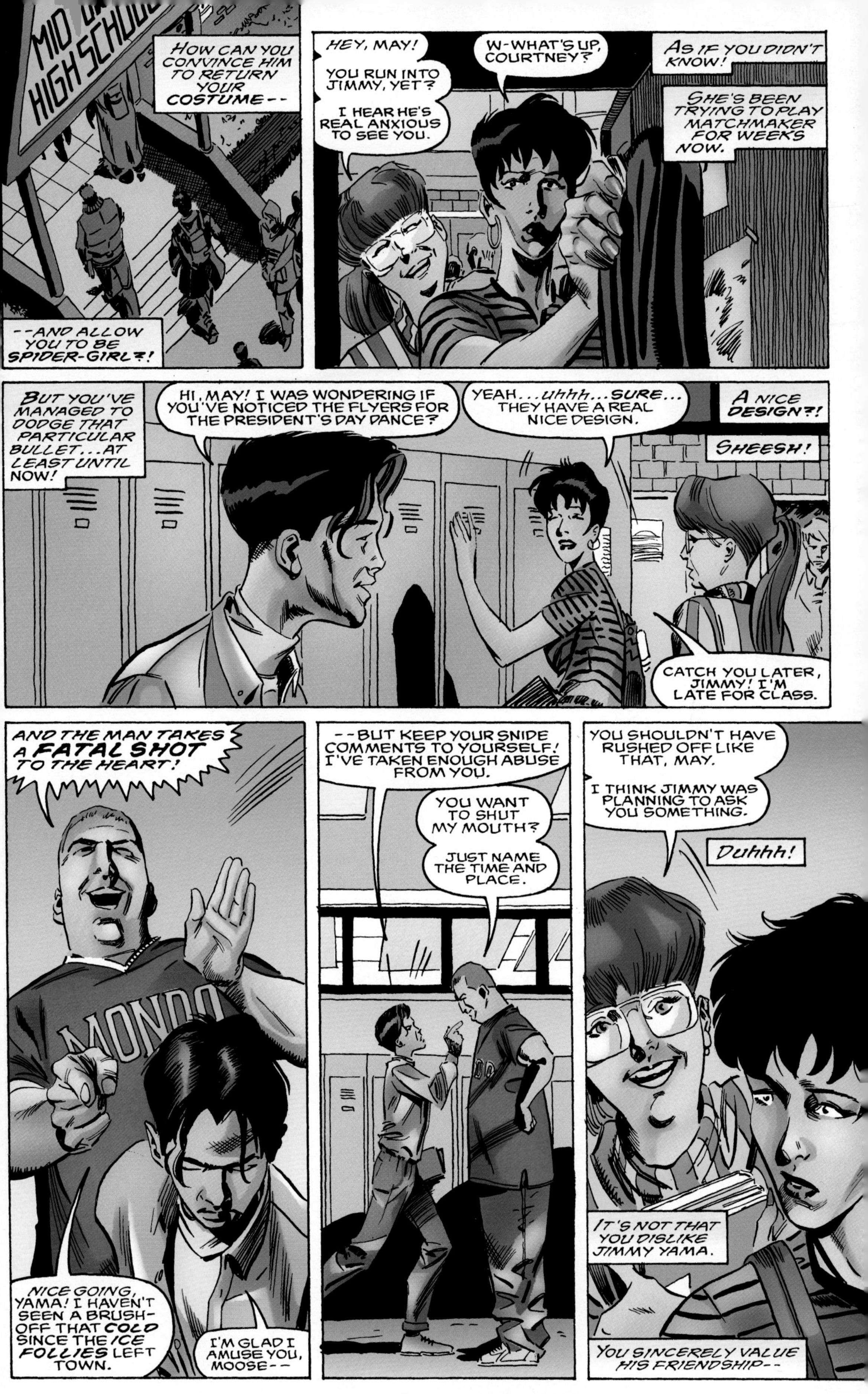
MID
HIGH SCHOO
HOW CAN YOU CONVINCE HIM TO RETURN YOUR COSTUME--
--AND ALLOW YOU TO BE SPIDER-GIRL?!
HEY, MAY!
YOU RUN INTO JIMMY, YET?
I HEAR HE'S REAL ANXIOUS TO SEE YOU.
W-WHAT'S UP, COURTNEY?
AS IF YOU DIDN'T KNOW!
SHE'S BEEN TRYING TO PLAY MATCHMAKER FOR WEEKS NOW.
BUT YOU'VE MANAGED TO DODGE THAT PARTICULAR BULLET...AT LEAST UNTIL NOW!
HI, MAY! I WAS WONDERING IF YOU'VE NOTICED THE FLYERS FOR THE PRESIDENT'S DAY DANCE?
YEAH...uhhh...SURE... THEY HAVE A REAL NICE DESIGN.
A NICE DESIGN?!
SHEESH!
CATCH YOU LATER, JIMMY! I'M LATE FOR CLASS.
AND THE MAN TAKES A FATAL SHOT TO THE HEART!
MONDO
NICE GOING, YAMA! I HAVEN'T SEEN A BRUSH-OFF THAT COLD SINCE THE ICE FOLLIES LEFT TOWN.
I'M GLAD I AMUSE YOU, MOOSE--
--BUT KEEP YOUR SNIDE COMMENTS TO YOURSELF! I'VE TAKEN ENOUGH ABUSE FROM YOU.
YOU WANT TO SHUT MY MOUTH?
JUST NAME THE TIME AND PLACE.
YOU SHOULDN'T HAVE RUSHED OFF LIKE THAT, MAY.
I THINK JIMMY WAS PLANNING TO ASK YOU SOMETHING.
Duhhh!
IT'S NOT THAT YOU DISLIKE JIMMY YAMA.
YOU SINCERELY VALUE HIS FRIENDSHIP--

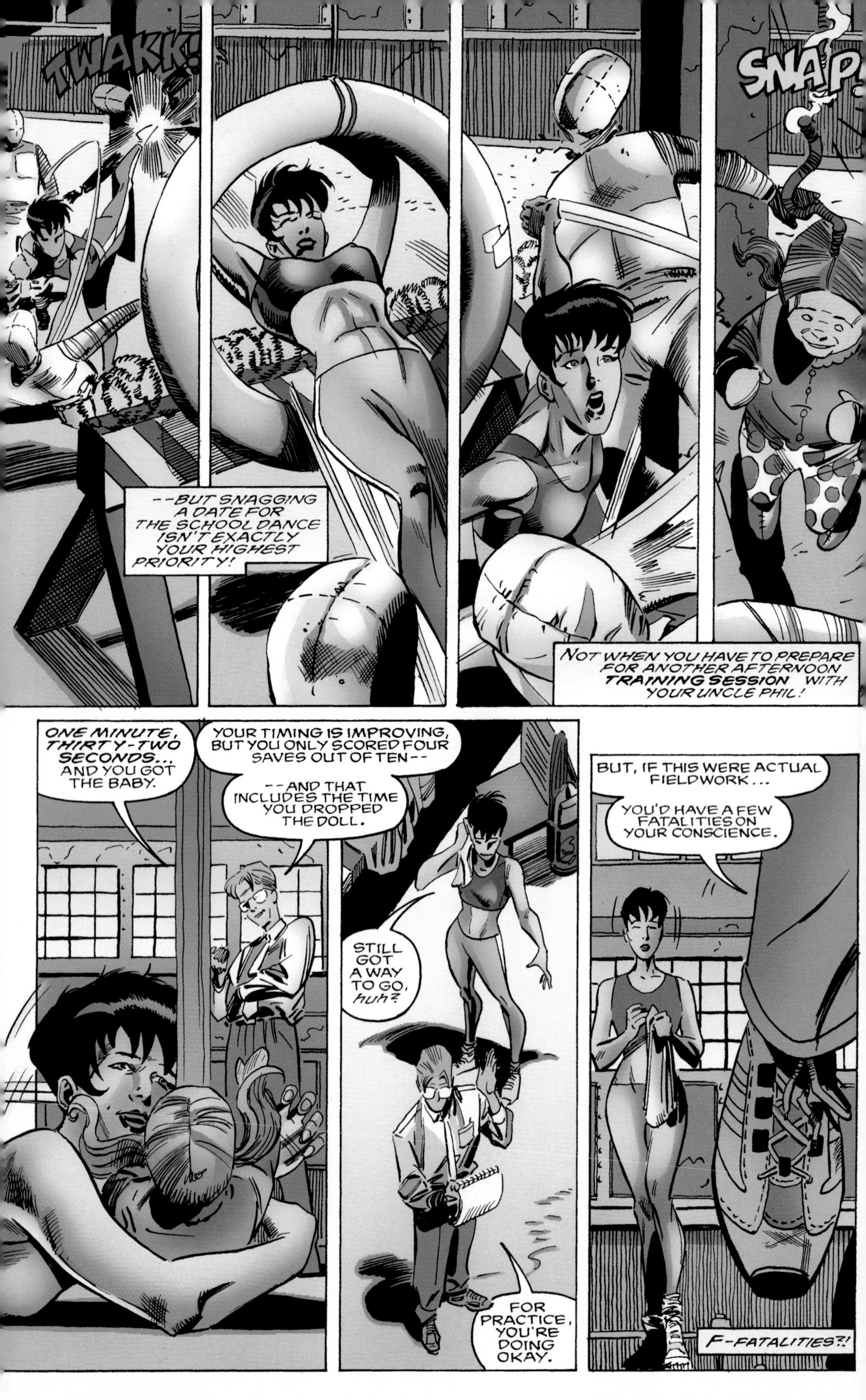
TWAKK!
SNAP!
--BUT SNAGGING A DATE FOR THE SCHOOL DANCE ISN'T EXACTLY YOUR HIGHEST PRIORITY!
NOT WHEN YOU HAVE TO PREPARE FOR ANOTHER AFTERNOON TRAINING SESSION WITH YOUR UNCLE PHIL!
ONE MINUTE, THIRTY-TWO SECONDS... AND YOU GOT THE BABY.
YOUR TIMING IS IMPROVING, BUT YOU ONLY SCORED FOUR SAVES OUT OF TEN--
--AND THAT INCLUDES THE TIME YOU DROPPED THE DOLL.
STILL GOT A WAY TO GO, huh?
FOR PRACTICE, YOU'RE DOING OKAY.
BUT, IF THIS WERE ACTUAL FIELDWORK...
YOU'D HAVE A FEW FATALITIES ON YOUR CONSCIENCE.
F-FATALITIES?!

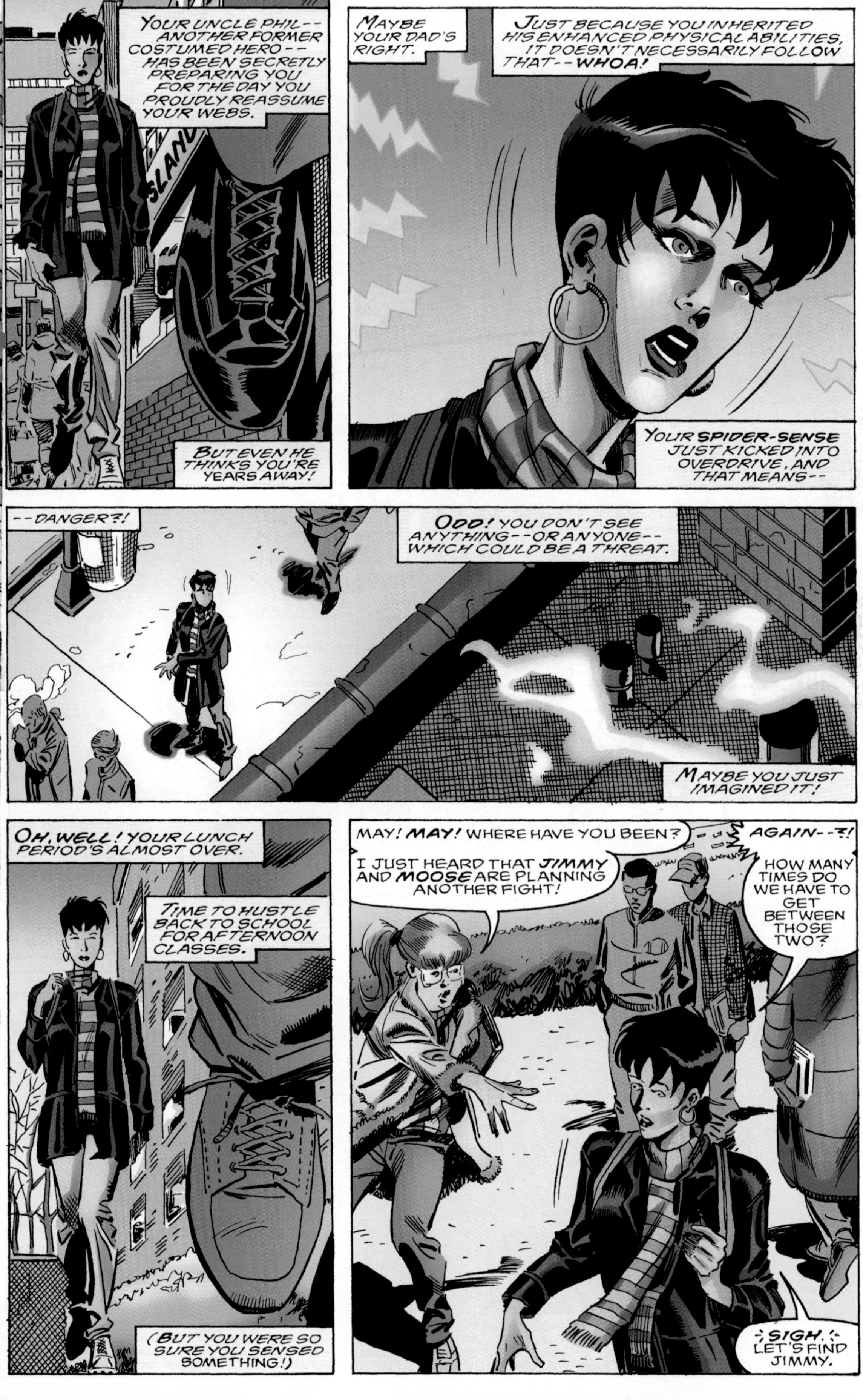

YOUR UNCLE PHIL-- ANOTHER FORMER COSTUMED HERO-- HAS BEEN SECRETLY PREPARING YOU FOR THE DAY YOU PROUDLY REASSUME YOUR WEBS.
BUT EVEN HE THINKS YOU'RE YEARS AWAY!
MAYBE YOUR DAD'S RIGHT.
JUST BECAUSE YOU INHERITED HIS ENHANCED PHYSICAL ABILITIES, IT DOESN'T NECESSARILY FOLLOW THAT--WHOA!
YOUR SPIDER-SENSE JUST KICKED INTO OVERDRIVE, AND THAT MEANS--
--DANGER?!
ODD! YOU DON'T SEE ANYTHING--OR ANYONE-- WHICH COULD BE A THREAT.
MAYBE YOU JUST IMAGINED IT!
OH, WELL! YOUR LUNCH PERIOD'S ALMOST OVER.
TIME TO HUSTLE BACK TO SCHOOL FOR AFTERNOON CLASSES.
(BUT YOU WERE SO SURE YOU SENSED SOMETHING!)
MAY! MAY! WHERE HAVE YOU BEEN?
I JUST HEARD THAT JIMMY AND MOOSE ARE PLANNING ANOTHER FIGHT!
AGAIN--?!
HOW MANY TIMES DO WE HAVE TO GET BETWEEN THOSE TWO?
SIGH. LET'S FIND JIMMY.

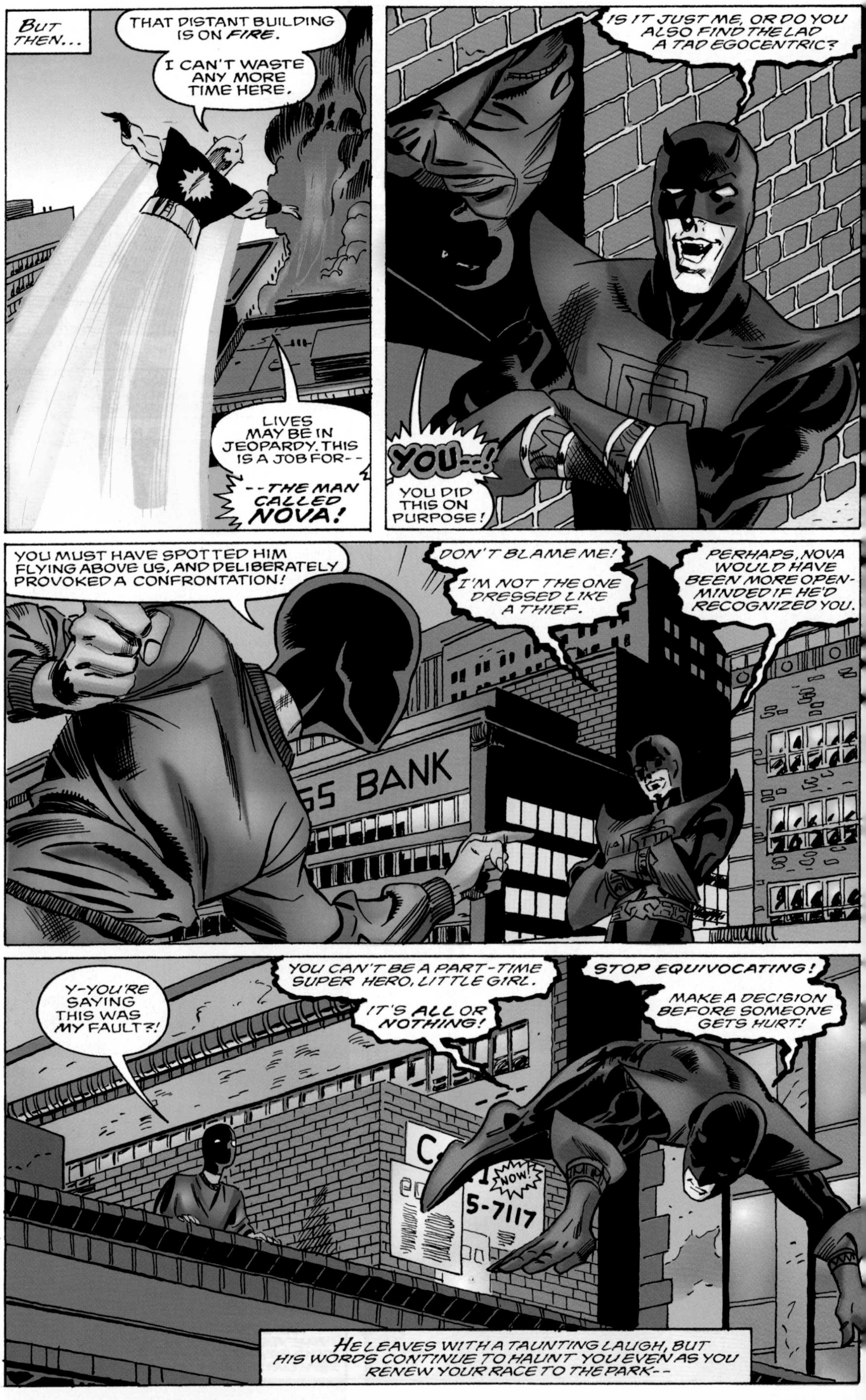

BUT THEN...
THAT DISTANT BUILDING IS ON FIRE.
I CAN'T WASTE ANY MORE TIME HERE.
LIVES MAY BE IN JEOPARDY. THIS IS A JOB FOR--
--THE MAN CALLED NOVA!
IS IT JUST ME, OR DO YOU ALSO FIND THE LAD A TAD EGOCENTRIC?
YOU--!
YOU DID THIS ON PURPOSE!
YOU MUST HAVE SPOTTED HIM FLYING ABOVE US, AND DELIBERATELY PROVOKED A CONFRONTATION!
DON'T BLAME ME!
I'M NOT THE ONE DRESSED LIKE A THIEF.
PERHAPS, NOVA WOULD HAVE BEEN MORE OPEN-MINDED IF HE'D RECOGNIZED YOU.
GS BANK
Y-YOU'RE SAYING THIS WAS MY FAULT?!
YOU CAN'T BE A PART-TIME SUPER HERO, LITTLE GIRL.
IT'S ALL OR NOTHING!
STOP EQUIVOCATING!
MAKE A DECISION BEFORE SOMEONE GETS HURT!
NOW!
5-7117
HE LEAVES WITH A TAUNTING LAUGH, BUT HIS WORDS CONTINUE TO HAUNT YOU EVEN AS YOU RENEW YOUR RACE TO THE PARK--

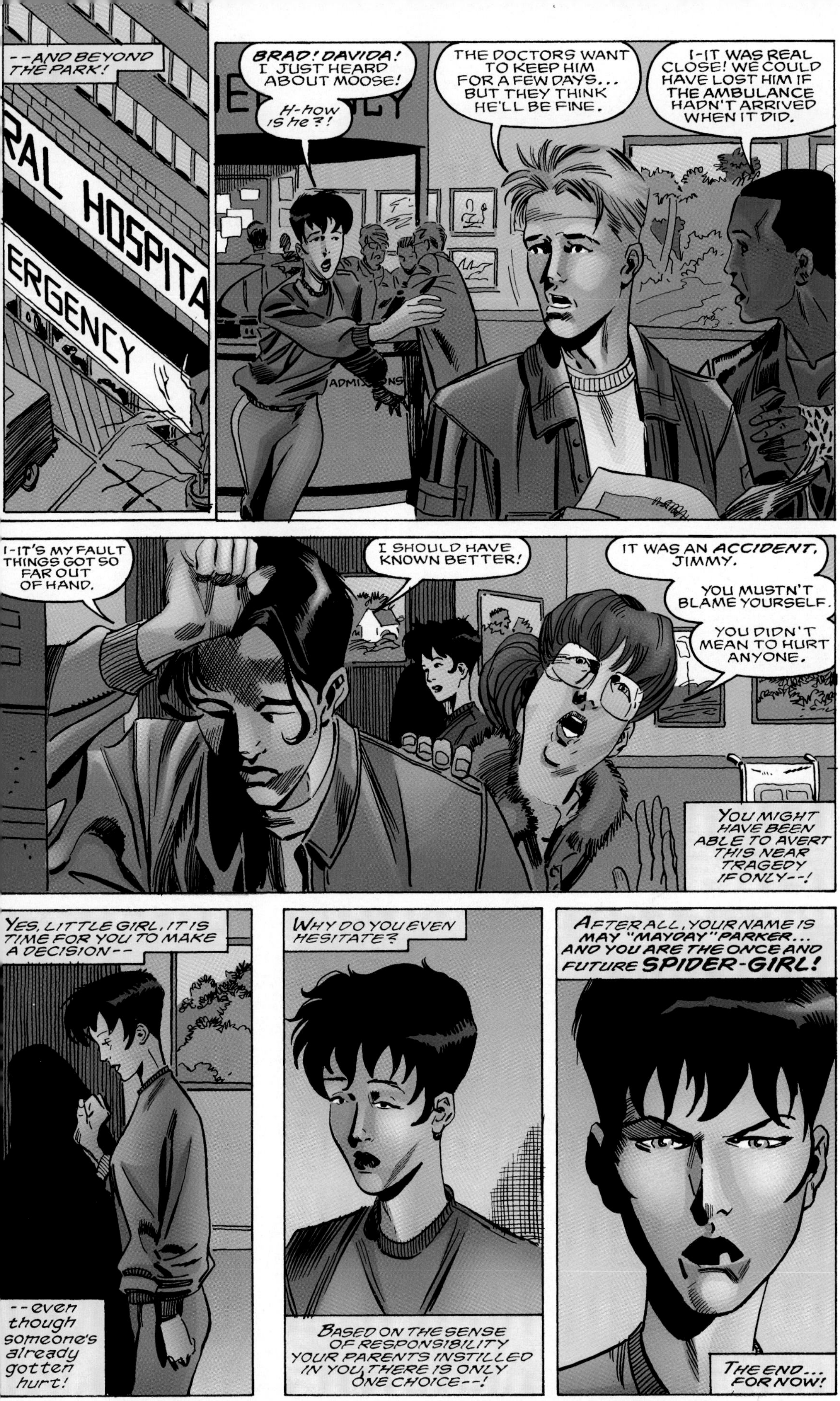
--AND BEYOND THE PARK!
RAL HOSPITA
ERGENCY
BRAD! DAVIDA! I JUST HEARD ABOUT MOOSE!
H-HOW IS HE?!
THE DOCTORS WANT TO KEEP HIM FOR A FEW DAYS... BUT THEY THINK HE'LL BE FINE.
I-IT WAS REAL CLOSE! WE COULD HAVE LOST HIM IF THE AMBULANCE HADN'T ARRIVED WHEN IT DID.
ADMISSIONS
I-IT'S MY FAULT THINGS GOT SO FAR OUT OF HAND.
I SHOULD HAVE KNOWN BETTER!
IT WAS AN ACCIDENT, JIMMY.
YOU MUSTN'T BLAME YOURSELF.
YOU DIDN'T MEAN TO HURT ANYONE.
YOU MIGHT HAVE BEEN ABLE TO AVERT THIS NEAR TRAGEDY IF ONLY--!
YES, LITTLE GIRL, IT IS TIME FOR YOU TO MAKE A DECISION--
--even though someone's already gotten hurt!
WHY DO YOU EVEN HESITATE?
BASED ON THE SENSE OF RESPONSIBILITY YOUR PARENTS INSTILLED IN YOU, THERE IS ONLY ONE CHOICE--!
AFTER ALL, YOUR NAME IS MAY "MAYDAY" PARKER... AND YOU ARE THE ONCE AND FUTURE SPIDER-GIRL!
THE END... FOR NOW!

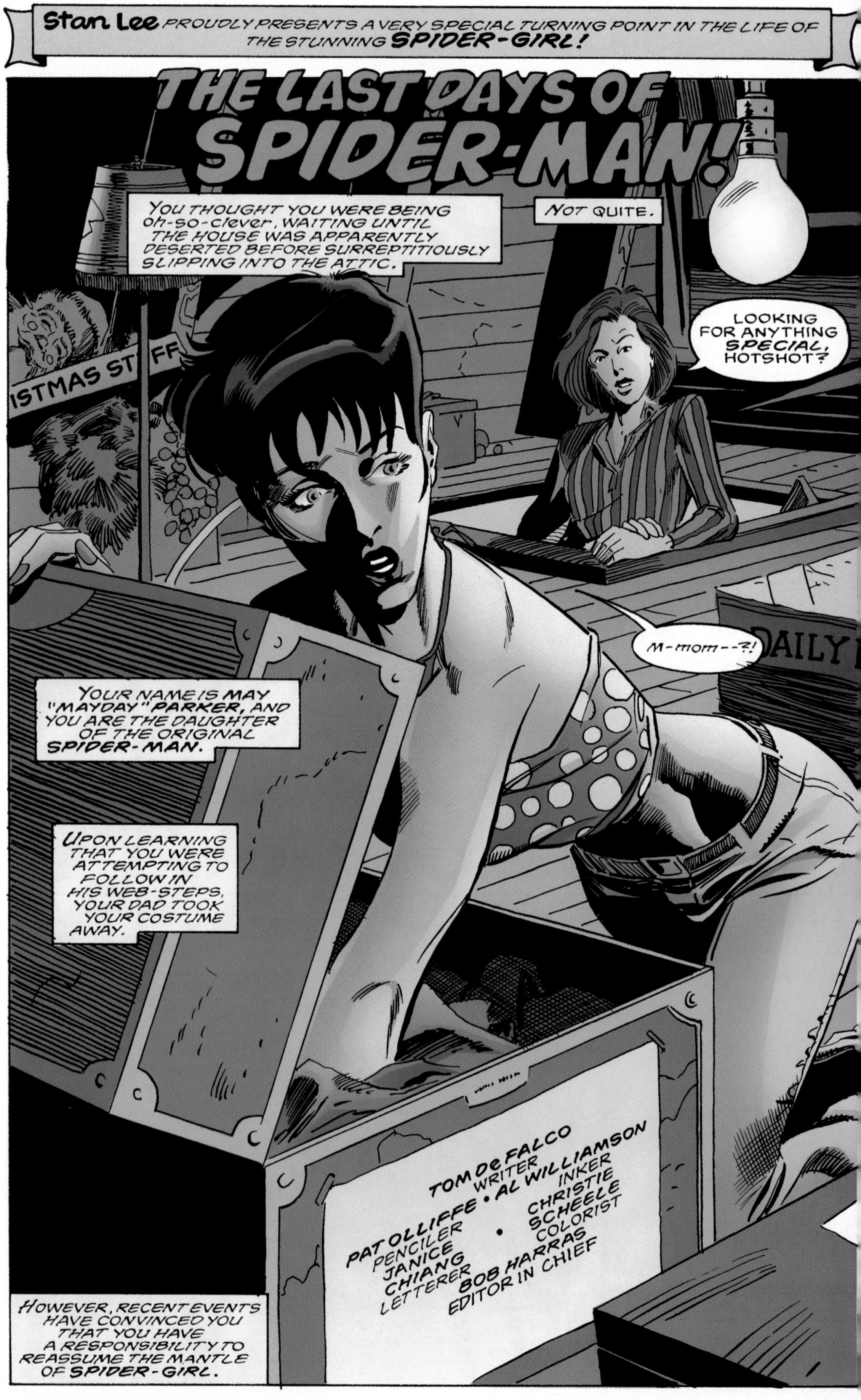
Stan Lee PROUDLY PRESENTS A VERY SPECIAL TURNING POINT IN THE LIFE OF THE STUNNING SPIDER-GIRL!
THE LAST DAYS OF SPIDER-MAN!
YOU THOUGHT YOU WERE BEING oh-so-clever, WAITING UNTIL THE HOUSE WAS APPARENTLY DESERTED BEFORE SURREPTITIOUSLY SLIPPING INTO THE ATTIC.
NOT QUITE.
LOOKING FOR ANYTHING SPECIAL, HOTSHOT?
M-mom--?!
YOUR NAME IS MAY "MAYDAY" PARKER, AND YOU ARE THE DAUGHTER OF THE ORIGINAL SPIDER-MAN.
UPON LEARNING THAT YOU WERE ATTEMPTING TO FOLLOW IN HIS WEB-STEPS, YOUR DAD TOOK YOUR COSTUME AWAY.
HOWEVER, RECENT EVENTS HAVE CONVINCED YOU THAT YOU HAVE A RESPONSIBILITY TO REASSUME THE MANTLE OF SPIDER-GIRL.
TOM DeFALCO WRITER
PAT OLLIFFE PENCILER • AL WILLIAMSON INKER
JANICE CHIANG LETTERER • CHRISTIE SCHEELE COLORIST
BOB HARRAS EDITOR IN CHIEF

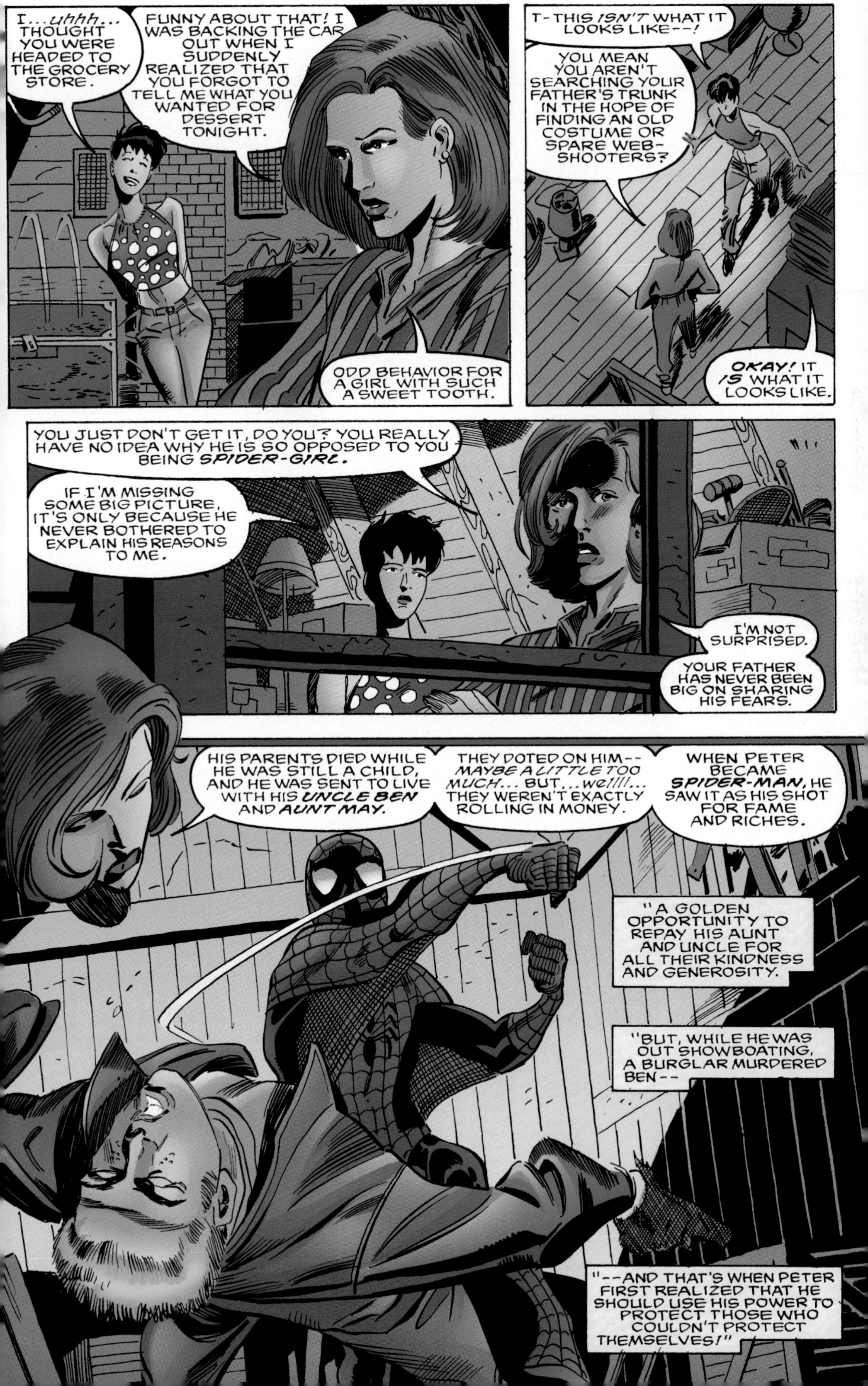
I... uhhh... THOUGHT YOU WERE HEADED TO THE GROCERY STORE.
FUNNY ABOUT THAT! I WAS BACKING THE CAR OUT WHEN I SUDDENLY REALIZED THAT YOU FORGOT TO TELL ME WHAT YOU WANTED FOR DESSERT TONIGHT.
ODD BEHAVIOR FOR A GIRL WITH SUCH A SWEET TOOTH.
T-THIS ISN'T WHAT IT LOOKS LIKE--!
YOU MEAN YOU AREN'T SEARCHING YOUR FATHER'S TRUNK IN THE HOPE OF FINDING AN OLD COSTUME OR SPARE WEB-SHOOTERS?
OKAY! IT IS WHAT IT LOOKS LIKE.
YOU JUST DON'T GET IT, DO YOU? YOU REALLY HAVE NO IDEA WHY HE IS SO OPPOSED TO YOU BEING SPIDER-GIRL.
IF I'M MISSING SOME BIG PICTURE, IT'S ONLY BECAUSE HE NEVER BOTHERED TO EXPLAIN HIS REASONS TO ME.
I'M NOT SURPRISED.
YOUR FATHER HAS NEVER BEEN BIG ON SHARING HIS FEARS.
HIS PARENTS DIED WHILE HE WAS STILL A CHILD, AND HE WAS SENT TO LIVE WITH HIS UNCLE BEN AND AUNT MAY.
THEY DOTED ON HIM-- MAYBE A LITTLE TOO MUCH... BUT... welllll... THEY WEREN'T EXACTLY ROLLING IN MONEY.
WHEN PETER BECAME SPIDER-MAN, HE SAW IT AS HIS SHOT FOR FAME AND RICHES.
"A GOLDEN OPPORTUNITY TO REPAY HIS AUNT AND UNCLE FOR ALL THEIR KINDNESS AND GENEROSITY.
"BUT, WHILE HE WAS OUT SHOWBOATING, A BURGLAR MURDERED BEN--
"--AND THAT'S WHEN PETER FIRST REALIZED THAT HE SHOULD USE HIS POWER TO PROTECT THOSE WHO COULDN'T PROTECT THEMSELVES!"

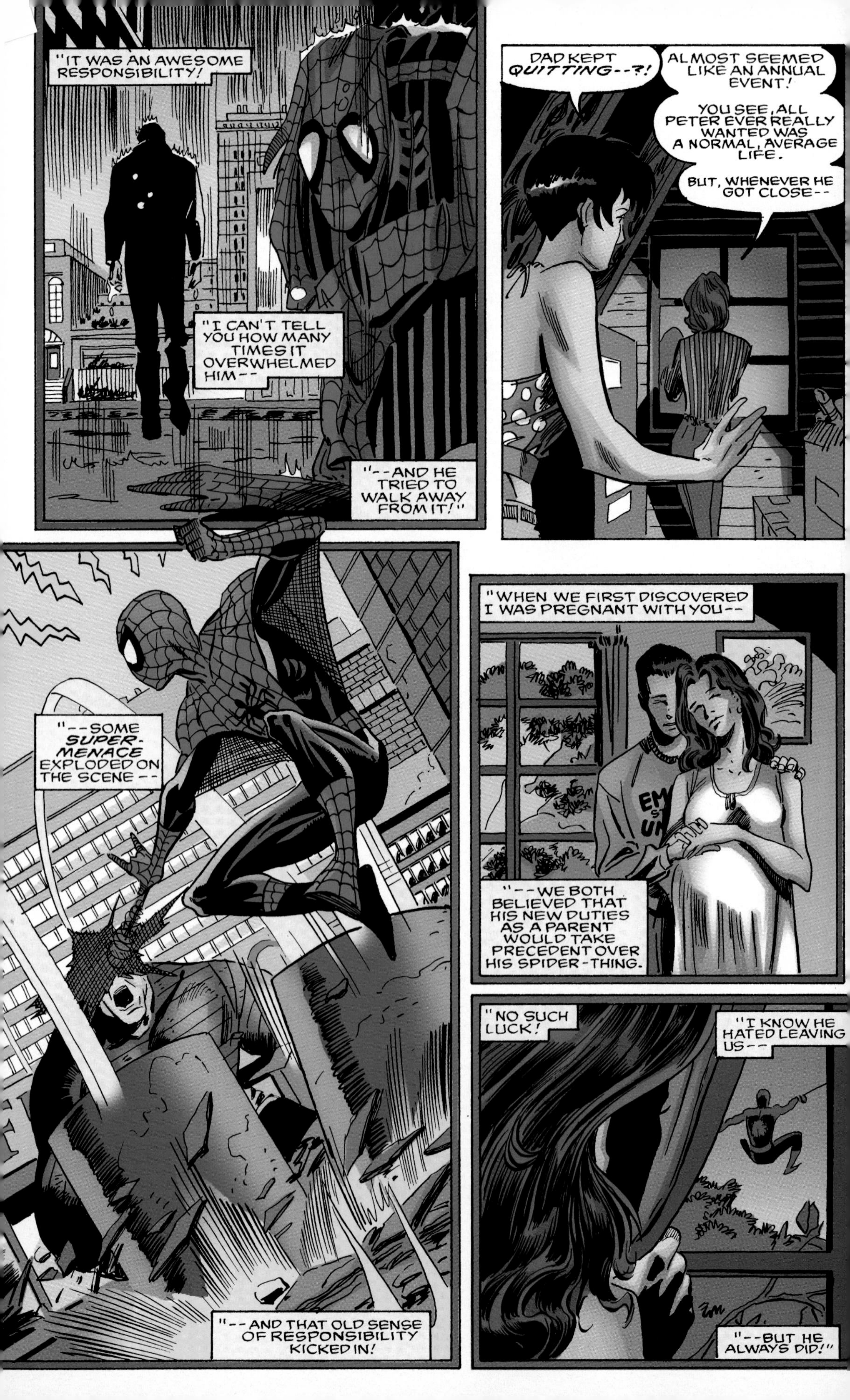
"IT WAS AN AWESOME RESPONSIBILITY!
"I CAN'T TELL YOU HOW MANY TIMES IT OVERWHELMED HIM--
"--AND HE TRIED TO WALK AWAY FROM IT!"
DAD KEPT QUITTING--?!
ALMOST SEEMED LIKE AN ANNUAL EVENT!
YOU SEE, ALL PETER EVER REALLY WANTED WAS A NORMAL, AVERAGE LIFE.
BUT, WHENEVER HE GOT CLOSE--
"--SOME SUPER-MENACE EXPLODED ON THE SCENE--
"--AND THAT OLD SENSE OF RESPONSIBILITY KICKED IN!
"WHEN WE FIRST DISCOVERED I WAS PREGNANT WITH YOU--
"--WE BOTH BELIEVED THAT HIS NEW DUTIES AS A PARENT WOULD TAKE PRECEDENT OVER HIS SPIDER-THING.
"NO SUCH LUCK!
"I KNOW HE HATED LEAVING US--
"--BUT HE ALWAYS DID!"

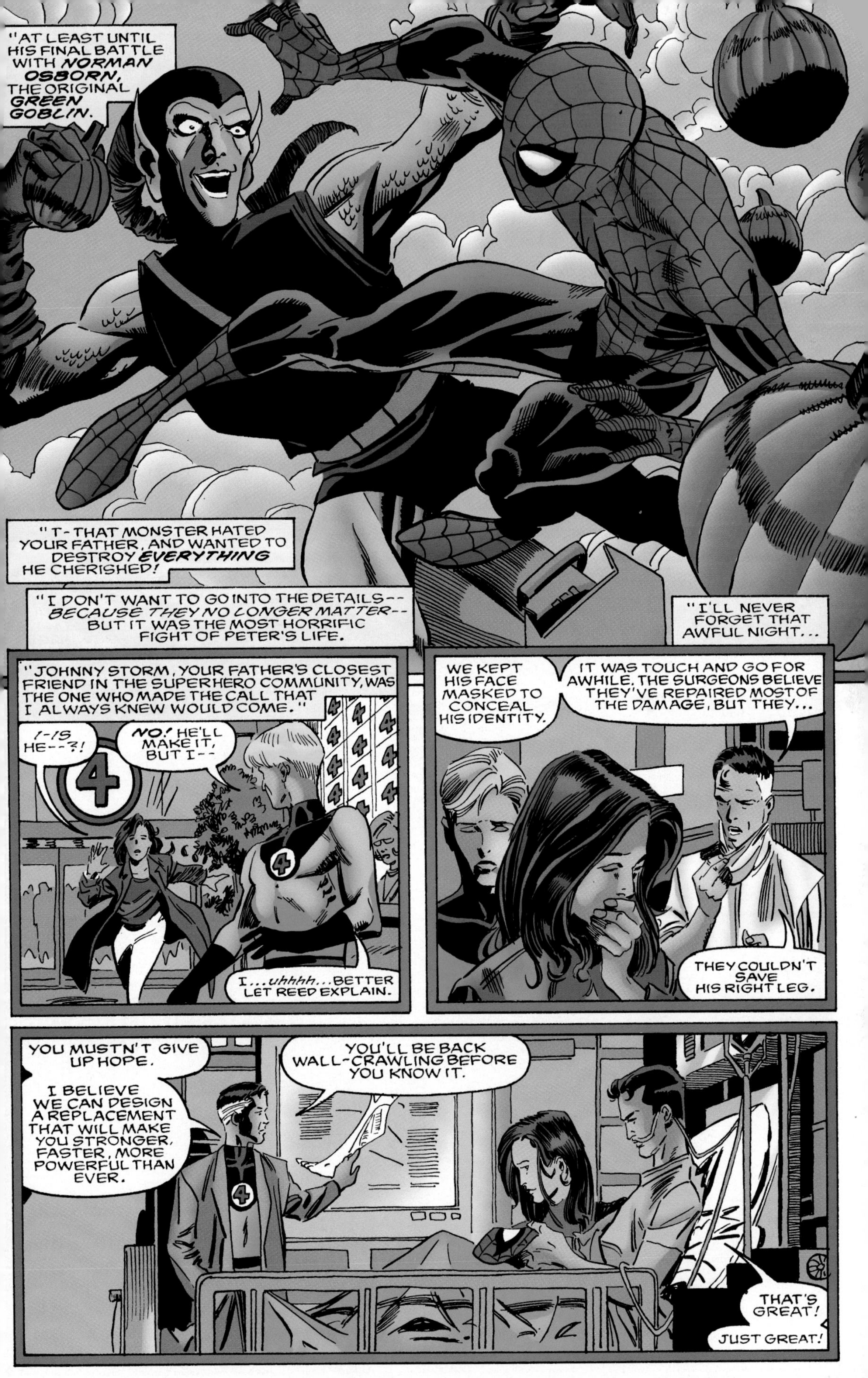
"AT LEAST UNTIL HIS FINAL BATTLE WITH NORMAN OSBORN, THE ORIGINAL GREEN GOBLIN.
"T-THAT MONSTER HATED YOUR FATHER, AND WANTED TO DESTROY EVERYTHING HE CHERISHED!
"I DON'T WANT TO GO INTO THE DETAILS-- BECAUSE THEY NO LONGER MATTER-- BUT IT WAS THE MOST HORRIFIC FIGHT OF PETER'S LIFE.
"I'LL NEVER FORGET THAT AWFUL NIGHT...
"JOHNNY STORM, YOUR FATHER'S CLOSEST FRIEND IN THE SUPERHERO COMMUNITY, WAS THE ONE WHO MADE THE CALL THAT I ALWAYS KNEW WOULD COME."
I-IS HE--?!
NO! HE'LL MAKE IT, BUT I--
I...uhhhh...BETTER LET REED EXPLAIN.
WE KEPT HIS FACE MASKED TO CONCEAL HIS IDENTITY.
IT WAS TOUCH AND GO FOR AWHILE. THE SURGEONS BELIEVE THEY'VE REPAIRED MOST OF THE DAMAGE, BUT THEY...
THEY COULDN'T SAVE HIS RIGHT LEG.
YOU MUSTN'T GIVE UP HOPE.
I BELIEVE WE CAN DESIGN A REPLACEMENT THAT WILL MAKE YOU STRONGER, FASTER, MORE POWERFUL THAN EVER.
YOU'LL BE BACK WALL-CRAWLING BEFORE YOU KNOW IT.
THAT'S GREAT!
JUST GREAT!

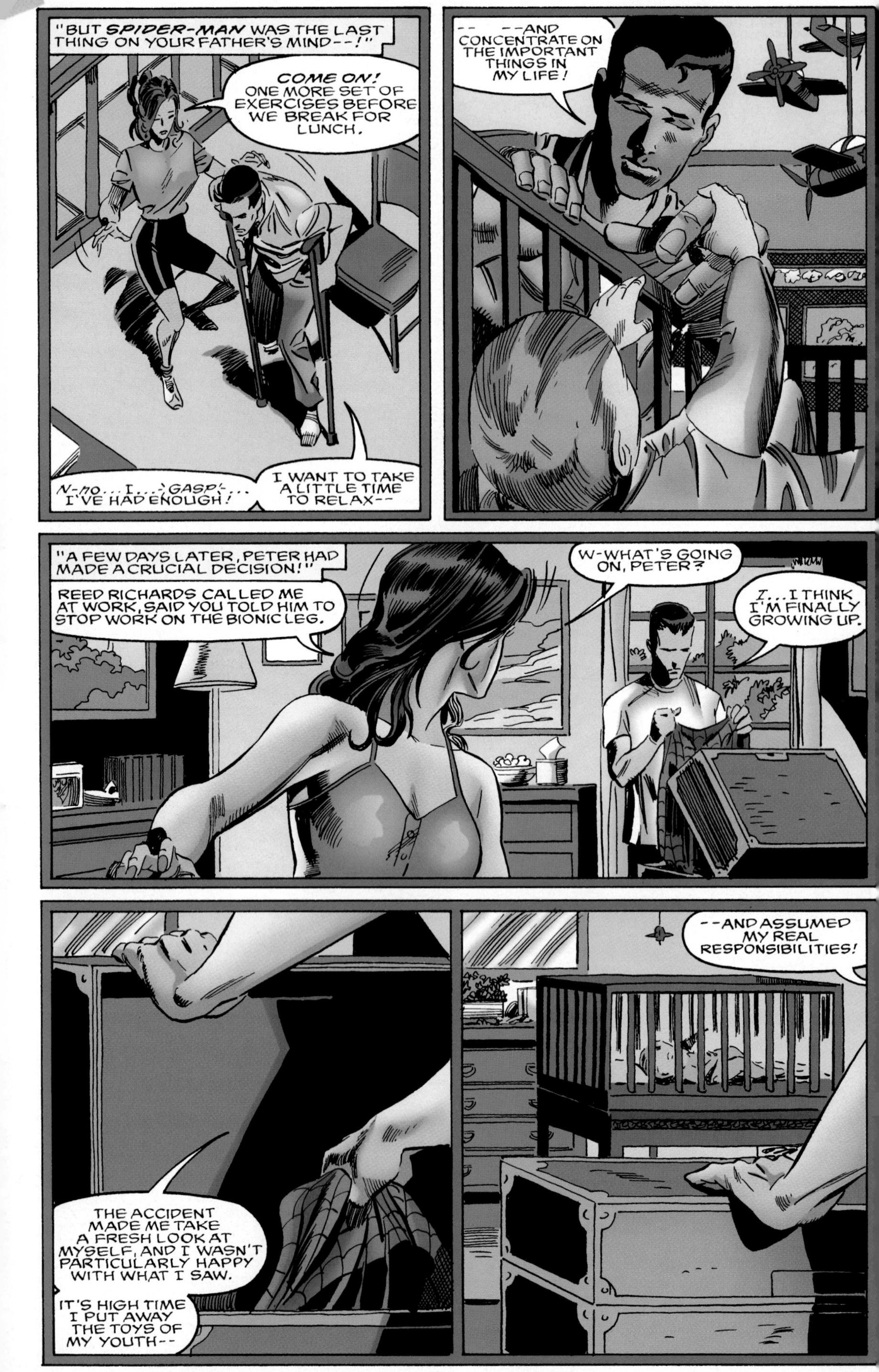
"BUT SPIDER-MAN WAS THE LAST THING ON YOUR FATHER'S MIND--!"
COME ON! ONE MORE SET OF EXERCISES BEFORE WE BREAK FOR LUNCH.
N-NO... I... GASP... I'VE HAD ENOUGH!
I WANT TO TAKE A LITTLE TIME TO RELAX--
--AND CONCENTRATE ON THE IMPORTANT THINGS IN MY LIFE!
"A FEW DAYS LATER, PETER HAD MADE A CRUCIAL DECISION!"
REED RICHARDS CALLED ME AT WORK, SAID YOU TOLD HIM TO STOP WORK ON THE BIONIC LEG.
W-WHAT'S GOING ON, PETER?
I... I THINK I'M FINALLY GROWING UP.
THE ACCIDENT MADE ME TAKE A FRESH LOOK AT MYSELF, AND I WASN'T PARTICULARLY HAPPY WITH WHAT I SAW.
IT'S HIGH TIME I PUT AWAY THE TOYS OF MY YOUTH--
--AND ASSUMED MY REAL RESPONSIBILITIES!

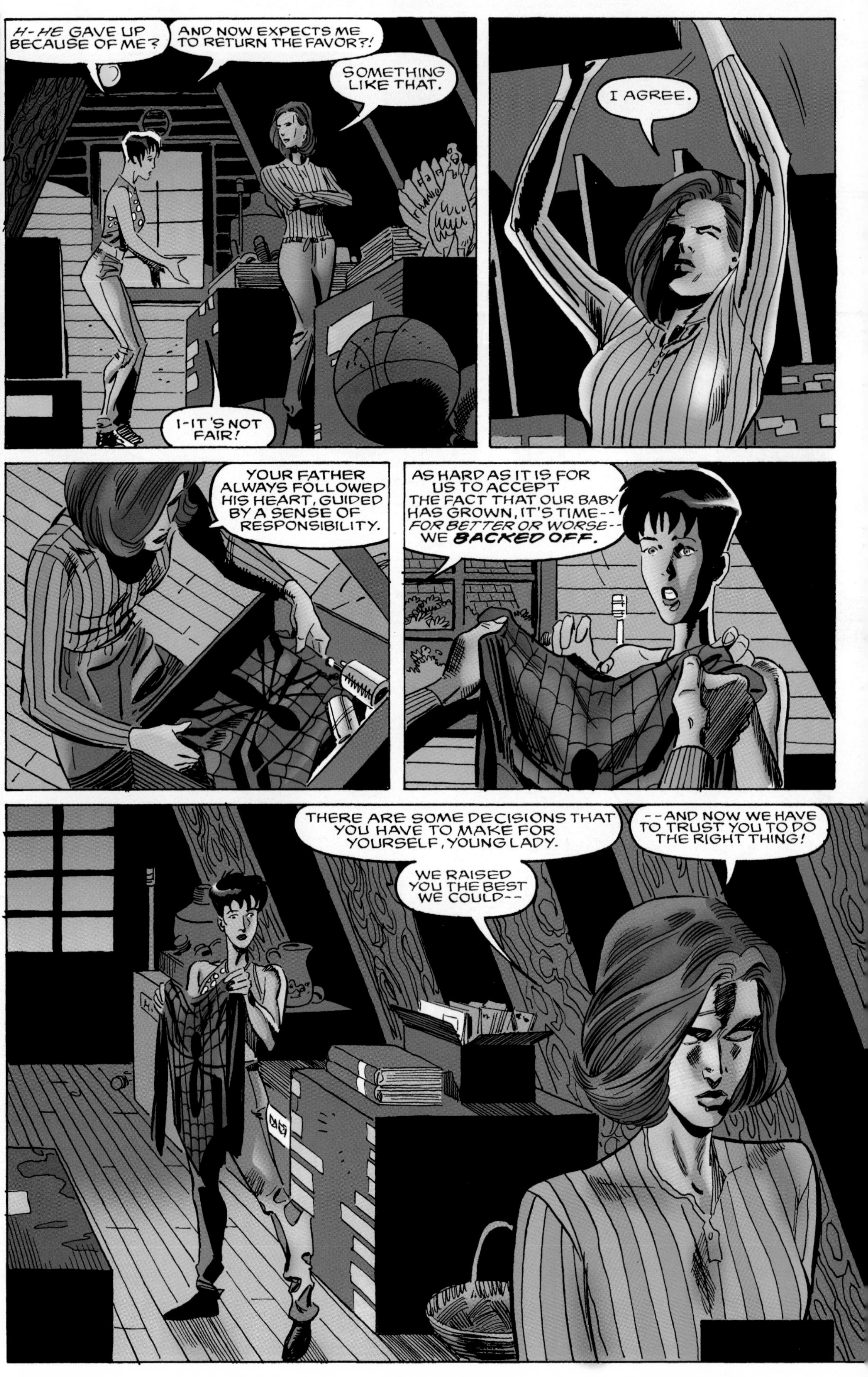

H-HE GAVE UP BECAUSE OF ME?
AND NOW EXPECTS ME TO RETURN THE FAVOR?!
SOMETHING LIKE THAT.
I-IT'S NOT FAIR!
I AGREE.
YOUR FATHER ALWAYS FOLLOWED HIS HEART, GUIDED BY A SENSE OF RESPONSIBILITY.
AS HARD AS IT IS FOR US TO ACCEPT THE FACT THAT OUR BABY HAS GROWN, IT'S TIME-- *FOR BETTER OR WORSE*-- WE **BACKED OFF.**
THERE ARE SOME DECISIONS THAT YOU HAVE TO MAKE FOR YOURSELF, YOUNG LADY.
WE RAISED YOU THE BEST WE COULD--
--AND NOW WE HAVE TO TRUST YOU TO DO THE RIGHT THING!

LET'S GET THIS STRAIGHT, YOUNG MAN--

QUEENS COUNTY COURTHOUSE

--YOU SCREWED UP!

I...I KNOW, AUNT SACHI... AND I'M REAL SORRY!

I NEVER MEANT TO HURT MOOSE--

WE WERE JUST--

:ugggggg:

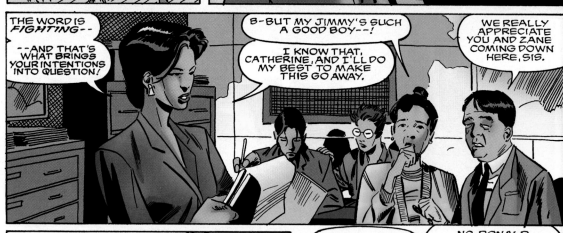

THE WORD IS FIGHTING--

--AND THAT'S WHAT BRINGS YOUR INTENTIONS INTO QUESTION!

B-BUT MY JIMMY'S SUCH A GOOD BOY--!

I KNOW THAT, CATHERINE, AND I'LL DO MY BEST TO MAKE THIS GO AWAY.

WE REALLY APPRECIATE YOU AND ZANE COMING DOWN HERE, SIS.

YOU SHOULD HAVE CALLED ME WHEN THAT BIG DOPE STARTED HASSLING YOU, JIMMY.

YEAH, ZANE... SURE!

I'M SERIOUS, MAN! I'M A LOT TOUGHER THAN I LOOK!

SHOULD WE ACCOMPANY YOU, SACHI?

NO, DONALD, IT'LL BE BETTER IF I TALK TO JIMMY'S PROSECUTOR ALONE.

YOU CAN USE THIS INTERVIEW ROOM UNTIL I RETURN.

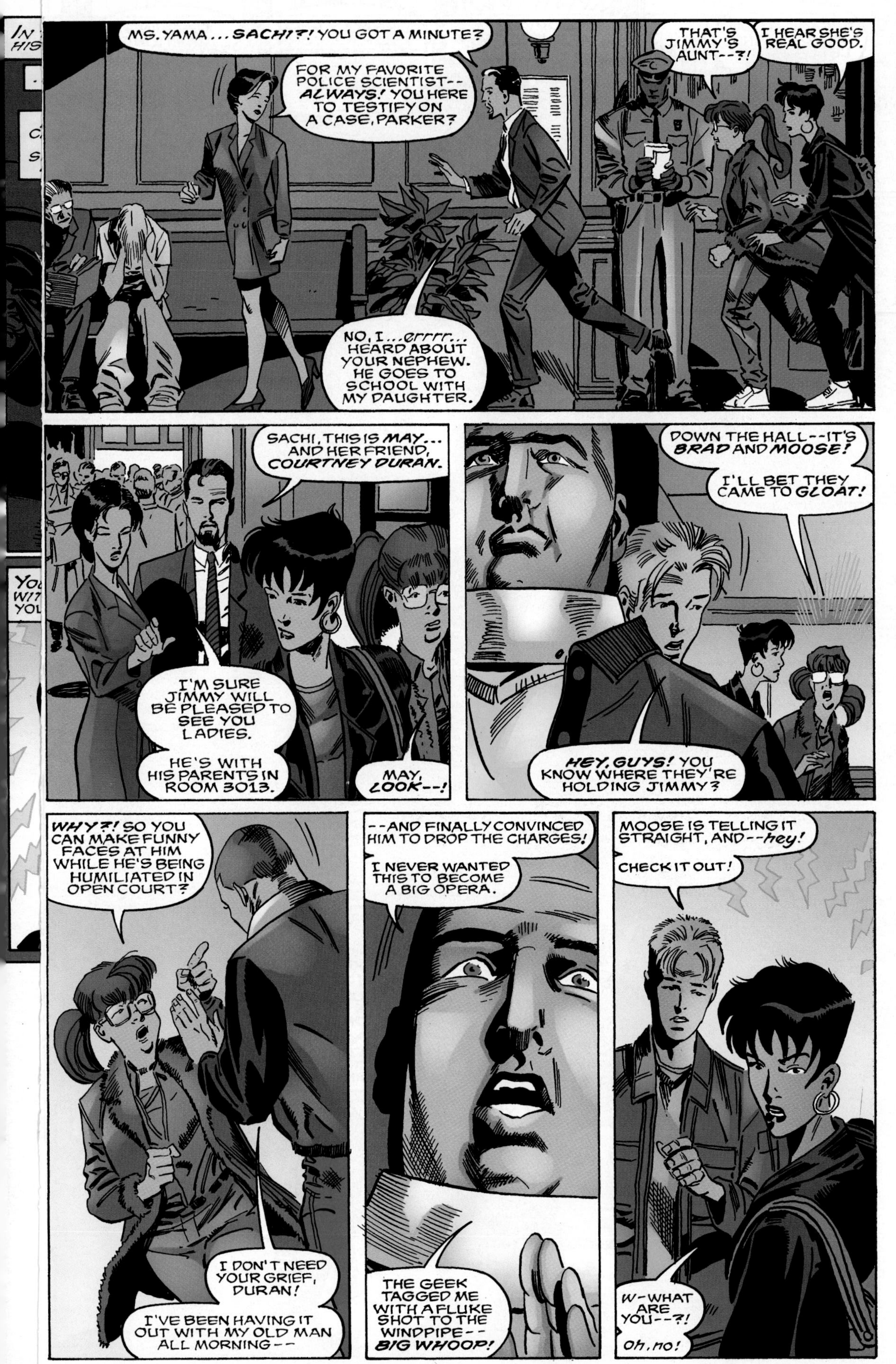
MS. YAMA ... SACHI?! YOU GOT A MINUTE?
FOR MY FAVORITE POLICE SCIENTIST-- ALWAYS! YOU HERE TO TESTIFY ON A CASE, PARKER?
NO, I ... errrr... HEARD ABOUT YOUR NEPHEW. HE GOES TO SCHOOL WITH MY DAUGHTER.
THAT'S JIMMY'S AUNT--?!
I HEAR SHE'S REAL GOOD.
SACHI, THIS IS MAY... AND HER FRIEND, COURTNEY DURAN.
I'M SURE JIMMY WILL BE PLEASED TO SEE YOU LADIES.
HE'S WITH HIS PARENTS IN ROOM 3013.
MAY, LOOK--!
DOWN THE HALL--IT'S BRAD AND MOOSE!
I'LL BET THEY CAME TO GLOAT!
HEY, GUYS! YOU KNOW WHERE THEY'RE HOLDING JIMMY?
WHY?! SO YOU CAN MAKE FUNNY FACES AT HIM WHILE HE'S BEING HUMILIATED IN OPEN COURT?
I DON'T NEED YOUR GRIEF, DURAN!
I'VE BEEN HAVING IT OUT WITH MY OLD MAN ALL MORNING--
--AND FINALLY CONVINCED HIM TO DROP THE CHARGES!
I NEVER WANTED THIS TO BECOME A BIG OPERA.
THE GEEK TAGGED ME WITH A FLUKE SHOT TO THE WINDPIPE-- BIG WHOOP!
MOOSE IS TELLING IT STRAIGHT, AND--hey!
CHECK IT OUT!
W-WHAT ARE YOU--?!
oh, no!

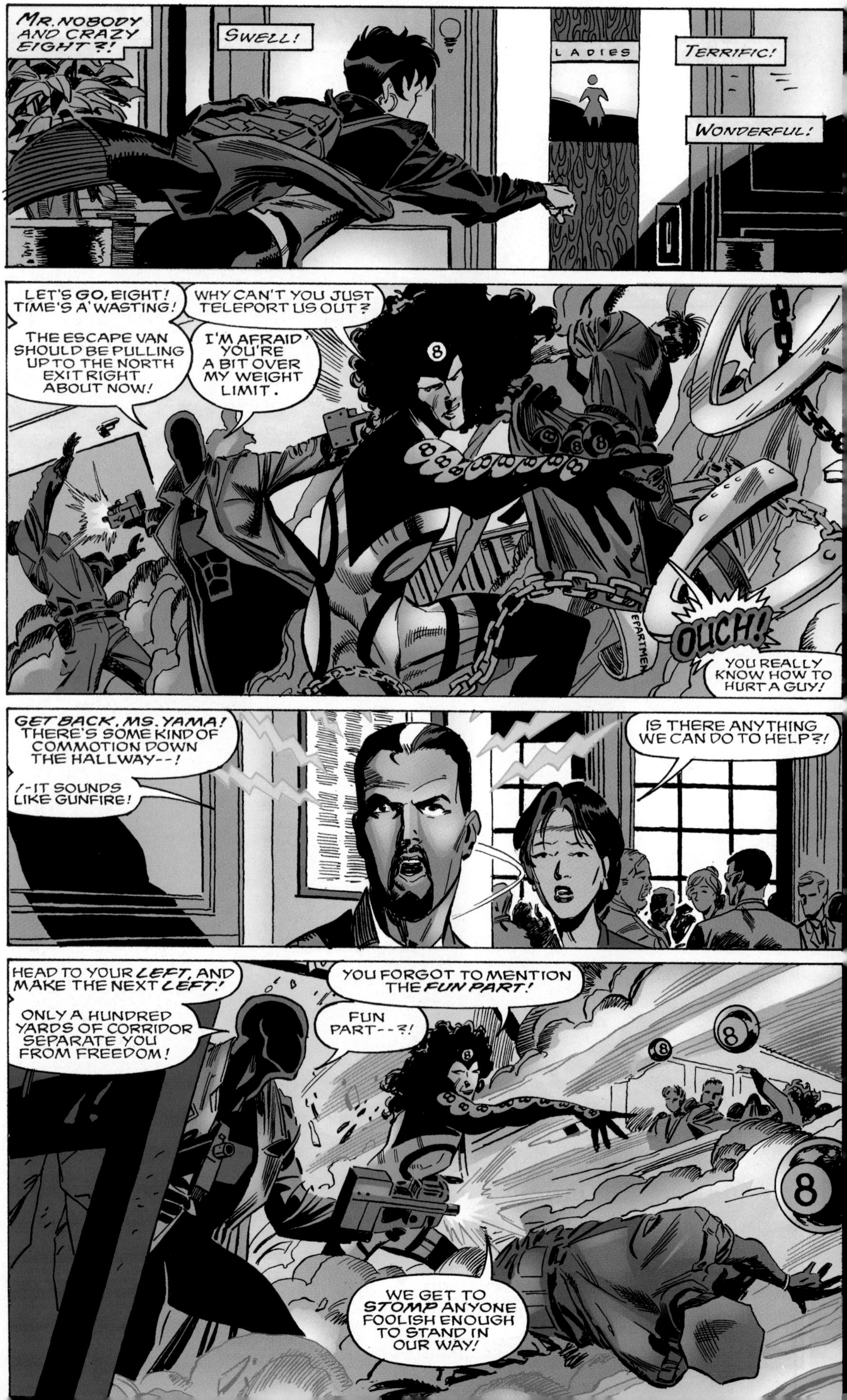
MR. NOBODY AND CRAZY EIGHT?!
SWELL!
LADIES
TERRIFIC!
WONDERFUL!
LET'S GO, EIGHT! TIME'S A'WASTING!
THE ESCAPE VAN SHOULD BE PULLING UP TO THE NORTH EXIT RIGHT ABOUT NOW!
WHY CAN'T YOU JUST TELEPORT US OUT?
I'M AFRAID YOU'RE A BIT OVER MY WEIGHT LIMIT.
OUCH!
YOU REALLY KNOW HOW TO HURT A GUY!
GET BACK, MS. YAMA! THERE'S SOME KIND OF COMMOTION DOWN THE HALLWAY--!
/-IT SOUNDS LIKE GUNFIRE!
IS THERE ANYTHING WE CAN DO TO HELP?!
HEAD TO YOUR LEFT, AND MAKE THE NEXT LEFT!
ONLY A HUNDRED YARDS OF CORRIDOR SEPARATE YOU FROM FREEDOM!
YOU FORGOT TO MENTION THE FUN PART!
FUN PART--?!
WE GET TO STOMP ANYONE FOOLISH ENOUGH TO STAND IN OUR WAY!

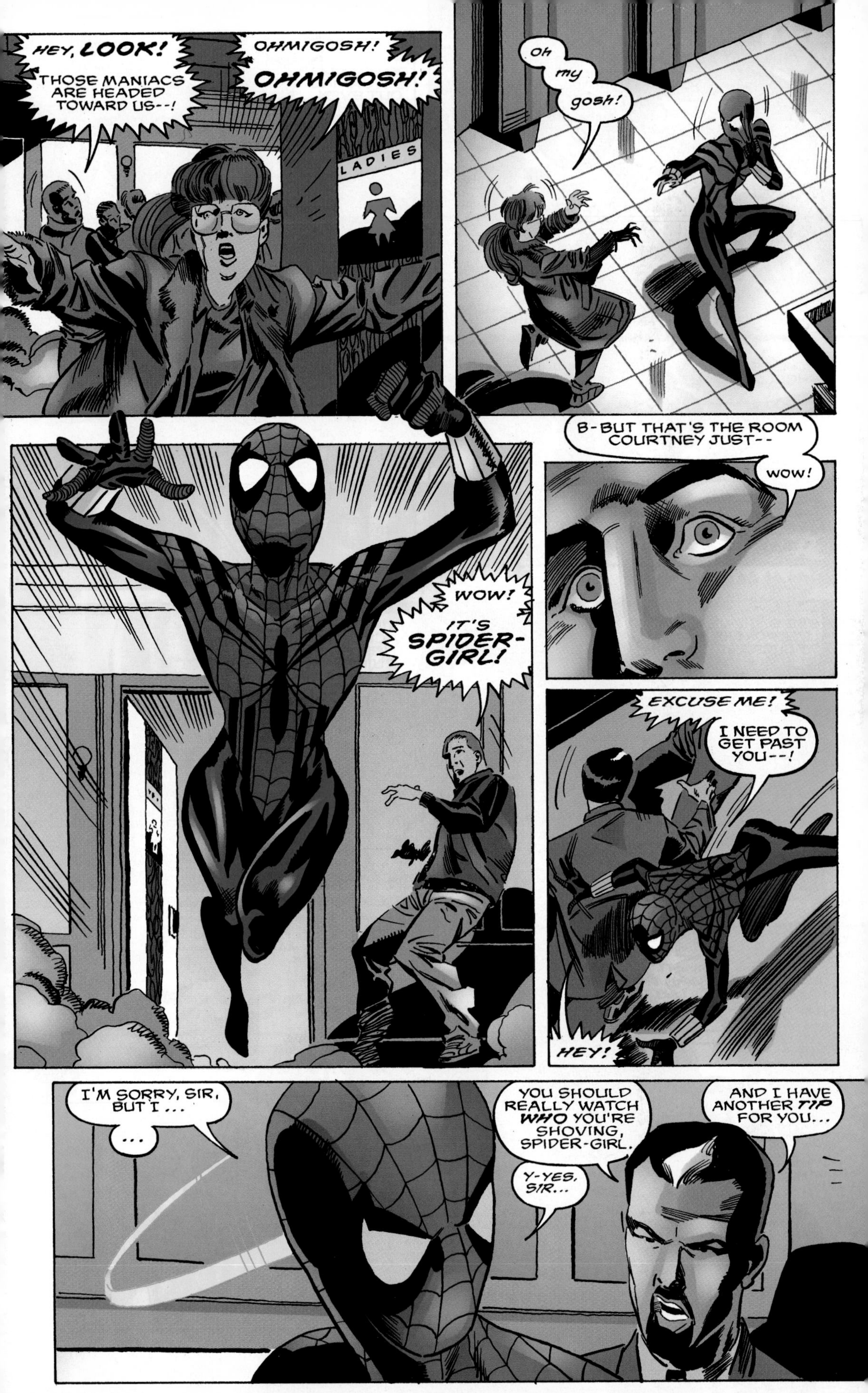
HEY, LOOK!
THOSE MANIACS ARE HEADED TOWARD US--!
OHMIGOSH!
OHMIGOSH!
LADIES
Oh my gosh!
B-BUT THAT'S THE ROOM COURTNEY JUST--
WOW!
WOW!
IT'S SPIDER-GIRL!
EXCUSE ME!
I NEED TO GET PAST YOU--!
HEY!
I'M SORRY, SIR, BUT I...
...
YOU SHOULD REALLY WATCH WHO YOU'RE SHOVING, SPIDER-GIRL.
Y-YES, SIR...
AND I HAVE ANOTHER TIP FOR YOU...

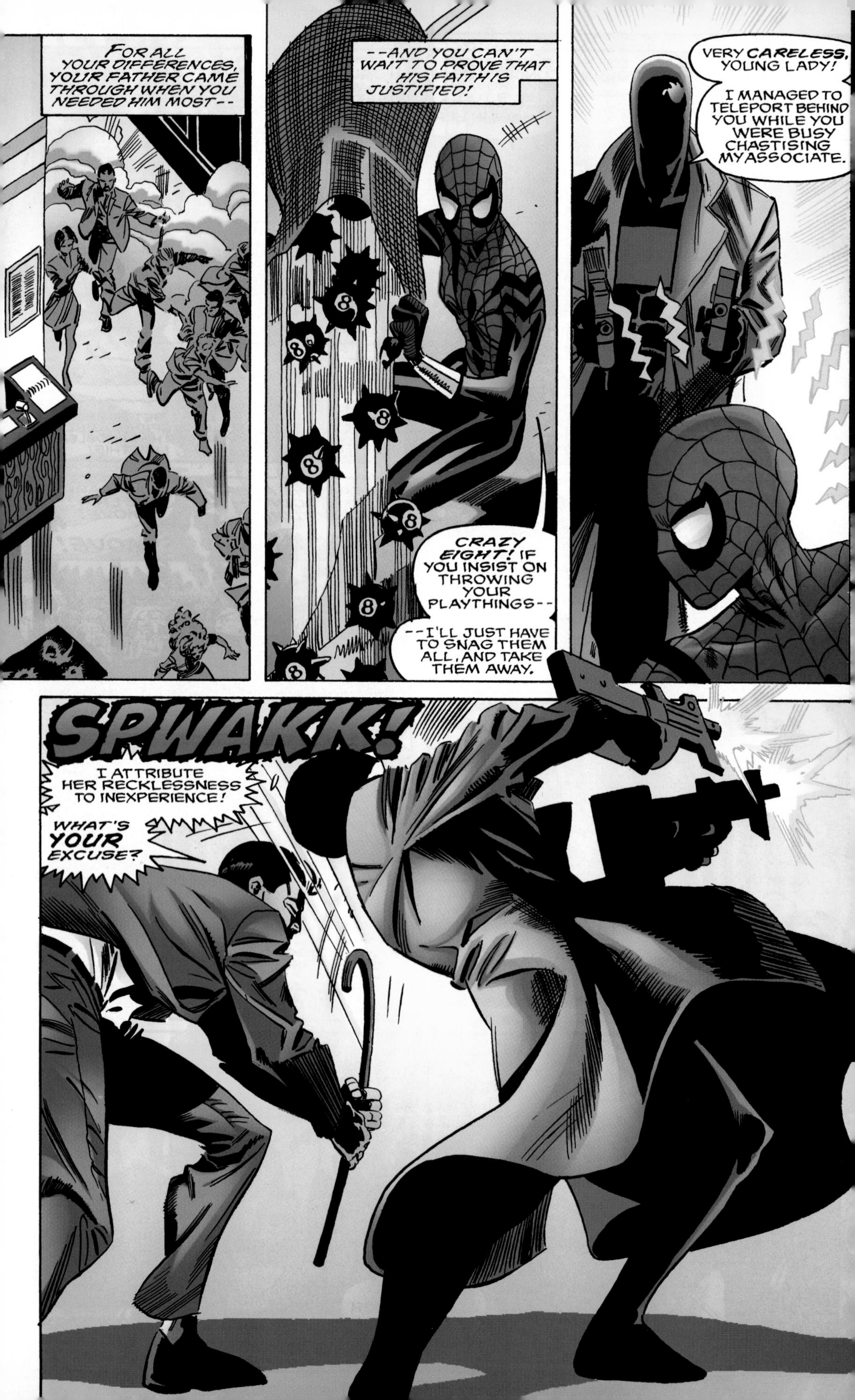

FOR ALL YOUR DIFFERENCES, YOUR FATHER CAME THROUGH WHEN YOU NEEDED HIM MOST--
--AND YOU CAN'T WAIT TO PROVE THAT HIS FAITH IS JUSTIFIED!
CRAZY EIGHT! IF YOU INSIST ON THROWING YOUR PLAYTHINGS--
--I'LL JUST HAVE TO SNAG THEM ALL, AND TAKE THEM AWAY.
VERY CARELESS, YOUNG LADY!
I MANAGED TO TELEPORT BEHIND YOU WHILE YOU WERE BUSY CHASTISING MY ASSOCIATE.
SPWAKK!
I ATTRIBUTE HER RECKLESSNESS TO INEXPERIENCE!
WHAT'S YOUR EXCUSE?

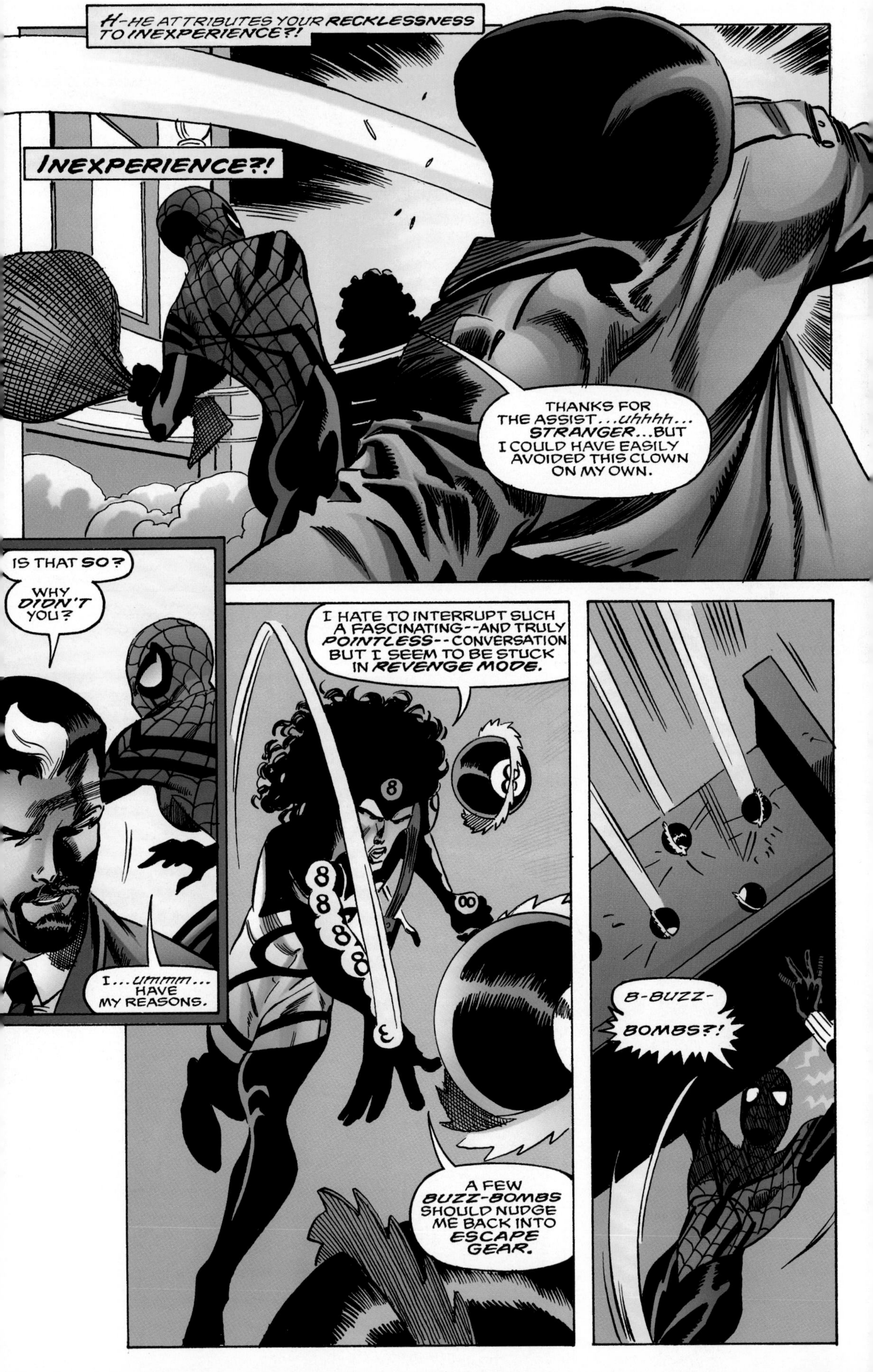
H-HE ATTRIBUTES YOUR RECKLESSNESS TO INEXPERIENCE?!
INEXPERIENCE?!
THANKS FOR THE ASSIST...uhhhh... STRANGER...BUT I COULD HAVE EASILY AVOIDED THIS CLOWN ON MY OWN.
IS THAT SO?
WHY DIDN'T YOU?
I...ummm... HAVE MY REASONS.
I HATE TO INTERRUPT SUCH A FASCINATING--AND TRULY POINTLESS--CONVERSATION BUT I SEEM TO BE STUCK IN REVENGE MODE.
A FEW BUZZ-BOMBS SHOULD NUDGE ME BACK INTO ESCAPE GEAR.
B-BUZZ-
BOMBS?!

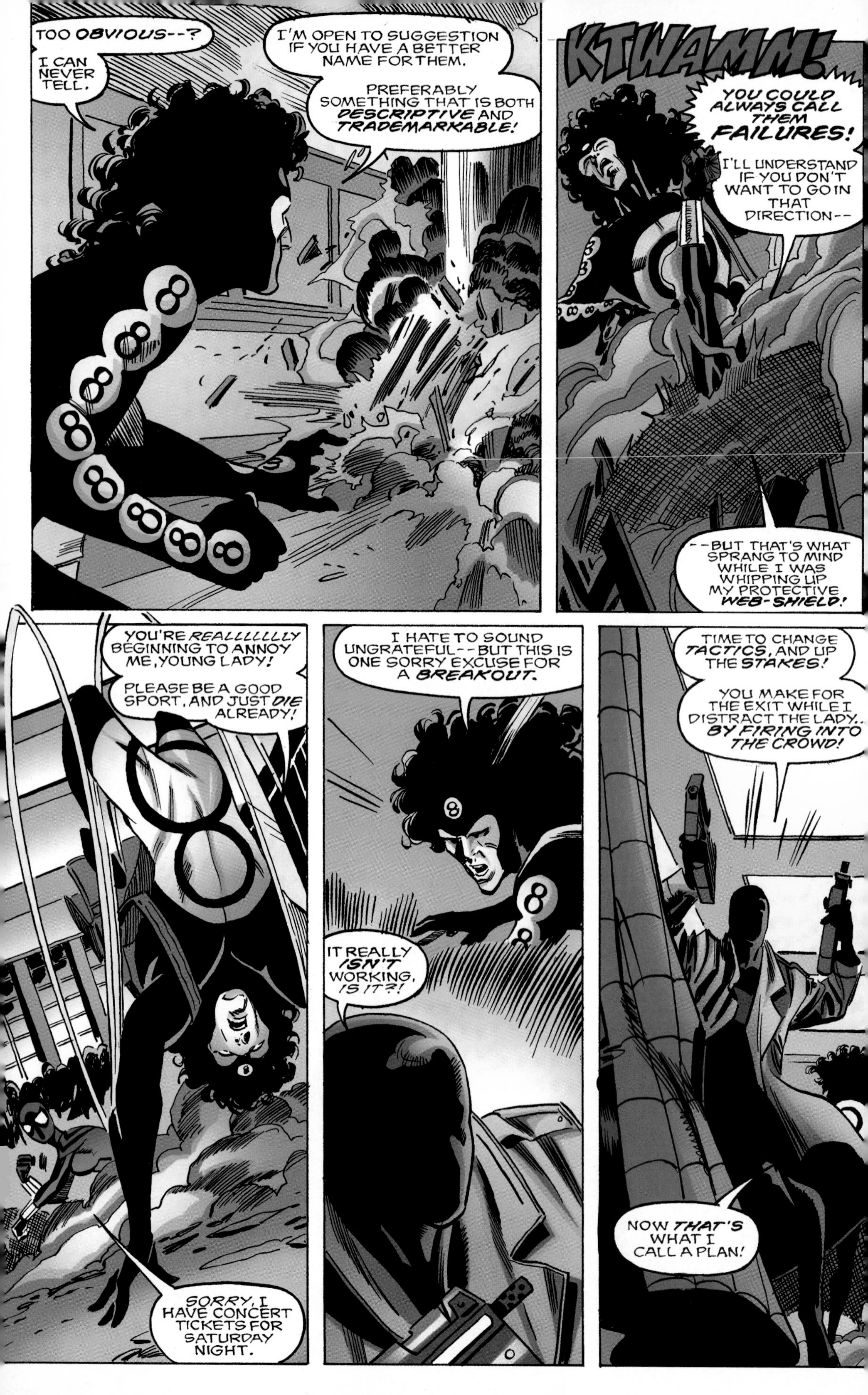
TOO OBVIOUS--?
I CAN NEVER TELL.
I'M OPEN TO SUGGESTION IF YOU HAVE A BETTER NAME FOR THEM.
PREFERABLY SOMETHING THAT IS BOTH DESCRIPTIVE AND TRADEMARKABLE!
KTWAMM!
YOU COULD ALWAYS CALL THEM FAILURES!
I'LL UNDERSTAND IF YOU DON'T WANT TO GO IN THAT DIRECTION--
--BUT THAT'S WHAT SPRANG TO MIND WHILE I WAS WHIPPING UP MY PROTECTIVE WEB-SHIELD!
YOU'RE REALLLLLLLY BEGINNING TO ANNOY ME, YOUNG LADY!
PLEASE BE A GOOD SPORT, AND JUST DIE ALREADY!
SORRY, I HAVE CONCERT TICKETS FOR SATURDAY NIGHT.
I HATE TO SOUND UNGRATEFUL--BUT THIS IS ONE SORRY EXCUSE FOR A BREAKOUT.
IT REALLY ISN'T WORKING, IS IT?!
TIME TO CHANGE TACTICS, AND UP THE STAKES!
YOU MAKE FOR THE EXIT WHILE I DISTRACT THE LADY.. BY FIRING INTO THE CROWD!
NOW THAT'S WHAT I CALL A PLAN!

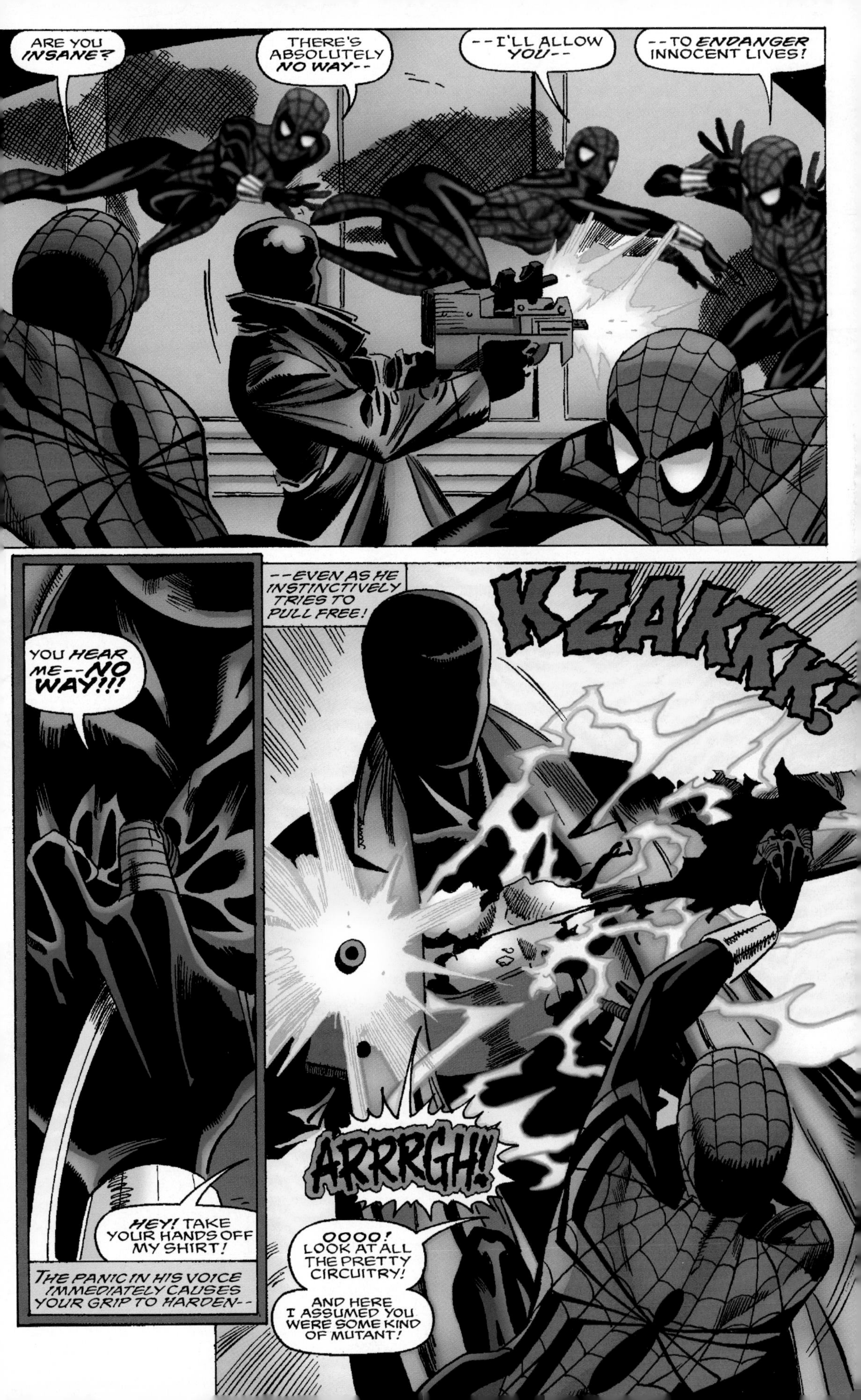
ARE YOU INSANE?
THERE'S ABSOLUTELY NO WAY--
--I'LL ALLOW YOU--
--TO ENDANGER INNOCENT LIVES!
YOU HEAR ME--NO WAY!!!
HEY! TAKE YOUR HANDS OFF MY SHIRT!
THE PANIC IN HIS VOICE IMMEDIATELY CAUSES YOUR GRIP TO HARDEN--
--EVEN AS HE INSTINCTIVELY TRIES TO PULL FREE!
KZAKKK!
ARRRGH!
OOOO! LOOK AT ALL THE PRETTY CIRCUITRY!
AND HERE I ASSUMED YOU WERE SOME KIND OF MUTANT!

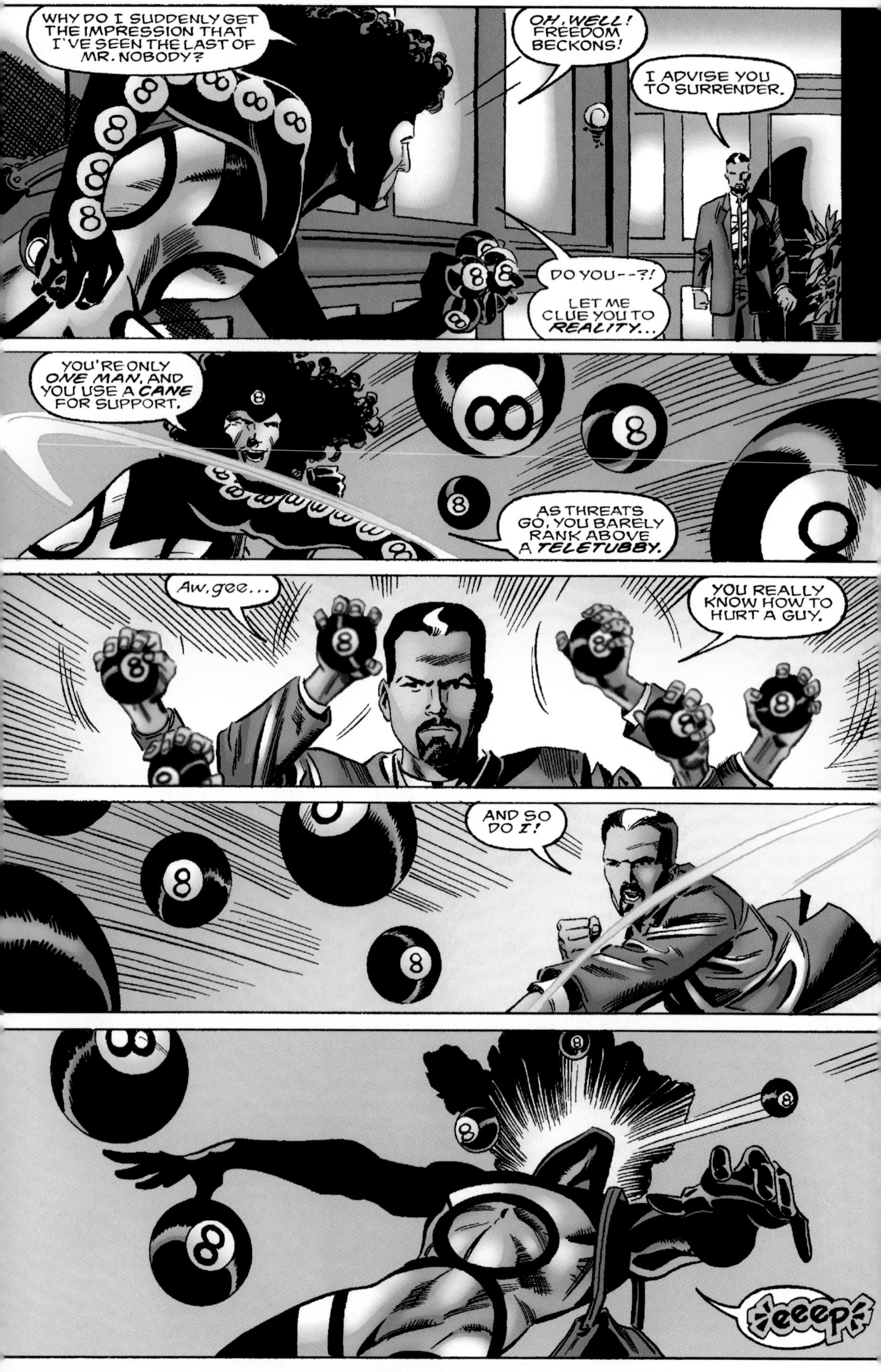
WHY DO I SUDDENLY GET THE IMPRESSION THAT I'VE SEEN THE LAST OF MR. NOBODY?
OH, WELL! FREEDOM BECKONS!
I ADVISE YOU TO SURRENDER.
DO YOU--?!
LET ME CLUE YOU TO REALITY...
YOU'RE ONLY ONE MAN, AND YOU USE A CANE FOR SUPPORT.
AS THREATS GO, YOU BARELY RANK ABOVE A TELETUBBY.
Aw, gee...
YOU REALLY KNOW HOW TO HURT A GUY.
AND SO DO I!
eeep

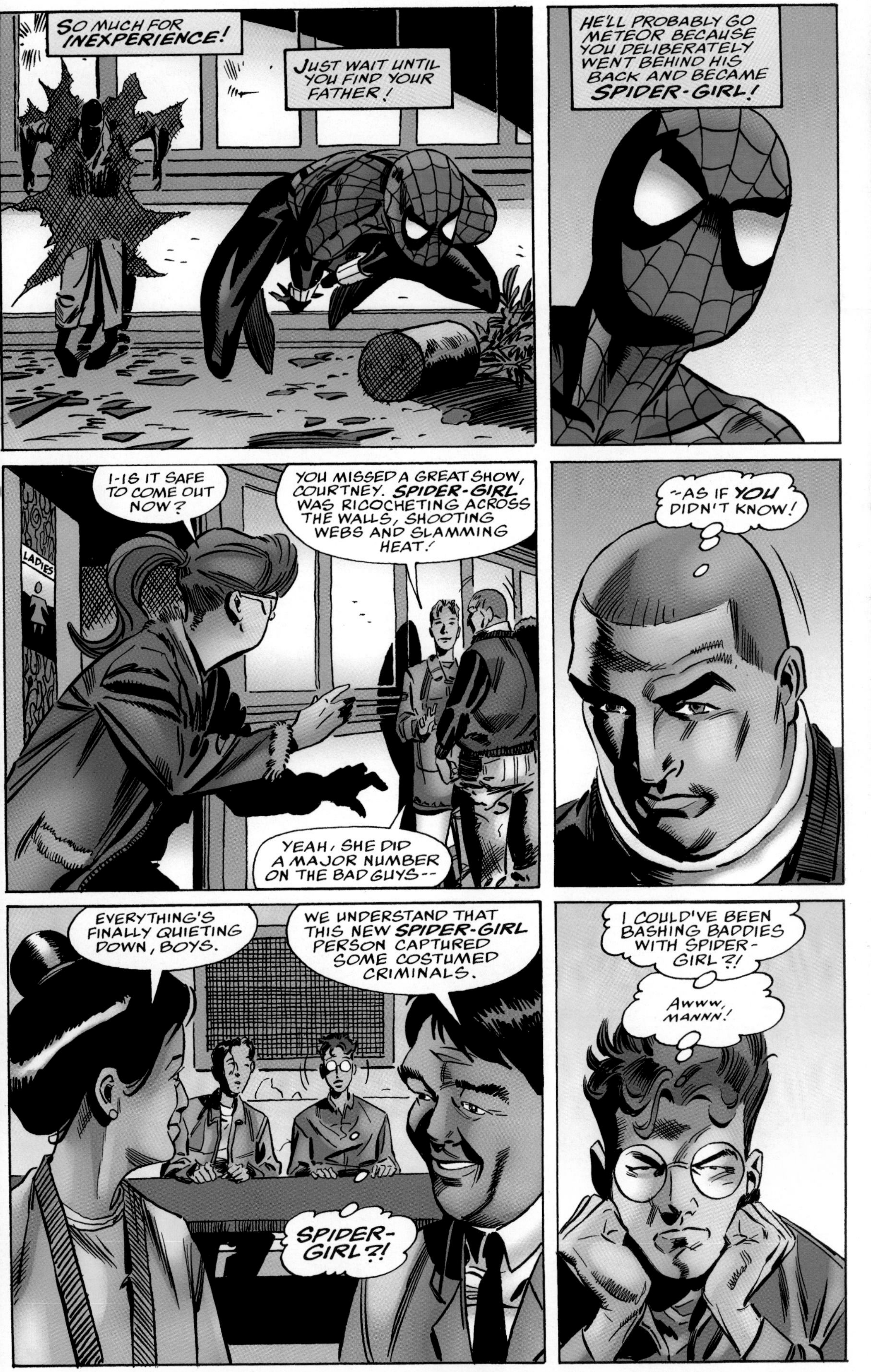
SO MUCH FOR INEXPERIENCE!
JUST WAIT UNTIL YOU FIND YOUR FATHER!
HE'LL PROBABLY GO METEOR BECAUSE YOU DELIBERATELY WENT BEHIND HIS BACK AND BECAME SPIDER-GIRL!
I-IS IT SAFE TO COME OUT NOW?
YOU MISSED A GREAT SHOW, COURTNEY. SPIDER-GIRL WAS RICOCHETING ACROSS THE WALLS, SHOOTING WEBS AND SLAMMING HEAT!
YEAH, SHE DID A MAJOR NUMBER ON THE BAD GUYS--
LADIES
--AS IF YOU DIDN'T KNOW!
EVERYTHING'S FINALLY QUIETING DOWN, BOYS.
WE UNDERSTAND THAT THIS NEW SPIDER-GIRL PERSON CAPTURED SOME COSTUMED CRIMINALS.
SPIDER-GIRL?!
I COULD'VE BEEN BASHING BADDIES WITH SPIDER-GIRL?!
AWWW, MANNN!

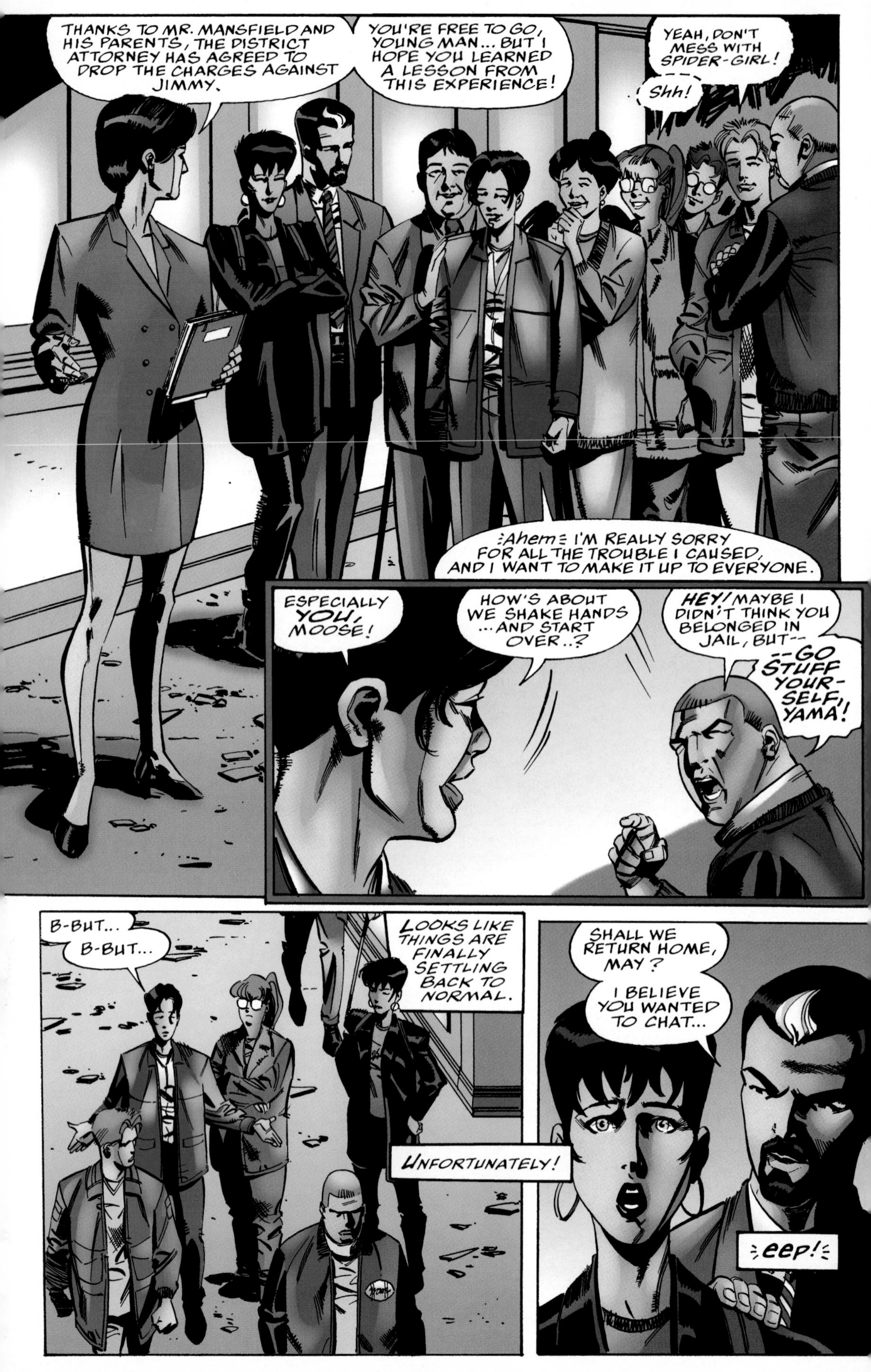
THANKS TO MR. MANSFIELD AND HIS PARENTS, THE DISTRICT ATTORNEY HAS AGREED TO DROP THE CHARGES AGAINST JIMMY.
YOU'RE FREE TO GO, YOUNG MAN... BUT I HOPE YOU LEARNED A LESSON FROM THIS EXPERIENCE!
YEAH, DON'T MESS WITH SPIDER-GIRL!
Shh!
:Ahem: I'M REALLY SORRY FOR ALL THE TROUBLE I CAUSED, AND I WANT TO MAKE IT UP TO EVERYONE.
ESPECIALLY YOU, MOOSE!
HOW'S ABOUT WE SHAKE HANDS ...AND START OVER..?
HEY! MAYBE I DIDN'T THINK YOU BELONGED IN JAIL, BUT--
--GO STUFF YOURSELF, YAMA!
B-BUT...
B-BUT...
LOOKS LIKE THINGS ARE FINALLY SETTLING BACK TO NORMAL.
UNFORTUNATELY!
SHALL WE RETURN HOME, MAY?
I BELIEVE YOU WANTED TO CHAT...
:eep!:

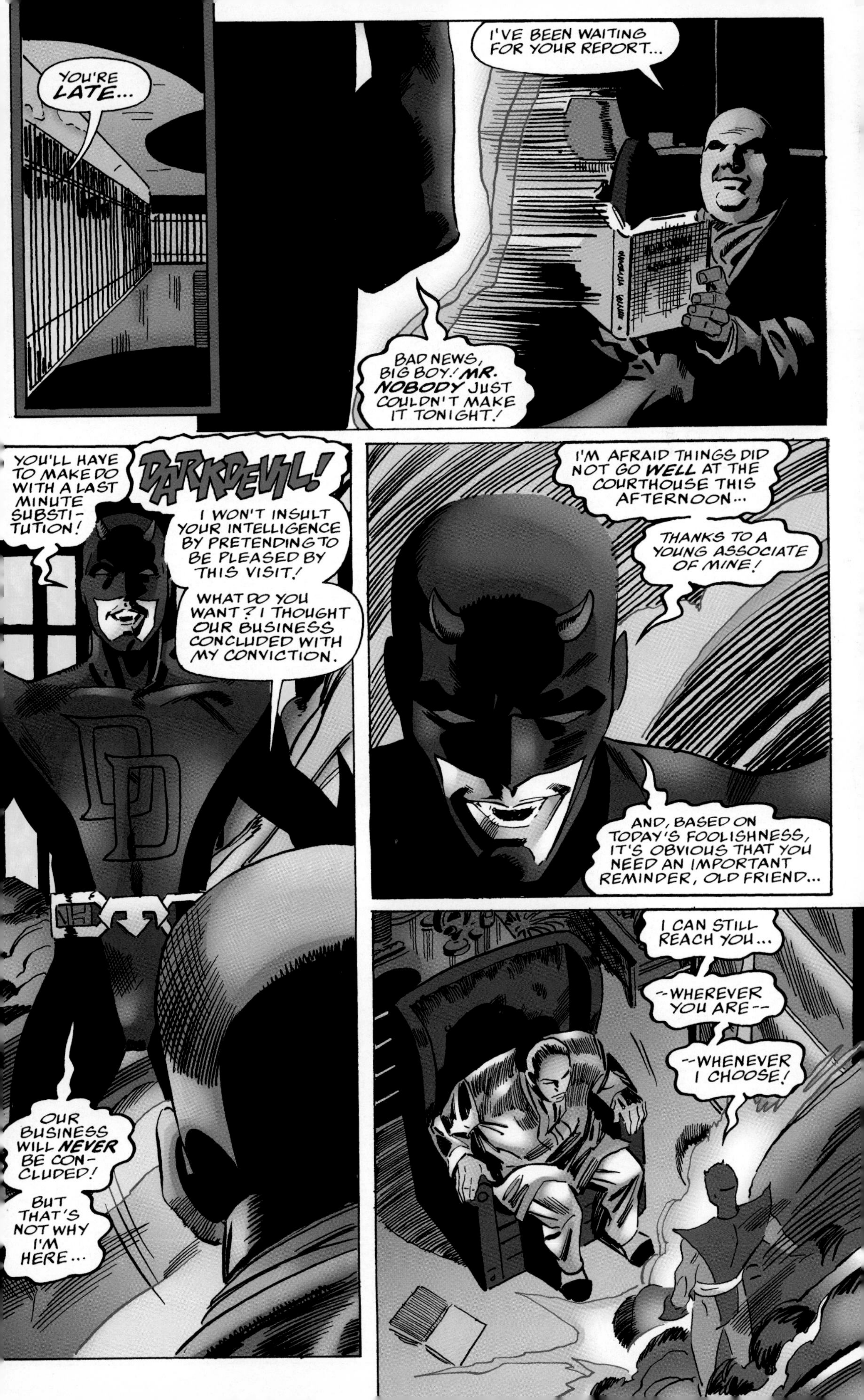

YOU'RE LATE...
I'VE BEEN WAITING FOR YOUR REPORT...
BAD NEWS, BIG BOY! MR. NOBODY JUST COULDN'T MAKE IT TONIGHT!
YOU'LL HAVE TO MAKE DO WITH A LAST MINUTE SUBSTITUTION!
DARKDEVIL!
I WON'T INSULT YOUR INTELLIGENCE BY PRETENDING TO BE PLEASED BY THIS VISIT!
WHAT DO YOU WANT? I THOUGHT OUR BUSINESS CONCLUDED WITH MY CONVICTION.
OUR BUSINESS WILL NEVER BE CONCLUDED!
BUT THAT'S NOT WHY I'M HERE...
I'M AFRAID THINGS DID NOT GO WELL AT THE COURTHOUSE THIS AFTERNOON...
THANKS TO A YOUNG ASSOCIATE OF MINE!
AND, BASED ON TODAY'S FOOLISHNESS, IT'S OBVIOUS THAT YOU NEED AN IMPORTANT REMINDER, OLD FRIEND...
I CAN STILL REACH YOU...
--WHEREVER YOU ARE--
--WHENEVER I CHOOSE!

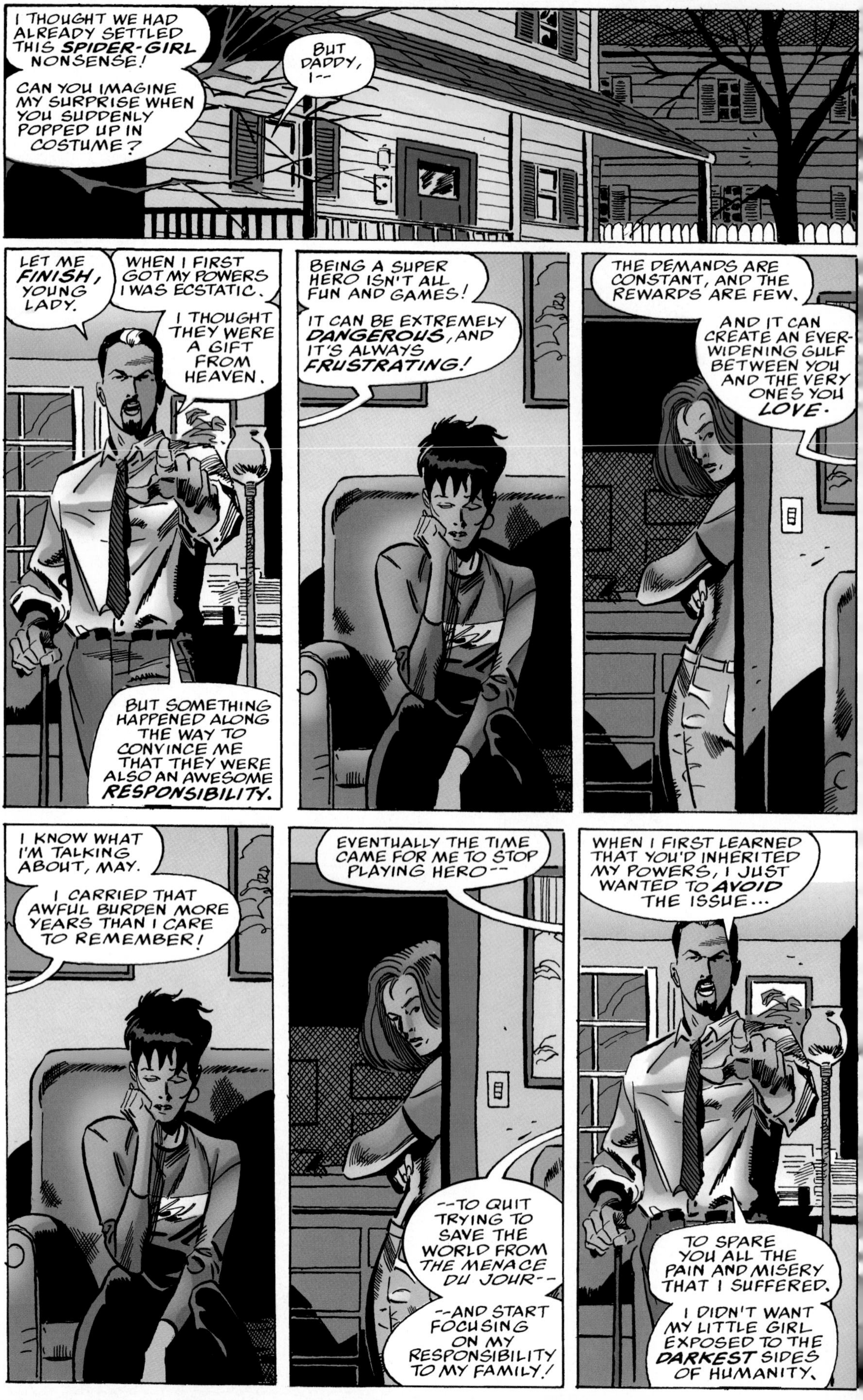
I THOUGHT WE HAD ALREADY SETTLED THIS SPIDER-GIRL NONSENSE!
CAN YOU IMAGINE MY SURPRISE WHEN YOU SUDDENLY POPPED UP IN COSTUME?
BUT DADDY, I--
LET ME FINISH, YOUNG LADY.
WHEN I FIRST GOT MY POWERS I WAS ECSTATIC.
I THOUGHT THEY WERE A GIFT FROM HEAVEN.
BUT SOMETHING HAPPENED ALONG THE WAY TO CONVINCE ME THAT THEY WERE ALSO AN AWESOME RESPONSIBILITY.
BEING A SUPER HERO ISN'T ALL FUN AND GAMES!
IT CAN BE EXTREMELY DANGEROUS, AND IT'S ALWAYS FRUSTRATING!
THE DEMANDS ARE CONSTANT, AND THE REWARDS ARE FEW.
AND IT CAN CREATE AN EVER-WIDENING GULF BETWEEN YOU AND THE VERY ONES YOU LOVE.
I KNOW WHAT I'M TALKING ABOUT, MAY.
I CARRIED THAT AWFUL BURDEN MORE YEARS THAN I CARE TO REMEMBER!
EVENTUALLY THE TIME CAME FOR ME TO STOP PLAYING HERO--
--TO QUIT TRYING TO SAVE THE WORLD FROM THE MENACE DU JOUR--
--AND START FOCUSING ON MY RESPONSIBILITY TO MY FAMILY!
WHEN I FIRST LEARNED THAT YOU'D INHERITED MY POWERS, I JUST WANTED TO AVOID THE ISSUE...
TO SPARE YOU ALL THE PAIN AND MISERY THAT I SUFFERED.
I DIDN'T WANT MY LITTLE GIRL EXPOSED TO THE DARKEST SIDES OF HUMANITY.

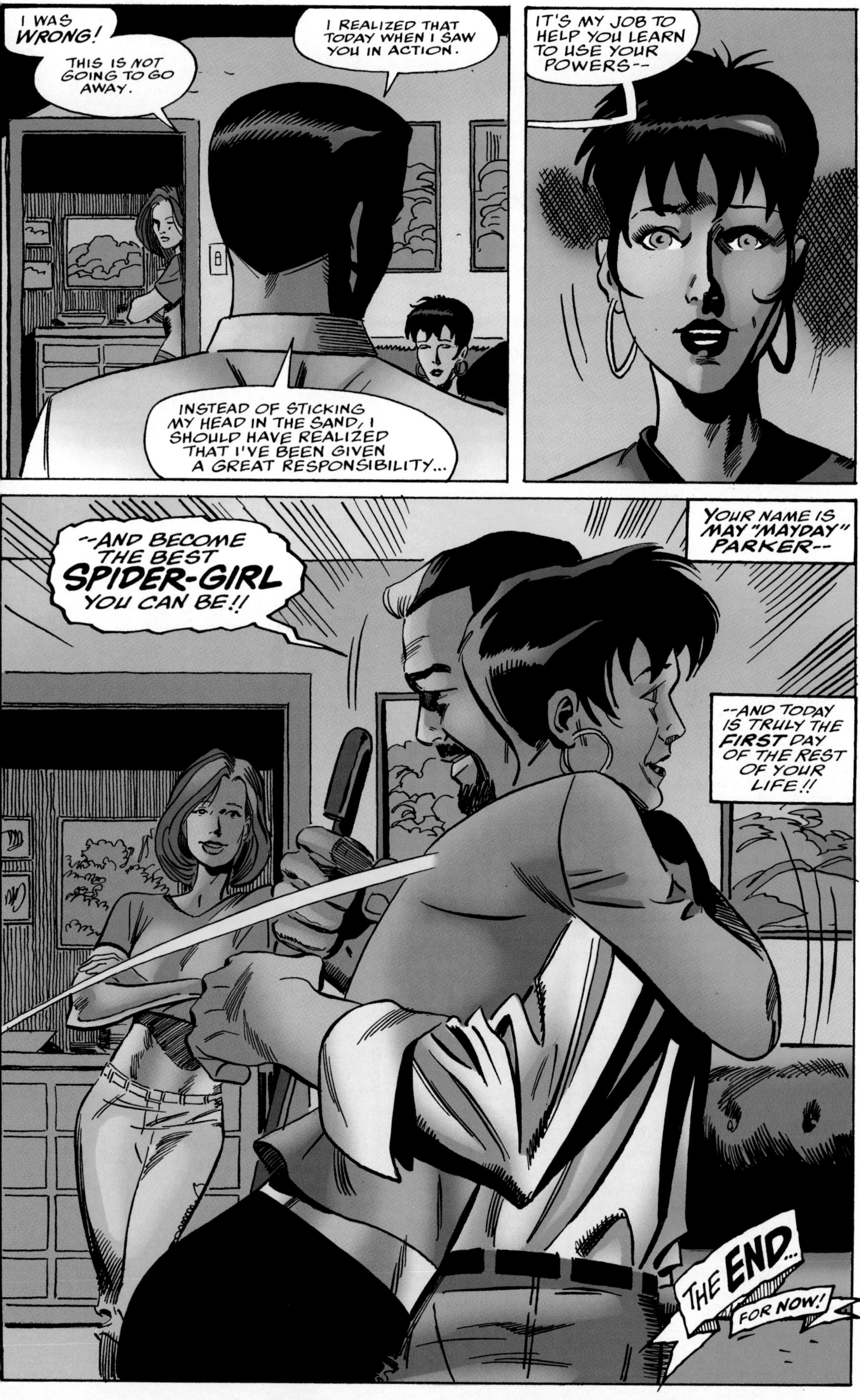

I WAS WRONG!
THIS IS NOT GOING TO GO AWAY.
I REALIZED THAT TODAY WHEN I SAW YOU IN ACTION.
INSTEAD OF STICKING MY HEAD IN THE SAND, I SHOULD HAVE REALIZED THAT I'VE BEEN GIVEN A GREAT RESPONSIBILITY...
IT'S MY JOB TO HELP YOU LEARN TO USE YOUR POWERS--
--AND BECOME THE BEST SPIDER-GIRL YOU CAN BE!!
YOUR NAME IS MAY "MAYDAY" PARKER--
--AND TODAY IS TRULY THE FIRST DAY OF THE REST OF YOUR LIFE!!
THE END... FOR NOW!

# SPIDER-GIRL COVER GALLERY

#0

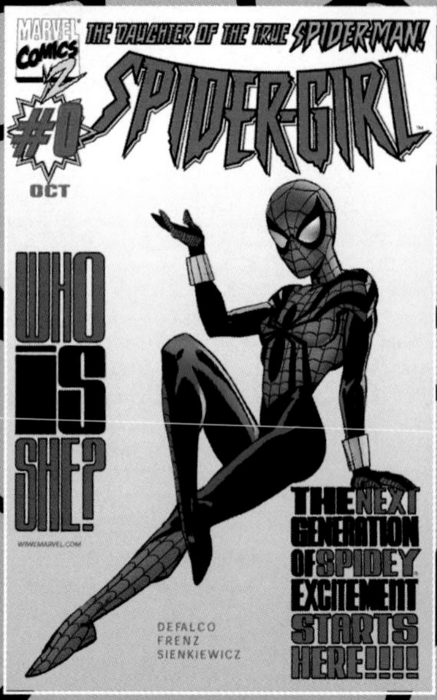
MARVEL COMICS 2
THE DAUGHTER OF THE TRUE SPIDER-MAN!
SPIDER-GIRL
#0
OCT
WHO IS SHE?
THE NEXT GENERATION OF SPIDEY EXCITEMENT STARTS HERE!!!!
DEFALCO
FRENZ
SIENKIEWICZ

#1

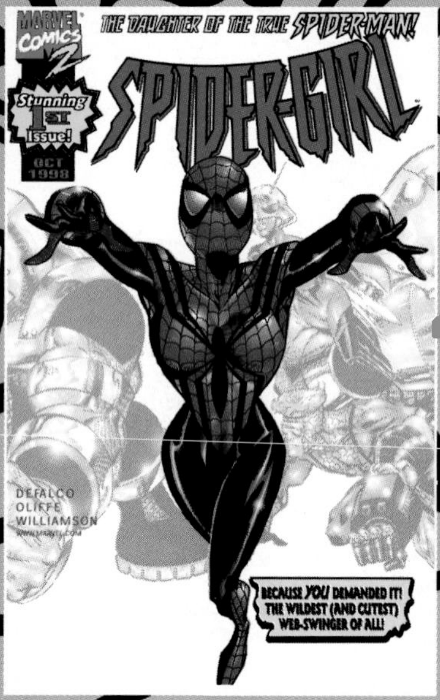
MARVEL COMICS 2
THE DAUGHTER OF THE TRUE SPIDER-MAN!
SPIDER-GIRL
Stunning 1st Issue!
OCT 1998
DEFALCO
OLIFFE
WILLIAMSON
BECAUSE YOU DEMANDED IT! THE WILDEST (AND CUTEST) WEB-SWINGER OF ALL!

#2

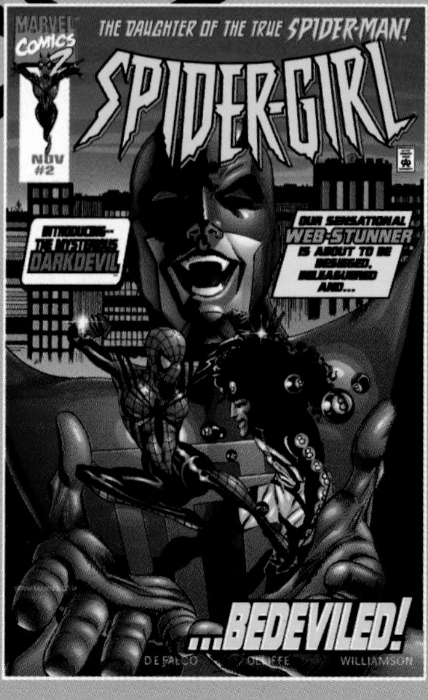
MARVEL COMICS 2
THE DAUGHTER OF THE TRUE SPIDER-MAN!
SPIDER-GIRL
NOV #2
INTRODUCING— THE MYSTERIOUS DARKDEVIL
OUR SENSATIONAL WEB-STUNNER IS ABOUT TO BE ...
...BEDEVILED!
DEFALCO
WILLIAMSON

#3

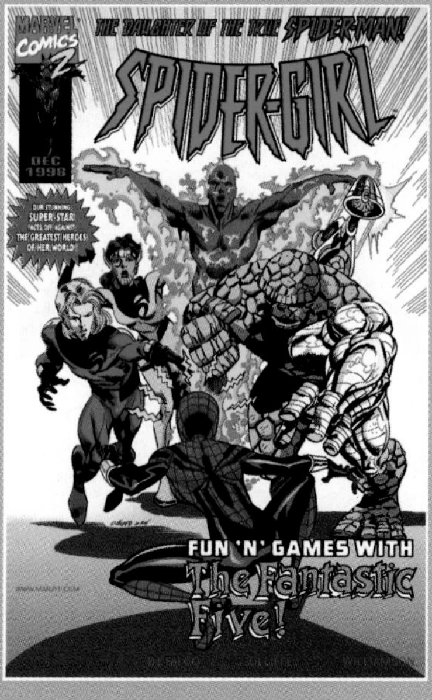
MARVEL COMICS 2
THE DAUGHTER OF THE TRUE SPIDER-MAN!
SPIDER-GIRL
DEC 1998
FUN 'N' GAMES WITH
The Fantastic Five!

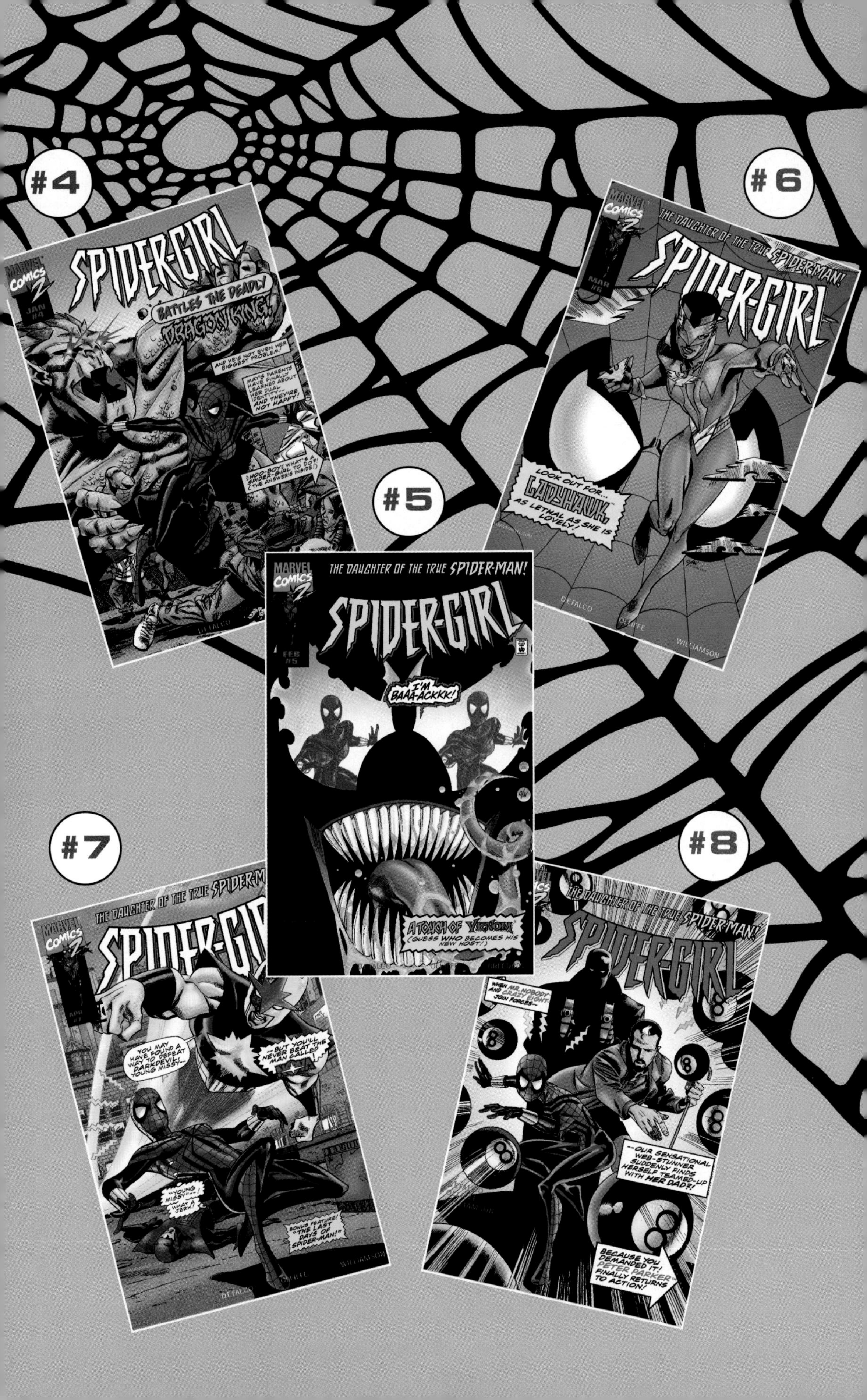
#4
MARVEL COMICS 2
SPIDER-GIRL
JAN #4
BATTLES THE DEADLY DRAGON KING!
AND HE'S NOT EVEN HER BIGGEST PROBLEM!
MAY'S PARENTS HAVE FINALLY LEARNED ABOUT HER DUAL IDENTITY-- AND THEY'RE NOT HAPPY!
HOO-BOY! WHAT'S A SPIDER-GIRL TO DO? (THE ANSWER'S INSIDE!)
#5
MARVEL COMICS 2
THE DAUGHTER OF THE TRUE SPIDER-MAN!
SPIDER-GIRL
FEB #5
I'M BAAA-ACKKK!
A TOUCH OF VENOM
(GUESS WHO BECOMES HIS NEW HOST!)
#6
MARVEL COMICS 2
THE DAUGHTER OF THE TRUE SPIDER-MAN!
SPIDER-GIRL
MAR #6
LOOK OUT FOR... LADYHAWK, AS LETHAL AS SHE IS LOVELY!
DEFALCO
OLLIFFE
WILLIAMSON
#7
MARVEL COMICS 2
THE DAUGHTER OF THE TRUE SPIDER-MA
SPIDER-GI
YOU MAY HAVE FOUND A WAY TO DEFEAT DARKDEVIL, YOUNG MISSY--
--BUT YOU'LL NEVER BEAT THE MAN CALLED
"YOUNG MISSY"--? WHAT A JERK!
BONUS FEATURE! "THE LAST DAYS OF SPIDER-MAN!"
DEFALCO
OLLIFFE
WILLIAMSON
#8
THE DAUGHTER OF THE TRUE SPIDER-MAN!
SPIDER-GIRL
WHEN MR. NOBODY AND CRAZY EIGHT JOIN FORCES--
--OUR SENSATIONAL WEB-STUNNER SUDDENLY FINDS HERSELF TEAMED-UP WITH HER DAD?!
BECAUSE YOU DEMANDED IT! PETER PARKER FINALLY RETURNS TO ACTION!

# Also Available From

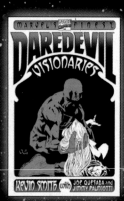

# COMETS AND METEOR SHOWERS

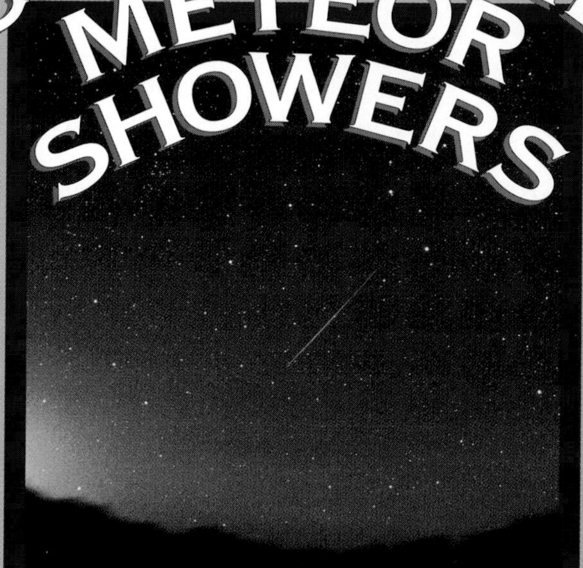

A TRUE BOOK

by

**Paul P. Sipiera**

Children's Press®
A Division of Grolier Publishing
New York London Hong Kong Sydney
Danbury, Connecticut

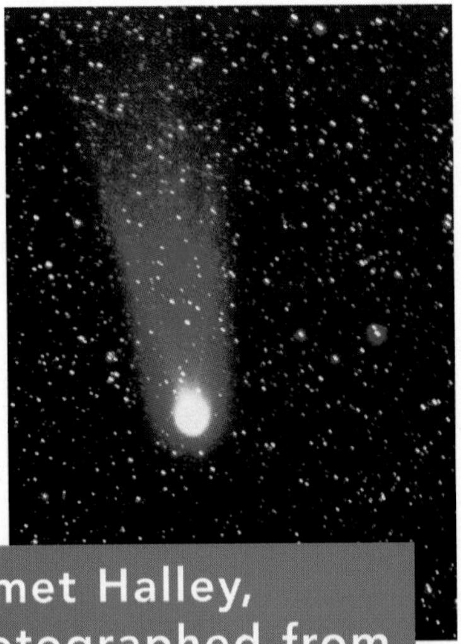

Comet Halley, photographed from Australia in 1986

*Reading Consultant*
**Linda Cornwell**
*Learning Resource Consultant*
*Indiana Department of Education*

*Science Consultant*
**Samuel Storch**
*Lecturer,*
*American Museum-Hayden Planetarium, New York City*

*Dedicated to my friend Herbert Windolf, a student of nature*

Library of Congress Cataloging-in-Publication Data

Sipiera, Paul P.
Comets and Meteor Showers / by Paul Sipiera.
p. cm. — (A true book)
Includes bibliographical references and index.
Summary: Provides an introduction to comets, covering where they come from, how they travel, their importance to astronomers, as well as their relationship to meteor showers.
ISBN 0-516-20330-4 (lib. bdg.) 0-516-26166-5 (pbk.)
1. Comets—Juvenile literature. 2. Meteorites—Juvenile literature. [1. Comets. 2. Meteors.] I. Title. II. Series.
QB721.5.S56 1997
523.6—dc20 96-31711
CIP
AC


Printed in the United States of America.
10 R 06 05

# Contents

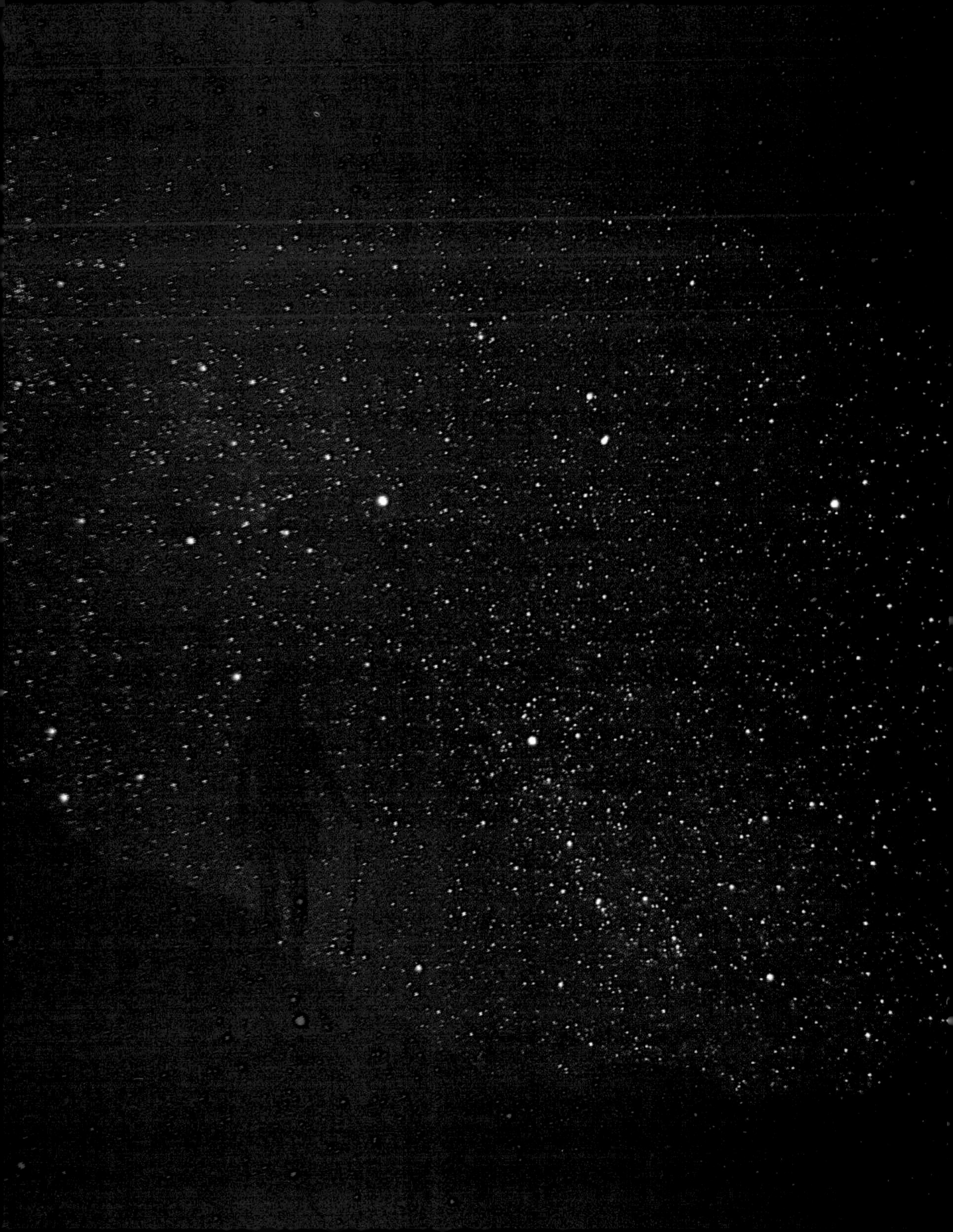

# The Night Sky

For thousands of years, people have looked up into the night sky and wondered about the stars. Ancient people made patterns from the brightest stars and called them constellations. These stars seemed to remain the same from year to year.

Against this background of stars moved five bright objects. These became known as the planets.

People learned to use the stars to tell time and to predict the seasons. Knowledge of the night sky became important in many cultures.

# What Is a Comet?

Every now and then, a new object was seen in the night sky. It was neither a star nor a planet. What was it? Many people saw it as a "hairy star" because of its fuzzy appearance and long tail. Today, we call these objects comets.

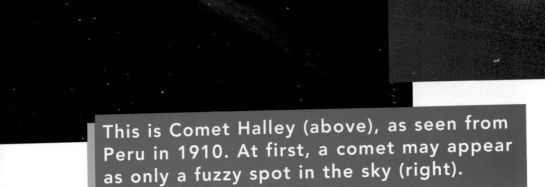

This is Comet Halley (above), as seen from Peru in 1910. At first, a comet may appear as only a fuzzy spot in the sky (right).

A comet is a chunk of ice and rock that orbits the Sun. It spends most of its life far from the Sun, where the temperatures are very cold.

Comets are very small, usually about 10 miles

(16 kilometers) across. When a comet is very far from the Sun, it cannot be seen from Earth. But when a comet's orbit brings it close to the Sun, a large cloud of gas forms around it. It is at this point that astronomers can usually first see it.

The central core of a comet, called the nucleus, is small, solid, and made of ice and bits of rock. The comet usually remains solid until it nears the orbit of Uranus, where the Sun's

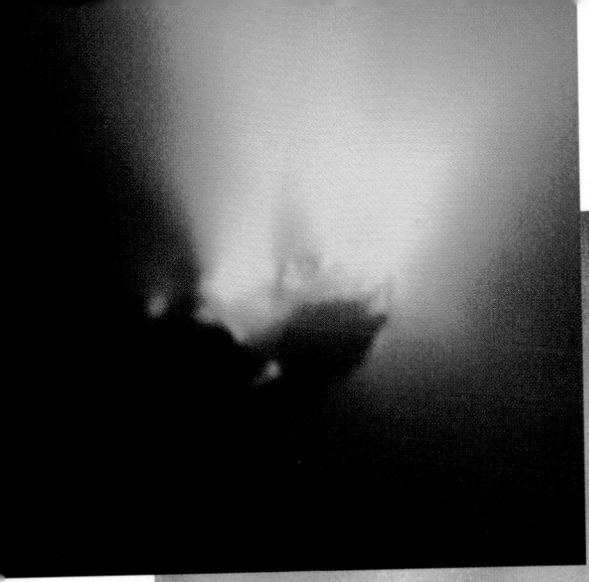

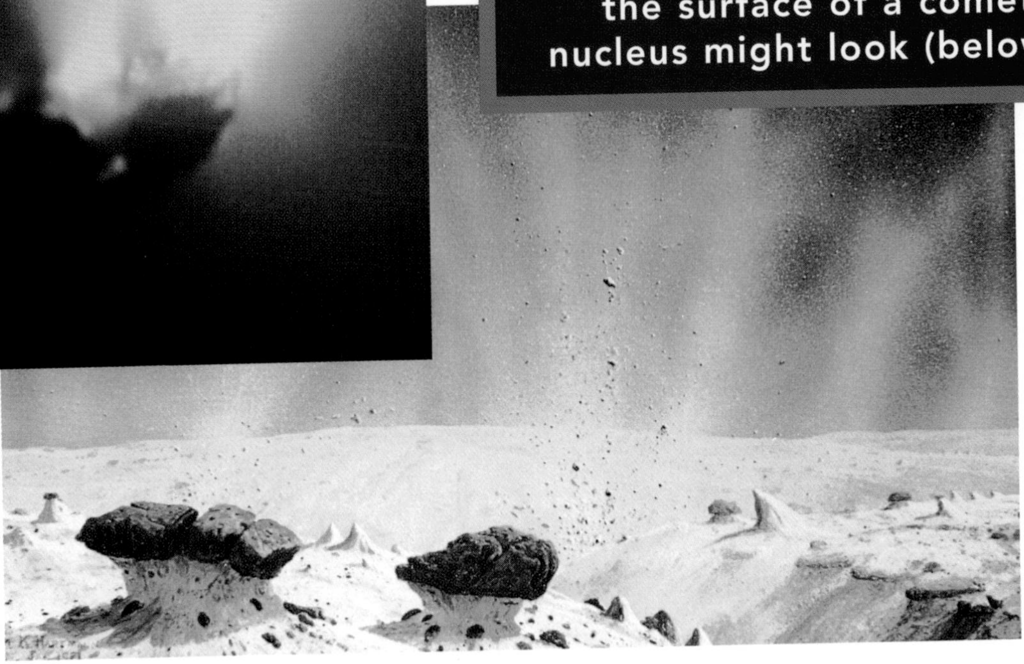

The nucleus of a comet (left) and an illustration of how the surface of a comet's nucleus might look (below)

heat causes the ice to evaporate. This evaporation forms a gas cloud, called a coma, around the nucleus. At this point, the comet can be seen through the largest telescopes.

As the comet gets closer to the Sun, more and more ice evaporates. The coma becomes bigger and brighter.

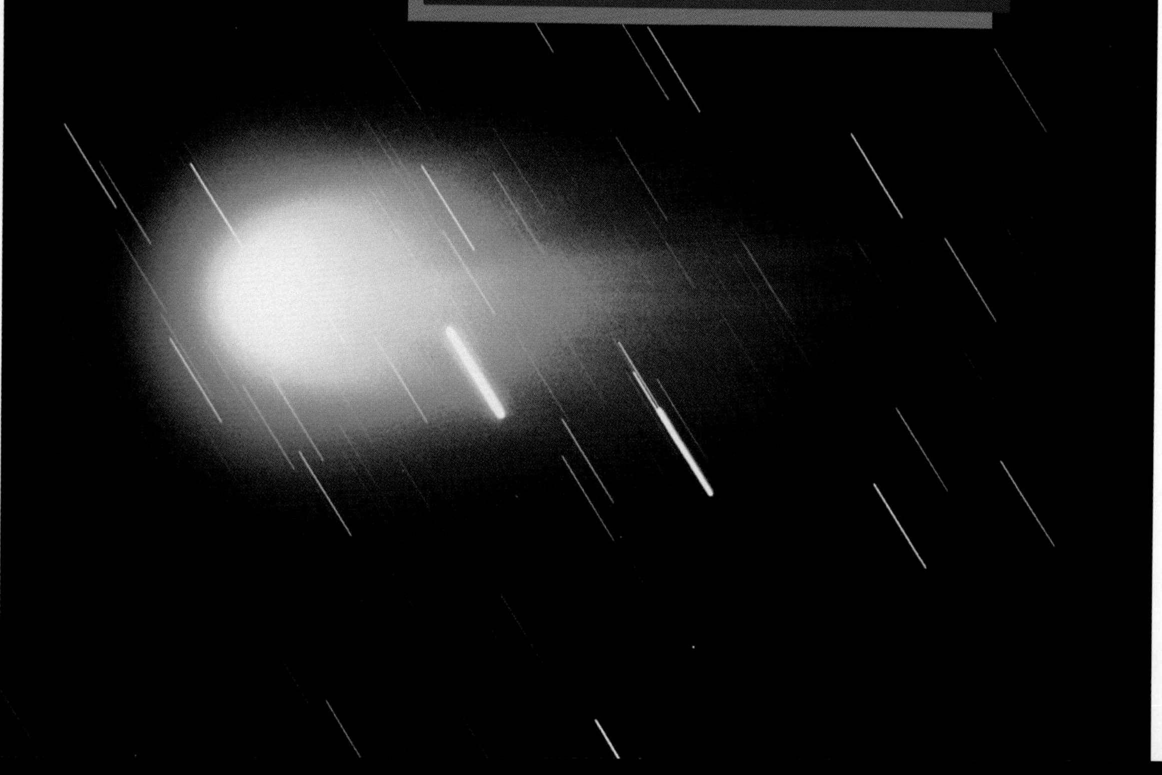

As a comet comes closer to the hot sun, its ice begins to evaporate, forming a gas cloud called a coma.

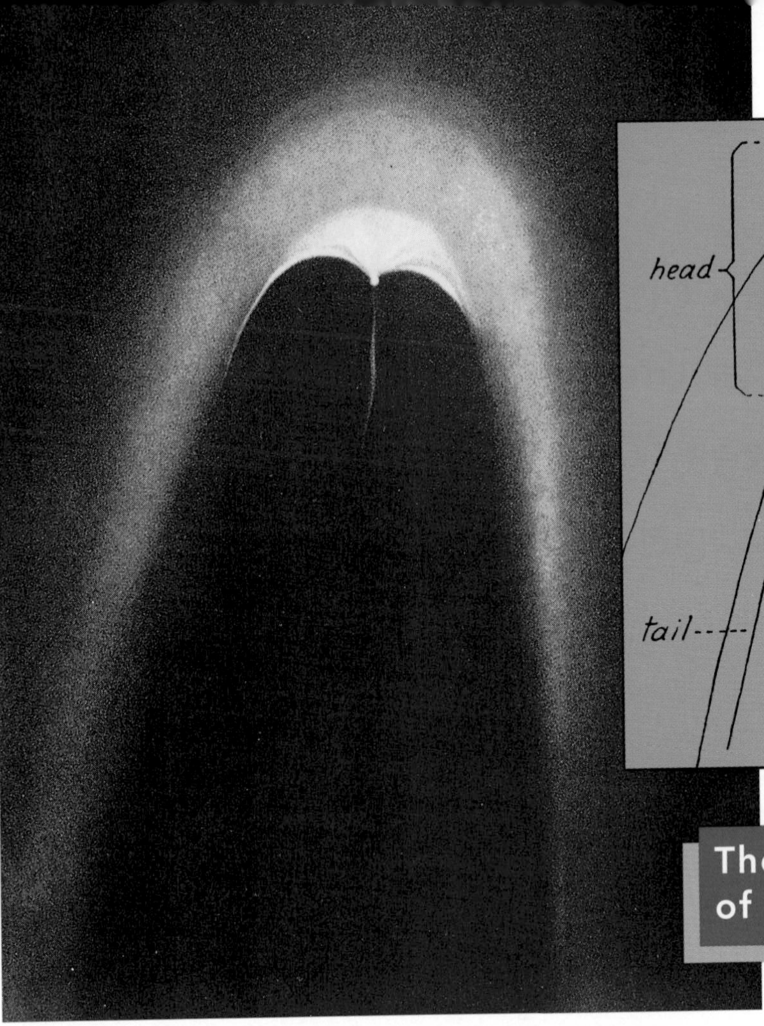

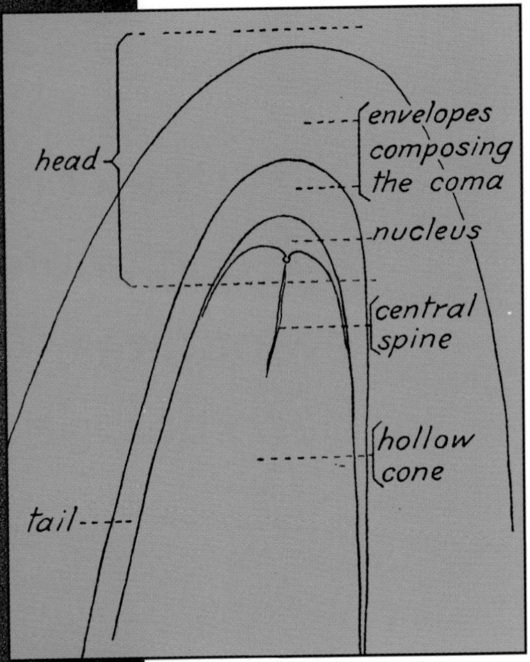
envelopes composing the coma
head
nucleus
central spine
hollow cone
tail

The parts of a comet

By the time the comet reaches the orbit of Mars, a small tail may develop. The tail is formed when powerful solar wind blows gas away from the coma. The tail grows as the comet approaches Earth's orbit. Now, if they know where to look, people can see the comet with binoculars.

At about the time when the comet is as close to the Sun as Earth is, it may actually have two tails. One tail is straight and looks bluish-white. The second tail is curved and has a yellowish color. The bluish-white tail is made of glowing

As it gets closer to the Sun, a comet develops two tails.

gas blown away from the coma. It is always straight and points away from the Sun.

The yellowish curved tail is made of small grains of rock and metal. It is yellow because it reflects the Sun's yellow light. Its curved shape is caused by the motion of the comet as it swings around the Sun. The solar wind does not blow this material away as it does the gas. As these particles melt out of the nucleus, they follow behind the comet like people in a parade.

In this photo of a comet, you can see both the straight, bluish tail and the curved, yellowish tail.

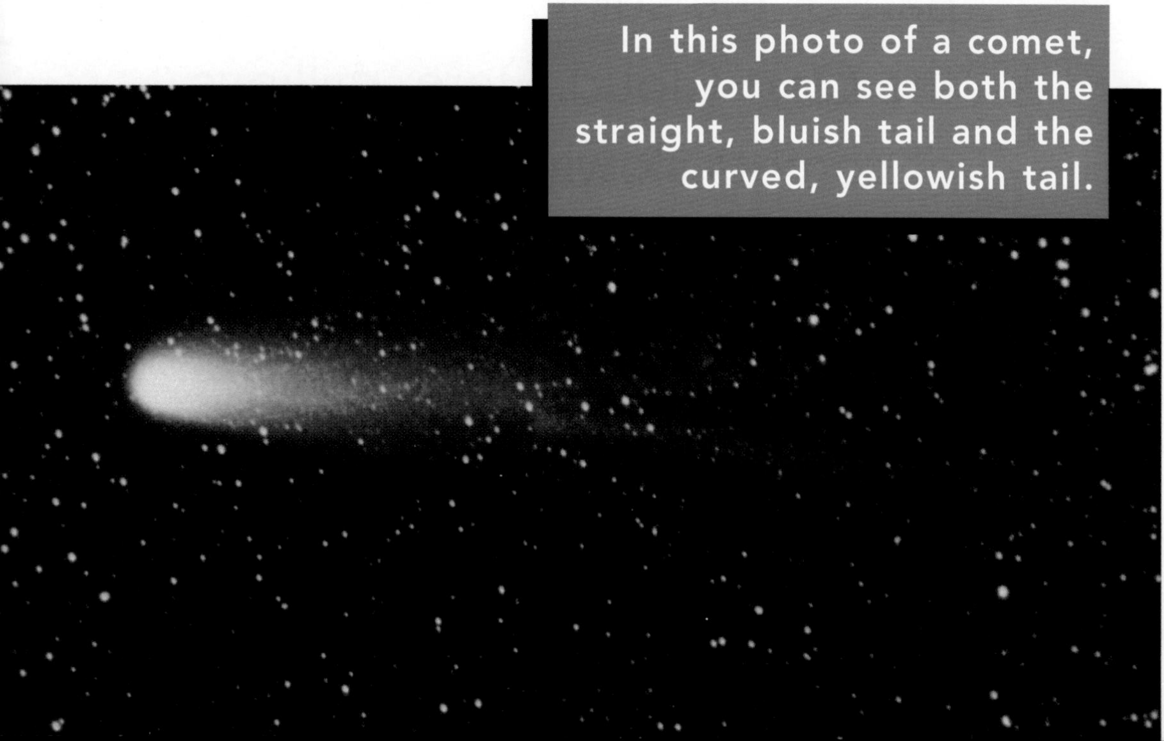

# Where Do Comets Come From?

Comets come from a distant part of the solar system called the Oort Cloud. Here, millions of comets slowly orbit the Sun. Sometimes, two comets collide with one another and one is bumped toward the Sun. Sometimes, the gravity of a

A diagram showing the oval-shaped orbits of various comets around the Sun

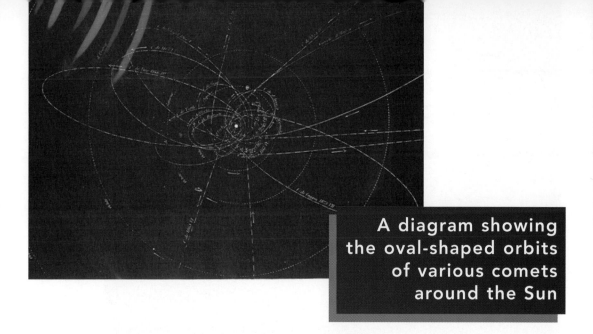

nearby star pulls a comet out of its orbit around the Sun. In turn, the Sun may pull comets away from other stars.

Most comets follow an oval-shaped path around the Sun called an ellipse. Some comets take thousands of years to complete one orbit. Comet

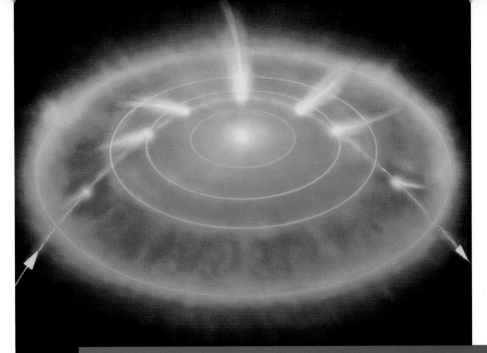

In this drawing, one comet is show in seven different positions of its orbit. The length and direction of the tail changes as the comet travels around the Sun and is shaped by solar wind.

Halley has one of the shorter orbits. It takes about 75 years to travel around the Sun—the average person's lifetime. Author Mark Twain was born in 1835, when Comet Halley was near Earth. In 1910, when it returned, Twain died. He had always said that he came in with the comet and that he would go out with it, too!

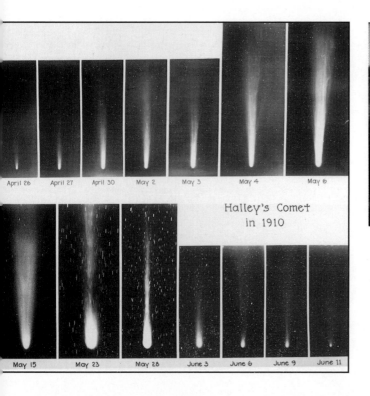

Halley's Comet in 1910

April 26  April 27  April 30  May 2  May 3  May 4  May 6

May 15  May 23  May 28  June 3  June 6  June 9  June 11

This is how Comet Halley looked on different days during its 1910 appearance (left). Author Mark Twain (right) died that same year.

# Comet Halley

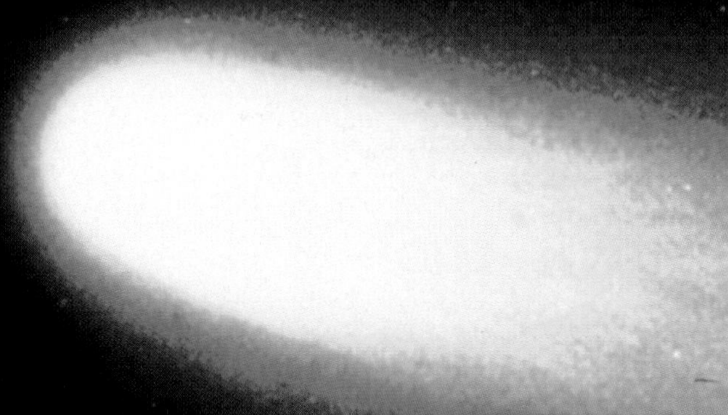

Comet Halley was the first comet shown to have an orbit. In 1705, English astronomer Edmond Halley showed that comets seen in 1531, 1607, and 1682 were really one comet. He predicted that this comet would continue to reappear about every 75 years. The comet was later named after him. Today, new comets are named after whoever discovers them!

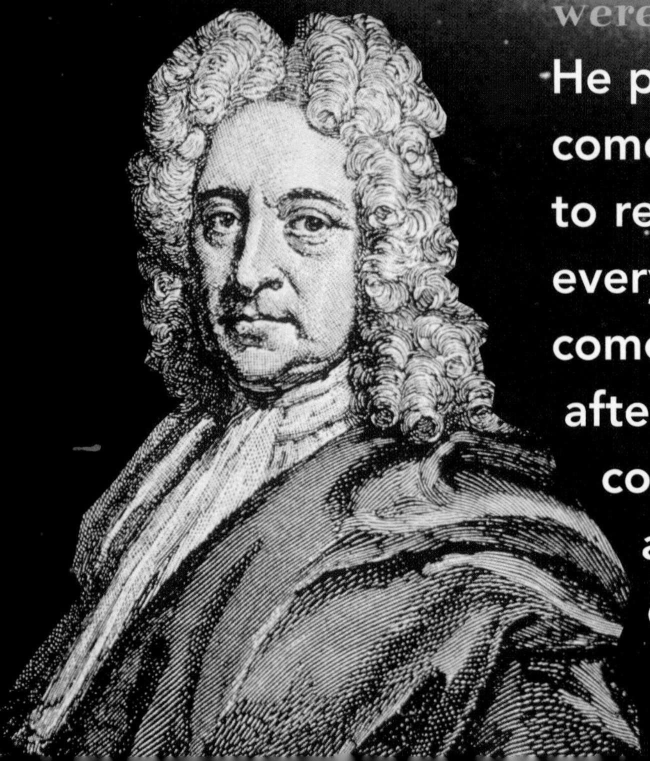

Some comets take only a few years to orbit the Sun. Other comets have orbits that bring them close to the Sun once in a 100,000 years, and still others may come only once and never return. It is fun to see the same comet at different times in your life. Seeing it several years apart may bring back good memories.

Unlike the stars and the motion of the planets, comets can be unpredictable.

Sometimes they show up a little earlier—or later—than expected. This depends partly on how close a comet gets to one of the planets. The planet's gravity may pull the comet into a new orbit. The new orbit may be either shorter or longer depending on how great the effect of the gravity. The gas and other material evaporating from the comet can also change its path through space.

# Light Shows in the Sky

As a comet passes through the solar system, it leaves behind a trail of dust and rock. Long after a comet has passed, its trail remains in orbit around the Sun. When Earth runs into these old comet trails, the result is a light show in the night sky.

A meteor, also called a "falling star"

A meteor is a small piece of rock or metal that enters the Earth's atmosphere at high speeds and burns up. It is often called a "shooting" or "falling" star. When a number of meteors come from the same direction in the sky, we

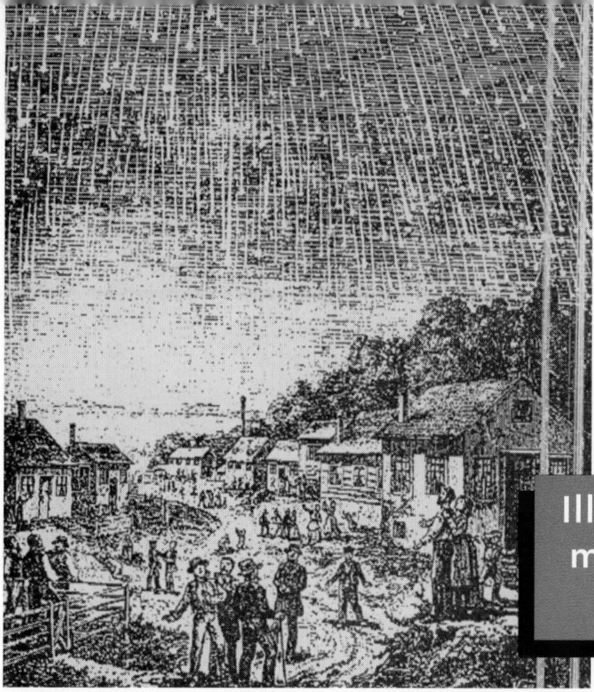

Illustration of a meteor shower in 1833

call it a meteor shower. When a very large number of meteors appear together, we call it a meteor storm.

Meteor showers and storms are named for the constellations they seem to be near. One of the best-known

A Perseid meteor over a campsite in California

showers is the Perseids. These
meteors appear to come from
the direction of the constella-
tion Perseus on the night of
August 11. On a clear, moon-
less night away from bright
city lights, a person may see
more than 60 meteors per

hour. They appear as fast but rather faint streaks of light.

Meteor storms are less frequent, but last longer and look brighter. This is true of the Leonids, from the direction

A false-color photograph of a Leonid meteor shower

of Leo. The Leonid storm can be seen once every 33 years. At the height of the storm, there may be more than 100,000 meteors per hour. This happens because Earth passes through a very dense region of the dust trail. These meteors light up the sky all night long. The next Leonid meteor storm will occur on the night of November 17, 1999. After that, you'll have to wait till 2032!

# Why Are Comets Important?

Comets are believed to be the leftover material from the formation of the solar system. They may be more than 4.6 billion years old.

Some scientists believe that comets may have brought the chemical compounds that first

An artist's impression of a meteor (left), a comet (center), and the path of a comet around the Sun (right)

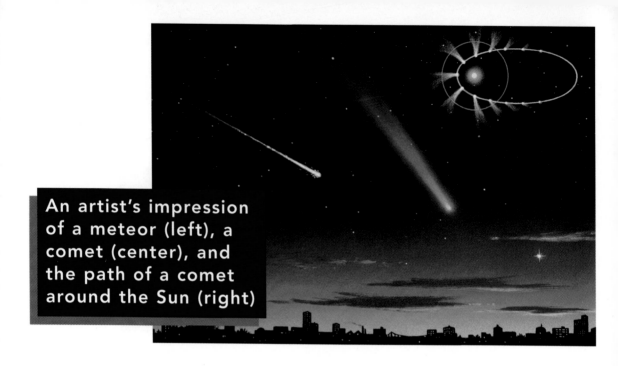

formed life on Earth. Comets contain water and certain chemicals that life depends on. One day soon, scientists will send a spacecraft to a comet to sample it. Then we will have a better idea of how comets may have contributed to life on Earth.

# Did a Comet Kill the Dinosaurs?

Just as comets may have brought life to Earth, they may also have brought death. Many scientists believe that a large comet caused the extinction of the dinosaurs.

Every now and then, a comet hits Earth. When this happens, Earth's climate can change and many different life forms may die.

An artist's impression of dinosaurs being startled by a huge comet heading toward Earth

About 65 million years ago, all the dinosaurs died. For more than 150 million years before that, dinosaurs had populated Earth. Many grew to an enormous size, and some were able to fly. Then, they suddenly disappeared. Many scientists believe that a giant comet or a small asteroid struck Earth. A large crater formed, and dust was thrown high into the atmosphere. This may have blocked out sunlight and darkened the skies for several years, producing what is called a "global winter."

Many scientists believe that the dinosaurs died out because of a "global winter" caused by a giant comet hitting Earth. This would have thrown dust high into the air, blocking out the sun's light and heat for perhaps several years.

Many dinosaurs died from the effects of the blast. Those that survived slowly starved to death. Most dinosaurs were plant-eaters. Without sunlight, most plants died out, and there was no food for the dinosaurs. By the time the skies cleared, the dinosaurs were all gone.

# Are Comets Bad Luck?

Today, most people do not fear comets—they look forward to seeing them. But that has not always been true. In the past, some people thought comets brought bad luck. Whenever anything really bad happened, there seemed to be a comet in the sky. When a terrible sickness killed thousands of people, or

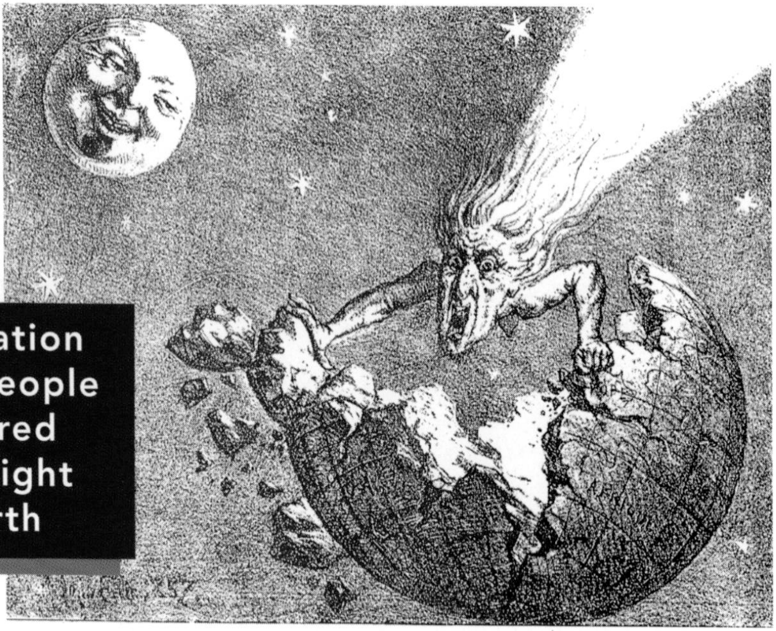

An 1857 illustration showing how people of the time feared that a comet might destroy the Earth

when a city was destroyed by fire, there was a comet to blame.

Today, we know that the comets we see in the sky have no effect on what happens on Earth. People long ago had to blame disasters on something, and a comet sometimes just happened to be there.

# How to Find a Comet

Most comets are discovered by accident. An astronomer may be taking photographs of stars when a new comet happens to appear in the sky. However, some astronomers conduct comet hunts. They search the sky night after night, looking for a fuzzy spot

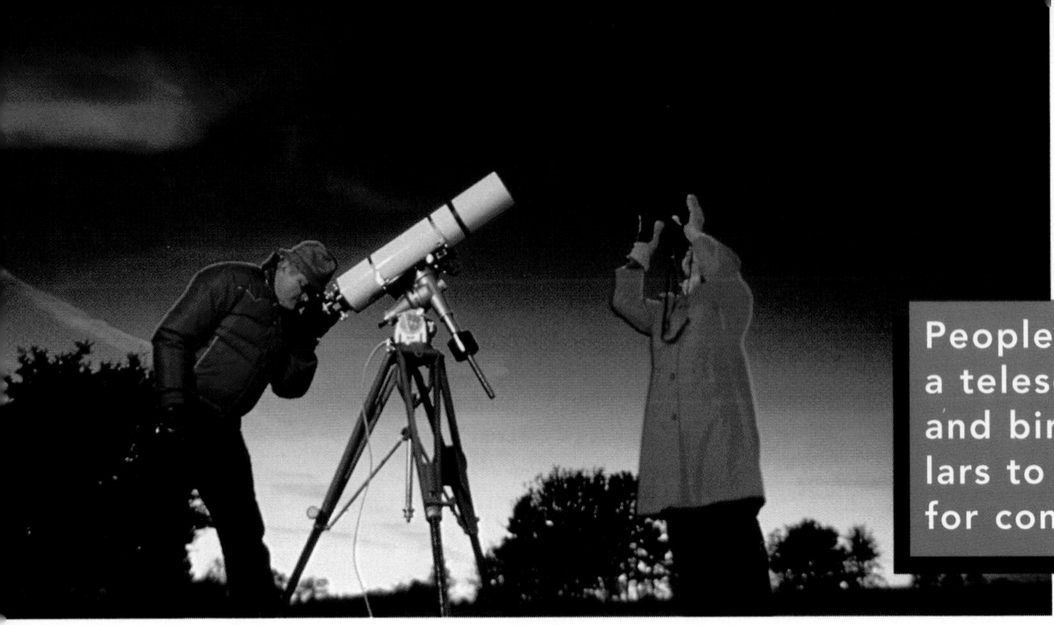

People using a telescope and binoculars to search for comets

that moves. Once a comet has been seen, no one is sure if it will become big and bright, or remain just a faint object in the telescope.

The brightness of a comet is hard to predict. Some comets that astronomers think will be spectacular fizzle out and never get bright. Others provide pleasant surprises. In 1976, a comet named West was just average at best before it passed around the Sun. As it came around, it broke into five pieces. This produced a beautiful tail that was very easy to see.

Comet West, which last appeared in 1976

Comet
Hale-Bopp

In 1995, a comet named
Hale-Bopp was discovered at
a point very far from the Sun.
Since it was seen from such a
great distance, it was predicted to be very bright when it
passed Earth in April 1997. In
January 1996, as astronomers

waited for Hale-Bopp, an unexpected bright comet was discovered—Comet Hyakutake. It was a beautiful sight in the evening sky for

Comet Hyakutake

more than two months. Many people got their first look at a comet at this time.

A great number of comets are discovered by amateur astronomers. If you are lucky enough to find one, it will be named after you. Someday, you might become very interested in astronomy and search for comets. If you succeed, your name will be among the stars.

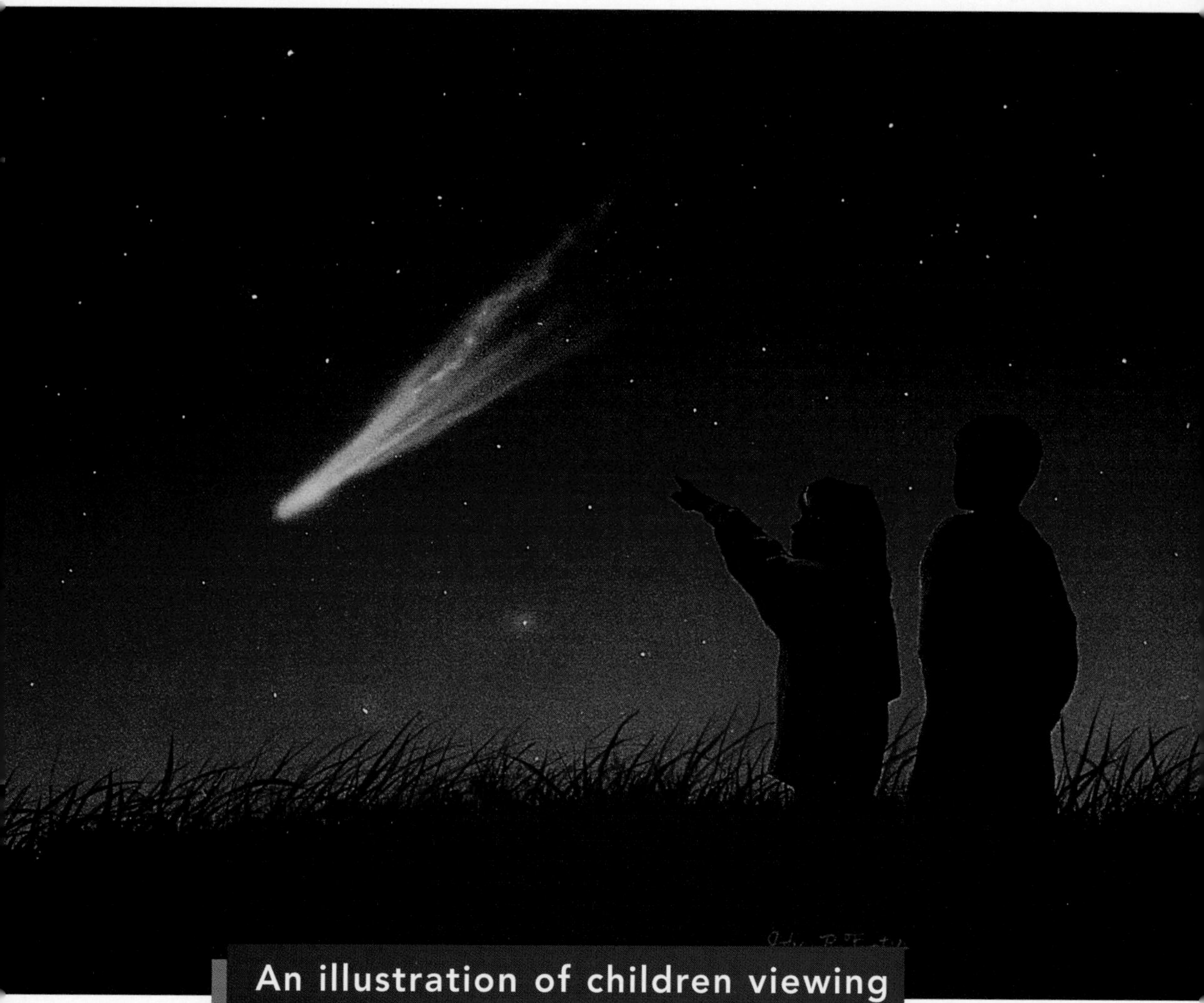

An illustration of children viewing a comet in the night sky

# To Find Out More

Here are some additional resources to help you learn more about comets and meteor showers:

 **Books**

 **Organizations**

Burrows, William E,.
**Mission to Deep Space: Voyagers' Journey of Discovery.** W.H. Freeman and Company, 1993.

Curtis, Anthony R., ed.,
**Space Almanac.** Gulf Publishing Company, 1992.

Van Cleave, Janice,
**Astronomy for Every Kid: 101 Easy Experiments that Really Work.** John Wiley & Sons, 1991.

**Astronomical Society of the Pacific**
1290 24th Avenue
San Francisco, CA 94122
*http://www.physics.sfsu.edu /asp*

**Junior Astronomical Society**
58 Vaughan Gardens
Ilford Essex IG1 3PD
England

**The Planetary Society**
5 North Catalina Avenue
Pasadena, CA 91106
e-mail: *tps.lc@genie.geis. com*

# Online Sites

**Astronomy Online!**
*http://www.eaglequest.com
/%7Eastro/*

**Comets and Meteor
Showers**
*http://medinfo.wustl.edu
/%7Ekronkg/index.html*

**Comet Hale-Bopp Online**
*www.halebopp.com*

**Comet Hyakutake
Information**
*http://www.sji.org/ed/
hyakinfo.html*

**Sky and Telescope's
Comet Page**
*http:/www.skypub.com/
comets/comets.html*

**The Comet Watch
Program - Last Night's
Comets**
*http://www.mindspring.com
/%7Etpuckett/comets.html*

# Important Words

*atmosphere* the gases that surround a planet; the air

*asteroid* small planetlike object that orbits the Sun between Mars and Jupiter

*coma* large gas cloud that surrounds the solid part of a comet

*ellipse* oval or egg-shaped path or orbit

*extinction* when all members of a certain kind of plant or animal die out

*evaporate* when a solid or liquid turns into a gas from being heated

*gravity* the force of attraction between two objects

*solar wind* gaslike substance constantly being thrown off by the Sun into space

# Index

# Meet the Author

Paul P. Sipiera is a professor of geology and astronomy at William Rainey Harper College in Palatine, Illinois. His main area of research is meteorites. When he is not studying science, he can be found working on his farm in Galena, Illinois, with his wife, Diane, and their three daughters, Andrea, Paula Frances, and Carrie Ann.

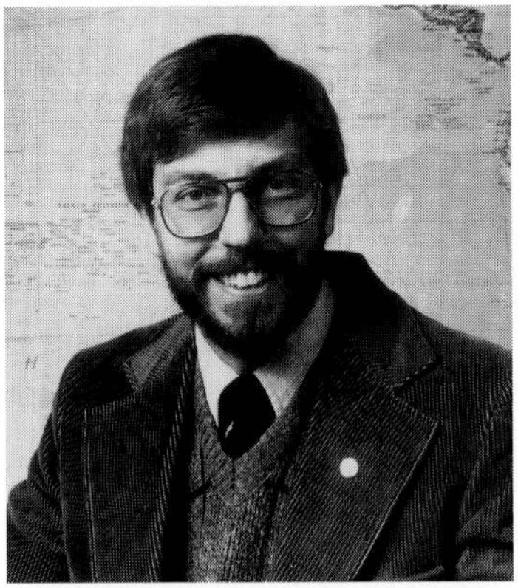

Photo Credits ©: American Museum of Natural History, Courtesy Department of Library Services: 17; Courtesy of American Museum of Natural History: 12, 36; Corbis-Bettmann: 19 right, 25; Mount Wilson and Las Campanas Observatories of the Carnegie Institution of Washington: 14, 19 left; NASA: 8 right; Photo Researchers: 10 right (ASP/SS), 18, 32, 34 (Julian Baum/SPL), 20 bottom inset (Dr. Jeremy Burgess/SPL), 11 (John Chumack/SS), 10 left (European Space Agency/SPL), 4, 43 (John R. Foster/SS), 30 (David Hardy/SPL), 8 left (Harvard College Observatory/SPL), cover, 38 (Jerry Lodriguss/SS), 1, 24 (Pekka Parviainen/SPL), 20 (Royal Greenwich Observatory/ SPL), 39 (Royal Observatory, Edinburgh/ SPL), 2 (Ronald Royer/SPL), 26, 41 (Jerry Schad/SS), 40 (Space Telescope Institute/NASA/SPL), 27 (Jay Stevens/ SPL); Royer: 15.